Technological Applications in Adult and Vocational Education Advancement

Victor C.X. Wang
Florida Atlantic University, USA

Managing Director:	Lindsay Johnston
Senior Editorial Director:	Heather A. Probst
Development Manager:	Joel Gamon
Assistant Acquisitions Editor:	Kayla Wolfe
Typesetter:	Deanna Jo Zombro
Cover Design:	Nick Newcomer

Published in the United States of America by
Information Science Reference (an imprint of IGI Global)
701 E. Chocolate Avenue
Hershey PA 17033
Tel: 717-533-8845
Fax: 717-533-8661
E-mail: cust@igi-global.com
Web site: http://www.igi-global.com

Library of Congress Cataloging-in-Publication Data

Technological applications in adult and vocational education advancement / Victor C.X. Wang, editor.
     p. cm.
  Includes bibliographical references and index. ISBN 978-1-4666-2062-9 (hardcover) -- ISBN 978-1-4666-2063-6 (ebook) -- ISBN 978-1-4666-2064-3 (print & perpetual access) 1. Adult education--Computer-assisted instruction. 2. Vocational education--Computer-assisted instruction.
I. Wang, Victor C. X.
  LC5225.D38T43 2013
  374'.26--dc23
                                          2012013059

British Cataloguing in Publication Data
A Cataloguing in Publication record for this book is available from the British Library.

The views expressed in this book are those of the authors, but not necessarily of the publisher.

Table of Contents

Detailed Table of Contents

Chapter 1

Today, in a globalised, digital world, leadership challenges in the adoption and integration of emerging social software tools to support learning abound. Today's students, who have grown up in technology saturated environments, have never known a world without the internet, mobile phones, video on demand and personal computers. Leaders and educators must know their students, and cater for their diverse needs. Educational institutions in the 21st century must learn how to adopt social software tools and apply sound pedagogical strategies to add value to existing practices and enhance the learning process. ICT supplements and enhances learning and student engagement through access to global learning communities and rich resources, requiring educators to be conversant with the technology, able to lead by example and capable of creating authentic contexts and environments for learning. Educators in today's media rich society must be ready to grapple with the significant pedagogic, cultural and social changes associated with technological innovation.

Chapter 2

This study investigates the andragogical and pedagogical teaching philosophies of online instructors at the California State University, Long Beach in the Spring Semester of 2010. Drawing from reflective adult education theory, this article proposes a new model for this reflective adult education theory. It is either the helping relationship (andragogical philosophy) or the directing relationship (pedagogical philosophy) plus the learning environment (the Internet) that leads to adult learners' critical reflection in Mezirow's (1991) terms. A researcher-designed survey instrument called Online Philosophy of Adult Education Scale (OPAES) was used to measure instructional preferences of these instructors in the electronic classroom to determine their andragogical or pedagogical teaching philosophies. Data were collected from 37 online instructors regarding their instructional preferences. Nine qualitative questions were designed to parallel the Likert scale OPAES to determine why these online adult education instructors chose their pedagogical or andragogical teaching philosophies. The results of the study demonstrate that these online adult education instructors support both the teacher-centered approach and the student-centered approach to teaching online.

This paper examines the critical issue of assuring quality online course delivery by examining four key components of online teaching and learning. The topic of course delivery is viewed as a cultural issue that permeates processes from the design of an online course to its evaluation. First, the authors examine and review key components of and tools for designing high impact online courses that support student learning. Second, in this paper, the authors provide suggestions for faculty teaching online courses to assist in creating high quality online courses that supports teaching and, consequently, facilitates opportunities for student learning. Quality online course delivery is also contingent on the support of faculty by administration. Lastly, this paper provides suggestions for conducting course evaluation and feedback loops for the continual improvement of online learning and teaching. These four components are essential elements in assuring quality online courses.

Senior citizens are comparatively vulnerable in accessing learning opportunities offered on the Internet due to usability problems in current web design. In an effort to build a senior-friendly learning web as a part of the Life-long Learning Network in Shanghai, usability studies of two websites currently available to Shanghai senior citizens were conducted, with the intention of integrating these websites into a senior learning web as well as promoting accessibility for senior users. Through this study usability problems were identified generating suggested changes for designing websites focused on learning by seniors. This study contributes empirical findings to the field of information system design and its accessibility for seniors.

This paper investigates the prevalence of coworker and supervisor incivility in the context of K-12 schools and incivility's possible link to teachers' commitment to the school and turnover intent. The data were collected via surveys from 94 middle school teachers in the United States. Results indicated that 85% of the teachers experienced coworker incivility over the past year; 71% experienced supervisor incivility. MANOVA results suggested no statistically significant differences in incivility by gender or ethnicity. Hierarchical regression results suggested that supervisor incivility was associated negatively with commitment and positively associated with turnover intent. Coworker incivility was not a significant predictor in the regression equations. Macro- and micro-level human resource strategies are offered as possible tools to lessen the likelihood of uncivil behavior.

Chapter 6
Literacy Level and Vocational Training for Substance-Using Hispanic Adults 69

Michele M. Wood, California State University, Fullerton, USA

Dennis G. Fisher, California State University, Long Beach, USA

Grace L. Reynolds, California State University, Long Beach, USA

Yesenia Guzman, California State University, Long Beach, USA

William C. Pedersen, California State University, Long Beach, USA

The Hispanic population has become the largest ethnic minority group in the United States. To successfully incorporate this population in adult vocational training, social service, and health programs, it is essential that programs design and implement materials at a reading level appropriate for the population served. This study determines the reading level in a population of Hispanic adult substance users receiving HIV prevention services in Long Beach, California. One hundred seven Spanish speakers were administered the Spanish Reading Comprehension Test. Spanish reading ability was determined to be at the third grade level for this sample. Results suggest that substance-using subpopulations of Spanish speakers in the Southwest United States face considerable language and literacy barriers. Findings have implications for adult vocational training as well as social service and health programs that include Hispanic subpopulations, and highlight the importance of designing materials that do not exceed the reading abilities of target populations.

Victor C. X. Wang, California State University at Long Beach, USA

Judith Parker, Columbia University, USA

This article addresses the traditional instructional leadership (characterized with Tyler's four questions; teachers prescribe a curriculum; learners assume a submissive role of following instructors) in comparison with the andragogical or innovative instructional leadership. As more and more scholars cast their doubt on this particular instructional mode (traditional instructional leadership), especially when compared with the innovative instructional leadership, this article seeks to draw on traditional instructional leadership that revolves around Ralph Tyler's model. In doing so, instructors and practitioners will see clearly what the traditional instructional leadership may bring to most education settings and above all, they may rely on a ready-made formula when planning curriculums, instruction, program planning, or evaluation. While traditional instructional leadership may have come under much criticism, there is much to learn from it.

Lila Holt, University of Tennessee, USA

Mary Ziegler, University of Tennessee, USA

The new workplace is a key arena for learning in today's society. The spiraling demand for knowledge in the workplace has increased interest in learning, especially team learning. Team learning can be viewed from multiple perspectives, making it difficult for career and technical educators (CTEs) to know how to prepare students for a team-based work environment, especially one that includes virtual teams. In addition, emerging technology adds to the confusion about how to provide effective learning experiences that mirror what is occurring in the workplace. To prepare the workforce of tomorrow, CTE instructors can become facilitators of team learning by providing ample opportunity for learners to practice team skills in a low-risk learning environment. By providing the exposure and practice to team learning skills and technology tools, CTEs may help equip students with added skills in entering a global workplace.

Chapter 9

Norhayati Ibrahim, Iowa State University, USA
Steven A. Freeman, Iowa State University, USA
Mack C. Shelley, Iowa State University, USA

A central challenge for higher education today is to understand the diversity and complexity of non-traditional students' life experiences and how these factors influence their academic success. To better understand these issues, this study explored the role of demographic characteristics and employment variables in predicting the academic success of part-time students at four polytechnic institutes in Malaysia. Demographic characteristics studied included respondent's age, gender, marital status, number of children, parent's educational level, and financial resources. Employment variables assessed were number of years working, job relatedness to the program, job satisfaction, and monthly salary. A total of 614 part-time students completed the survey. Results indicated that being an older student, being female, paying for their own education, and having high job satisfaction were statistically significant predictors of part-time students' academic success. Understanding the effects of demographic characteristics and employment variables on students' academic success might help administrators and educators to develop teaching and learning processes, support services, and policies to enhance part-time students' academic success.

Chapter 10

Victor C. X. Wang, California State University - Long Beach, USA

This article argues that E-leadership emerged out of technological development among all other major developments in our society. In the virtual environment, leaders are required to lead followers by using different approaches. This is not to say that traditional leadership has no place in the new virtual environment characterized by the constant use of technology. Rather, traditional leadership and leadership style studied and conceptualized by researchers and scholars enhance E-leadership supported by Rogers' facilitative leadership. Leadership theories are meant to be applied to practice. Further, leadership theories can be applied in part or in whole. They are not ideologies that must be followed to the letter.

Chapter 11

Beth Kania-Gosche, Lindenwood University, USA
Lynda Leavitt, Lindenwood University, USA

Dissertation writing is often the most challenging aspect of the doctoral program. In an effort to raise completion rates and lower time-to-degree as well as increase student satisfaction with the program, professors in an Ed.D. program developed a semester-long course to support students writing their dissertations. This case study describes the development of the course and the implementation of the first semester. The course consisted of a series of workshops on various aspects of dissertation writing as well as various other activities such as peer review. The students did not receive a grade for the course. After reviewing data, students in the course were classified by their productivity that semester and engagement in the course. Students who were highly engaged but not highly productive were the most prevalent group. In this article, the authors also provide follow-up, including changes made the next semester and data on student completion.

Chapter 12

Mark E. Johnson, University of Alaska Anchorage, USA

Grace Reynolds, California State University Long Beach, USA

Dennis G. Fisher, California State University Long Beach, USA

Colin R. Harbke, Western Illinois University, USA

Vocational assessment data were collected from 94 low-education adults with severe substance abuse problems not currently in treatment. Participants completed the My Vocational Situation (MVS), Self-Directed Search (SDS), and Reading-Free Vocational Interest Inventory (R-FVII). Lower scores than the normative sample were revealed on all MVS scales, with scores for men being significantly lower than the normative sample. These findings indicate that these participants, particularly the men, lack a clear and stable view of their occupational future, need information to clarify their occupational options and goals, and perceive multiple barriers in attaining employment. SDS and R-FVII results provide detailed information about these participants' occupational interests and vocational likes and dislikes. These findings highlight vocational counseling and guidance as critical needs for individuals with severe substance abuse problems who are unable or unwilling to seek treatment. Providing vocational services to this out-of-treatment population may be an essential pathway for their long-term recovery.

Chapter 13

Suwithida Charungkaittikul, Chulalongkorn University, Thailand

This study uses a prospective qualitative approach. The Ethnographic Delphi Futures Research (EDFR) technique is used to propose a learning society model. The data include a review of peer-reviewed literature, a field study visit and observation of five best practices communities in Thailand, in-depth interviews to gain experts' perspectives, mini-Delphi techniques questionnaires, focus group discussions, and model evaluation. Qualitative data were transcribed and analyzed using content-analysis. Policy makers, practitioners from public and private agencies, educational personnel, and community leaders were among the 42 individuals involved in the data collection effort. Results revealed essential elements for development of a learning society including, principles, developmental processes, strategies, and key success factors to enhance a positive paradigm shift for communities. It is anticipated that the findings will (1) add meaningful information and practical guidelines for developing a learning society, (2) contribute to ensuring the quality of citizen participation and ensure balanced and sustainable development of communities and societies, and (3) serve as a basis for further research.

Chapter 14

Edward C. Fletcher, University of South Florida, USA

Kathy Mountjoy, Illinois State University, USA

Glenn Bailey, Illinois State University, USA

Applying a modified-Delphi technique, this research study sought consensus from business education mentor teachers regarding the top three areas in which business education student teachers were prepared as well as underprepared for their roles as teachers. Further, the mentor teachers provided recommendations for business education teacher preparation programs to implement to better prepare their teacher candidates for the student teaching internship. To that end, the mentor teachers did not gain consensus on the top three areas their student teachers were most prepared. However, they did agree classroom management and working with special needs' students were among the top three areas their student teachers were least prepared. The mentor teachers agreed business education teacher preparation programs could provide more experiences with classroom management in public schools and provide their teacher candidates with more information about the workload and commitment needed to be effective teachers.

Chapter 15
Stephen Asunka, Regent University College of Science & Technology, Ghana

In the present knowledge economy, individuals, particularly working adults, need to continuously acquire purposeful knowledge and skills so they can better contribute towards addressing society's ever-changing developmental challenges. In the developing world however, few opportunities exist for working adults to acquire such new learning experiences through the formal education sector, and this makes it imperative for organizations to develop non-formal education and training programs to help address this need. With the proliferation of Information and Communication Technologies (ICTs) worldwide, this article recommends the adoption of Collaborative Online Learning (COL) by non-formal learning organizations as a means of helping address the education and training needs of working adults. The article thus provides an overview of COL, and then draws on the research literature on relevant theories to recommend best-practice strategies for designing and delivering effective and workable COL initiatives within non-formal education settings, particularly in the developing world.

Chapter 16
Lesley Farmer, California State University - Long Beach, USA

Intellectual pursuit and the recognition of ideas is a central concept. Copyrights protect the rights of intellectual creators while balancing those rights with the needs for access. As technologies have expanded, and production has become more sophisticated, the legal regulations surrounding their use have become more complex. With the advent of the interactive web 2.0 and increased resource sharing, as well as growth in distance learning opportunities, complying with the legal use of information technology can be daunting. In any case, leaders and other educators should be aware of the more important aspects of technology-related copyright laws and regulations. This article provides an overview of copyright law and fair use for educational research purposes. It explains different options for intellectual production and sharing, and notes administrative actions to support copyright compliance.

Chapter 17
Lantana M. Usman, University of Northern British Columbia, Canada

In northern Nigeria, widows' identities and status are defined within the mores, norms, traditional religions, and legal institutions of the cultures of the community. The ethnic cultural laws are oppressive and retrogressive. The nexus of these cultural pressures trigger discriminatory practices that deny school attending widows' access, and completion of primary and secondary levels of education, leaving them literacy bankrupt and unskilled to fend for themselves and their children. These experiences motivated an all women Community Based Organization (CBO) to establish a Widows Training School to educate widows in vocational skills and basic literacy and numeracy. This paper examines research that was conducted with a sample of former graduates and attendees of the Widows Training School (WTS). The study is based on a qualitative educational research orientation, and the case study design. Multi-modal data were derived from Focused Group Interviews (FGIs) and Non Participant Observation (NPO) with a sample population of the widows. Data analysis engaged the qualitative process of transcription, categorization, and generation of codes that were merged into major themes, and presented in the as socio cultural status of the widows in the community; historical foundation, nature and curriculum implementation of the school; and the facets of sustainable learning outcome of the widows.

Victor C. X. Wang, Florida Atlantic University, USA
Patricia Cranton, University of New Brunswick, Canada

The theory of transformative learning has been explored by different theorists and scholars. However, few scholars have made an attempt to make a comparison between transformative learning and Confucianism or between transformative learning and andragogy. The authors of this article address these comparisons to develop new and different insights to guide Web-based teaching and learning. Indeed, as Web-based teaching and learning has become popular in the 21st century, the theory of transformative learning should help Web-based teaching and learning. The authors of this article demonstrate different ways whereby the theory of transformative learning can be used to stimulate critical self-reflection and potentially transformative learning.

Preface

INTRODUCTION

The most common misconception is that technology can replace adult employees in vocational and adult education as the power of technologies has been exaggerated in the 21st century. From newspaper/ magazine articles to want advertisements, employers place more emphasis on the effective use of technologies. Without adequate skills in the use of appropriate technologies, adult workers are faced with challenges in finding employment.

As an essential component of our social environment, technology cannot replace adult employees in vocational and adult education. In other words, it provides a powerful teaching/learning tool used to "enhance" learning, hence learners changed in the three most often talked about domains. This book addresses technological applications in vocational and adult education advancement from different perspectives. However, technology does help transform the adult learners that seek perspective transformation via critical theory and epistemological positions in the virtual environment. Technology, together with adult course instructors play a helping role in terms of helping learners attain changed behavior. Through the discussion of the above pertinent issues, an insightful model titled *Learners'Seeking Transformation via Web 2.0 Technologies*, has emerged.

Researchers and educators have been addressing the issue: can technology replace adult workers in vocational and adult education? There is no doubt that learners engage in learning through technology in order to seek change in Bloom's (1956) three domains: 1, cognitive domain; 2, psychomotor domain; and 3, affective domain. Educators and researchers strive to find out whether adult learners have learned anything from their courses through the use of technology; they can ask the following questions:

1. Do the learners think differently after completing this class via technology?
2. Do the learners act differently after completing this class via technology?
3. Do the learners feel differently after completing this class via technology?

The three questions revolve around the three domains of educational objectives. Once these objectives are achieved on the part of learners, it may be possible to say that the learners are transformed. The potential for transformative learning exists; however, the question remains unanswered: who has transformed these adult learners? Course instructors, Web 2.0 technologies? Or the learners themselves?

Course instructors may have the highest degree in a specific discipline. Then, based on their knowledge base and instructional experience, they are hired by universities or colleges to "teach" adult learners through the use of technology. To be successful, they must possess a certain body of knowledge that they can impart to their learners one way or the other. In Western cultures, an instructor's teaching is constantly evaluated by students. If instructors keep receiving low ratings from students, they may be subject to instructional development related to teaching and learning or further training in their subject area. In rare cases, some unqualified instructors' employment as professional teachers may be terminated. Those who remain in the academy based on consistently good teaching evaluations are considered knowledgeable in the field or at least have the ability to impress their students enough to warrant a good review of their teaching abilities. They have the potential to inspire learners to transform themselves via their teachings or their being a role model. There has been considerable literature on how course instructors can set up an environment in their classrooms that fosters and supports transformative learning for adult learners.

What about technology? How can technology foster transformative learning for adults? Since education was delivered via technology in the early 21st century, scholars have been asking this question. Some say, "yes, technology transforms adultlearners in a big way." Others say, "technology provides only teaching and learning tools; it is only the learners that can seek transformation themselves." At least two points of view exist, either or both of which could be valid. Perhaps too many exaggerations regarding the power of technology have been heard of in vocational and adult education. Some have become rather cliché. For example, people have been known to say, "technology will replace human beings." "Technology will lead to the demise of the instruction inside four-walled classrooms." "Intelligent computers will replace classroom teachers." While some educators feel threatened by these exaggerations, others choose to explore the power of technology by conducting research. Programmed instruction was introduced even before the advent of computers—paper and pencil modules and "teaching machines" existed in the early 1960s. Computer-assisted instruction in the 1960s and 1970s relied on behaviorism as advanced by Watson and Skinner (1967; 1968). Some central themes about the power of technology can be found in the literature:

1. Learners research technology as technology represents a core body of knowledge.
2. Learners learn from technology as technology complements and supplements learners' existing knowledge base.
3. Learners learn with technology as technology represents one access point to knowledge.

However, little can be found regarding whether technology supports learner transformation. It was Marx that advanced critical theory and it was Habermas who advanced three basic human interests and the kinds of knowledge generated by these interests. Mezirow began the development of transformative learning theory in 1975 and presented a fully comprehensive theory to adult educations in his 1991 book, *Transformative Dimensions of Adult Learning*, in which he drew on the work of Habermas, Freire, and many others. The theory of transformative learning helps interpret how learners seek change in the in different domains of educational objectives and different kinds of knowledge. Mezirow addresses perspective transformation (Paulo Freire emphasized "social cultural aspect); that is, the cognitive/rational and affective/emotional domains. A brief summary of perspective transformation is outlined below.

Transformative learning is a process that describes how learners transform a habit of thought by redefining a problem and examining their assumptions, content, or process for problem solving (Mezirow, 2000). When asking learners to think "outside the box," they are being asked to redefine a problem and reexamine their own assumptions—the content or process for problem solving. In other cultures, they say, "think above the thinking process," which essentially means the same as thinking outside the box. Learners who progress through a transforming event critically reflect on their assumptions and examine their points of view to determine how they approached solving problems presented by that event. Those transformations may be dramatic and epochal or take place over time with small or incremental changes and shifts in one's thought process. Steps that lead to a transformation typically begin with what Mezirow calls a "disorienting dilemma" (p. 22). From that dilemma, the learner examines his or her feelings and evaluates the assumptions that lead up to the disorienting dilemma. At this point, the person can ignore the event and its effects or recognize that they are not the only ones going through such an event and explore ways to prevent the disorienting dilemma from occurring again. If transformation is to take place, the person becomes a learner and sets out on a process of exploring new ways to approach the dilemma. Once new approaches are discovered, the learner can develop a plan, try different approaches, and learn from the experiences. The outcome of this process is a deep shift in perspective in which the learner's frame of reference becomes more open, better justified, and discriminating. As they work towards avoiding the disorienting dilemma, their new perspective and understanding is integrated back into one's life. The core of this process of transformative learning is the use of critical reflection. Cranton (1994, 2006) helps educators of adults better understand the essential features of Mezirow's theory of transformative learning via her book titled *Understanding and Promoting Transformative Learning: A guide for educators of adults.* Her unique way of interpreting/illustrating this theory with her own style of writing/professional experiences helps readers understand the theory from rather a different angle. More importantly, Cranton's writing has enhanced this theory of transformative learning and readers can understand how the theory has been applied in the field.

In Mezirow's approach to transformative learning, perspectives are made up of frames of references or, "the structure of assumptions and expectations through which we filter sense impressions" (p. 16). Our frames of references are shaped by our experiences and how we interpret them and can represent cultural values or personal beliefs. A frame of reference is made up of two parts: habit of mind and a point of view. Our habit of mind is based on the assumptions we hold regarding social, ethical, philosophical, psychological, and aesthetic values (Mezirow, 2000). Our point of view is how we express those assumptions. To put it differently, how we act upon those habits of mind becomes our point of view. Points of view are made up of a group of meaning schemes, or how we feel, believe, judge, or react to events or objects in the real world. As we are often times unaware of the meaning schemes we hold, they have the ability to impact how we interpret the world around us. Our meaning schemes inform our frame of reference and impact how we express those frames of references to the rest of the world. People rely on those frames of reference as a touchstone for their existence and sense of identity. When alternative points of view are expressed that challenge existing frames of reference, it is more likely that the person will disregard them. However, if a disorienting dilemma challenges those frames of reference to the point that they cannot be dismissed, it is likely the person will experience transformative learning.

Set up in contrast to Mezirow's work is the extrarational approach which substitutes imagination, intuition, and emotion for critical reflection (Dirkx, 2001). Also focusing on the individual is a developmental perspective. As is the case in developmental psychology in general, transformative learning in this framework describes shifts in the way we make meaning—moving from a simplistic reliance on authority through to more complex ways of knowing or higher orders or consciousness (Kegan, 2000). Belenky and Stanton (2000) report on a similar change in epistemology, but they emphasize connected knowing (through collaboration and acceptance of others' views rather than autonomous, independent knowing.

Some theorists, including Mezirow and Dirkx, focus on the individual, and others are interested in the social context of transformative learning, social change as a goal, or the transformation undergone by groups and organizations. Social transformation is a view of transformative learning of a socially constructed individual who "is contextualized in the history, culture, and social fabric of the society in which he/she lives… at the intersection of the personal biography and societal structure" (Cunningham, 1998, p. 16). This view reflects a shift from the individual to the individual within the context of society. It is concerned with how public knowledge is created, as well as emphasizing the importance of fostering an awareness of the dominant culture and its relationship to power and positionality in defining what is and is not knowledge in society.

Although this appears to be a divide in theoretical positions, there is no reason that both the individual and the social perspectives cannot peacefully coexist; one does not deny the existence of the other, but rather they share common characteristics and can inform each other. If technology is considered part of the social context, it comes back to the same question: Can technology foster transformative learning among adult learners as it is described in transformative learning theory?

In the field of vocational and adult education, what plays a major role in terms of learners' transformation, technology or the learners themselves via epistemological positions? This preface seeks to shed some light on how adult learners seek to transform themselves through different epistemological positions in relation to the theory of transformative learning and even the much debated theory of andragogy advanced by Knowles (1970, 1975). It does not seek to underestimate the power of technology. Rather, technology provides excellent teaching and learning tools in vocational and adult education. Please note, vocational and adult education, in many cases, have been replaced by newer terms such as career and technical education (vocational education) and lifelong learning (adult education). It is like putting the old wine in a new bottle. Tools are to be manipulated by humans, hence adult learners and instructors in vocational and adult education. As Olgren (2000) indicates, "technology invites a tools-first emphasis, but technology is only as good as our knowledge of how to use it to enhance learning" (p. 7).

For years, scholars and educators have been relying on the theory of andragogy (Knowles, 1984), or principles of adult learning, to help understand how learners seek change in the field. In the early 1990s, scholars such as Mezirow, Dirkx, and Cranton began to advance a new theory, the theory of transformative learning to help interpret how learners seek transformation, especially a deep shift in perspective. According to Mezirow and Cranton (1991, 2000; 2010) the process of transformative learning focuses on critical reflection and critical self-reflection whereas other scholars may place imagination, intuition, and emotion at the heart of transformation (Dirkx, 2001). Although Mezirow's theory was based on a study of women who found that their experience of returning to college led them to question and revise their personal beliefs and values in a fairly linear ten-step process, theoretically, he drew on Habermas's (1971) three kinds of human interest and the resulting three kinds of knowledge—instrument, practical, and emancipatory. The goal in using transformative learning theory is for learners to attain emancipatory knowledge by critically reflecting upon the first two kinds of knowledge—instrumental and practical (communicative in Mezirow's terms). Further, Mezirow (2000) addressed six types of meaning perspectives—epistemic (about knowledge and how we acquire knowledge), sociolinguistic (understanding ourselves and social world through language), psychological (concerned with our perception of ourselves largely based on childhood experiences), moral-ethical (conscience and morality), philosophical (concerned with worldview, philosophy, or religious doctrine), and aesthetic (attitudes, tastes, and standards about beauty). Mezirow appears to focus more on the cognitive domain of educational objectives.

However, critics of Mezirow's theory fail to understand that in order for learners to become meaningful doers, perspectives must be changed first. Consider Kacirek, Beck, and Grover's quote, "even the early Greeks believed that working people didn't think and thinking people didn't work" (as cited in Kacirek, Beck, & Grover, 2010, p. 32). Although Mezirow was modest and humble by saying that his theory is a theory in progress, his emphasis on cognitive and affective domains was well justified by even early Greeks.

The next question to ask is how helpful is the theory of transformative learning when interpreting whether technology, as part of the social context, can support transformative learning. Or is it as powerful as the traditional theory of andragogy in terms of interpreting the relationship between technology and adult learners? In the next section, we address how learners acquire knowledge in the virtual learning environment by reflecting on the theoretical framework.

EPISTEMOLOGICAL POSITIONS AND VOCATIONAL AND ADULT EDUCATION

Learners engage in adult learning for a variety of reasons. The asynchronous nature of online-learning is so conspicuous and returning students especially enjoy this feature of online-learning because of their multiple work/family responsibilities (Wang, 2006, 2008). Some employees take courses via technology because learners are limited to those courses provided via Blackboard or WebCT programs. More and more universities turn to Blackboard, Moodle, or Desire2Learn as the platform for delivering instructions to learners at a distance. Learners, as a result, can save money on gas and have the flexibility of taking asynchronous courses anytime throughout the day rather than adhering to a set schedule. Other learners take courses via Blackboard because it is mandated by their employers. Those organizations that wish to remain competitive in this global economy must seek to train and retrain their employees in the new century. Having employees take university courses is a primary method of training employees. Needless to say traditional age students can take Blackboard courses to attain career and life goals. Given the downturn of the economy, universities wishing to save money offer Blackboard courses and, thus, do not have to pay for brick and mortar buildings, construction of parking lots, nor their upkeep. All these reasons may point to one direction, that is, online--learning as predicted by Knowles (1975) has become popular in the new century. And the popularity of e-learning is driven by four epistemological positions: postpositivism, constructivism, advocacy/participatory, and pragmatism. These four positions are closely related to Mezirow's theory of transformative learning. The heart of his theory is for learners to experience perspective change via critical reflection and critical reflection must be based on Habermas's three kinds of knowledge and the four epistemological positions. Without interpreting the four positions, readers may wonder how learners engage in learning via technology. It comes back to the central question: can technology promote transformation among adult learners? By expanding the four positions in the following section, readers will see clearly that it is the learners who seek to transform themselves while technology is meant only to be used to enhance learning.

Postpositivists believe that knowledge is created by humans conjecturing and that, for learners to create an understanding, it is important that they work with and challenge the conjectures (Bettis & Gregson, 2001). In the virtual environment, course instructors can arrange knowledge by specifying course syllabus, course assignments, discussion topics, course evaluation methods and learning resources. Then adult learners come to the virtual environment to study, observe and even challenge these conjectures in order to determine effects or outcomes. Course instructors justify the course's existence by saying, "there are laws or theories that govern the world, and these need to be tested or verified and refined so that you, as learners, can understand the world." If we try to connect this position with instructional methods, we can likely say that this position is in agreement with andragogy instead of pedagogy simply because instructors link learners to learning resources. Learners do the "legwork" by embarking on Habermas's instrumental knowledge and practical knowledge in order to attain emancipatory knowledge—perspective transformation in Mezirow's terms.

Constructivists assume that individuals seek an understanding of the world in which they live and work. Individuals develop subjective meanings of their experiences—meanings directed toward certain objects or things (Creswell, 2009, p. 8). Creswell further indicates that these meanings are varied and multiple, leading the learner to look for the complexity of views rather than narrowing meanings into a few categories or ideas. Based on this position, adult learners' tasks are clear: learners construct the meaning of a situation, typically forged in discussions or interactions with other persons. Then course instructors may arrange more open-ended questioning, case studies, analyzing personal experiences. These instructional methods all fit well with this position. In adult education, this epistemological position penetrated into the field a long time ago. When scholars address "experiential learning", they want learners to make meaning out of their experience. Some universities in the United States grant college credits to adult learners based on experiential learning. If learners can turn their prior experience into knowledge, skills or attitudes, why require them to take redundant courses to waste their time or money? In the virtual learning environment, instructors may arrange learning activities around learners' prior experience. Again, we can tell that learners seek change in the cognitive domain or affective domain based on the reflection of their experiential learning or prior learning. Technology is used as an external environment. To further elaborate on the constructivist position, I focus on the following central themes:

1.   Meanings are constructed by learners as they engage with the virtual learning environment. Course instructors tend to use open-ended questions so that the learners can share their views and generate knowledge through their sharing.
2.   Learners engage with the virtual learning environment and make sense of it based on their historical and social perspectives. Course instructors may remind learners to seek to understand the context or setting by visiting this context and gathering information personally via the use of technology.
3.   The basic generation of meaning is always social, arising in and out of interaction with an adult learning community. The goal of course instructors is to foster an adult learning community.

Scholars and educators feel that postpositivist and constructivists do not go far enough in advocating for an action agenda to help marginalized peoples in society. Therefore, they developed advocacy/participatory worldview by drawing on the writings of Marx and Freire (Neuman, 2000). According to Creswell (2009), an advocacy/participatory worldview holds that learners need to become radical philosophers, that is, they need to have an action agenda for reform that may change the lives of themselves, the institutions in which they work or live, and perhaps the larger society. The course instructor's role is to have learners speak to important social issues of the day, issues such as empowerment, inequality, oppression, domination, suppression, and alienation. Learners should be considered equals of their course instructors. Therefore, learners may help design learning questions, collect data, and analyze information together with their course instructors via the use of technology. Since this epistemological position focuses on the needs of the learners and learners in society that may be marginalized or disenfranchised, we can tell the ultimate goal of this position is for learners to develop emancipatory knowledge. Specifically, learners can seek to do the following in order to develop a perspective change:

1.   Learners advance an action agenda for change based on this worldview.
2.   Learners seek to free themselves from constraints found in the media, in language, in work procedures, and in the relationships of power in educational settings.

3. Learners began with an important issue or stance about the problems in society.
4. Learners seek to create a political debate so that real change will occur.
5. Course instructors consider their learners as active collaborators in the learning process in the virtual environment.

The fourth epistemological position is pragmatism that maintains that a worldview arises out of actions, situations, and consequences rather than antecedent conditions as in postpositivism (Creswell, 2009). Learners are required to use all approaches available to understand problems. To understand problems, learners are free to choose the methods, techniques, and procedures that best meet their needs or purposes. Learners may use multiple methods to understand a particular problem. The emphasis in pragmatism is on hands-on application and practical solutions to problems rather than esoteric or theoretical approaches.

In short, the four epistemological positions together with the theory of transformative learning and principles of andragogy all translate into instructional methods either in the traditional classroom setting or virtual learning environment. These positions view knowledge acquisition differently, yet they share some commonality. It seems that no single position seeks to specify pedagogical instructional methods. Rather, they all prompt course instructors to provide "andragogical" instructional methods, which were vividly described by Knowles, Holton and Swanson (1998) as follows:

Finally, I found myself performing a different set of functions that required a different set of skills. Instead of performing the function of content planner and transmitter, which required primarily presentation skills, I was performing the function of process designer and manager, which required relationship building, needs assessment, involvement of students in planning, linking students to learning resources, and encouraging student initiative. (p. 201)

Indeed, both instructors and technology play a helping role rather than a directing role in the virtual learning environment (Wang, 2005). For any change in the three domains of educational objectives to occur, it is the learners that seek to transform themselves and their transformation can be clearly expounded by the prevalent theories or epistemological positions.

Figure 1 has emerged from this preface and several points are worth emphasizing.

Figure 1. Learners' seeking transformation via Web 2.0 technologies

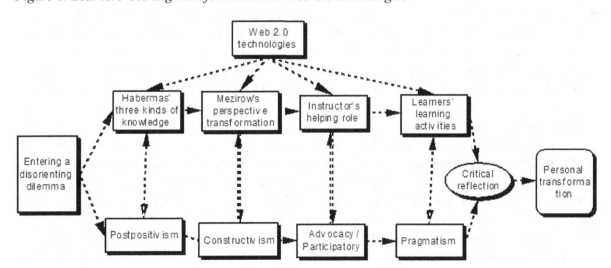

Technology as a teaching/learning took provides an interactive learning environment to enhancing learning.

1.   Instructors play a secondary helping role by providing a conducive environment via putting their course syllabi, assignments and discussion forums online.
2.   It is the learners that seek to transform themselves and their transformation is driven by learning theories and epistemological positions.
3.   Change, whether more in cognitive or affective domains, is bound to occur because of the nature of epistemological positions and our worldviews.
4.   Relying too much on technology without taking into consideration learning theories or epistemological positions will prevent instructors from prescribing the much needed andragogical instructional methods.
5.   What really contributes to learners' transformation is the learners themselves. Change must come from within the learners not from outside the learners.

CRITICAL REFLECTION

Technology was designed and built by intelligent humans and it is supposed to serve the learning needs of learners and instructional needs of instructors in this information age. We have advanced into this information age simply because education is being delivered electronically. And technology has permeated society in general, and major government and economic stakeholders have recognized the importance of incorporating technology throughout education in order to prepare a competitive workforce in a global economy (Farmer, 2010, p. 276). However interactive technology can be used in the teaching/learning arena, it is only one access point to knowledge, skills and attitudes. Learners have to do the learning in order to achieve perspective transformation in Mezirow's terms. Learners learn in traditional classroom settings and learners learn in virtual environment. If learners are not motivated to learn, if learners are not self-directed to learn and if learners do not use the basic five senses to acquire knowledge, perspective transformation is not likely to occur. What really contributes to learners' transformation are Habermas's three kinds of knowledge, Mezirow's interpretation of critical reflection, epistemological positions, and even Knowles (1984) principles of andragogy. As a tool to enhance learning, technology does play a major role. However, technology itself cannot enable transformation of adult learners if learners are not engaged in actual learning themselves. As a tool, learners should take advantage of it. Some senior learners may be anxious when they think of learning via technology. Some younger learners may take technology for granted, believing they can be multi-tasked in terms of learning. Having the right attitude towards using technology as a tool to enhance learning is key to successful perspective transformation on the part of learners.

In addition to learning to be technology savvy, learners need to be internally motivated to learn. Confucius's "silent reflection" is not outmoded in terms of promoting transformative learning. Schutz (1967) argues, "I live in my Acts and by reflecting upon them" (p. 51). Once we do this, we begin the process of critical reflection or meaning-making in our lives. The process of meaning making is a great way to transform oneself and it is such an essential part of the theory of transformative learning. Although technology serves as one access point to knowledge, it can also serve as a subject matter for learners. Do we not have universities where instructional technology is treated as an academic discipline? Learners can even obtain doctorate degrees in technology. Once learners obtain their degrees, they can practice in the field of technology. Professionals in the field teach "technology" as a subject. A subject of an academic discipline does not seek to transform adult learners if learners decide to have nothing to do with it. It is when learners have made learning decisions to study such a subject or academic discipline that perspective transformation can begin to occur. To achieve three domains of educational objectives, learners need to be immersed in learning the subject matter. After this rigorous process of learning, learners can be totally transformed. Technology as an enhancing tool also provides a learning environment. As to whether learning will occur, Rogers' (1969) hypotheses regarding learning should be taken into consideration by instructors:

1. Human beings have a natural potential for learning. They are curious about their world, until and unless their curiosity is blunted by their experience in our educational system. They are ambivalently eager to develop and learn. The reason for the ambivalence is that any significant learning involves a certain amount of pain, either pain connected with the learning itself or distress connected with giving up certain previous learning.
2. Significant learning takes place when the subject matter is perceived by the student as relevant for his/her own purpose. A person learns significantly only those things which he perceives as being involved in the maintenance of, or the enhancement of, his own self.
3. Learning which involves change in self-organization—in the perception of oneself—is threatening and tends to be resisted.
4. Those learning experiences, which are threatening to the self, are more easily perceived and assimilated when external threats are at a minimum.
5. When threats to the self are low, experience can be perceived in a different fashion and learning can proceed.
6. Much significant learning is acquired through doing.
7. Learning is facilitated when the student participates responsibly in the learning process.
8. Self-initiated learning which involves the whole person of the learner—feelings as well as intellect—is the most lasting and pervasive.
9. Independence, creativity, and self-reliance are all facilitated when self-criticism and self-evaluation are basic and evaluation by others is of secondary importance.
10. The most socially useful learning in the modern world is the learning of the process of learning, a continuing openness to experience and incorporation into oneself of the process of change.

All these hypotheses are important, but involving the whole learner—feelings as well as intellect should be the most important in terms of helping learners achieve perspective transformation. Without going through this process, learners' behavior can be changed to a certain extent. As Rogers put it, to achieve the most lasting and pervasive change, learners should involve the whole person in learning. To do so, learners also need to be engaged on multiple levels and with multiple experiences and technology can help provide those experiences.

SUMMARY

This preface has posited that technology cannot transform or replace adult learners. Rather, it is the learners themselves that can transform themselves by using technology as a tool to enhance learning. Therefore, technological applications should be placed more emphasis in vocational and adult education or in any other field. The power of technology should not be exaggerated. After all, it is humans who develop and invent new technology at all times. The theory of transformative learning has developed as a different branch of the theory of andragogy in adult education. It is based on Habermas's three kinds of knowledge, Marx's critical theory and Freire's radical philosophy. Learners seek to transform themselves via four epistemological positions. No one single theory of learning is more important than another. As Knowles's prediction about E-Learning came true in the new century, technology has provided an additional learning environment for learners to engage in transformative learning. In a sense, this additional access point to knowledge has accelerated learning, which means that learners do learn at a faster pace than in the past when technology was not available. Learning anywhere, anytime is needed in the information age when speed is used to measure learning or progress. Does more time on critical reflection mean more learning? Supposedly so. According to Rogers (1969), learning involves the whole person of the learner... and the whole person needs more critical reflection.

Victor C. X. Wang
Florida Atlantic University, USA
April 7, 2012

REFERENCES

Belenky, M., & Stanton, A. (2000). Inequality, development, and connectedknowing. In Mezirow, J. (Eds.), *Learning as transformation: Critical perspectives on a theory in progress* (pp. 71–102). San Francisco, CA: Jossey-Bass.

Bettis, P. J., & Gregson, J. A. (2001). The why of research: Paradigmatic and pragmatic considerations. In Farmer, E. I., & Rojewski, J. W. (Eds.), *Research pathways: Writing professional papers, theses, and dissertations in workforce education* (pp. 1–21). New York, NY: University Press of America.

Bloom, B. S. (1956). *Taxonomy of educational objectives: The classification of educational goals – Handbook one: Cognitive domain*. New York, NY: Longman.

Cranton, P. (1994). *Understanding and promoting transformative learning: A guide for educators of adults*. San Francisco, CA: Jossey-Bass.

Cranton, P. (2006). *Understanding and promoting transformative learning: A guide for educators of adults* (2nd ed.). San Francisco, CA: Jossey-Bass.

Cranton, P. (2010). Working towards self-evaluation. In Wang, V. C. X. (Ed.), *Assessing and evaluating adult learning in career and technical education* (pp. 2–11). Hangzhou, China: ZUP.

Creswell, J. W. (2009). *Research design: Qualitative, quantitative, and mixed methods research* (3rd ed.). Los Angeles, CA: SAGE.

Cunningham, P. M. (1998). The social dimension of transformative learning. *PAACE Journal of Lifelong Learning, 7*, 15–28.

Dirkx, J. (2001). Images, transformative learning and the work of soul. *Adult Learning, 12*(3), 15–16.

Farmer, L. (2010). Career and technical education technology: Three decades in review and technological trends in the future. In Wang, V. C. X. (Ed.), *Definitive readings in the history, philosophy, practice and theories of career and technical education* (pp. 259–277). Hershey, PA: Information Science Reference.

Habermas, J. (1971). *Knowledge and human interests*. Boston, MA: Beacon Press.

Kacirek, K., Beck, J. K., & Grover, K. S. (2010). Career and technical education: Myths, metrics, and metamorphosis. In Wang, V. C. X. (Ed.), *Definitive readings in the history, philosophy, practice and theories of career and technical education* (pp. 31–49). Hangzhou, China: ZUP.

Kegan, R. (2000). What 'form' transforms? A constructivist-developmental approach to transformative learning. In Mezirow, J. (Eds.), *Learning as transformation: Critical perspectives on a theory in progress* (pp. 35–70). San Francisco, CA: Jossey-Bass.

Knowles, M. S. (1970). *The modern practice of adult education: Andragogy versus pedagogy*. New York, NY: Association Press.

Knowles, M. S. (1975). *Self-directed learning: A guide for learners and teachers*. New York, NY: Association Press.

Knowles, M. S. (1984). Introduction: The art and science of helping adults learn. In Knowles, M. S. (Eds.), *Andragogy in action* (pp. 1–21). San Francisco, CA: Jossey-Bass.

Knowles, M. S., Holton, E., & Swanson, A. (1998). *The adult learner*. Houston, TX: Gulf Publishing Company.

Mezirow, J. (1991). *Transformative dimensions of adult learning*. San Francisco, CA: Jossey-Bass.

Mezirow, J. (2000). Learning to think like an adult. In Mezirow, J. (Eds.), *Learning as transformation: Critical perspectives on a theory in progress* (pp. 3–34). San Francisco, CA: Jossey-Bass.

Neuman, W. L. (2000). *Social research methods: Qualitative and quantitative approaches* (4th ed.). Boston, MA: Allyn & Bacon.

Olgren, C. H. (2000). Learning strategies for learning technologies. In E. J. Burge (Ed.), *The strategic use of learning technologies* (pp. 7-16). New Directions for Adult Continuing Education, No. 88. San Francisco, CA: Jossey-Bass.

Rogers, C. R. (1969). *Freedom to learn*. Columbus, OH: Merrill.

Schutz, A. (1967). *The phenomenology of the social world*. London, UK: Heinemann.

Skinner, B. F. (1968). *The technology of teaching*. New York, NY: Appleton-Century-Crofts.

Tu, W. M. (1979). *Humanity and self-cultivation: Essays in Confucian thought*. Berkeley, CA: Asian Humanities Press.

Wang, V. C. X. (2006). *Essential elements for andragogical styles and methods: How to create andragogical modes in adult education.* Boston, MA: Pearson Education.

Wang, V. C. X. (2008). *Facilitating adult learning: A comprehensive guide for successful instruction* (Rev. ed.). Boston, MA: Pearson Education.

Watson, G. (Ed.). (1967). *Concepts for social change.* Washington, DC: National Training Laboratories Institute for Applied Behavioral Science.

Chapter 1
Leading Pedagogical Change with Innovative Web Tools and Social Media

Catherine McLoughlin
Australian Catholic University, Australia

ABSTRACT

Today, in a globalised, digital world, leadership challenges in the adoption and integration of emerging social software tools to support learning abound. Today's students, who have grown up in technology saturated environments, have never known a world without the internet, mobile phones, video on demand and personal computers. Leaders and educators must know their students, and cater for their diverse needs. Educational institutions in the 21st century must learn how to adopt social software tools and apply sound pedagogical strategies to add value to existing practices and enhance the learning process. ICT supplements and enhances learning and student engagement through access to global learning communities and rich resources, requiring educators to be conversant with the technology, able to lead by example and capable of creating authentic contexts and environments for learning. Educators in today's media rich society must be ready to grapple with the significant pedagogic, cultural and social changes associated with technological innovation.

INTRODUCTION

The development and uptake of digital tools and social software is bringing about massive societal and economic change. Yet, technology's impact on education, teaching, and learning has been

DOI: 10.4018/978-1-4666-2062-9.ch001

rather limited. While expectations have run high about web-based instruction, personal computers, computer-based instruction, social media and the raft of "Web 2.0" tools, the impact on teaching and learning is not well documented. While there are cases of innovation and transformation of pedagogies, there remain many exemplars of outmoded, traditional curricula and didactic instruction that merely replicate face-to-face teaching rather than innovations that make best use of interactive tools and technologies (Schrum & Leven, 2009).

The paper will focus on leadership challenges that educators need to be fully aware of in the adoption of emerging social software tools, and the need for educators to embrace innovative pedagogies in order to capitalise on Web 2.0 applications to support teaching and assessment in meaningful and authentic ways. The adoption of social software tools need to be integrated into sound pedagogical strategies in order to add value to existing practices and to enhance the learning process. The article supports the notion that ICT supplements and enhances learning and student engagement through access to global learning communities and rich resources, thereby creating opportunities for dialogue with others, for broadening understanding and participation leading to improved social and learning outcomes. The realization of these benefits can only come through institutional leadership that is focused on adoption of appropriate pedagogies, learner centred curricula and the design of effective learning environments and learning activities.

CHALLENGES IN THE DIGITAL AGE: STUDENTS AND LEARNING ENVIRONMENTS IN TRANSITION

Worldwide, higher education institutions today are confronted by considerable change driven by a myriad of external factors. The current learning landscape is characterized by constant connectivity, networked spaces, web-based tools and virtual learning environments. Mobile devices and social media abound, and the dramatic shift in learner characteristics and demands is evidenced by the emergence of "millennial students" who are digitally literate, always on, communicative, and experimental and community oriented (Oblinger & Oblinger, 2005). The terms "learner voice" and "learner experience" are central to today's

technology supported learning environments, and a number of studies have emphasized how ICT tools can facilitate learner engagement and participation (Conole, 2008). Today's students demand interactivity and thus there is a pressing need to meet t their needs and to rethink approaches to teaching and learning in order to replace outmoded didactic pedagogies, which place emphasis on the delivery of content from a textbook or website rather than being learner-centric and to allowing for self-paced flexible learning. Clearly, many popular learning management systems (LMS's) and virtual learning environments (VLE's) used by educational institutions to support e-learning perceive the student as "information consumer" thereby reinforcing instructor and content-centered approaches to teaching, learning, and cognition. Many commonly used learning management systems simply feed information or content to students and do not include social engagement, peer learning or creative inquiry by students. In the Web 2.0 era, such approaches no longer meet student needs. Tim Berners-Lee (2000, p. 216), the inventor of the World Wide Web, foreshadowed a more open, social raft of tools that are not simply about learners downloading and consuming information when he stated, "I have always imagined the information space as something to which everyone has immediate and intuitive access, and not just to browse, but to create" (p. 169). These words foreshadowed the Web 2.0 era, with its raft of social tools (Flickr, Facebook, Twitter, and MySpace) which allow users expanded capacities for creative, collaborative and communicative responses, often leading to idea generation and knowledge creation. The rise of learner generated content is captured by Wheeler, Yeoman and Wheeler (2008) who state *"The social network provides opportunities for the individual learner to create sound and viable knowledge syntheses from fractured and inchoate information"* (p. 989). For digital age learners, Web 2.0 tools are part of the learning landscape, and are therefore worthy of consideration by educators and instructional designers.

LEARNING PARADIGMS IN TRANSITION: M-LEARNING, B-LEARNING AND HYBRID LEARNING

Learning paradigms are moving beyond offering prepackaged information to students, as mobile devices and social media allow for connectivity beyond the classroom and for engagement with global communities. Efforts aimed at moving the learning environment beyond the classroom seem to be gaining momentum on campuses worldwide, evidenced by the emerging paradigms on m-learning and b-learning (mobile learning and blended learning). The terms "hybrid learning" and "blended learning" have been found to represent many levels of meaning and many encompass multiple different perspectives (Sharpe, Benfield, Roberts, & Francis, 2006). Since the advent of e-learning, however, the focus in the literature has appeared to be predominantly focused on the combination of delivery modes, i.e. face-to-face (F2F) and web-based. Blended learning programs are designed to take advantage of the relative strengths of the various instructional modes - the really important factor is not the blend of online and face to face, but what that blend enables. The right "mix" should enable mass customization of the creation and use of learning resources, more flexibility in terms of learner participation and time-on-task, multimodalities of presentation and creation. The distinctions between hybrid learning and e-learning may become decreasingly significant or even irrelevant in a networked society (New Media Consortium, 2007) where ICT tools, including Web 2.0 and mobile technologies, are becoming increasingly pervasive. What we are seeing is the blending of all elements of a successful learning environment-the courses, time, mode of delivery, media, technologies, and all of this is to accommodate learner choice, lifestyle convenience, flexibility and cognitive style.

More recently, mobile devices have become commonplace tools used in teaching, learning, work and leisure, hence the word m-learning. At societal level we are also witnessing wider, societal shifts such as the merging of formal and informal learning as social network communities function as personal and personalisable spaces for online conversations and sharing of content. The current wave of ubiquitous computing and social software tools enable an expanded repertoire of learner-teacher interaction, distributed collaboration, and communication, and their transformative effects on society, learning, and networking are becoming increasingly visible. Social networking sites can be characterized as environments for democratic forms of self-expression and as they support interaction and exchange of ideas between users they are also spaces for informal learning.

Hybrid learning experiences offer great potential for enhancing the learning experience as they use multiple modalities and technologies. Institutions are offering significant variations on the blended and online learning paradigms models with many options for choice and participation. Leadership issues are still paramount and it is critical that institutions understand and respond to learner expectations and capabilities, while ensuring that staff have the skills to use the technology creatively, and to adopt innovative pedagogies that engage and retain students.

THE CHANGING TEACHING AND LEARNING LANDSCAPE

Recent changes to the global adoption of information and communications technologies (ICT's) place higher education institutions at the forefront of pedagogical practice and require them to constantly reevaluate their approaches to curriculum, student support and the creation of physical and virtual learning environments. The Horizon (2010) report offers insights into the major challenges facing higher education providers, and signals not only technological change, but also identifies emerging trends relating to pedagogy, learner needs and design of learning technologies. A number of salient trends is identified below, and each is discussed each with issues for pedagogical leadership.

Revisiting the Role of Educators in Teaching

There is now an abundance of resources and relationships which are easily accessible via the Internet the challenge for universities is to offer quality degrees and a unique learning experience. The Open Education movement allows personalization, customization and re-use of learning resources, and reduces the cost of materials and texts. Initiatives such as MIT's OpenCourseWare marked the start of the Open Educational Resource (OER) movement, a movement largely strategically driven on institutional levels. With this movement good quality tools and educational materials are made freely available to educators and learners throughout the globe. During the past years many institutions followed this move indicating that there is a growing trend within traditional education to 'open up' (UNESCO, 2009). The Open Educational Resource movement has emerged as what might be seen as an alternative to traditional educational environments, aiming at broadening access to education for the next generation. The current OER movement is tackling perhaps one of the most crucial aspects for education: free and open access to educational resources being released under a commons license and thus the possibility to re-use those resources and to adapt them. This form of sharing and re-use gradually taking off and there is growing number of open access publishers where users can view books and monographs online for free. In the process, The OER movement creating a culture of lifelong learning that spans the distance between formal and informal education and opens pathways for development and innovation on a global scale. One of the challenges is that while universities have always been seen as the gold standard for

educational credentialing, there are now alternative programs from other providers that are now competing for the same clients. The Open Education movement emphasises community building, participation and user generated content. Examples are The Open University (Open learn Labspace), Wikibooks and Wikiversity.

Changes to Pedagogy: Demands for Flexibility

Life in an increasingly busy world means that learners must balance demands from home, work, school, and family. Demands for professional growth pose a host of logistical challenges with which today's ever more mobile students must cope. Informal learning in the workplace forms part of the lifelong learning policy in Europe and elsewhere (OECD, 2003). Increasingly the trend for consumption, creation and sharing of ideas and knowledge with Web 2.0 applications is set to continue (Shirky, 2003), in what O'Reilly called the architecture of participation. People want easy and timely access not only to the information on the network, but to their social networks that can help them to interpret it and maximize its value. The implications for informal learning are profound, as are the notions of "just-in-time" learning and "found" learning, both ways of maximizing the impact of learning by ensuring it is timely and efficient (2010, Horizon Report). For educational leaders, the challenge is now to develop more personalized learning environments that allow flexibility and choice, and that cater to the social and cultural needs of the students.

Learning Outcomes as a Portfolio of Literacies

Worldwide, universities now acknowledge that they have a key role in providing students with strategies and competences to allow them to be part of the current information society and to be able to graduate and take up a productive career. Learning outcomes now include what are known as digital or media literacies, a term that has a number of definitions (Beetham, McGill & Littlejohn). What constitutes new media literacies also known as *transliteracies* i.e. the notion that effective communication requires using, producing and interacting across multiple media and social platforms and contexts. The concept includes the kind of capabilities that are essential in self managing learning and in managing and choosing strategies to enable them to thrive in a networked world with ubiquitous, embedded digital technologies. Graduates from universities should be critical, evaluative, self-aware, confident and skilled individuals capable of using technologies to work live and engage in lifelong learning. However, this trend is also impacting and bringing to the fore the importance on a growing range of other literacies. Two examples of this are: (i) *civic literacies* where participatory media coupled with the 21st century digital generation bring collective action and more openness/transparency to the civic arena (Jenkins, 2007), (ii) *ecoliteracies*- education and knowledge-based action for sustainable living. It has been claimed that universities have tended to dismiss the importance of this form of knowledge, preferring to focus upon attitudes/values in the teaching of environmental education. More recently, there have been arguments that identify eco-literacy as the "missing paradigm" in education more broadly.

The leadership challenges are that institutions worldwide must consider the unique value that each form of literacy adds to student capability in a globalised world where information is abundant and the need for practical, ecological skills is becoming more important. More than ever, digital literacy, ie sense-making and the ability to assess the credibility of information are paramount. Mentoring and preparing students for the world in which they will live, is at the forefront, and the goals of universities worldwide acknowledge that they have key role in this area.

Adoption of Social Media as a Classroom Resource is more Common

Students are already making friends and connecting via social spaces, and turning to the Web to navigate their academic lives. With expectations for greater ICT integrating and round the clock connectivity, students are the drivers of change in pedagogy, and social media are being hailed as essential to a 21st-century education. Teachers can become involved in professional or interest-based social communities using social networking tools, and thereby engage in professional learning online. The big challenge is that more teachers/ instructional designers have to understand how to effectively use social media as an engaging learning resource rather than assuming they can simply upload content and facts and require learners to regurgitate content to earn grades. Merely grafting social media onto old paradigms of teaching/ testing leads to dismal failures and disengaged students. Social media and their affordances alert us to the poverty of old teaching paradigms that disrupt those traditional practices and offer students an opportunity to create knowledge and engage deeply with ideas, peers and the global learning community (Lee, McLoughlin & Chan, 2008). An example of changing practices is the new focus on engaging students by using Web 2.0 tools and social media, called *Pedagogy 2.0* (McLoughlin & Lee, 2008).

Change to Teaching and Learning Roles: From Andragogy to Heutagogy

Pedagogy 2.0 is a framework that aims to focus on desired learning outcomes in order to exploit more fully the affordances and potential for connectivity enabled by Web 2.0 and social software tools. It is envisioned as an overarching concept for an emerging cluster of practices that advocates learner choice and self-direction, and engagement in flexible, relevant learning tasks and strategies. Though not intended a prescriptive framework, it distills a number of guidelines characterizing effective learning environments, such as choice of resources, tasks, learning supports, and communication modalities, as follows:

- *Content:* micro units of content that augment thinking and cognition; may include a wide variety of learner-generated resources accruing from students creating, sharing, and revising ideas;
- *Curriculum:* dynamic, open to negotiation and learner input, consisting of "bite-sized" modules, inter-disciplinary in focus, and blending formal and informal learning;
- *Communication:* multiple opportunities for open, social, peer-to-peer, and multi-faceted forms of visual, verbal, and auditory communication, using multiple media types to achieve relevance, immediacy, and clarity;
- *Learning processes:* situated, contextualized, reflective, integrated with thinking processes, iterative, dynamic, performance, and inquiry-based;
- *Resources:* multiple informal and formal sources that are media rich, interdisciplinary, and global in reach;
- *Scaffolds:* student support should come from a network of peers, teachers, experts, and communities;
- *Learning tasks:* authentic, personalized, experiential, and learner driven and designed, and enable the creation of content and innovative ideas by learners.

These principles represent the intersection between established instructional design principles for the creation of constructivist, student-centered learning environments (e.g. open-ended learning, authentic learning, and inquiry-based learning) and emerging perspectives on cognition including connectionism. They are evident in and have been derived from the exemplary practices of a growing number of teachers in tertiary education who have begun to demonstrate how social software tools offer rich possibilities for students to create and share ideas, connect, and participate in broader learning communities that are not confined to the spaces in which formal teaching and learning activities take place. Nevertheless, the rapid social and socio-technical changes adoption of innovative practices presents universities with challenges. Universities have to prepare themselves and not just their learners for an uncertain future. However, a cautionary note is needed: in some cases, staff may assume that students are more digitally capable than they really are, and therefore both academic support structures and training in learning technology are very important (Kennedy et al., 2008).

DIGITAL AGE LEARNING: FORMAL AND INFORMAL

Globally we are witnessing the uptake of a rich and diverse set of digital tools that should be able to support many new ways to support learning. The devices include: smart personal phones, mobile devices supporting access to media such as music, tools to sense and capture activity, e-book readers, tablets, laptops, desktops, collaborative devices such as e-whiteboards and tabletops, with cloud and internet based integration of services. This array of tools appears to have the potential to support many new ways to learn, in formal and informal settings. Debate about some of the possibilities offered by mobile and social media tools for new visions of education and the challenges, such as effective assessment, empowering the classroom teacher and enabling new forms of learner control.

This paper has presented the major leadership challenges in higher education that are associated with fostering learning processes that encourage the production and use of student centred learning, and curricula that integrate learner-generated content. Nevertheless, there is still a need for accountability and recognition of authoritative sources of information. Content supplied by teachers and textbook authors is but one of many resources available to assist students in developing knowledge and skills, and may have limitations, particularly if it pre-empts learner exploration and discovery, and active student involvement in the knowledge creation process. At the same time, in their desire to engage emerging forms of collaborative scholarship and self-expression, students must be made aware of the expectations from the point of view of academic integrity (Edson, 2007). There is also a need for quality assurance mechanisms to maximise the validity and reliability of learner-generated content. Moving away from teacher-centred models of evaluation and assessment, the review, editing and quality assurance of content can be done collaboratively and in partnership with learners, while simultaneously drawing on input from the wider community (i.e., "wisdom of crowds").

Teachers who adopt social software tools need to integrate the tools into sound pedagogical strategies in order to transform and improve existing courses, and facilitate authentic exchange and dialogue with and among students (Berg, Berquam, & Christoph, 2007). They need to convince their students' that social networks and communities add value to the learning process, and ensure that social spaces and networks are use to support both formal and informal learning activities (Jenkins, 2007).

A FOCUS ON DIGITAL SKILLS: HOW TO MEET THE CHALLENGE

It must be recognised that the implementation of new pedagogies that utilise web 2.0 tools is not without its issues and challenges. For example, although the advent of Web 2.0 and Web 3.0 and the open content movement significantly increases the volume of information available to students

and exposes them to a raft of ideas and representations, many higher education students currently lack the competencies necessary to navigate and use the overabundance of information available, including the skills required to locate quality sources and assess them for objectivity, reliability and currency (Windham, 2005; Katz & Macklin, 2007). In recently published reports it is recommended that students develop sound information literacy skills in effectively finding, evaluating, and creating information (Beetham et al., 2009). Additionally, beyond search and retrieval, information is contextualised, analyzed, visualised and synthesised, which involves complex critical thinking skills and evaluation by learners.

The need is to balance the demands for these tools, which fall into the realm of Web 2.0 and are often user controlled, against the need for central IT leadership to assert an appropriate amount of control, reliability and security. This is often seen as the choice between using open source software as opposed to using a closed learning management system or "walled garden". With the Open Education movement there is an emerging "open source leadership" style that university leaders must accommodate and learn to value the contributions of community rather than control them (Hilton, 2006).

There is a growing body of research that demonstrates that in combination with appropriate strategies, social software can also serve as levers for such critical thinking and meta-cognitive development (e.g., Sener, 2007b; Lee & McLoughlin, 2010). There is a growing willingness on the part of administrators to consider new approaches to combining face-to-face and technology-assisted instruction. Initiatives such as the Gates Foundation's *"Next Generation Learning Challenges"* will likely move this trend forward in the near future. How universities balance the demands for these new tools with centralised administrative systems and learning management systems that do not allow students to personalise their learning experiences is a further challenge.

FUTURE TRENDS

While there is a great deal of enthusiasm about the potential of new tools and social media, there are leadership challenges as higher education explores dozens of e-learning technologies to support learning (for example, electronic books, virtual worlds, text messaging, podcasting, wikis, blogs), with new ones seeming to emerge each week. Such innovative technologies confront instructors and administrators at a time of continued budget retrenchments and rethinking of the role of the 21st century university. Adding to this, there is increase competition among universities for students and concerns that bored students may drop out of online classes as they are expecting and demanding richer and more engaging online learning experiences. Given the demand for e-Learning, the abundance of social media and Web 2.0 tools that are being grafted into teaching there are expanded opportunities for innovation. However, there are tensions between centralized, institution supported virtual learning environments and learner configured personalized spaces. Universities are therefore facing are a "perfect storm," that threatens to shift pedagogy, learning spaces and the unique role of educational institutions.

A major report published by UNESCO (2009) signals the major changes that are occurring worldwide in higher education and mentions that internationalisation and catering to diversity are prominent challenges across the globe. The realities of the 21st century have magnified these challenges and there is a need to diversify student support and services to meet the needs of diversification and multiculturalism. Universities may offer study abroad program, curriculum differentiation, or inter-institutional partnerships. Alongside these trends, Web 2.0 tools are giving students and academics access to wider, global communities, to tap into the affordances of social networking, where learners from multiple cultural backgrounds can share ideas, communicate and generate new ideas. Technology can be seen as a driver of change, and a tool for empowerment at an individual level, but also at community and institutional level as globalisation has made interconnectivity a focal point. Leadership in higher education, whether it is by individuals, teams or consortia must be systemic and transformational, that is it must have an outlook that considers how change in one area impacts on other areas.

Systemic changes leadership models hold promise for the future as they are complex and non-linear and involve all participants and players, and have quality improvement, progress and open communication as essential elements. Leadership in a Web 2.0 world needs these qualities and a vision of how to harness technology to improve learning and meet the needs of a diverse student population. Part of the 21st century leaders' job will be to help change pedagogy and to ensure that university teaching is not about being "sage on the stage" but is about mentoring, coaching, personalising and facilitating lifelong learning, while allowing students to create and shape their own learning pathways.

CONCLUSION: LEADERSHIP CHALLENGES TO HIGHER EDUCATION PRACTITIONERS

Innovative practices supported by social media provide an opportunity for higher education institutions to look at wider implementation issues around technical infrastructure, but they must also address pedagogical challenges such as the integration of informal learning experiences, the limitations of existing physical and virtual learning environments and the personalisation of learning experiences (Alexander, 2006). Student diversity, expectations for technology saturated environments and the demand for skills that offer potential for employment are the main agendas driving change in provision for pedagogical innovation and teaching of digital literacy skills. Curricula are being revised and each individual has responsibility to respond to change and progress by utilising current learning technologies to achieve the best outcomes. Worldwide, schools and universities are seeking to move into the 21st century, and needs models of leadership that embrace change, quality improvement and progress.

Often, educators may be confronted with the expectation of working in unfamiliar environments and scenarios, and with tools with which they lack expertise and confidence. Leaders need to make time for professional learning, awareness raising, and discussion of what pedagogic approaches and tools best target the desired learning outcomes. The goal is to be flexible and to meet students' expectations, be less prescriptive, and be open to new media, tools and strategies, while nurturing innovation and creativity, independent inquiry and digital literacy skills (Barnes & Tynan, 2007). Overall, for the power and potential of innovative web tools and social media to be realised, institutional change combined with systemic leadership is needed.

REFERENCES

Alexander, B. (2006). Web 2.0: a new wave of innovation for teaching and learning? *EDUCAUSE Review*, *41*(2), 33–44.

Anderson, T. (2007, June 25-29). Social Learning 2.0. In *Proceedings of ED-MEDIA 2007: World Conference on Educational Multimedia, Hypermedia & Telecommunications,* Vancouver, BC, Canada. Retrieved from http://www.slideshare.net/terrya/educational-social-software-edmedia-2007/

Barnes, C., & Tynan, B. (2007). The adventures of Miranda in the brave new world: learning in a Web 2.0 millennium. *ALT-J. Research in Learning Technology*, *15*(3), 189–200.

Beetham, H., McGill, L., & Littlejohn, A. (2009). *Thriving in the 21st century: Learning literacies for the Digital Age*. Retrieved from http://elearning. jiscinvolve.org/wp/2009/06/11/thriving-in-the-21st-century-learning-literacies-for-the-digital-age/: JISC, UK

Berg, J., Berquam, L., & Christoph, K. (2007). Social networking technologies: a "poke" for campus services. *EDUCAUSE Review*, *42*(2), 32–44.

Bryant, T. (2006). Social software in academia. *EDUCAUSE Quarterly*, *29*(2), 61–64.

Conole, G. (2008). listening to the learner voice: The ever changing landscape of technology use for language students. *ReCALL*, *20*, 124–140. doi:10.1017/S0958344008000220

Edson, J. (2007). Curriculum 2.0: user-driven education. *The Huffington Post*. Retrieved from http://www.huffingtonpost.com/jonathan-edson/curriculum-20-userdri_b_53690.html

Goodman, E., & Moed, A. (2006, November 4-8). Community in mashups: the case of personal geodata. In *Proceedings of the 20th ACM Conference on Computer Supported Cooperative Work*, Banff, AB, Canada. Retrieved from http://mashworks.net/images/5/59/Goodman_Moed_2006.pdf

Hilton, J. (2006). The future for higher education: sunrise or perfect storm. *EDUCAUSE Review*, *41*(2), 58–71.

Jenkins, H. (2007). *Confronting the challenges of participatory culture: media education for the 21st Century*. Chicago: MacArthur Foundation. Retrieved from http://www.digitallearning.macfound. org/atf/cf/%7B7E45C7E0-A3E0-4B89-AC9C-E807E1B0AE4E%7D/JENKINS_WHITE_PAPER.PDF

Katz, I. R., & Macklin, A. S. (2007). Information and communication technology (ICT) literacy: integration and assessment in higher education. *Systemics. Cybernetics and Informatics*, *5*(4), 50–55.

Kennedy, G., Dalgarno, B., Bennett, S., Judd, T., Gray, K., et al. (2008). *Immigrants and Natives: Investigating differences between staff and students' use of technology*. Paper presented at Hello! Where are you in the landscape of educational technology? 25th Annual Conference of the Australasian Society for Computers in Learning in Tertiary Education (ASCILITE), Melbourne, Australia.

Lee, M. J. W., & McLoughlin, C. (Eds.). (2010). *Web 2.0-based e-learning: Applying social informatics for tertiary teaching*. Hershey, PA: Information Science Reference.

Lee, M. J. W., McLoughlin, C., & Chan, A. (2008). Talk the talk: learner-generated podcasts as catalysts for knowledge creation. *British Journal of Educational Technology*, *39*(3), 501–521. doi:10.1111/j.1467-8535.2007.00746.x

McLoughlin, C., & Lee, M. J. W. (2008). Future learning landscapes: transforming pedagogy through social software. *Innovate: Journal of Online Education, 4*(5). Retrieved from http://innovateonline.info/index.php?view=article&id=539

New Media Consortium. (2007). *A global imperative: the report of the 21st Century literacy summit*. Retrieved from http://www.nmc.org/pdf/Global_Imperative.pdf

O'Reilly, T. (2005). *What is Web 2.0: design patterns and business models for the next generation of software*. Retrieved from http://www.oreillynet.com/pub/a/oreilly/tim/news/2005/09/30/what-is-web-20.html

Oblinger, D. G., & Oblinger, J. L. (Eds.). (2005). *Educating the net generation*. Washington, DC: EDUCAUSE.

OECD. (2003). *ICT and Economic Growth: Evidence from OECD countries, industries and firms*. Paris: Author.

Report, H. (2010). *2010 horizon report*. Retrieved from http://wp.nmc.org/horizon2010/

Schrum, L., & Levin, B. (2009). *Leading 21st Century schools: Harnessing technology for engagement and achievement*. Thousand Oak, CA: Corwin.

Sharpe, R., Benfield, G., Roberts, G., & Francis, R. (2006). *The undergraduate experience of blended e-learning: a review of UK literature and practice*. York, UK: The Higher Education Academy.

Shirky, C. (2003). *Social software and the politics of groups*. Retrieved November 2, 2010, from http://www.shirky.com/writings/group_politics.html

UNESCO. (2009). *Trends in Global Higher Education: Tracking an academic revolution*. Paris: Author.

Wheeler, S., Yeomans, P., & Wheeler, S. (2008). The good, the bad and the wiki: Evaluating student-generated content for collaborative learning. *British Journal of Educational Technology*, *39*(6), 987–995. doi:10.1111/j.1467-8535.2007.00799.x

Windham, C. (2005). The student's perspective. In Oblinger, D. G., & Oblinger, J. L. (Eds.), *Educating the Net Generation* (pp. 5.1–5.16). Washington, DC: EDUCAUSE.

This work was previously published in the International Journal of Adult Vocational Education and Technology, Volume 2, Issue 1, edited by Victor C.X. Wang, pp. 13-22, copyright 2011 by IGI Publishing (an imprint of IGI Global).

Chapter 2
Online Instructors:
Andragogical or Pedagogical Teaching?

Victor C. X. Wang
California State University at Long Beach, USA

Beth Kania-Gosche
Lindenwood University, USA

ABSTRACT

This study investigates the andragogical and pedagogical teaching philosophies of online instructors at the California State University, Long Beach in the Spring Semester of 2010. Drawing from reflective adult education theory, this article proposes a new model for this reflective adult education theory. It is either the helping relationship (andragogical philosophy) or the directing relationship (pedagogical philosophy) plus the learning environment (the Internet) that leads to adult learners' critical reflection in Mezirow's (1991) terms. A researcher-designed survey instrument called Online Philosophy of Adult Education Scale (OPAES) was used to measure instructional preferences of these instructors in the electronic classroom to determine their andragogical or pedagogical teaching philosophies. Data were collected from 37 online instructors regarding their instructional preferences. Nine qualitative questions were designed to parallel the Likert scale OPAES to determine why these online adult education instructors chose their pedagogical or andragogical teaching philosophies. The results of the study demonstrate that these online adult education instructors support both the teacher-centered approach and the student-centered approach to teaching online.

INTRODUCTION

Since current theories of transformative learning generally rest on humanistic philosophy and Knowles' version of andragogy is based on humanistic psychology, online learning for adults and

DOI: 10.4018/978-1-4666-2062-9.ch002

principles of andragogy have become inseparable, especially because of the asynchronous nature of many online courses. Although adults are responsive to external motivators, such as grades or verbal praise, adults are basically internally motivated. When it comes to online transformation, adults' real interest is in how to maximize their learning without the benefit of having a face-to-face discussion with their instructors. Adult learners may hold full time jobs and have family responsibilities, which may make physical travel to a campus for class difficult or even impossible, thus online courses are appealing.

To some extent, andragogy was designed to maximize adult learning especially adults' online transformation where the individual adult learner is a "free-agent" in his or her own learning. To some scholars, andragogy is more a technological application of psychological and sociological knowledge. However, to Knowles, it became a continuum from teacher-directed to student-directed learning. This student-centered learning is a democratic approach to teaching and learning. Influential scholars have delved into the principles of andragogy such as self-concept of adult learners (Tough, 1967, 1971; Knowles, 1975; Mezirow, 1985; Brookfield, 1986; Pratt, 1988, 1993; Brockett & Hiemstra, 1991; Candy, 1991; Merriam & Caffarella, 1999; Merriam, 2001). Because adult learners are capable of self-direction in learning, some scholars doubt whether a teacher-learner relationship is really needed given the asynchronous nature of cyberspace learning. Rhode (2009) investigated adult learners' preferences in a self-paced online environment, rather than the traditional course calendar many higher education institutions utilize.

However, to say this teacher-learner relationship is not needed is to overemphasize the power of self-direction. Even when adult learners are highly self-directed, an andragogical type of teacher-learner relationship may facilitate adult learning. When adult learners are highly self-directed, they may also require the traditional pedagogical teacher-learner relationship because of speed, convenience, previous experience in courses, or learning styles. Not only is this relationship necessary, but also the kinds of andragogical and pedagogical teaching philosophies online instructors may hold strongly affecting this relationship, hence adult online transformation. "Most students have a tendency for sensing, visual, and active

styles of learning. However, most college courses follow the lecture teaching style" (Wirz, 2004, p. 2). The instructors' teaching philosophies lead to the methods and art of teaching. Ultimately, students' critical reflection is affected by these methods and art of teaching. However, no empirical study has been conducted to determine online instructors' teaching philosophies. Most literature has focused on the learners' preferences (Rhodes, 2009) rather than the instructor's.

The present study is an investigation to determine and describe online instructors' andragogical and /or pedagogical teaching philosophies. The humanistic principles of andragogy support a helping relationship (andragogical philosophy) between teachers and learners whereas principles of pedagogy indicate a directing relationship (pedagogical philosophy) between teachers and learners. This exploratory study is only a first step to examining this concept.

"Although a learner-centered approach is strongly supported in the literature, a teacher-centered approach is widely practiced in community college and university settings" wrote Kraska and Harris (2007, p. 19) in their study of cognitive style and teaching style. They found no relationship between the two in a sample of 65 students enrolled in Air Force Reserve Officer Training. Their study emphasized the importance of innovating in teaching, rather than recruiting those with the same style. However, this study did not specifically examine online learning, although the sample did consist of adult educators.

For self-directed adult learners, online learning requires an andragogical relationship with their instructors. As a consultant or delegator, instructors link their students to learning resources. In contrast, the pedagogical information transmitter will only disappoint self-directed adult learners who are experienced with a subject matter and are capable of teaching themselves. However, the information transmitter is highly helpful when adult learners are inexperienced with a subject matter and do not have independent learning skills.

The andragogical instructor should provide topics-driven courses with open-ended questions. Such online activities leave much room for adult learners' prior experience, which serves as the best resource for learning. "Online learners desire an instructor who addresses them as individuals and offers supportive comments" (Dennen et al., 2007, p. 68). When online topics-driven courses with open-ended questions are designed to accept their viewpoints (Wang, 2003), adult learners feel they are treated with dignity and respect. In this context, online adult education becomes andragogical education. For this to occur, students must interact with the instructor, with each other, and with the content (Dennen et al., 2007; Rhode, 2009). In Rhode's (2009) study of college students in a self-paced environment, students consistently rated interactions with the content and the instructor as more important than interactions with other learners. However, in a self-paced course, learner-to-learner interactions are obviously more difficult as each student is in a different place. Adapting to meet individual needs may also require sacrifice of other elements, such as peer knowledge sharing.

Thoughtful comments by the instructor may further facilitate online learning. Palloff and Pratt's (1999) research indicated that by providing thought-provoking comments, the instructor truly involves herself or himself in the learning process. Therefore, the instructor is viewed as a co-learner in the online educational process (Price, 1999). However, Dennen, Darabi, and Smith (2007) found that timeliness of feedback was more important than quantity of feedback, at least from the students' perspectives. The instructor should resist the urge to respond to every comment posted by a student and allow the class to share with each other, creating a community (Dennen et al., 2007). As adult learners and the instructor learn together, a helping relationship instead of a directing relationship emerges. In their study of college students, Ravert and Evans found (2007)

A continuing trend in all levels of education is toward creating constructivist and student-centered learning environments. The interest is particularly evident in literature on e-learning, where researchers and designers are enthusiastic regarding the potential of technology to allow for constructivist-oriented pedagogical approaches that have heretofore been difficult to accomplish (p. 321).

Drawing on the literature of college student development, Ravert and Evans (2007) suggested that early college students may have difficulty with a course where the instructor follows andragogical principles or constructivism. They found a statistically significant negative relationship between grade level and "(a) absolute knowledge that is factual and unambiguous and (b) absolute perspective, with the learning process being singularly controlled and orchestrated by the instructor" (p. 325). The sample of Ravert and Evans' (2007) study was, presumably, traditional college students as no mention was made of the demographics. Thus, it is difficult to generalize the results of their study to adult learners.

Contrary to the helping relationship, the directing relationship reveals that an online instructor manages courses by learning objectives. These objectives may stem from certification standards or departmental benchmarks. The pedagogical instructor tends to follow a behaviorist philosophy of teaching, which is driven by behavioral objectives. This is not to suggest that the helping relationship does not utilize any learning objectives. Rather, the andragogical instructor encourages adult learners to go beyond stated learning objectives or to create the learning objectives together. The directing relationship reflects competency-based teacher education. In this mode, teachers prefer to be regarded by their students as an unchallengeable authority. The more control the instructors have over the learners, the better they believe their learners can learn. The instructor may feel uncomfortable if she or he loses control of the learners. In an online environment especially, trust is essential between instructor and students for the course to be successful.

Without question, learning takes place in relationship with teachers, whether it is through direct interaction with the instructor or through direct interaction with content created or organized by the instructor. When it comes to online transformative learning, a teacher-learner relationship plus Internet Environment plus learners' critical reflection equal learner changed (transformation and emancipation in Mezirow and Freirian terms). The researchers sought to determine whether online adult education instructors preferred andragogical philosophies over pedagogical philosophies. Specifically, the researchers wanted to know what were the preferences of online adult education instructors relative to the following:

1. Liberal philosophy of teaching (Pedagogical).
2. Progressive philosophy of teaching (Andragogical).
3. Behavioral philosophy of teaching (Pedagogical).
4. Humanistic philosophy of teaching (Andragogical).
5. Radical philosophy of teaching (Andragogical; Paulo Freire's problem posing education).
6. Analytic philosophy of teaching (Andragogical; could be pedagogical).

Each of these philosophies of teaching will be explained in more detail in the Theoretical Framework section of this article. The authors seek to examine whether there is an intersection of andragogy (helping relationship between teachers and learners) and pedagogy (directing relationship between teachers and learners). It begins with an overview of online learning, moves into theoretical framework, and is followed by the procedure and results of a mixed-methods research study.

BACKGROUND: OVERVIEW OF ONLINE LEARNING

Knowles predicted that teaching, especially teaching of adults for the 21st century would be delivered electronically. Knowles also predicted that the de-institutionalization of education, in the form of open and independent learning systems, is creating a need for learners to develop appropriate skills. "Students entering into these programs without having learned the skills of self-directed inquiry will experience anxiety, frustration and often failure, and so will their teachers" (Knowles, 1975). The connection Knowles drew between adults' online transformation and principles of andragogy, especially self-concept of adult learners is clear. Today's academic institutions are in transition. According to the National Center for Education Statistics (2009),

The number of young students has been growing more rapidly than the number of older students, but this pattern is expected to shift. Between 1995 and 2006, the enrollment of students under age 25 increased by 33 percent. Enrollment of people 25 and over rose by 13 percent during the same period. From 2006 to 2017, NCES projects a rise of 10 percent in enrollments of people under 25, and a rise of 19 percent in enrollments of people 25 and over.

Kraska and Harris (2007) noted, "increased diversity of students may frustrate instructors. Unfamiliar with many of the new student characteristics, instructors see contemporary students as hopelessly unprepared" (p. 8). Thus, any instructor in higher education should be familiar with andragogical learning, as more learners are adults returning to class. One of the characteristics of nontraditional students (adult learners) is that they perform multiple roles and responsibilities (Wang, 2003). To accommodate adult learners' needs, more and more institutions of higher learning have responded to Knowles' call 20 years ago by turning to the use of the Internet to deliver courses to students at a distance, as well as to enhance educational programs that are delivered on campus. Some adult learners choose to take online courses, for they may be self-directed learners in that they do not need much direction and support from their instructors. Others may choose to take online courses simply because they have no other choices due to employment and family responsibilities. Universities have to meet the needs of this new population of students. Institutions of higher learning are faced with the pressure to control costs, improve quality, focus directly on customer needs, and respond to competitive pressures.

Information technology (IT) has the potential to solve many of the problems. It can change the roles of students and faculty. Although Knowles made a successful prediction about the use of electronic media for the education and training of adult learners in the 21st century, he did not spell out the connections between andragogical/pedagogical orientations and the teaching philosophies of online instructors. It is researcher's responsibility to align these orientations with the preferred teaching philosophies of online instructors. "If students' learning styles are compatible with the teaching style of their instructors, they tend to retain more information, effectively apply it, and have a better attitude toward the subject" (Wirz, 2004, p. 1). Instructors must be able to recognize their own teaching philosophies and teaching styles to be able to meet the needs of learners.

Dennen et al. (2007) examined how learners and instructors perceived a list of 19 practices of online instruction using a survey. For most items, instructors and students prioritized similarly; however, "timeliness was more important to students than the extent of feedback" (p. 76). However, this could be because of the students' focus on a grade rather than if learning is occurring. Their study indicated that instructors should be responsive to learner communication, especially through email. Dennen et al. (2007) also recommended

that instructors model assignments and behavior, which is consistent with andragogical principles.

THEORETICAL FRAMEWORK

Action without philosophical reflection leads to a mindless activism (Elias & Merriam, 1995, p. 4). Philosophies of teaching lead to meaningful practice. Humanistic philosophy of teaching is characterized by freedom and autonomy, trust, active cooperation and participation, and self-directed learning. Therefore this mode of teaching is andragogical in nature. According to Wang and Sarbo (2004), humanistic instructors tend to enhance personal growth and development, facilitate self-actualization, and reform society. The prominent leader, Knowles advocated needs-meeting and student-centered andragogical approach to adult learning. Since progressive philosophy of teaching emphasizes experience-centered education and democratic education, it falls squarely in line with the Need to Know and Prior Experience principles of andragogy.

Progressive adult educators give adult learners the practical knowledge and problem-solving skills necessary to reform society.

Radical philosophy of teaching proposes education as a force for achieving radical social, political and economic changes in society. A chief proponent of this philosophy of education is Freire (1970, 2003) who advocated radical conscientization as the true function of education among the oppressed (Elias & Merriam, 1995, p. 11). This philosophy's problem posing method of teaching can be andragogical, for it takes into consideration learner's readiness to learn and orientation to learning principles of andragogy. Radical adult educators work to change culture and its social structures.

Analytic philosophy of teaching can be highly andragogical, for it emphasizes the need for clarifying concepts, arguments, and policy statements used in adult education. This logical and scientific positivism of analytic philosophy again indicates a democratic andragogical approach to adult learning. Elias and Merriam (1995) posit that the role of the analytic adult educators is not to construct explanations about reality but to eliminate language confusions (p. 181).

Liberal philosophy of teaching characterized by organized knowledge is pedagogical by nature, for lecture method is the most used and the most abused method by those who hold this kind of teaching philosophy. Liberal adult educators tend to make adult learners literate in the broadest sense—intellectually, morally, and spiritually.

Behaviorist philosophy of teaching characterized by programmed learning, behavioral objectives, and competency-based teacher-education can be highly pedagogical. It is top-down education, an essential form of pedagogical philosophy of teaching in adult learning. The purpose of behaviorist education is to bring about behavior that will ensure survival of the human species, societies, and individuals and the role of behaviorist adult educators is to promote behavior change.

Wang (2005) maintains that a key concept in reflective adult education theory is critical reflection (p. 18). The three types of reflection identified by Mezirow (1991, 2000) are as follows: content reflection (i.e., an examination of the content or description of a problem); process reflection (i.e., checking on the problem-solving strategies); premise reflection (i.e., questioning the problem). Although reflective adult education theory by Mezirow (1991, 2000) and Brookfield (1991, 1995) seems to work well with adults' online transformation and emancipation, it focuses on a set of skills or processes possessed by individuals to teach (Boxler, 2004). This theory does not take into consideration the immediate situation that an adult learner is involved in. It is in relationship with teachers (either a helping relationship or a directing relationship) that causes learners' critical reflection to occur whether in the electronic classroom or in the traditional classroom. Failure to acknowledge this relationship (andragogical

philosophy or pedagogical philosophy) is to deny the need for an intersection of andragogy and pedagogy. To ignore students' relationship with teachers is to say that reflective adult education theory takes effect without students' social interaction with their teachers in the electronic classroom. Reflective adult education theory has been criticized for its lack of attention to any relationship between teachers and students. Since andragogy's inception, adult learning professionals have been labeling themselves as "trained" learning facilitators. Any connection with pedagogy is viewed as negative. For this study, the researcher seeks to shed light on the convergence of andragogical teaching philosophies and pedagogical teaching philosophies.

METHODOLOGY

Participants

As technology comes into greater use, faculty and students alike are grappling with changes it brings to the educational environment. The Occupational Studies Department of California State University, Long Beach (CSULB) has seized the chance and enrolls approximately 1500 adult students in its distance education programs every semester. Students in the CSULB Occupational Studies Programs usually are classified as non-traditional students; they come from such backgrounds as police and military officers, firefighters, secondary and postsecondary instructors and teachers, corporate employees, and many others. This study does not focus on all students; rather, it focuses on the students who have been teaching adult students in their own disciplines and those adult credential students who will become instructors of adult students in the future. Because of the nature of their work, these adult students take courses related to Adult Education via the Internet offered through Occupational Studies Department at CSULB. Regardless of their career path, they have one common goal that is to acquire adequate skills to facilitate the learning of adult learners either in the traditional classroom or in the electronic classroom. One of the purposes of offering courses in adult education online by CSULB is to equip online instructors with sound teaching philosophies so that adult learning can be maximized. These adult students themselves are bone fide nontraditional students that seek transformation and emancipation in learning via the Internet. Therefore, in this study they were identified as a group of "online instructors and /or adult educators." In the Spring Semester of 2010, a survey of 37 online instructors at CSULB was conducted. The online instructors taking courses of Adult Education via the Internet from the Department of Occupational Studies at CSULB were from 25 to 65 years old. These adult educators (online instructors) chose to take the online courses because they either liked the online version of the courses or they had no other choices due to their full time employment, family responsibilities or transportation constraint. This convenience sample is just the first step in this exploratory study; further research is needed to draw any conclusions.

Instruments

The study employed a quantitative design supplemented with a qualitative element. First, the researcher designed a survey instrument called Online Philosophies of Adult Education Scale (OPAES) to determine and describe online instructors' andragogical and /or pedagogical teaching philosophies in the electronic classroom (cyberspace learning). The survey instrument was designed based on Elias and Merriam's (1995) and Knowles, Holton, and Swanson's (1998) description of what adult educators may do if they possess certain andragogical/pedagogical teaching philosophies either in a traditional classroom setting or in a cyberspace learning situation. The survey utilizes a Likert scale from five to zero with five being the highest (support for the student-centered approach to learning) and zero the lowest (support for the teacher-directed approach to learning). For this study, survey responses were used to determine and describe online instructors' andragogical and /or pedagogical teaching philosophies in cyberspace in order to develop the base of data. The adult educators' mean scores were calculated using the Statistical Package for Social Sciences (SPSS-16.0 for Windows). The mean score of 2.5 represents the midpoint between 0 and 5.

High mean scores represent support for the student-centered approach (andragogical) to teaching. Low mean scores indicate support for the teacher-directed approach (pedagogical) to teaching. If a mean score nears the mean score (2.5), it may indicate support for the andragogical philosophy; it may also indicate support for the pedagogical philosophy.

In addition, the study, while primarily quantitative in design, included qualitative data regarding why these adult educators chose certain andragogical philosophies in preference to others. To collect this qualitative information, a series of nine open-ended questions were designed to parallel the quantitative survey questionnaire. The participants surveyed answered the nine open-ended questions by using paper and pencil. The quantitative design by the researcher together with the qualitative element ensures the comprehensiveness of the study. The quantitative survey instrument, together with the qualitative survey instrument for this study, was posted inside Beachboard (a version of Blackboard used to teach courses at California State University, Long Beach). The survey was available to 60 adult educators who were taking the courses via the Internet offered through Occupational Studies Department at CSULB in the Spring Semester of 2010. Thirty-seven (62%) of these adult educators volunteered to respond to the survey instrument and their survey was submitted to the researcher through a feature called digital drop box inside Beachboard. While this is a small sample size, this study is exploratory in nature, and the response rate was high.

A group of three adult education instructors in the department of Occupational Studies, California State University, Long Beach, California, who were not included in the sample, were used in a pilot study to validate the instrument. Data gathered from the validation study were not included in the study but were used to determine whether revisions to the instrument were needed. The validation study was also used to test to clarity and comprehensibility of the questionnaire items. Validation study results indicated revisions to the instrument were not needed since the adult education instructors in the validation study understood the questions in the survey instrument. In sum, the questions used could be considered content valid. The alpha reliability coefficient for the instrument was .92. (N of cases = 37, N of items = 19).

DATA ANALYSIS

Data collected in this study were analyzed using SPSS (16.0 for Windows) software. Since the survey instrument (OPAES) contain positive items and negative items, different values were assigned to these items. For positive items, the following values are assigned: "Always" equals five, "almost always" equals four, "often" equals three, "seldom" equals two, "almost never" equals one and "never" equals zero. For negative items, the following values are assigned. "Always" equals zero, "almost always" equals one, "often" equals two, "seldom" equals three, "almost never" equals four and "never" equals five. Omitted items are assigned a neutral value of 2.5.

Analysis was conducted for each item in the research question. For descriptive statistics, mean scores and standard deviations were reported for adult education educators' responses. To provide a better picture of the population surveyed, the overall scale mean scores and standard deviations were also calculated. The findings were entered

into tables and figures, and a narrative was developed to report the findings.

To provide greater depth of analysis, patterns and themes in qualitative data were reported to supplement and complement quantitative findings. First, the textual data was organized categorically, reviewed repeatedly, and continually coded. Second, patterns and themes from the perspective of the participants were identified and described. The patterns and themes were listed using percentages in the section of findings. Third, these patterns and themes were analyzed and compared to the findings from the quantitative data analysis, and the literature review of the study. The data analysis process was not aided by the use of a qualitative data analysis computer program since the qualitative database is small (e.g., less than 500 pages of transcription) (Creswell, 2003).

FINDINGS

The purpose of the study was to determine and describe online instructors' andragogical and / or pedagogical teaching philosophies. Research questions revolved around Knowles' principles of andragogy and Freire's problem posing education. The questions were developed out of Elias and Merriam's (1995) and Knowles, Holton, and Swanson's (1998) description of what adult educators may do if they possess certain andragogical/pedagogical teaching philosophies either in a traditional classroom setting or in a cyberspace learning situation. Thirty-seven adult educators answered survey questions via the Internet, using the survey instruments.

Tables 1 through 6 summarize the analysis of survey results. The mean scores for these adult education instructors on each of the six principles of andragogy are presented in separate tables. Each of the tables contains several items that determine and describe online instructors' andragogical and /or pedagogical teaching philosophies. The standard deviation scores for these online adult education

Table 1. Online adult educators' responses for liberal teaching philosophy

Mode One: Liberal Teaching Philosophy Responses	n=37 M	N=60 SD
1. I use the lecture method as an efficient instructional strategy	3.00	1.41
19. I develop students' intellect through reading, reflection, and production	4.00	1.00

instructors are also provided in the tables. Table 1 summarizes the online adult educators' responses for Liberal Teaching Philosophy.

Table 1 indicates that online adult education instructors had high scores in the two variables. The results suggest that these instructors favored the liberal Teaching Philosophy. When conducting teaching, they tended to use the lecture method as an efficient instructional strategy and supported the notion of developing students' intellect through reading, reflection, and production. The use of the lecture method is greatly supported in the literature.

Table 2 shows that the online adult education instructors had high scores on the four variables. These results indicate that these instructors applied the experiential learning principle of andragogy in their learning and teaching. First, they provided a learning setting in which they became a co-learner, a helper, guide, encourager, consultant and resource person. They also organized, stimulated,

Table 2. Progressive teaching philosophy responses

Mode Two: Progressive Teaching Philosophy Responses	n=37 M	N=60 SD
3. I organize, stimulate, instigate and evaluate the highly complex process of education	3.65	1.18
6. I am a helper, guide, encourager, consultant, and resource instead of a transmitter, disciplinarian, judge and authority	4.22	1.18
7. I provide the setting that is conducive to learning	4.30	1.08
8. I become a learner in the learning process	4.30	1.08

instigated, and evaluated the highly complex process of education.

Table 3 indicates that these online adult education instructors had high scores on the variables in Behavioral Teaching Philosophy. The results show that these instructors designed an environment that elicited desired behavior toward meeting educational goals and to extinguish behavior that was not desirable. They were contingency managers, environmental controllers or behavior engineers who planned in detail the conditions necessary to bring about desired behavior. These results indicate that these online adult education instructors favored behavioral Teaching Philosophy.

Table 4 indicates that online adult education instructors had high scores in four of the five variables that make up humanistic Teaching Philosophy. These results suggest that these instructors basically favored humanistic Teaching Philosophy except that they provided information to their students, which is something humanistic instructors do not do. The results show that these instructors were facilitators, helpers, and partners in the learning process; they created the conditions within which learning could take place; they trusted students to assume responsibilities for their learning and respected and utilized the experiences and potentialities of students. Humanists do not provide information to students. However, these online adult education instructors provided information to their students.

Table 3. Behavioral teaching philosophy responses

Mode Three: Behavioral Teaching Philosophy Responses	n=37 M	N=60 SD
4. I design an environment that elicits desired behavior toward meeting educational goals and the extinguish behavior that is not desireable	3.89	1.13
5. I am a contingency manager, an environmental controller, or behavioral engineer who plans in detail the conditions necessary to bring about desired behavior	2.97	1.24

Table 5 shows that these online adult education instructors had high scores in three of the four variables that comprise radical Teaching Philosophy. These results indicate that these instructors generally applied radical Teaching Philosophy except that they determined the themes that served to organize the content of the dialogues, which is something radical instructors do not do.

Table 6 indicates that these online adult education instructors did not favor analytic Teaching Philosophy. Although they eliminated language confusions, they constructed explanations about reality, which is something analytic instructors do not do.

Table 7 shows that online adult education instructors had high scores on Mode One, Two, Three, Four and Five. This result suggests that these instructors applied liberal Teaching Philosophy, experiential approach to teaching, behavioral Teaching Philosophy, humanistic Teaching Philosophy and radical Teaching Philosophy. Although relatively a little higher than the mean score 2.5, their score on the Analytic Teaching Philosophy was low in comparison with other scores, indicating that these instructors might not favor the analytic Teaching Philosophy.

The nine qualitative questions (Table 8) included in the survey were designed to parallel the quantitative portion of the survey developed out of Elias and Merriam's (1995) and Knowles, Holton, and Swanson's (1998) description of what adult educators may do if they possess certain andragogical/pedagogical teaching philosophies either in a traditional classroom setting or in a cyberspace learning situation. For the first two questions, 30 (81%) of 37 adult education instructors indicated "yes" as their answer. For question three, 22 (59%) of 37 adult education instructors gave yes as their answer. For question four, 29 (78%) of 37 adult education instructors indicated "yes" as their answer. For question five, 10 (27%) of 37 adult education instructors indicated "yes" as their answer.

Table 4. Humanistic teaching philosophy responses

Mode Four: Humanistic Teaching Philosophy Responses	n=37 M	N=60 SD
11. I trust students to assume responsibility for their learning	3.97	1.07
12. I respect and utilize the experiences and potentialities of students	4.46	0.77
13. I provide information to my students	0.49	0.77
14. I am a facilitator, helper, and partner in the learning process	4.49	0.69
15. I create the conditions within which learning can take place	4.30	0.91

Table 5. Radical teaching philosophy responses

Mode Five: Radical Teaching Philosophy Responses	n=37 M	N=60 SD
9. I offer a libertarian, dialogic, and problem-posing education	3.27	1.07
10. I emphasize the importance of dialogue and equality between teacher and learners	4.08	0.95
16. I am open to clarifications and modifications	4.65	0.63
17. I determine the themes that serve to organize the content of the dialogues	1.35	0.79

Table 6. Analytic teaching philosophy responses

Mode Six: Analytic Teaching Philosophy Responses	n=37 M	N=60 SD
2. I eliminate language confusions	3.95	1.08
18. I construct explanations about reality	1.54	1.37

Table 7. Thirty-seven online adult education instructors on overall scale means and standard deviations on the six teaching philosophies

Six Teaching Philosophies	n=37 M	N=60 SD
1. Liberal Teaching Philosophy	3.50	1.21
2. Progressive Teaching Philosophy	4.12	1.13
3. Behavioral Teaching Philosophy	3.43	1.19
4. Humanistic Teaching Philosophy	3.54	0.84
5. Radical Teaching Philosophy	3.34	0.86
6. Analytic Teaching Philosophy	2.75	1.23

Table 8. Nine Qualitative Questions to supplement and complement the Quantitative

Analysis
1. Briefly identify the following individuals: Malcolm Knowles, Jack Mezirow, Peter Jarvis, Stephen Brookfield, Kathleen King, and Sharan B. Merriam. Please indicate "unknown" for individuals you cannot identify.
2. Briefly explain the difference between andragogy and pedagogy.
3. Do you negotiate curricular priorities with your adult students at the beginning of each course you teach? Why or why not?
4. Do you take into account your adult learners' prior experience when planning your lessons?
5. Do you believe that the lecture method is superior to facilitating learning? Why or why not?
6. Do you use a learning contract when assessing adult students' learning? Why or why not?
7. Do you think it should be a goal of adult educators to help all adult learners become self-directed?
8. Do you design activities that build students' self-esteem and sense of accomplishment while delivering course content? Why or why not?
9. Do you encourage a search for real-life examples, develop assignments related to real-life situations and embed the content of your course in everyday life? Why or why not?

For question six, 26 (70%) of 37 adult education instructors indicated that they did not use a learning contract when assessing adult students' learning. For question seven, 33 (89%) of 37 adult education instructors indicated "yes" as their answer. For question eight, 33 (89%) of 37 adult education instructors indicated "yes" as their answer. For question nine, 33 (89%) of 37 adult education instructors indicated "yes" as their answer.

DISCUSSION

The purpose of the study was to determine and describe online instructors' andragogical and /or pedagogical teaching philosophies. The findings of the quantitative portion of the study showed that the 37 online adult education instructors surveyed supported both a teacher-centered (pedagogical) approach to teaching and a student-centered (andragogical) approach to teaching in the electronic classroom setting (cyberspace learning). Future studies using a larger sample size would further validate the instrument. Additional questions, such as length of time teaching online, could determine if experience was a predictor. Future studies using online observations of the participants' classrooms

could also determine if the self-report items on the survey were actually occurring.

For the pedagogical approach to teaching, these adult education instructors tended to use the lecture method as an efficient instructional strategy and supported the notion of developing students' intellect through reading, reflection, and production. They designed an environment that elicited desired behavior for meeting educational goals and that extinguished behavior that was not desirable. They were contingency managers, environmental controllers or behavior engineers who planned in detail the conditions necessary to bring about desired behavior. The use of this pedagogical approach in the online environment may reflect several psychological and spiritual issues: our online adult learning professionals may have a fear of losing control or a fear of losing authority over students. If they do not stay highly connected with students by being liberal and behaviorist, they feel that adult learners' online transformation may never take place. The use of this pedagogical approach in the online environment may also reflect the fact that some of our online adult learners may constantly search for connection, interdependence, intimacy, and safety. If their instructors are not "there" for them, these adult learners may feel isolated, aimlessly wandering (Rhode, 2009). Palloff and Pratt's (1999) research reveals that extroverted adult learners in cyberspace learning environments require their instructors to be pedagogical in their instruction.

For the andragogical approach to teaching, these adult education instructors applied the experiential learning principle in their teaching and learning. They provided a learning setting in which they became a co-learner, a helper, guide, encourager, consultant and resource person. They organized, stimulated, instigated, and evaluated the highly complex process of education. The instructors surveyed were facilitators, helpers, and partners in the learning process; they trusted students to assume responsibilities for their learning and respected and utilized the experiences and potentialities of students. This preference for the andragogical approach to teaching in the online environment appears related to Knowles' humanistic assumption that every adult learner has unlimited potential for learning. All adult learners have enormous pent up energy. Once stimulated, low achievers can become high achievers under the influence of an andragogical facilitator. Palloff and Pratt (1999) took this approach further by stating:

Our online instructors may provide general topics within the body of knowledge about which students together might read and make comment. Or the instructor may ask open-ended questions designed to stimulate critical thinking about the topics being discussed. Additionally, it is important for the instructor to make thoughtful comments on student posts, designed again to stimulate further discussion (p. 74).

Although they are the beneficiaries of principles of andragogy, these online adult education instructors violated Knowles' humanistic principles and Freire's principle of problem-posing education. For example, these instructors provided information to their students, which is something humanistic instructors do not do. They determined the themes that served to organize the content of the dialogues, which is something Freire's followers would not do. However, these violations of andragogical principles can be justified if we consider Grow's (1991) Stages in Learning Autonomy.

Grow (1991) suggested the four stages and corresponding teaching methods/styles presented in Table 9.

Grow's Stages in Learning Autonomy suggest that learners' stages of learning determine the situational roles of adult educators. It must be noted that the order of learners' stages of learning may not be sequential, for some adult learners may not necessarily go through stage 1 and stage 2 before they reach stage 4 (W. McWhinney, personal communication, February 12, 2004). Grow's Stages in Learning Autonomy illustrate the situational roles of adult educators also for the online learning environment. If adult learners are still at Stage 1 and Stage 2, online adult education instructors do not need to be andragogical. Following a humanistic and Freirian approach at this point may frustrate and lose adult learners in the online learning environment.

Findings of the qualitative portion of the study revealed surprising results. Responses to the qualitative questions also indicated that the 37

Table 9. Grow's Stages in Learning Autonomy

Stages	Learner	Educator	Methods/Styles
Stage 1	Dependent	Coach	Coaching with immediate feedback, drill. Informational lecture.
Stage 2	Interested	Motivator	Inspiring lecture plus guided discussion. Goal setting.
Stage 3	Involved	Facilitator	Discussion facilitated by teacher who participates as equal.
Stage 4	Self-directed	Consultant	Internship, dissertation, self-study

online adult education instructors surveyed supported both the andragogical approach to teaching and the pedagogical approach to teaching in the electronic classroom setting (cyberspace learning). What was surprising for Western adult learning professionals was that 27% of the 37 online adult education instructors surveyed indicated that they believed the lecture method is superior to facilitating learning. For example, 27% of the 37 online adult education instructors claimed:

Lecture has its place when utilized for specific technical information provided to those who do not have a base knowledge and when time is of the essence. Yes, the lecture method is a needed tool when the learner has no clue as to the subject matter. Otherwise the teacher needs to determine what it is she/he is hiding. Yes, lecture will define the material and process...

This result confirmed that the teaching philosophies preferred by Chinese adult educators may also be preferred by American adult learning professionals. Wang and Bott's (2004) research showed that in general, political, economic, and social context determined Chinese adult educators' preference for the pedagogical methods in their instruction of adult learners.

Another surprising result was that 70% of the 37 adult education instructors surveyed indicated that they did not believe in using a learning contract when assessing adult students' learning. This response is surprising in light of the fact that the Western form of andragogy (student-centered teaching) is characterized by using learning contracts to structure coursework, negotiating the syllabus, asking students to compile personal learning journals, and relying on open-ended discussion methods. They further indicated that using Knowles' learning contract may undermine the self-directed learning preference of adult learners. They claimed that using a learning contract is very pedagogical and that it is most appropriate for pre-adults and immature learners. In this view, self-directed learners should not be bound by a learning contract, for they know exactly whether

learning has taken place or whether learning has illuminated the dark areas of ignorance in the online learning environment.

The response to other qualitative questions confirmed the quantitative portion of the study. Thirty-three (89%) of 37 adult education instructors indicated that being self-directed in learning allows their students to be in control of their education. They further indicated that designing activities that build students' self-esteem and sense of accomplishment while delivering course content could better motivate adult learners. By using real-life examples, developing assignments related to real-life situations and embedding the content of courses in everyday life, online adult education instructors could make their course more relevant and meaningful. A crucial part of Mezirow's Transformative Learning Theory (1991, 2000) is reflection on the part of the adult learners themselves. By being andragogical facilitators in the online learning environment, instructors make space for perspective transformation (King, 2000). The online classroom is fertile territory for transformational learning.

The significance of this study is that its results corroborated Hase and Kenyon's (2000) research, which suggested that Knowles set the foundation for principles of adult learning, but these principles still include a teacher-student relationship. If this is true, then the current study takes this teacher-student relationship one step further. It is either the helping relationship (andragogical philosophy) or the directing relationship (pedagogical philosophy) plus the learning environment (i.e., the Internet, Cyberspace) that leads to adult learners' online critical reflection in Mezirow's (1991) terms.

In light of these findings, adult learning professionals should be encouraged to stop labeling themselves as "trained" online facilitators just because they wish to show that they are true followers of such andragogical leaders as Knowles, Rogers, Mezirow, Jarvis, Brookfield and Merriam. For adults' online transformation, andragogy is not the only way. Pedagogy still has its place. It is in relationship with others that learners learn. This relationship could be a helping relationship; it could be a directing relationship. Only when these adult learning professionals move in and out of the pedagogical and andragogical philosophies freely, can they really become successful online "facilitators" of adult learners in electronic classroom settings.

The results of this study confirmed Hersey and Blanchard's (1969) situational leadership styles in that when followers (learners in cyberspace learning) have low need for direction and low need for support, leaders (teachers in cyberspace learning) become consultants or delegators. Self-directed as learners are in cyberspace learning, they still need a relationship with their teachers, and this relationship reflects a humanistic helping relationship, which is the andragogical teaching philosophy. When followers (learners in cyberspace learning) have high need for direction and high need for support, leaders (teachers in cyberspace learning) become directors/coaches. When such a situation occurs, teachers have to switch to the pedagogical teaching philosophy, which is characterized by being liberal and behaviorist in teaching.

IMPLICATIONS FOR ADULT EDUCATION THEORY AND PRACTICE

Since Knowles predicted that teaching, especially teaching of adults for the 21st century, would be delivered electronically, adults' online transformation and principles of andragogy have become inseparable. However, this is not to say that the teacher-centered approach to teaching and learning does not have its place among adult learners/educators. To try to restrict online teaching/learning to the andragogical method is to fail to understand the teaching and learning process. Certain aims and objectives of a lesson and the content to be taught may leave adult learning

professionals with no room for their andragogical preference. To restrict teaching exclusively to an andragogical method may allow for the possibility of irresponsibility and unacceptable eccentricities especially when andragogy is referred to more as an art rather than a science.

To try to say which of the two methods of teaching (pedagogical and andragogical) affects adults' online transformation more is extremely difficult since each of us who teaches engages not only in a time-honored process but one that is quite unique to the immediate situation in which we are actually teaching. The more we understand the difference between pedagogical philosophies and andragogical philosophies, the more likely we are to understand those whom we are privileged to teach online. Perhaps it is safe and beneficial to conform to Knowles' reminder that "an essential feature of andragogy is flexibility" (Knowles, 1984, p. 418). By being flexible, adult learning professionals accommodate both andragogical philosophies and pedagogical philosophies. A linear mode of teaching (either solely andragogical or solely pedagogical) can be detrimental in helping adults learn.

The issues of pedagogy and andragogy have ignited a tremendous amount of research into adult learning since Knowles advanced the principles of andragogy. These issues (i.e., pedagogy versus andragogy) will continue to spark further and subsequent research given the nature of the 21st century online transformation and emancipation. Finally, can we conclude that pedagogy is as important as andragogy in the process of teaching and learning based on the finding that some aspects of Knowles' humanistic principles and Freire's problem-posing education were violated by the 37 online adult education instructors surveyed? Further research is clearly needed to answer this question.

In the meantime, a new model has emerged from this study that can serve as the theoretical basis for further research to refine reflective adult education theory in the context of cyberspace learning. Both the helping relationship (andragogical philosophy) and the directing relationship (pedagogical philosophy) of adult learning professionals either *facilitate* or *inhibit* critical reflection of adult learners because these two relationships determine either the andragogical methods/styles or the pedagogical methods/styles, which eventually impact adult learners' critical reflection. The process by which these two relationships contribute to critical reflection in transformative learning in the online environment is illustrated in the model presented below.

Figure 1 illustrates the dynamic interaction of factors that contribute to learners' critical reflection in Mezirow's terms. A number of significant points are worth noting.

1. The helping relationship between adult learners and adult learning professionals comes from both the adult learning professionals' internal beliefs and the adult learners' self-direction in learning. This relationship inherently leads to andragogical methods and styles. The relationship provides the guiding principles for teachers of adult learners.

2. The directing relationship between adult learners and adult learning professionals may come from the adult learning professionals' internal beliefs. However, more often this relationship is determined by external factors such as the adult learners' need for direction and support. Naturally, this directing relationship leads to pedagogical methods and styles. This relationship may coexist with the helping relationship.

3. Both andragogical methods/styles and pedagogical methods/styles impact the learning environment. The online environment is ***not*** a vacuum. It is filled with human interaction.

4. Adult learners' critical reflection may occur by its self. That is, critical reflection depends on a set of individual skills and processes to teach. However, it is largely in relationship with others and with the environment that adult learners' critical reflection occurs.

5. Although from time to time, adult learners' critical reflection may be determined by factors other than those proposed on the model, this model illustrates the essential roles the two relationships play in impacting adult learners' critical reflection.

As more students turn to online learning, researchers must study this setting just as they would the face-to-face classroom. Findings from traditional classrooms settings may not translate into the online environment. Adult learners in an online environment require specific strategies, and instructors must be willing to meet their needs.

Figure 1. Model of reflective adult education theory

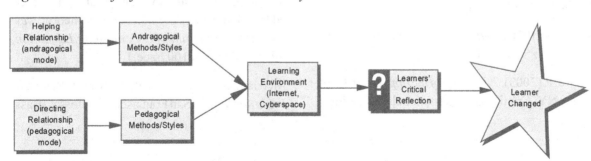

REFERENCES

Boxler, H. N. (2004). Grounded practice: Exploring criticalities in a job reeducation setting. *Adult Education Quarterly*, *54*(3), 210–223. doi:10.1177/0741713604263052

Brockett, R. B., & Hiemstra, R. (1991). *Self-direction in adult learning: Perspectives on theory, research, and practice*. London, UK: Routledge.

Brookfield, S. D. (1986). *Understanding and facilitating adult learning*. San Francisco, CA: Jossey-Bass.

Brookfield, S. D. (1991). On ideology, pillage, language and risk: Critical thinking and tensions of critical practice. *Studies in Continuing Education*, *13*(1), 1–14. doi:10.1080/0158037910130101

Brookfield, S. D. (1995). *Becoming a critically reflective teacher*. San Francisco, CA: Jossey-Bass.

Candy, P. C. (1991). *Self-direction for lifelong learning*. San Francisco, CA: Jossey-Bass.

Creswell, J. W. (2003). *Research design: Qualitative, quantitative, and mixed methods approaches* (2nd ed.). Thousand Oaks, CA: Sage.

Dennen, V. P., Darabi, A. A., & Smith, L. J. (2007). Instructor-learner interaction in online courses: The relative perceived importance of particular instructor actions on performance and satisfaction. *Distance Education*, *28*(1), 65–79. doi:10.1080/01587910701305319

Elias, J. L., & Merriam, S. B. (1995). *Philosophical foundations of adult education. Malabar*. Malabar, FL: Krieger Publishing.

Freire, P. (1970). *Pedagogy of the oppressed*. New York, NY: Seabury Press.

Freire, P. (2003). *Pedagogy of the oppressed*. New York, NY: Continuum International Publishing.

Grow, G. O. (1991). Teaching learners to be self-directed. *Adult Education Quarterly*, *41*(3), 125–149. doi:10.1177/0001848191041003001

Hammonds, K., Jackson, S., DeGeorge, G., & Morris, K. (1997). *The new university: A tough market is reshaping colleges*. Retrieved from http://www.businessweek.com/1997/51/b3558139.htm

Hase, S., & Kenyon, C. (2000). *From andragogy to heutagogy*. Retrieved from http://ultibase.rmit.edu.au

Hersey, P., & Blanchard, K. (1969). *Management of organizational behavior: Utilizing human resources*. Upper Saddle River, NJ: Prentice-Hall.

King, K. P. (2000). Educational technology that transforms: Educators' transformational learning experiences in professional development. In *Proceedings of the 42nd Annual Adult Education Research Conference*, Vancouver, BC, Canada.

Knowles, M. S. (1975). *Self-directed learning*. New York, NY: Association Press.

Knowles, M. S. (1984). *Andragogy in action*. San Francisco, CA: Jossey-Bass.

Knowles, M. S., Holton, E. III, & Swanson, A. (1998). *The adult learner*. Houston, TX: Gulf Publishing.

Kraska, M., & Harris, S. (2007). Cognitive and teaching style preferences of officers attending the Air Force Reserve Office Training Instructor Course. *Journal of Industrial Teacher Education*, *44*(5), 5–24.

Merriam, S. B. (2001). Andragogy and self-directed learning: Pillars of adult learning theory. *New Directions for Adult and Continuing Education*, *89*, 3–13. doi:10.1002/ace.3

Merriam, S. B., & Caffarella, R. S. (1999). *Learning in adulthood*. San Francisco, CA: Jossey-Bass.

Mezirow, J. (1985). A critical theory of self-directed learning. In Brookfield, S. (Ed.), *Self-directed learning: From theory to practice: New directions for continuing education, No. 25*. San Francisco, CA: Jossey-Bass.

Mezirow, J. (1990). *Fostering critical reflection in adulthood: A guide to transformative and emancipatory learning*. San Francisco, CA: Jossey-Bass.

Mezirow, J. (1991). *Transformative dimensions of adult learning*. San Francisco, CA: Jossey-Bass.

Mezirow, J. (Ed.). (2000). *Learning as transformation: Critical perspectives on a theory in progress*. San Francisco, CA: Jossey-Bass.

National Center for Education Statistics. (2009). *Fast facts*. Retrieved from http://nces.ed.gov/fastfacts/display.asp?id+98

Palloff, R. M., & Pratt, K. (1999). *Building learning communities in cyberspace*. San Francisco, CA: Jossey-Bass.

Pratt, D. D. (1988). Andragogy as a relational construct. *Adult Education Quarterly*, *38*, 160–181. doi:10.1177/0001848188038003004

Pratt, D. D. (1993). Andragogy after twenty-five years. *New Directions for Adult and Continuing Education*, 57.

Price, D. M. (1999). Philosophy and the adult learner. *Adult Learning*, *11*(2), 3–5.

Ravert, R. D. (2007). College student preferences for absolute knowledge and perspective in instruction: Implications for traditional and online learning environments. *Quarterly Review of Distance Education*, *8*(4), 321–328.

Rhode, J. F. (2009). Interaction equivalency in self-paced online learning environments: An exploration of learner preferences. *International Review of Research in Open and Distance Learning*, *10*(1), 1–23.

Tough, A. (1967). Learning without a teacher. *Educational Research Series, 3*.

Tough, A. (1971). *The adult's learning project*. Toronto, ON, Canada: Ontario Institute for Studies in Education.

Twigg, C. (1994). The need for a national learning infrastructure. *Educause, 29*(4-6).

Wang, V. (2003). *Principles of adult education*. Boston, MA: Pearson.

Wang, V. (2005). Adult education reality: Three generations, different transformation the impact of social context: Three generations of Chinese adult learners. *New York Journal of Adult Learning*, *3*(1), 17–32.

Wang, V., & Bott, P. A. (2004). Modes of teaching of Chinese adult educators. *New York Journal of Adult Learning*, *2*(2), 32–51.

Wang, V., & Sarbo, L. (2004). Philosophy, role of adult educators, and learning how contextually adapted philosophies and the situational role of adult educators affect learners' transformation and emancipation. *Journal of Transformative Education*, *2*(3), 204–214. doi:10.1177/1541344604265105

Wirz, D. (2004). Students' learning styles vs. professors' teaching styles. *Inquiry*, *9*(1).

This work was previously published in the International Journal of Adult Vocational Education and Technology, Volume 2, Issue 3, edited by Victor C.X. Wang, pp. 12-29, copyright 2011 by IGI Publishing (an imprint of IGI Global).

Chapter 3
Assuring Quality in Online Course Delivery

Julia M. Matuga
Bowling Green State University, USA

Deborah G. Wooldridge
Bowling Green State University, USA

Sandra Poirier
Middle Tennessee State University, USA

ABSTRACT

This paper examines the critical issue of assuring quality online course delivery by examining four key components of online teaching and learning. The topic of course delivery is viewed as a cultural issue that permeates processes from the design of an online course to its evaluation. First, the authors examine and review key components of and tools for designing high impact online courses that support student learning. Second, in this paper, the authors provide suggestions for faculty teaching online courses to assist in creating high quality online courses that supports teaching and, consequently, facilitates opportunities for student learning. Quality online course delivery is also contingent on the support of faculty by administration. Lastly, this paper provides suggestions for conducting course evaluation and feedback loops for the continual improvement of online learning and teaching. These four components are essential elements in assuring quality online courses.

INTRODUCTION

Few would argue that online teaching and learning has been and is on a meteoric rise. David Nagel (2009), in fact, predicted that by 2014 over 10 Million PreK-12 students will be taking online courses. A cursory search in Google Scholar

DOI: 10.4018/978-1-4666-2062-9.ch003

showed that over 2.3 million hits were found when searching for "online education". However, when the precursor "quality" was added to "online education" the search results declined to 1,050 articles. While this is a somewhat flawed example, it does illustrate a dilemma that has faced the field of online teaching and learning—ensuring quality while delivering course content and engaging students within online environments has not garnered the attention that it has deserved. The topic of course delivery to ensure quality within this paper is viewed as a cultural issue that permeates processes from the design to the evaluation of an online course.

It may first be helpful to highlight three myths and misconceptions about online teaching and learning. These myths/misconceptions are held by students, faculty, and administrators and influence any discussion about the quality of online course delivery (e.g., White, n.d.):

1. Online teaching and learning is 'worse' (or 'better') for meeting student learning outcomes than face-to-face courses.
2. Online teaching and learning is easier and more convenient for students and faculty than face-to-face courses.
3. Online teaching and learning is less interactive for both student and faculty than face-to-face courses.

All of these statements are based upon the premise that there are no special affordances or constraints of the environment, either online or face-to-face, when it comes to teaching or learning-that we are comparing apples to apples. It has been argued elsewhere that this is not the case, that there are many fundamental differences that the educational environment both affords or constraints (Anderson, 2004; Matuga, 2001, 2005, 2007) and that establishing a dichotomistic relationship does not adequately reflect the complexity of teaching or learning within either environment. In essence, learning and teaching within online environments is fundamentally *different* than learning and teaching in face-to-face environments. One is not comparing apples to apples, but more like apples to oranges.

A useful concept to use as a framework, one that more adequately reflects the complexity of online teaching and learning, would be to view both through the lens of a cultural system. There are many definitions of culture and descriptions of

what constitute a cultural system. LeVine (1984), for example, defined culture as "a shared organization of ideas that includes the intellectual, moral, and aesthetic standards prevalent in a community and the meanings of communicative actions" (p. 67). Others have claimed that these organizations of ideas and meanings derived from actions are not static and that culture should be thought of as systems that may be more complicated and organic collections of cognitive functions, practices, and meaning (D'Andrade, 2001; Giddens, 1984; Kitayama, 2002). Online teaching and learning may be viewed as cultural systems in that understandings and meanings are socially shared within online environments (Courtney, 2001; Mehlinger & Powers, 2002). There are also cultural practices and customs within these environments that may be linked, in various ways, to the values and beliefs of larger cultural systems, like face-to-face educational environments (Courtney, 2001; LeVine, 1984).

A more traditional view of cultural systems, for example, is based upon the idea that they contain within them, nested systems that are interdependent to the functioning of the system as a whole (White, 1975). This view holds that technological (or physical subsystem), social, and psychological factors guide a multitude of functions and influence the behaviors of individuals that are participating in cultural communities (Kityama, 2002; White, 1975). For example, Kitayama (2002) stated that "each person's psychological processes and structures are organized though the active effort to coordinate his or her behaviors with the pertinent cultural systems of practices and public meanings" (p. 92). While this is may be viewed as a valid preposition, this view does imply that there are somewhat distinct sub-systems that guide or organize psychological processes and practices. It may be quite common to reduce discussions regarding online teaching and learning to cultural sub-systems, like technological ones, for example, because the impact of technology may be seen as more explicit within online teaching and learning environments.

This position is arguable in light of contemporary pedagogical theory, however, which would hold that psychological and social factors need to be explored in conjunction with technological ones. Perhaps one of the most critical characteristic of a cultural system is that they support the development and transmission of meaning and understanding within and between participants. Rosaldo (1984) stated that "we must appreciate the ways in which such understandings grow, not from an "inner" essence relatively independent of the social world, but from experience in a world of meanings, images, and social bonds, in which all persons are inevitable involved" (p. 139). In the case of meaning making and understanding within online teaching and learning environments, the importance of viewing the psychological in conjunction with social and technological dimensions of cultural systems is implied. These are important points that frame the conversation of designing high impact online courses, providing suggestions for faculty teaching online courses, describing critical administrative support of faculty, and conducting course evaluation and feedback loops for continual improvement of online learning and teaching.

DESIGNING HIGH IMPACT ONLINE COURSES

Viewing online teaching and learning as a cultural system provides a framework to describe and understand 'high impact' online courses. Within education, 'high impact' refers to educational experiences that are meaningful, require student action and participation, and that contribute to the life-long learning of the student (Kuh, 2008). It is important to note that the examples illustrating high impact practices within online courses in this paper do not represent an exhaustive or comprehensive list, but serve as important points

of reference for discussion within this paper. Two such high impact practices that assist in the design of online courses are pedagogical alignment and meaning making.

Pedagogical Alignment

Pedagogical alignment, also called systematic instructional design (Gagne, Briggs, & Wagner, 1992), entails aligning instructional variables to provide the fundamental framework for online cultural systems, conveying meanings to community participants, and defining cultural activity. Instructional design is currently in the midst of a paradigm shift towards a more situated view of design activity within cultural systems (Anderson, 2004; Derry & Lesgold, 1996). When designing high impact online courses, pedagogical alignment involves the optimum use of a wide array of instructional features including, but not limited to, instructional goals, instructional strategies, and assessment measures and evaluation practices that support teaching and learning (see Matuga, 2005).

When instructional features do not align, then teaching and learning may be seriously undermined and compromised. A good example of this is a teacher who wants to teach students critical thinking skills (goal), has students participate in small group discussions or problem-solving activities (instructional strategies), but assesses students utilizing a multiple-choice examination (assessment) in which very little critical thinking is involved. While the goal and instructional strategies to obtain the goal are appropriately aligned with the other, the tool used to assess student learning is out of alignment.

The issue of pedagogical alignment in an online course is an important one, for several reasons. While in a face-to-face environment, instructional design and alignment may occur in conjunction with the other during instruction, alignment in an online course, in contrast, is often completed *a priori*. In fact, a clear, comprehensive, and logical course structure may be one of the primary factors which students use to judge whether or not an online course is an effective one. Online course alignment is further complicated by the affordances and constraints stemming from technology and the social and psychological composition of community participants. Each instructional variable is influenced by the affordances and constraints that influence technological, social, and psychological subsystems. For example, discussions regarding effective online course alignment must also incorporate pedagogical and technological expertise of students and teachers in the design process.

There may be several methods in which to assess whether or not pedagogical alignment was effective, more often than not, discussions regarding the effectiveness of online activities are reduced to formal, summative assessment practices such as tests, quizzes, projects, or portfolios. Pedagogical decisions regarding the selection of formal, summative assessments within online courses are important, especially when designing instructional strategies (see Duffy & Cunningham, 2001). However, it is equally important to plan for the manner in which formative assessments and other evaluative information will be utilized to inform other educational practices within the online environment. Teacher and student self-reflection, as a formative, informal assessment to inform learning is a potentially powerful tool for evaluating pedagogical effectiveness.

Another tool to assess pedagogical alignment is peer evaluation of the course itself. There may be many mechanisms and tools that faculty and administration can use that carry out the peer evaluation of online courses. One is a tiered method at the local level asking more experienced faculty or if available, online instructional designers within the institution to review and constructively evaluate the pedagogical alignment of a particular course. Another method may be to request the course be formally evaluated by peers through organizations such as Quality Matters. Quality Matters is a peer review system of online courses utilizing a rubric that examines pedagogical alignment. While there are costs involved in the later, the former would take some due diligence on the part of the faculty members involved but would one step towards assuring quality in online course design.

MEANING MAKING

Cultural meaning making is a complex activity tied to the cultural systems in which they are created and shared. One concept that is interesting to explore and is of particular importance to the development of quality online courses is the concept of intersubjectivity. Intersubjectivity is a term associated with Vygotskian theory of cognitive development and refers to the shared cultural understanding between two people (Rogoff, 1990; Rosaldo, 1999; Wertsch, 1985). If there is no shared understanding between two people, for example a teacher and a student, then attempts to communicate, create meaning, and establish understanding are somewhat fruitless endeavors. If the teacher is unable to understand the misconceptions, questions, or understanding of his or her students, then that teacher will not be able to address the student needs and learning will be hampered. It is in this manner that the constraints of an online environment may present challenges to establishment of intersubjectivity (Anderson, 2004). There is the suggestion, that like culture, some meanings may be more explicit due to the "pragmatics of social life and their history for a given society" but not all meanings may be "reduced to its explicit or implicit dimensions" (Le Vine, 1984, p. 77). Social referencing (i.e., gesture, gaze, and other nonverbal communication cues) which is critical for establishing intersubjectivity (Rogoff, 1990) in a face-to-face environment is not impossible to establish in an online environment, it does, however, take a more concentrated effort in high impact online courses.

Another component of cultural systems are social acts, or activities, in which meanings are negotiated, established, presented, or shared between participants within cultural systems. Gardner (1984) explained that individuals utilizing social acts may not actively reflect upon their participation in meaning making activities and in fact the participation in social activities may be more intuitive. It is only when, he stated, that individuals become more reflective upon their own participation within social activities do shifts of knowing how to participate becomes more explicit. Reflecting upon participation in cultural activities, thereby making implicit acts explicit is one step towards making those processes, which are critical for navigating teaching and student, transparent. One suggestion for faculty teaching online courses that would promote meaning making within online educational environments would be to maintain a (Weekly? Daily?) blog documenting the faculty's own experiences as an online teacher, how they learned the course material, personal stories and examples illustrating important concepts, etc. This makes those processes, so necessary for meaning making within electronic environments, explicit.

The culture of online teaching and learning may share similar characteristics with traditional, face-to-face teaching and learning and there may also be new territory for future investigations. The critical investigation of how teachers and learners understand, navigate, and utilize the culture of online learning environments to become competent participants is critical to the future of designing high impact courses. As Gardner (1984) has stated, "the human being, who, starting from a state of total ignorance about his or her particular culture, must within a decade or two acquire sufficient competence so that he or she can carry out productive work and interact effectively with other individuals to achieve valued ends" (p. 261). The enculturation of teachers and students within online teaching and learning environments requires learning how to use psychological tools within similar, yet dramatically different cultural systems, systems that have different environmental affordances and constraints.

SUGGESTIONS FOR FACULTY TEACHING ONLINE COURSES

There are many resources, books and websites, to assist faculty when teaching high quality online courses (e.g., Ko & Rossen, 2001; Koszalka & Ganesan, 2004). There is also assistance to help faculty effectively utilize discussion boards, online tools, blogs, wikis, open source programs, iPads, iPods, the iGoogle suite, cell phones, etc. within their online courses. Returning to the framework of viewing online courses as cultural systems, two inter-related important considerations are outlined within this paper for faculty teaching high quality online courses: rituals of participation and co-regulation.

Rituals of Participation

One of the ways in which individuals navigate technological, social, and psychological systems are what Courtney (2001) called "rituals of participation" (p. 236). These rituals for participation encompass the norms and behaviour for participating in cultural activities. Learning how to "do school," or mastering implicit and explicit academic and social knowledge needed to be successful in school, is an important ritual of participation required for effective teaching and learning (Westby, 1997). This issue is critically important due to the alarming drop rates from online courses by students (Diaz, 2002). Two popular explanations of why online students fail to complete online courses seem to be individual (demographic and/or learning style) or performance (low) differences (Diaz, 2002). However, researchers have suggested that the issue of student preparedness for online classes may be more complicated and include a variety of factors including student, situational, and educational factors (Gibson, 1998).

There may be cross cultural interference between how students conceptualize "doing school" within face-to-face environments and how this concept is challenged and, by necessity, altered within online teaching and learning environments. For example, one affordance within online environments is the ability, on the part of the faculty, to "hear" what every student thinks about a particular subject by requiring all students to post on a discussion board, for example. This, of course, requires that each student contributes to the conversation in a concrete and physical way that reflects what was read, in this there is simply a lot of individual accountability. and challenges what a student may view of 'doing school'. Many students, it could be argued, have learned what it means to "do school" by either engaging in discussion or gaining enough inference from what others are discussing in class to participate adequately, or simply keep quiet during discussion.

There may be several strategies to help online students assimilate to "doing school' online. Perhaps the most utilized strategy is to give student a pre-assessment evaluating certain skills that are needed to be a successful online student. Many universities now utilize some sort of instrument that asks students a variety of questions about their learning habits to find a "goodness of fit." For example, the University of Georgia uses the Readiness for Education at a Distance Indicator (READI @ http://goml.readi.info/) which is a self-assessment in which the student evaluates him- or herself on a variety of indicators like: life factors, personal attributes, learning styles, reading rate and recall, technical competency, technical knowledge, and typing speed and accuracy. There may be other ways to address the issue of student readiness within online courses, including scaffolding student learning at the beginning of the class and providing assistance with establishing regular activities and other strategies mentioned in this paper. Another potential powerful strategy is assigning student-student pairs or each student to a small group and requiring they participate in activities in which they form a bond or rely upon each other to complete course tasks. For example, you may ask groups to define expectations about

group standards of behaviour or something a little more fun like identifying a group name, wiki, or mascot. All of these activities are socially binding acts that may help students from dropping out if they feel they have more connections and support for learning in online environments.

Co-Regulation

What then happens when students move from one environment in which "doing school" is sufficient to another in which the concept of "doing school" is fundamentally different? Wesby (1997) stated that:

It may be like "coming from cultures that value interdependence, obedience to authority, and learning by watching rather than talking, [students] will be delayed in the development of self-control and self-regulation. Development of these skills will require not only environments that expect such skills, but that also foster such skills by providing the necessary scaffolding. (p. 286)

Navigating online teaching and learning, or becoming an efficient online teacher and/or online learner, requires that an individual is able to adequately use processes, strategies, and responses to plan and monitor his or her participation in pedagogical activity (Zimmerman, 2001, 1994). This concept, known as self-regulation, reflects those processes that occur at an individual level that play an important role in student academic achievement (Zimmerman, 1994). In many cases, online students are ill-prepared for online courses or drop out of online courses due to their inability to regulate (i.e., plan or monitor) their own learning. Ironically, this is also related to the convenience myths/misconceptions of online teaching and learning—a teacher or student need not go to a bricks-and-mortar classroom at a prescribed time, one can learn anytime and anyplace. In reality, it is very difficult for some students to be self-regulated enough to complete a course online.

McCaslin and Hickey (2001) proposed, however, that co-regulation is a more appropriate concept when discussing regulation of the teaching and learning process within socio-cultural contexts from a Vygotskian perspective (Courtney, 2001). In reference to this position, Zimmerman (1986) stated that "self-regulation is not an idiosyncratic product of the child's own discovery experiences; but rather, it is a culturally transmitted method for optimizing and controlling learning events" (p. 311). The processes of regulating teaching and learning does not fall simply on the isolated individual, but is shared between and among students and teachers. In this sense, the self-regulatory functions of the student are influenced by others within the socio-cultural environment (i.e., peers and the teacher), just as others' self-regulatory functions are influenced by that individual student.

Another aspect of co-regulated learning is monitoring strategies. Self-monitoring strategies refer "to students' efforts to observe themselves as they evaluate information about specific personal processes or actions that affect their learning and achievement in school" (Zimmerman & Paulsen, 1995, p. 14). Students who have effective self-monitoring strategies are able to evaluate their own progress towards an established goal, making appropriate strategy changes as they proceed to regulate their learning effectively (Zimmerman & Paulsen, 1995).

The ability to effectively monitor ones own learning processes are also dependent upon a wide array of technical, social, and psychological variables (see Zimmerman & Paulsen, 1995). Let us briefly discuss self-monitoring of the writing process as an example. Writing the "old way," in other words before word processing was pretty rudimentary and in retrospect seems almost primitive. An individual first had to prepare quite thoroughly before writing, often generating a detailed outline and/or completing a rough draft in long hand, before moving to type the paper on a typewriter. There was a certain diligence required on the part of the individual for if a mistake was made,

it could necessitate starting the entire process all over (unless your professor did not mind a lot of liquid paper). The process described was necessary because there were constraints associated with the technological tool that was utilized to write (i.e., typewriters…an electric one if you were lucky). The process, itself also served as a self-regulatory strategy that monitored the writing process. The invention and utilization of word processors has, however, altered the procedural script of writing used by students and, essentially, made obsolete a monitoring strategy used for writing.

There are three primary suggestions for faculty when teaching high quality online courses. First, it is important for faculty to be explicit about how to "do school" online and ways to assist in the co-regulation of student learning in your course. One promising practice in online courses is to keep the patterns of behavior or interactions similar throughout the duration of the course. For example, always 'open' online course discussions on Mondays and students are expected to have their points posted by Friday. Second, faculty should plan for activities to help students identify and address the ways in which there may be differences in how to "do school" in their online course. Faculty should also assist students in how they plan to work their online course requirement into their calendar; this is also referred to as an 'orienting activity' (see Olgren, 1998). Third, faculty should provide guidelines for activities and assessments that address both issues, rituals of participation and co-regulation, to help scaffold these skills throughout the duration of the course. Scaffolding simply means that the faculty member should provide a lot of assistance with these activities at the beginning of the course and as the course progresses; the faculty member slowly withdraws that help as the student gains confidence and masters course material.

ADMINISTRATIVE SUPPORT OF FACULTY

Quality online course delivery is contingent upon administrative support of faculty. Additionally "administrators need to understand their faculty population if they are to support faculty participation in [online teaching and learning]" (Schifter, 2004, p. 25). However, according to Jorge Gaytan (2009) while all valued online teaching and learning there was little agreement among deans, vice presidents for academic affairs, and administrators of distance learning at campuses regarding the organizational structures that would support online teaching and learning. It could be that online teaching and learning as a field has, traditionally, been focused upon the pedagogy of teaching and learning that takes place within online learning environments and contributes to institutional culture. Two important factors that face administrative support of faculty and delivering quality online courses and programs are adequate support for planning and faculty workload.

Adequate Support for Planning

Osika (2006) warns that there are many administrative issues that need to be addressed within and across institutions to provide support for online students and faculty beyond the borders of the virtual learning environment. The issue of adequate faculty support, however, is perhaps the most examined administrative issue in distance learning literature (see Ko & Rossen, 2001). Levy (2003) outlined critical factors for administrators to take into account when planning for online courses and/or programs; she proposed that planning be systematic and strategic. Levy (2003) stated that "the challenge to colleges in the 21st century is not to decide why they should have an online distance learning program, but to decide how to design and implement such a program" (p. 3).

Effective and innovative leadership plays an important role in the development and delivery of online course and programs (see Latchem & Hanna, 2001). Beaudoin (2003) stated that "any focused consideration of the dimension of leadership and its impact on the growth and apparent success of distance education at literally hundreds of institutions worldwide" has been largely absent from the literature (p. 3). There appear to be some disconnect, however, between the roles that faculty and administrators play in the development of quality online courses and programs and this disconnect is reflected recent studies on the topic.

One of the first steps for administrators to support online students, faculty, and programs would be to understand the demands on online faculty when designing and planning for online courses and programs. Administrators should clarify, in discussions with their faculty, any misconceptions about developing and offering a high quality online course/program. For example, Gaytan (2009) found that there was a disconnect between administrators' rhetoric and practice and that there was still, on the part of administrators, "an emphasis is on cost savings, remaining competitive, and delivery of information as opposed to instructional quality" (p. 69).

Howell, Williams, and Lindsay (2003) stated that there is a need to pose difficult questions about online programs, but a need to address those questions "from an informed perspective" (p. 1). As Gaytan (2009) found, there were many instances in which administrators and faculty differed in important ways when discussing online teaching and learning. For example, "while online education coordinators and faculty [in his study] were thinking about the ways to improve the quality of online education, academic administrators had other priorities such as being able to remain competitive" (Gaytan, 2009, p. 69). This illustrates a common assumption, on the part of institutional administrators, that online courses will address the need to service more students for the same costs, often by increasing the number of students within online courses (Concieção & Baldor, 2009). As stated in the beginning of the paper, there are also myths and misconceptions about online teaching and learning that may be held by both administrators and faculty. Assumptions, myths, and misconceptions need to be examined and discussed by administrators and faculty members within the context and characteristics (i.e., pedagogical alignment) of a particular course or program. This is a critical first step during the design and planning stage of online courses and programs. Administrative support of faculty for high quality online courses needs, however, to extend beyond support to encompass adequate planning (Osika, 2006).

Faculty Workload

One issue that has received some attention in the online teaching and learning literature has been that of faculty workload. Lehmann and Chamberlin (2009), for example, illustrate the number and variety of hats that online faculty wear when teaching a high quality online course: (1) teacher, (2) facilitator, (3) instructional technologist, (4) course designer, (5) writer, editor, and proofreader, (6) counselor and mediator, and (7) advisor and registrar. Wearing more hats, however, may not necessarily result in increased compensation for the online faculty member. For example, in Schifter's (2004) research surveying administrators about online teaching and learning issues, both found that there was little consistency with faculty compensation. Additionally, faculty may not be prepared to wear many of those hats and professional development, mentoring programs, or providing other models to those faculties may be critical (Blythe, 2001).

The complications and added workload for the online faculty member is debated in the research literature. Some researchers have found that more students in an online course increases workload due to more student-teacher interactions and/or more individual feedback on assessments, particularly if a pedagogical alignment is used for the course that is more student-centered (Matuga,

2005). Other researchers, however, have found that placing additional students within an online course may not increase faculty workload substantially, especially if the online faculty member has previous online teaching experience or the course's pedagogical alignment is more teacher-centered and does not require a lot of student-teacher interaction and student monitoring (Anderson & Avery, 2008; DiBiase & Rademacher, 2005; Matuga, 2005). It is very important, however, to realize that many of the studies investigating faculty workload were comparison studies with face-to-face faculty. As stated in the introduction of this paper, this premise may be flawed as we are not comparing apples-to-apples therefore, investigating faculty workload from a comparison perspective may not adequately reflect what an online faculty *does*.

Just as it may be more accurate to examine online teaching and learning as a cultural system, it may be necessary to redefine the roles, responsibilities, and what it means to be an online faculty member. The supposition that online faculty is treated differently at educational institutions, and this may be a threat to academic quality, has been a recurring theme in the research literature (Concieção & Baldor, 2009). Schifter (2004) found that faculty workload for those teaching online courses were not to consistent within and across institutions (Schifter, 2004). This has given rise to a trend at educational institutions of hiring online adjunct faculty to teach online courses (Puzziferro & Shelton, 2009). On the one hand, while this group of faculty may have highly specialized skills to teach online there may still be a perceived threat to the online quality of courses and programs. Regardless, the rise of the online adjunct faculty illustrates the need for an examination of knowledge and skills required to be an effective online faculty member and support from administration for quality online course delivery. It also necessitates the transformation of how we assess and evaluate effective online faculty, especially if we look at online learning environments as complex, cultural systems. A cornerstone of support for online faculty from an administrative perspective should include support for the systematic assessment and evaluation of online courses with an eye toward continual improvement.

CONTINUAL IMPROVEMENT

The last issue explored in this paper, which of continual improvement, encompasses the various aspects for all the topics features highlighted in this paper: pedagogical alignment, meaning making, rituals of participation, co-regulation, administrative support for faculty planning courses/programs, and faculty workload. The relationships between and among these different factors illuminate themselves to be reciprocal in nature through the process of continual improvement. It is in this sense that online teaching and learning contributes to the notion of cultural systems discussed at the beginning of the article.

Continual improvement is the act of reflecting on the effectiveness of pedagogical alignment within the context of the constraints and affordances of the online teaching and learning environment. Perhaps the most important component for continual improvement, for example, is pedagogical alignment which, as stated earlier, requires that instructional variables like student learning outcomes, learning activities, and assessment and evaluation practices, that support student success and learning, be selected with care during the planning process (Matuga, 2005). Pedagogical alignment provides a blueprint for continual improvement. However, continual improvement also mandates the re-visitation of pedagogical alignment during and after the course has been taught with the goal of perfecting the course with an eye towards assuring quality.

Sims and Jones (2002) proposed a three-phased model for continuous improvement in online classes that emphasizes the importance of pedagogical alignment and instructional design. They proposed that there be a "Pre-Delivery" phase in which the focus is on the functionality of the newly designed course be peer evaluated. This could be by utilizing some of the peer-evaluation methods mentioned in this article. The second phase is that of an initial delivery, or enhancement stage, and the last stage is an ongoing delivery or course maintenance phase in which the course is modified based upon feedback from students and peers. This approach emphasizes a team approach to course design, evaluation, and redesign. This is also called within socio-cultural literature creating 'communities of practice'. Sims and Jones (2002) outline that building shared understanding, establishing rituals of participation, and maintaining communication are all critical components of their continuous improvement model. Continuous improvement is by its definition, a dynamic process that examines those shared ideas of what is quality online teaching and learning and is essential for assuring quality.

CONCLUSION

As a review of the online teaching and learning research by Tallen-Runnels and colleagues (2006) illustrated, online teaching and learning can be and has been a field typically organized by following four categories: course environment, learners' outcomes, learners' characteristics, and institutional and administrative factors. In this paper we have presented a foundation for viewing some of these topics through the lens of cultural systems.

Three common myths/misconceptions regarding online teaching and learning were presented at the beginning of this article to help frame the discussion presented. One last myth or misconception that was not highlighted in this paper is that online teaching and learning is less expensive than face-to-face teaching. Divorcing this myth from the comparison (apples to apples) metaphor, this is a topic that was touched upon when the subject of administrative support of faculty was discussed, but not fully examined. Colleges and universities are pressured into developing online courses and programs, in essence, to meet economic shortfalls. However, as Levy (2003) stated "the challenge to colleges in the 21st century is not to decide why they should have an online distance learning program, but to decide how to design and implement such a program" (p. 3). The subject or relationship between how much a course/program cost and quality of learning within that course/program remains a very complex and difficult topic to frame within the topic of assuring quality.

The issue of assuring quality in online courses and programs is a multifaceted one that requires we look at the online teaching and learning environment with a fundamentally different lens, that as a complex, cultural system with unique affordances and constraints. While an exhaustive list is not presented here, important factors that influence the design of high impact online courses, make suggestions for faculty who are teaching online classes that ensure quality, impact administrative support of online faculty, and offer a potential model for continual improvement. All of these factors are aligned with the central premise of this paper that assuring quality in online course delivery is a complicated communal activity focusing on the alignment of sound instructional features, meaning-making, working together with students to develop new ways 'to do school' online, recognition of faculty work, and continual improvement.

REFERENCES

Anderson, K. M., & Avery, M. D. (2008). Faculty teaching time: A comparison of web-based and face-to-face graduate nursing courses. *International Journal of Nursing Education Scholarship*, *5*(1), 1–12.

Anderson, T. (2004). Toward a theory of online learning. In T. Anderson & F. Elloumi (Eds.), *Theory and Practice of Online Learning* (pp. 33-60). Athabasca, AB, Canada: Athabasca University. Retrieved from http://cde.athabascau.ca/online_book/index.html

Beaudoin, M. F. (2003). Distance education leadership for the new century. *Online Journal of Distance Learning Administration*, *6*(2).

Blythe, S. (2001). Designing online courses: User-centered practices. *Computers and Composition*, *18*, 329–346. doi:10.1016/S8755-4615(01)00066-4

Conceição, S. C. O., & Baldor, M. J. (2009, October). *Faculty workload for online instruction: Individual barriers and institutional challenges.* Paper presented at the Midwest Research-to-Practice Conference in Adult, Continuing, and Community Education, Chicago.

Courtney, S. (2001). Technology and culture of teaching and learning. In Lieberman, D., & Wehlberg, C. (Eds.), *To Improve the Academy* (*Vol. 19*, pp. 232–249). Bolton, MA: Anker Publishing.

D'Andrade, R. (2001). A cognitivist's view of the units debate in cultural anthropology. *Cross-Cultural Research*, *35*, 242–257. doi:10.1177/106939710103500208

Derry, S., & Lesgold, A. (1996). Toward a situated social practice model for instructional design. In Berliner, D. C., & Calfee, R. C. (Eds.), *Handbook of Educational Psychology* (pp. 787–806). New York: Simon & Schuster Macmillan.

Diaz, D. P. (2002). *Online drop rates revisited.* Retrieved from http://technologysource.org/article/online_drop_rates_revisited/

DiBiase, D., & Rademacher, H. (2005). Scaling up: Faculty workload, class size, and student satisfaction in a distance learning course on Geographic Information Sciences. *Journal of Geography in Higher Education, 29*(1), 139–158. doi:10.1080/03098260500030520

Duffy, T. M., & Cunningham, D. J. (2001). Constructivism: Implications for the design and delivery of instruction. In Jonassen, D. H. (Ed.), *Handbook of research for educational communications and technology* (pp. 170–198). Mahwah, NJ: Erlbaum.

Gagne, R. M., Briggs, L. J., & Wagner, W. W. (1992). *Principles of instructional design.* Fort Worth, TX: Harcourt Brace Publishers.

Gardner, H. (1984). The development of competence in culturally defined domains: A preliminary framework. In Shweder, R. A., & LeVine, R. A. (Eds.), *Culture theory: Essay on mind, self, and emotion* (pp. 257–275). New York: Cambridge University Press.

Gaytan, J. (2009). Analyzing online education through the lens of institutional theory and practice: the need for research-based and –validated frameworks for planning, designing, delivering, and assessing online instruction. *Delta Pi Epsilon Journal, 51*(2), 62–75.

Gibson, C. C. (1998). The distance learner's academic self-concept. In Gibson, C. (Ed.), *Distance learners in higher education: Institutional responses for quality outcomes* (pp. 65–76). Madison, WI: Atwood.

Giddens, A. (1984). *The constitution of society.* Oxford, UK: Polity Press.

Howell, S. L., Williams, P. B., & Lindsay, N. K. (2003). Thirty-two trends affecting distance education: An informed foundation for strategic planning. *Online Journal of Distance Learning Administration, 6*(3).

Kirshner, D., & Whitson, J. A. (1997). *Situated cognition: Social, semiotic, and psychological Perspectives.* Mahwah, NJ: Erlbaum.

Kitayama, S. (2002). Culture and basic psychological processes—toward a system view of culture: Comment on Oyserman et al. *Psychological Bulletin, 128*(1), 89–96. doi:10.1037/0033-2909.128.1.89

Ko, S., & Rossen, S. (2001). *Teaching online: A practical guide.* Boston: Houghton Mifflin.

Koszalka, T. A., & Ganesan, R. (2004). Designing online courses: A taxonomy to guide strategic use of features available in course management systems (CMS) in distance education. *Distance Education, 25*(2), 243–256. doi:10.1080/0158791042000262111

Kuh, G. D. (2008). *High-impact educational practices: What they are, who has access to them, and why they matter.* Washington, DC: Association of American Colleges and Universities.

Latchem, C., & Hanna, D. E. (2001). Leadership in open and flexible learning. In Lathem, C., & Hanna, D. E. (Eds.), *Leadership for 21st Century Learning: Global Perspectives from Educational Innovators* (pp. 53–62). London: Kogan Page Limited.

Lehmann, K., & Chamberlin, L. (2009). *Making the move to elearning: Putting your course online.* Lanham, MD: Rowman & Littlefield.

LeVine, R. A. (1984). Properties of culture: Ethnographic view. In Shweder, R. A., & LeVine, R. A. (Eds.), *Culture theory: Essay on mind, self, and emotion* (pp. 67–87). New York: Cambridge University Press.

Levy, S. (2003). Six factors to consider when planning online distance learning programs in higher education. *Online Journal of Distance Learning Administration, 6*(1).

Matuga, J. M. (2001). Electronic pedagogical practice: The art and science of teaching and learning on-line. *Journal of Educational Technology & Society, 4*(3), 77–84.

Matuga, J. M. (2005). The role of assessment and evaluation in context: Pedagogical alignment in online courses. In Williams, D. D., Howell, S. L., & Hricko, M. (Eds.), *Online Assessment, Measurement and Evaluation* (pp. 316–330). Hershey, PA: Information Science Reference.

Matuga, J. M. (2007). Self-regulation and online learning: Theoretical issues and practical challenges to support life-long learning. In Inoue, Y. (Ed.), *Online Education for Lifelong Learning* (pp. 146–168). London: Information Science Publishing.

McCaslin, M., & Hickey, D. T. (2001). Self-regulated learning and academic achievement: A Vygotskian view. In Zimmerman, B. J., & Schunk, D. H. (Eds.), *Self-regulated learning and academic achievement: Theoretical perspectives* (pp. 227–252). Mahwah, NJ: Erlbaum.

Mehlinger, H. D., & Powers, S. M. (2002). *Technology and teacher education: A guide for educators and policymakers.* Boston: Houghton Mifflin Company.

Nagel, D. (2009). 10.5 Million preK-12 students will attend classes online by 2014. *The Journal: Transforming Education through Technology.* Retrieved from http://thejournal.com/articles/2009/10/28/10.5-million-prek-12-students-will-attend-classes-online-by-2014.aspx

Olgren, C. H. (1998). Improving learning outcomes: The effects of learning strategies and motivation. In Gibson, C. C. (Ed.), *Distance learners in higher education: Institutional responses for quality outcomes* (pp. 77–95). Madison, WI: Atwood Publishing.

Osika, E. (2006). The concentric support model: A model for planning and evaluation of distance learning programs. *Online Journal of Distance Learning Administration, 9*(3). Retrieved from http://www.westga.edu/~distance/ojdla/fall93/osika93.htm.

Puzziferro, M., & Shelton, K. (2009). Supporting online faculty – Revisiting the seven principles (A few years later). *Online Journal of Distance Learning Adminsration, 12*(3). Retrieved from http://www.westga.edu/~distance/ojdla/fall123/puzziferro123.html

Rogoff, B. (1990). *Apprenticeship in thinking: Cognitive development in social context.* New York: Oxford University Press.

Rosaldo, M. Z. (1984). Toward an anthropology on self and feeling. In Shweder, R. A., & LeVine, R. A. (Eds.), *Culture theory: Essay on mind, self, and emotion* (pp. 137–157). New York: Cambridge University Press.

Rosalso, R. I. Jr. (1999). A note on Geertz as a cultural essayist. In Ortner, S. B. (Ed.), *The fate of "culture": Geertz and beyond* (pp. 30–34). Los Angeles: University of California Press.

Schifter, C. (2004). Faculty participation in distance education programs: Practices and plans. In Monolescu, D., Schifter, C. C., & Greenwood, L. (Eds.), *The distance education evolution: Issues and case studies* (pp. 22–39). Hershey, PA: Information Science Publishing.

Sims, R., & Jones, D. (2002, December). *Continuous improvement through shared understanding: Reconceptualizing instructional design for online learning.* Paper presented at ASCILITE 2002, Auckland, New Zealand.

Tallent-Runnels, M. K., Thomas, J. A., Lan, W. Y., Cooper, S., Ahern, T. C., & Shaw, S. M. (2006). Teaching courses online: A review of the research. *Review of Educational Research, 76*(1), 93–135. doi:10.3102/00346543076001093

Wertsch, J. V. (1985). *Vygotsky and the social formation of mind*. Cambridge, MA: Harvard University Press.

Westby, C. (1997). There's more to passing than knowing the answers. *Language, Speech, and Hearing Services in Schools, 28*(3), 274–286.

White, L. A. (1975). *The concept of cultural systems: A key to understanding tribes and nations*. New York: Columbia University Press.

White, R. (n.d.). *Four myths about online learning*. Retrieved from http://www.learnnc.org/lp/pages/2720

Zimmerman, B. J. (1986). Becoming a self-regulated learner: Which are the key subprocesses? *Contemporary Educational Psychology, 11*, 307–313. doi:10.1016/0361-476X(86)90027-5

Zimmerman, B. J. (1994). Dimensions of academic self-regulation: A conceptual framework for education. In Schunk, D. H., & Zimmerman, B. J. (Eds.), *Self-regulation of learning and performance: Issues and educational implications* (pp. 3–20). Hillsdale, NJ: LEA.

Zimmerman, B. J. (2001). Theories of self-regulated learning and academic achievement: An overview and analysis. In Zimmerman, B. J., & Schunk, D. H. (Eds.), *Self-regulated learning and academic achievement: Theoretical perspectives* (pp. 1–38). Mahwah, NJ: Erlbaum.

Zimmerman, B. J., & Paulsen, A. S. (1995). Self-monitoring during collegiate studying: An Invaluable tool for academic self-regulation. In Pintrich, P. R. (Ed.), *Understanding self-regulated learning* (pp. 13–27). San Francisco: Jossey-Bass.

This work was previously published in the International Journal of Adult Vocational Education and Technology, Volume 2, Issue 1, edited by Victor C.X. Wang, pp. 36-49, copyright 2011 by IGI Publishing (an imprint of IGI Global).

Chapter 4
Improving Accessibility for Seniors in a Life–Long Learning Network:
A Usability Study of Learning Websites

Xiaoqing Gu
East China Normal University, China

Rui Ding
East China Normal University, China

Shirong Fu
East China Normal University, China

ABSTRACT

Senior citizens are comparatively vulnerable in accessing learning opportunities offered on the Internet due to usability problems in current web design. In an effort to build a senior-friendly learning web as a part of the Life-long Learning Network in Shanghai, usability studies of two websites currently available to Shanghai senior citizens were conducted, with the intention of integrating these websites into a senior learning web as well as promoting accessibility for senior users. Through this study usability problems were identified generating suggested changes for designing websites focused on learning by seniors. This study contributes empirical findings to the field of information system design and its accessibility for seniors.

1. INTRODUCTION

Life-long learning refers to a society in which learning possibilities exist for everyone who wants to learn (Aspin & Chapman, 2000; Fischer, 2001). With a senior population of 21.6% in Shanghai,

China and growing (Shanghai Civil Affairs Bureau, 2009), senior citizens of Shanghai are among the target users of a Life-long Learning Network. This network is an implementation of the Life-long Learning Initiative, which is being developed with the goal of building Shanghai into a learning city for 'anyone, anytime and anywhere' (SMC, 2006).

DOI: 10.4018/978-1-4666-2062-9.ch004

There is substantial growth in the use of the Internet by older people (Morrell, 2005; Becker, 2004a; Wick, 2004; Nahm et al., 2006; SCAB, SBSC, & SSB, 2009). However, many of the senior Internet users are not taking full advantage of online resources due to usability and accessibility issues common to elderly participants (Morrell, 2005; Dickinson & Gregor, 2006; Aula, 2005). Computer software and most web content are usually developed by and for younger users; lack of consideration for the elderly and the problems associated with aging, such as computer experience and attitude, age-related constrains, language barriers, and software complexity (Dickinson et al., 2005) contribute to the problems of usability and accessibility.

In the work reported here we consider the terms senior citizen or elderly refers to those who are 60 and older as is common in China (Chinese Government, 1996), while in most developed countries 65 has been accepted as definition of older people (Arch, 2008).

The Life-long Learning Network has identified a number of websites with content appropriate to the elderly with the intention of integrating these sites into the learning network for seniors in Shanghai. From the current set of websites identified as having the elderly as the target audience, a representative site from two groups has been chosen: one is from the group of the websites developed by senior related agencies, and the other is from the group of websites developed by corporations. The criteria for selection are that they are learning oriented, and the design of the website has been based on some kind of senior-friendly requirements. The objective of the current work was to examine these existing sites using usability guidelines for usage by the elderly so as to identify needed improvements in the sites as well as to build new knowledge about the use of guidelines in designing websites for the elderly. Thus, we conducted a usability study of each of these two selected learning websites. Lessons learned from the study will be used to improve the usability and therefore improve accessibility of the learning opportunities for seniors in life-long learning network. The usability requirements found in this study can also contribute to the field of information system design and its accessibility for seniors in general.

2. RELATED WORK

Research shows that seniors are increasingly using the Internet to access information, to meet their needs for fun and mental stimulation, for education, to increase their social interaction and to serve as a useful medium to provide them information with a high level of interest in health information (Hendrix, 2000; Nahm et al., 2006; Arch, 2008). However, even websites that are designed to be compliant with accessibility standards catering to specific impairments may be ineffective in enabling access for older adults (Dickinson et al., 2007). The accessibility problems aged people encounter are mainly attributed to the lack of awareness and implementation of usability design guidelines dedicated especially for the senior users group (Morrell, 2005; Dickinson et al., 2007; Aula, 2005).

As a group older adults are vulnerable with lower education, cognition effects and chronic disabilities normal for aging such as poor vision, hearing impairments, and declining motor skills (Becker, 2004b; Kurniawan et al., 2006; Wick, 2004; Emery et al., 2003; Arch, 2008).

A significant proportion of older adults have low literacy and also low computer literacy compared to young adults (Dickinson et al., 2007; NAAL, 2003; Department for Education, 2003; SCAB, SBSC, & SSB, 2009). A primary barrier older people face when trying to use the web is lack of familiarity with computers and the conventions used in computer software, especially for those with less education (Dickinson et al., 2005). To add to this, aging is associated with cognitive changes, such as reduction in the efficacy of short term memory, spatial memory and certain forms of reasoning and generalization of knowledge (Dickinson et al., 2007), thus accessibility barriers include difficulties in remembering task-related steps, understanding technical words and using the mouse (Sharit et al., 2008; Sayago & Blat, 2009). Research shows that older adults are less likely to complete tasks that require three moves or more, and they have more difficulty recalling previous actions and the locations of previously viewed information (Morrell, 2005).

Further, chronic disabilities, such as poor vision, hearing impairments, and declining motor skills also affect accessibility to information systems for the elderly. Typically, older adults may have impaired vision, thus they may lose the overall context of the current page in navigation, and encounter information overload because of excessive sequential reading (Leporini & Paternò, 2008). Their visual capacities diminish across visual acuity, contrast sensitivity, glare sensitivity, visual field and ability to discern colors; these all could affect how accurately seniors access information (Becker, 2004b).

In order to promote web accessibility to a wide population of users, including special categories such as seniors, the World Wide Web Consortium (W3C) proposed Web Accessibility Initiative (1999) and Web Content Accessibility Guidelines (Caldwell, Cooper, Guraino Reid, & Vanderheiden, 2004) to specify web design so as to remove the technical barriers that may prevent access to the information systems. With senior users in mind, guidelines for senior friendly information system design was also proposed by the U.S. National Institute on Aging (NIA) in conjunction with the U.S. National Library of Medicine (NLM) (NIA & NLM, 2002), with the overall objective of eliminating barriers to web use and promote information accessibility for elderly people.

Other guidelines also have been provided from specific studies to improve the design of information systems for aged populations. The impact of font sizes, the structure of content, complexity appropriate for targeted users, clear contrast between foreground and background, further text-enlarging, changing background or foreground colors are frequently mentioned in these guidelines for senior friendly interface design (Wick, 2004; Dickinson et al., 2007; Morrell, 2005; Kurniawan & Zaphiris, 2005). For example, to address low-literacy, Nielsen et al. (2005) suggested simplifying the text by using a 6th grade reading level on homepages and 8th grade reading level on other pages. Having impairments in cognition and motor skills in mind, Web designers should take into account the declining cognitive abilities of older adults (Sharit et al., 2008), by simplifying web design to ensure users are not overwhelmed by too many concepts and diverse content (Dickinson et al., 2007). For the performances such as drag-and-drop computer tasks, visual feedback combined with other modalities may be needed according to Emery et al. (2003). Additionally using tabs could eliminate the necessity of the user having to frequently move the cursor, and this consideration can be important for impaired people (Hendrix, 2000).

A draft guideline for making websites accessible to seniors has been proposed in Shanghai, in which specifications for style, color, font and layout have been identified (Gerontological Society of Shanghai, 2006). While this guideline will be helpful in guiding the design of websites for seniors in Shanghai, there is a need for empirical studies on the implications of applying the proposed design guidelines for making the Internet more accessible to seniors, and in particular a need for empirical studies of usability in life long learning systems for the elderly. In an effort to create a learning web by integrating currently available sites for senior citizens as a part of the Life-long Learning Network in Shanghai, we conducted usability studies of two websites which are targeted for integration into the network so as to find current usability problems, develop specific guidelines for future systems in

China and to improve accessibility for seniors to life-long learning. Additionally, while there is a substantial set of guidelines and requirements in place to make websites more accessible for the elderly, this study seeks to contribute to the ongoing work of information system design for seniors through an empirical study of the importance of these guidelines to how seniors make sense of information systems.

3. USABILITY STUDY

In this study, two current learning websites that are dedicated to elderly users were examined, in order to identify usability problems and promote accessibility for when these sites and others like them are integrated into the Life-long Learning Network. One is e60sh (http://www.e60sh.com, *e60sh*) and the other is The Home of Old Kids (http://www.oldkids.cn, *oldkids*). Both of them are well-known learning websites among Shanghai elders.

3.1. Description of the Learning Webs

With the aim of facilitating lifelong learning for seniors in Shanghai, the *e60sh* was co-sponsored by Shanghai Distance Education Group, University for the aged in Shanghai, and Shanghai Development Center on the Affairs of the Aged. There are five sections in the *e60sh*: news center, elders' plaza, consult center, learning events, and education forum. From elders' plaza, users can gain access to a variety of learning resources such as information and knowledge on health, finance or culture; the consult center provides an online platform for elders to consult health problems with experts; news center, learning events and education forum provide other related information that could be interested to elders.

The *oldkids* was founded by Shanghai Qifeng Science and Technology Development Co., Ltd.

Sections for learning, blogging and a bulletin board system (BBS) are the three main channels in this website, along with other channels dedicated to improving life quality of elders, such as entertainment, social interaction and shopping. From the learning channel, users can access various learning resources, which are presented as video, text or slides; while the blog and BBS channels serve as a kind of useful medium for seniors to exchange information for fun, for learning as well as for social connection.

These two websites share a lot of common ground in terms of the learning services that they provide: areas in which aged people may be interested, such as health care, finance and culture. Meanwhile, a variety of information including news, recommended books, as well as curriculum schedules for some universities that are available to the elderly are also presented. In addition, these two websites encourage users to participate in activities both on and off-line. However, differences between them also exist; for example, blog and BBS are used in *oldkids* as channels of interaction between users to facilitate learning; meanwhile, online consulting is used as an interaction channel in *e60sh* to provide health information for seniors.

Although these two websites are expected to be senior-accessible based on their applying the existing Gerontological Society of Shanghai (GSS) guidelines, there is a need for empirical studies on the implications of using these guidelines on usability and accessibility by the elderly to insure that seniors can take advantage of learning opportunities through the Internet. In the effort to modify and integrate these learning websites into the Life-long Learning Network for seniors all across the city, usability problems are expected to be found in this study.

3.2. Study Method

In this study, an extended guideline for designing for seniors on the Internet was developed by integrating the existing GSS guideline with the widely accepted NIA/NLM guidelines and additional themes found across relevant studies (Nahm et al., 2006; Leporini & Paternò, 2008; Dickinson et al., 2007; Web Accessibility Initiative, 1999; Kurniawan & Zaphiris, 2005). Specifically, design requirements such as highlight, form and search engine were added, while language-sensitive requirements including typeface, capital and lowercase letters, and phrasing were taken into consideration; for example, typeface was required to be Hei instead of Song. Based on the extended guideline, a comprehensive usability checklist was developed, which consists of thirty evaluation items in four categories of Readable Text, Information Presentation, Media, and Ease of Navigation (Appendix).

In addition, think-aloud protocol and user interview were used to conduct the usability studies. The abovementioned checklist was used as the framework of data collection and analysis. Thirteen tasks were designed along with thirteen think-aloud questions, with the former six for *e60sh* and the later seven for *oldKids*. Table 1 shows the tasks (phrasing was simplified) and their targeted usability categories from the evaluation framework.

According to Nielsen (2000), 85% of usability problems could usually be found in the first five users studied. Given that potential lifelong learners are voluntary Internet users, we recruited volunteers by randomly selecting and contacting subjects from a list of names from a local community. Once the potential subject was contacted, we provided further information about

Table 1. Testing tasks and targeted usability categories

NO.	Task	Category
1	Skim through the index page and read a piece of today's news	Readable Text Information presentation Increasing the Ease of Navigation
2	Watch a video about "harmonious family"	Media Increasing the Ease of Navigation
3	Consult a specialist with a health problem	Increasing the Ease of Navigation
4	Check out the reply of any specialist	Increasing the Ease of Navigation
5	Check out one of the activities for seniors that interests you.	Increasing the Ease of Navigation Information presentation
6	Try to use on-site search engine to find any passage about how to improve memory	Increasing the Ease of Navigation
7	Enter the learning channel and look for the curriculum schedule of *oldkids* training center (March)	Readable Text Information presentation
8	Try to find curriculum schedule of Luwan University for the Senior (2010).	Readable Text Information presentation
9	Enter the entertainment channel to watch a video that you are interested in.	Media Increasing the Ease of Navigation
10	Enter the blog channel and read a passage that you find interesting.	Readable Text: Increasing the Ease of Navigation
11	Post a comment on the passage you've just read	Increasing the Ease of Navigation
12	Sign in the BBS (username: app12; password: 111111), pick one topic about photography and add a comment to it	Readable Text Increasing the Ease of Navigation
13	Try to use on-site search engine to find any passage about how to improve memory	Increasing the Ease of Navigation

how we would carry out the testing, why we needed their help and how the data we collected would be used to those who were interested in this study. Once the first five volunteer evaluators were identified the time and the place of testing were arranged with them, and stipends for transportation were offered.

All five volunteers in this research were above the age of 60, with an average of 70 years with one female and four males. Those with and without rich computer experience were included during the enrollment. Since only those who have computer experience were interested in this study, these five volunteers had a higher education level compared to the average of the senior population. None of them had ever visited the websites to be tested. Table 2 is the demographic of the volunteers.

Evaluation data was collected in the fourth week of March in the Information Experience (IE) laboratory in our university. Each volunteer went through the testing procedure with one of our team members as moderator. In order to make sure that there was no jargon that needed to be explained to all the participants as well as to ensure that they have a thorough understanding of the tasks to be finished, task lists were given to them to go through before the evaluation session began. Also, the evaluators were reminded that it was the websites that we intend to evaluate instead of their competence before the testing. They were encouraged to tell moderators whenever they got confused by a task, and were urged to always express how they feel about the websites during the whole procedure. While the evaluators were engaged in the tasks, they were asked to talk aloud what they were looking for, where they were clicking on, and what kind of difficulties they were encountering. Meanwhile, the evaluators were allowed to give up on a task if they were unable to find the answer. They were also allowed to ask for help when they felt unable to handle any unexpected situations or errors during the evaluation process. After the tasks were finished, an exit interview was conducted with each evaluator. All sessions as well as synchronized screen recording of their web browsing behavior during the evaluation process were captured using Morae Recorder.

4. FINDINGS

4.1. General Results

Overall completion rate for all thirteen tasks was 67.7%. Specifically, task 3, task 6 and task 9 could not be completed by 4 out of 5 participants; task 4 could not be completed by 3 participants; task 11 was completed by 3 participants; task 2, task 5, task 12 and task 13 were completed by 4 participants. Only four tasks out of all the thirteen were successfully completed by all the participants: task 1, task 7, task 8 and task 10. Moreover, the gender, age and education level of participants had no differences in terms of the completion of all thirteen tasks.

Table 2. Demographic data

No.	Age	Gender	Highest Education Level	Computer Skills	Computer usage	Frequency of usage
1	75	Male	Bachelor's degree	Average	1-2 years	Monthly
2	74	Female	Bachelor's degree	Poor	3-5 years	Weekly
3	72	Male	Bachelor's degree	Poor	1-2 years	Weekly
4	63	Male	Master's degree	Average	5-10 years	Daily
5	64	Male	Bachelor's degree	Good	5-10 years	Daily

4.2. Findings in Readable Text

The design of the color, background and justification of text in these websites met the requirements of the guidelines. Within all of the thirteen tasks, the tasks that were designed to find out potential usability problems in text design category, namely task 7, 10 and 12, acquired comparatively higher performance; only one participant failed on task 12. From the exit interview, when asked about their perceptions of the text design in the tested websites, they verified that they felt comfortable with the color, background and justification of the text, which were mostly presented with black ink on a light-colored background, and only occasionally in red ink when it needs to be stand out. Also, they felt comfortable with the Song typeface with medium weight which both of the websites have used. This typeface and the left justification of all body text were thought in agreement with their established reading habits of all the participants.

On the other hand, major usability problems were found in the text design for the font size and physical spacing of the text. These were turned out in the task procedures when most of the participants had a difficult time reading the text of the task pages, although only one of them ended up as an *incompletion*. While the font size of web pages has been required to use at least 12 point or 14 point type size for seniors, and double space should be used, it was not up to this standard in these two webs: *e60sh* mainly uses 9 point type size on homepage and 10.5 point type size for other pages, while font size used on homepage of *oldkids* is also 9 point, and in some parts, 10.5 point and 12 point for other pages, moreover double space only has been used in few of the pages. In the exit interview, all of the participants claimed that they preferred the bigger font size, although two of them thought he/she could figure out the text with small font size. One participant said he normally did not care about line space very much, but when type size was small, the insufficient line space could make the text even harder to read. As

a matter of fact, in the blogs the elderly published in the *oldkids,* only size 14 or bigger with double space has been used.

In addition, another usability problem was found in the designers' effort to making the websites senior-friendly. Compliant with the requirement of "enlarge text available," both of the tested websites do provide buttons to enlarge the size of the page text. Unfortunately, this function was only provided in the news sections in both of the websites, but not all of the pages across the websites. Moreover, the design of the enlarge button was not obvious enough that two of the participants did not notice it on *e60sh* while the other three noticed and used it; it was provided in such an imperceptible way on *oldkids* that none of the participants even noticed it. All of them appreciated this function after they were showed this button and tried out how to make text larger with it.

4.3. Findings in Information Presentation

The style, simplicity, organization and highlight of information presentation in the tested websites confirmed the requirements of senior friendly design. All of the evaluators successfully completed the three tasks (task 1, task 7 and task 8) which were mainly dedicated to testing these features without any difficulties. Also, in the think aloud sessions, participants felt satisfied with the organization of information, and thought it was pretty easy for them to get the idea of the passages. Moreover, this was verified in the exit interview. When asked if they felt that the information of the websites were presented clearly and in their familiar way, and if there were any terms that made them confused or hard to understand, they reported that they did not have difficulty understanding the information presented in these two websites. Also they did not run into any jargon during the task process.

Yet usability problems were also found in both of the websites for the information presentation.

The major problem here was the use of scrolling. Being incompliant with the guidelines, scrolling has been used a lot in both of the websites. In the testing process, it acted as a distraction of the consistency of the task, and lead to four failures in task 9, two in task 11 and one in task 12. Most of the time, the evaluators did not even notice the scrolling bar and did not realize that they needed to drag it to catch the content out of the window. What makes the problem even worse was that most of them have not established the habits to maximize the windows, they tended to leave the windows as they were opened, even the participants with average computer competency. For example, in task 9, after they opened the window with video and saw the instruction of pushing the play button to play the video, the evaluators hadn't noticed that there was a scrolling bar that they could drag to locate the play button of the video, thus four of them failed in this task.

4.4. Findings of Media

Positive opinions as well as usability problems were found concerning the media design in these two websites. From the think aloud sessions and exit interview, evaluators consistently expressed their favor of the image design in both of the websites. Only text-relevant images were used in these two websites, and text alternatives were provided all of which were confirmed to the design guidelines. All the evaluators reported that they felt comfortable with the ratio of text and image in the interview. Moreover, the evaluators especially adored the images designed in *oldkids*, which not only make the columns in the page better structured, but also make the pages more attractive to the users. For example, during the task 2, we observed that some of the evaluators obviously were attracted right away by the "study" image in the webpage which was intentionally designed as an attraction for recommended content for users, and then found what the task required without trouble.

The major usability problem found in the media design was about the video (including animation video). Both of the two websites have used numerous video clips as main learning resources aside from the text. During the process of the two tasks related to media design, it revealed that the fixed location of video in the up-left side of the window and the fixed size of 320×240 were neither convenient nor comfortable to the users. While the segments of the video clips were suitable in terms of their download speed, the fact that they were not played automatically when the window was open failed to meet the evaluators' expectations. Two of them sat there waiting for at least fifteen seconds, and doubted aloud that the video didn't work. They also claimed in the interview that they were used to videos starting automatically in other websites.

In addition, other usability concerns for the media design were found out in our observation, think aloud session and interview, although they did not lead to task failures in testing. First, in one case the evaluator found either no hint or text alternatives for the video when its download speed was not fast enough. After waiting there for a while, he obviously thought something was wrong and closed the window. After he made sure that he followed the task instruction correctly, he clicked the video link and opened the window again and played the video. Next, both from think-aloud session and interview, evaluators reported that they would like a video control handle to be included underneath the video for users to pause, stop or hide it as they prefer while making it automatically play upon opening.

4.5. Findings of Ease of Navigation

The navigation in both of the two tested websites was the hardest part for the evaluators, where several usability problems were found out. Major usability problems were found in the design of hyperlinks and buttons, Backward/Forward Navigation design, and the Search design.

The most salient problem was the design of hyperlinks and buttons. From the task results, our observation and the think-aloud sessions, most of the evaluators had a hard time finding the button or hyperlinks, which should lead them to expected results. The two tasks (task 3 and task 4) which were dedicated to evaluating the buttons and hyperlinks acquired the lowest rate; only one and two out of the five evaluators ended up successfully after struggling during the process. This was also the case in task 2, where one of the evaluators could not finish the task due to his failure in finding the hyperlink. Our observation and the think-aloud sessions all showed that the evaluators always got confused with the poor design of the buttons or hyperlinks in both of the two websites, where many hyperlinks did not stand out in the page, or indeed were hidden within images. For example, three of the participants had to try to determine if there was the hyperlink by observing the variation of the shape of mouse, the color of text or if there was an underline beneath the text. Still there were a number of times they got confused and felt lost due to the inconsistency of the hyperlinks. The other two evaluators with lower computer competency simply failed the tasks in which hyperlinks were needed. While this problem was found in both of the websites, it was even worse in *e60sh*, where it occurred across all of the sections and pages while it only occurred in the blog and BBS channel in *oldkids*.

Another major usability problem found out in navigation design was the Backward/Forward Navigation in the websites. Different Backward/Forward Navigation methods have been used in these two websites, and led to different usability problems which emerged during the testing. Specifically, when the evaluators opened a link in a page of *e60sh*, there a new window always popped up where the users could not move back and forth to the Previous Page and Next Page other than closing this new window. This led the evaluators to accidently close all of the windows and start over several times in the testing process. Although

this design did not lead to failure of the testing task, it caused trouble for all of them. Therefore two of the evaluators requested to improve this design in the interview. On the other hand, a different usability problem occurred in *oldkids* in this design. When the evaluators opened a link in the navigation bar in a page of *oldkids*, there also a new window popped up. The problem here was too many windows left opened although no navigation problem like *e60sh* occurred. From our observation, all of the participants ended up with at least four more windows opened and it made them get lost in too many open windows.

The design of search engine in both of the websites caused major usability problems in our testing. Similarly, the tasks designed to test the search engine also acquired lower completion compared to others, where only one participant finished task 6, four had some struggle during the task 13 but finally finished it. In *e60sh*, only one out of the five evaluators found the search engine and found the expected information with it. Two of them could not tell the difference between different search engines within and out of the websites. They used the outside search engine and could not find the information within the *e60sh*. Other two users failed to find the search engine. Moreover, even the one who could find the search engine got confused and asked for assistance from the moderator when he pushed search button several times in vain because he did not allow the pop up window. On the other hand, while all of the evaluators had no problems in finding the search engine in the right upper corner of the window above the navigation bar in *oldkids*, they could not tell the difference between the search results with advertisements which were brought by search engine. Two of the evaluators failed the task by following the ads instead of the search result. Towards the requirement of error tolerance of search engines, neither of the two websites could recognize the any of errors in Chinese characters; only *oldkids* could recognize errors in English and provided prompts for users, but this was not the case for *e60sh*.

The strength of the navigation design was also confirmed in the testing, especially the design of navigation bar, the layout of the page, and help information, while some usability problems were also found in these aspects. From the task process, we observed that navigation bar was straightforward to the evaluators and the layout of the pages was explicit to them. This observation was confirmed in the interview by all of the evaluators. No dead link and no pop up menu were presented in all of the task process. Further, the help information which was provided in both of the websites was made use of in the task process; one of the evaluators looked for the help information in *oldkids* when he encountered difficulty in task 9 and found the instruction about how to tackle it. Yet he failed in this task due to the scrolling problem as aforementioned.

The usability problem found in regard to the design of "navigation" was the titles used in the navigation bar in *e60sh*. Although no problem was brought about in the tasks, they did cause some confusion to the evaluators. Three of them reported in the interview that they felt unsure about what each of the titles in the navigation bar referred to the real content page.

Finally, both positive and negative reports were collected for the design of Form in these two websites. First of all, explicit instruction regarding what should be filled in each box was provided in both of the websites made the Form-filling task pretty easy. From our observation for task 11 and task 12 which evaluators needed to fill in the form, they obviously had no problem with filling out the form following the instructions gained here. Moreover, the tab key was enabled in both of the websites, although no evaluators ever used it during the evaluation process. As well, most of the submit buttons were well designed except for that of BBS in *oldkids*, in which the submit button was separated from the last entry field. This design caused unnecessary trouble for

evaluators, three of them stopped for a while to read these rules. Also, not being close to the last entry field was more likely to failure. During the task process, one of the evaluators left the form page after she had filled all the required information without submitting it in task 11, while she finished task 12 which also needed filling and submitting. The explanation which she gave in the interview was that she was not aware of the necessity to push the button to submit as the final action of filling in a form. She pushed the submit button in task 12 since she saw it, but not in task 11. She also mentioned that for the elderly who were not familiar with computer applications, there should be explicit instructions of how-to-do steps included.

5. CONCLUSION AND FUTURE RESEARCH

With the application of the extended guideline in this usability study, the implications of using the guideline as well as the value for improving accessibility of learning websites being developed for seniors have been tested. Here are some conclusions from the results of the empirical investigation.

A key implication for the field of senior friendly information system design from the findings of the current study is to confirm many of the senior-friendly information system design guidelines. For example, for the elderly with poor vision, type size should be 12 point or bigger with double space, and the text should be provided with clear contrast between foreground and background (Wick, 2004; Dickinson et al., 2007; Morrell, 2005; Arch, 2008; NIA & NLM, 2002). Also aligned with NIA/NLM guidelines, only text-relevant images should be used, and text alternatives of video or audio should be provided (NIA & NLM, 2002).

However, this study also suggests some extensions to the current guidelines. For example, in the "Information presentation category", in addition to "Minimize the need for scrolling", explicit instruction should be provided if the use of scrolling is unavoidable for the elderly users who have lower computer competency and conventions. Next, this study shows that user control of video should be added as one of the guidelines in the media category especially for learning websites in which video clips will be used as one of the major resources. Meanwhile, in the category of "Increase the Ease of Navigation," avoid or minimize pop up windows should be added into the checklist so as not to add cognitive tension for senior users. Also, from the findings we learned that explicit step-by-step instruction presented along with the expected operations would be appreciated by senior users with low computer competency.

Furthermore, highlight, form and search engine could be added to the guidelines as this study shows. For the design of search engine, this study shows that an in-site search engine should be included only if indispensible, since it could increase the cognitive pressure to distinguish between the in-site search engine and the outside search engine which they might be more familiar with. Moreover, language sensitive modification should be made when the guideline is applied to websites employing languages other than English. From the findings of this study, the typeface of Song is acceptable for users since it is in agreement with their established reading habits.

In terms of practical implications for the two websites studied, the findings of this study show that substantial efforts are needed to integrate these two websites into a learning web for seniors in Life-long Learning Network. Improvements are needed to promote the usability as well as the accessibility of the learning web. For example, in order to accommodate their declining vision, the recommended font size with double space should be used consistently in all of the pages. Moreover, while an enlarge button is in place according to the existing guidelines, the button should be presented in the proper position as well as be available on all the pages across the website. Additionally the

suggested extension to the guidelines on explicit instruction for operations, limited use of pop up windows, and being cautious about including an in-site search engine should be applied in the re-development of these sites.

In addition, for learning websites in which video clips will be used as one of the major resources, the design of the video presentation should be improved according to the findings in this study: the location of the video should be adjusted to be more comfortable to users, and the control of the video should be provided to users for them to make choice for the size of the video, or the status of play. Also a hint feature or text alternatives for the video should be provided in case there might be a waiting time for the download of the video. Also, using the default of automatically playing video seems like an acceptable approach to use, at least in contexts similar to the two websites studied.

Although this study collected data only from fairly highly educated users, it seems reasonable to believe that the usability problems we have found could be even worse for less educated users. After a re-design and development of the two websites based on the extended guidelines, we plan a more comprehensive usability evaluation to be conducted by a larger group of seniors more varied by education level, so as to examine if accessibility has been improved by the application of the extended guidelines. Particular attention will be paid to the implications of applying the Simplicity of Information Presentation Guideline for the performance of less educated and those who are less experienced at using computers.

ACKNOWLEDGMENT

Source of Funding: Research on learning technology system for Lifelong Learning Network founded from Distance Education Group, Shanghai. The authors would like to thank Professor James M. Laffey for his constructive suggestions on this article. The authors would like thank Lori Younker for her help on editing of this article.

REFERENCES

Arch, A. (2008). *Web accessibility for older users: A literature review*. Retrieved from http://www.w3.org/TR/wai-age-literature/

Aspin, D. N., & Chapman, J. D. (2000). Lifelong learning: Concepts and conceptions. *International Journal of Lifelong Education, 19*(1), 2–19. doi:10.1080/026013700293421

Aula, A. (2005). User study on older adults' use of the Web and search engines. *Universal Access in the Information Society, 4*(1), 67–81. doi:10.1007/s10209-004-0097-7

Becker, S. A. (2004a). A study of web usability for older adults seeking online health resources. *ACM Transactions on Computer-Human Interaction, 11*(4), 387–406. doi:10.1145/1035575.1035578

Becker, S. A. (2004b). E-Government visual accessibility for older adults users. *Social Science Computer Review, 22*(1), 11–23. doi:10.1177/0894439303259876

Caldwell, B., Cooper, M., Guraino Reid, L., & Vanderheiden, G. (Eds.). (2004). *Web content accessibility guidelines 2.0 (WCAG)*. Retrieved from http://www.w3.org/WAI/GL/WCAG20/

Chinese Government. (1996, August 29). *Decree for protecting the right of senior citizens*. Retrieved from http://www.gov.cn/banshi/2005-08/04/content_20203.htm

Department for Education. (2003). *The skills for life survey: A national needs and impact survey of literacy, numeracy and ICT skills*. Retrieved from http://www.dcsf.gov.uk/research/data/uploadfiles/RB490.pdf

Dickinson, A., Eisma, R., Gregor, P., Syme, A., & Milne, S. (2005). Strategies for teaching older people to use the World Wide Web. *Universal Access in the Information Society, 4*(1), 3–15. doi:10.1007/s10209-003-0082-6

Dickinson, A., & Gregor, P. (2006). Computer use has no demonstrated impact on the well-being of older adults. *International Journal of Human-Computer Studies, 64*(8), 744–753. doi:10.1016/j.ijhcs.2006.03.001

Dickinson, A., Smith, M. J., Arnott, J. L., Newell, A. F., & Hill, R. L. (2007). Approaches to web search and navigation for older computer novices. In *Proceedings of the SIGCHI Conference on Human Factors in Computing Systems*, San Jose, CA (pp. 281-290).

Emery, V. K., Edwards, P. J., Jacko, J. A., Moloney, K. P., Barnard, L., Kongnakorn, T., et al. (2003). Toward achieving universal usability for older adults through multimodal feedback. In *Proceedings of the Conference on Universal Usability*, Vancouver, BC, Canada (pp. 46-53).

Fischer, G. (2001). Lifelong learning and its support with new media. In Smelser, N. J., & Baltes, P. B. (Eds.), *International encyclopedia of social and behavioral sciences, discipline cognitive psychology and cognitive science* (pp. 8836–8840). Oxford, UK: Pergamon.

Gerontological Society of Shanghai (GSS). (2006). *Guideline for design senior accessible website (for trial)*. Retrieved from http://www.shanghaigss.org.cn/news_view.asp?newsid=2400

Hendrix, C. (2000). Computer use among elderly people. *Computers in Nursing, 18*(2), 62–71.

Kurniawan, S., King, A., Evans, D., & Blenkhorn, P. (2006). Personalising web page presentation for older people. *Interacting with Computers, 18*(3), 457–477. doi:10.1016/j.intcom.2005.11.006

Kurniawan, S., & Zaphiris, P. (2005). Research-derived Web design guidelines for older people. In *Proceedings of the 7th International ACM SIGACCESS Conference on Computers and Accessibility*, Baltimore, MD (pp. 129-135).

Leporini, B., & Paternò, F. (2008). Applying Web usability criteria for vision-impaired users: Does it really improve task performance? *International Journal of Human-Computer Interaction, 24*(1), 17–47.

Morrell, R. W. (2005). The process of construction and revision in the development of a model site for use by older adults. *Universal Access in the Information Society, 4*(1), 24–38. doi:10.1007/s10209-003-0085-3

Nahm, E., Resnick, B., & Covington, B. (2006). Development of theory-based, online health learning modules for older adults: Lessons learned. *CIN: Computers, Informatics. Nursing, 24*(5), 261–268.

National Assessment of Adult Literacy (NAAL). (2003). *The 2003 national assessment of adult literacy.* Retrieved from http://nces.ed.gov/naal/

National Institute on Aging (NIA) & National Library of Medicine. (NLM). (2002). *Making your Web site senior-friendly: A checklist.* Retrieved from http://www.nlm.nih.gov/pubs/checklist.pdf

Nielsen, J. (2000). *Why you only need to test with 5 users.* Retrieved from http://www.useit.com/alertbox/20000319.html

Nielsen, J. (2005). *Lower-literacy users.* Retrieved from http://www.useit.com/alertbox/20050314.html

Sayago, S., & Blat, J. (2009). About the relevance of accessibility barriers in the everyday interactions of older people with the web. In *Proceedings of the International Cross-Disciplinary Conference on Web Accessibility*, Madrid, Spain (pp. 104-113).

Shanghai Civil Affair Bureau (SCAB). Shanghai Bureau for Senior Citizens' Work (SBSC), & Shanghai Statistic Bureau (SSB). (2009). *2009 annual report of the development of senior citizens' work in Shanghai.* Retrieved from http://www.shanghai60.org.cn/newsinfo.aspx?id=363

Shanghai Civil Affairs Bureau (SCAB). (2009). *2008 aging population and affairs. Monitoring Statistics.* Retrieved from http://www.shmzj.gov.cn/gb/shmzj/node6/node592/node596/userobject1ai22218.html

Shanghai Municipal Committee (SMC). (2006). *Guidelines on promoting the building of a learning society issued by CPC Shanghai Municipal Committee.* Retrieved from http://www.shanghai.gov.cn

Sharit, J., Hernández, M. A., Czaja, S. J., & Pirolli, P. (2008). Investigating the roles of knowledge and cognitive abilities in older adult information seeking on the Web. *ACM Transactions on Computer-Human Interaction, 15*(1), 1–25. doi:10.1145/1352782.1352785

Web Accessibility Initiative (WAI). (1999). *Accessibility guidelines.* Retrieved from http://www.w3.org/wai

Wick, D. A. (2004). Older adults and their information seeking. *Behavioral & Social Sciences Librarian, 22*(2), 1–26. doi:10.1300/J103v22n02_01

APPENDIX

Table Al. Evaluation checklist

Items	Guidelines/checklist
Readable Text	
Typeface	Use Hei typeface instead of Song typeface
Type size	Use 12 point or 14 point type size. Enlarge text available
Type weight	Use medium or bold face type
Physical spacing	Double space. Paragraph spacing should be at least 1.5 times larger than the line spacing.
Texts width	Width is no more than 40 characters in Chinese.
Justification	Left justify all body text.
Color	Avoid yellow and blue and green in close proximity.
Background	Clear contrast between foreground and background. Foreground and background colors can be selected by the user.
Information presentation	
Style	Present information in a clear and familiar way to reduce the number of inferences that must be made. Use positive statements.
Simplicity	Use 6th grade reading level on homepages and 8th grade reading level on other pages. Provide definition and explanation when have to use idioms, jargon and abbreviations.
organization	Organize the content in a standard format. Break lengthy documents into short sections.
Highlight	Highlight headlines and important information by changing color, type size or type weight.
Scrolling	Avoid automatically scrolling text. Minimize the need for scrolling.
Media	
Illustrations and Photo-graphs	Use text-relevant images only.
Images of text	Images of text are only used for pure decoration or where a particular presentation of text is essential to the information being conveyed.
Animation, Video and Audio	Use short segments to reduce download time on older computers.
Moving, linking, scrolling	Provide control handle to pause, stop or hide video or audio
Text Alternatives	Provide text alternatives such as open-captioning or access to a static version of the text for all animation, video and audio.
Increasing the Ease of Navigation	
Navigation	The organization of the web site should be simple and straightforward. Use explicit step-by-step navigation procedures whenever possible to ensure that people understand what follows. Web pages have titles that describe topic or purpose.
The Mouse	Use single mouse clicks to access information.
Layout	Always provide a clean and well organized page. Information about the user's location within a set of Web pages is available. Components that have the same functionality within a set of web pages are identified consistently and be set in the same place on each page.
Icons and Buttons	Incorporate text with the icon if possible. Use large buttons that do not require precise mouse movements for activation.
Menus	Use pull down menus sparingly.

continued on following page

Table A1. Continued

Items	Guidelines/checklist
Backward/Forward Navigation	Incorporate buttons such as Previous Page and Next Page to allow the reader to review or move forward.
Site Maps	Provide a site map to show how the site is organized.
Hyperlinks	Help user to understand it is a hyperlink and make obvious change when a mouse hover over hyperlinks. Make noticeable differences between visited and not visited place by changing color or underlining.
Help and Information	Provide various ways for users to get information or give comments. (telephone, email, etc)
Form	Gave instance or guidance to show what one should fill in. Enable the tab key. Put the submit button close to the last entry field.
Error	Describe the error to the user in text and provide suggestions if possible.
Search Engine	Offer a search engine that is tolerant spelling errors.

This work was previously published in the International Journal of Adult Vocational Education and Technology, Volume 2, Issue 2, edited by Victor C.X. Wang, pp. 11-24, copyright 2011 by IGI Publishing (an imprint of IGI Global).

Chapter 5
Workplace Incivility in Schools

Thomas G. Reio Jr.
Florida International University, USA

Stephanie M. Reio
University of Louisville, USA

ABSTRACT

This paper investigates the prevalence of coworker and supervisor incivility in the context of K-12 schools and incivility's possible link to teachers' commitment to the school and turnover intent. The data were collected via surveys from 94 middle school teachers in the United States. Results indicated that 85% of the teachers experienced coworker incivility over the past year; 71% experienced supervisor incivility. MANOVA results suggested no statistically significant differences in incivility by gender or ethnicity. Hierarchical regression results suggested that supervisor incivility was associated negatively with commitment and positively associated with turnover intent. Coworker incivility was not a significant predictor in the regression equations. Macro- and micro-level human resource strategies are offered as possible tools to lessen the likelihood of uncivil behavior.

INTRODUCTION

Workplace incivility is a growing challenge for all types of organizations (Porath & Pearson, 2010). In recognition of this mounting problem, researchers have investigated its prevalence in a broad range of organizational contexts, yet surprisingly little in K-12 schools. The lack of scholarly inquiry in this area is troubling considering the almost overwhelming difficulties facing the teaching

profession (Fox & Stallworth, 2010). For example, in our current lean economic times, schools are receiving less financial support, yet calls for accountability remain (Fox & Stallworth, 2010). Teachers continue to be under mounting pressure from a variety of sources to increase student learning performance (e.g., through federal and state legislative mandates, demanding parents, society in general), with little obvious relief in sight (Steffgen & Ewen, 2007). Educational policy makers and superintendents, and in-school instructional and administrative (e.g., principal) leaders need

DOI: 10.4018/978-1-4666-2062-9.ch005

to be aware that these stressful contingencies contribute to a school workplace context that may be less than ideal to work, setting the stage for increasing the likelihood of teachers' uncivil behaviors (Waggoner, 2003).

Andersson and Pearson (1999) define workplace incivility as "low intensity deviant behavior with ambiguous intent to harm the target, in violation of workplace norms for mutual respect. Uncivil behaviors are characteristically rude, discourteous, displaying a lack of respect for others" (p. 457). Incivility is not necessarily objective, as it is a reflection of an individual's interpretation about how an action made them feel; in other words, it is defined in the eyes of the beholder (Porath & Pearson, 2010). Scholars have cited several antecedents to uncivil behavior such as lack of establishing positive relationships in the organization (i.e., not learning to fit in with coworkers), negative affect (e.g., anxiety, frustration, anger), and demographic dissimilarity (e.g., age, gender) as some of the likely predictors of uncivil behavior in the workplace (Baron & Neuman, 1996; Chen & Eastman, 1997; Pearson, Andersson, & Porath, 2000). Numerous labels have been assigned to uncivil behaviors such as condescending, sarcastic, inconsiderate, rude, and insulting, among others (Andersson & Pearson, 1999). Increases in workplace incivility have also been associated with organizational outcomes like reduced organizational commitment and job satisfaction, and increased turnover intentions (Laschinger, Leiter, Day, & Gilin, 2009). Workplace incivility can dampen employee productivity and become an economic drain (Porath & Pearson, 2010), and even ruin an organization's reputation (Fox & Stallworth, 2010; Hutton & Gates, 2008). Because few studies have examined workplace incivility and its possible association with organizational outcomes in the context of a K-12 school, the aim of this research was to investigate the frequency of uncivil behavior among teachers and the influence of workplace incivility on teachers' commitment to the school and turnover intentions. Educational

leaders could use new information generated by this research to find ways to reduce the likelihood of uncivil behavior, increase teacher commitment, and decrease turnover intent among teachers at our schools.

REVIEW OF THE BACKGROUND LITERATURE

In this section, we demonstrate how workplace incivility can be associated with intentional acts of workplace aggression and physical violence (Fox & Stallworth, 2010; Lim et al., 2008; Porath & Pearson, 2010). Second, we link workplace incivility to school outcomes like teacher commitment to the school and turnover intentions.

Workplace incivility's link to aggression and physical violence. Workplace incivility is characterized as violating norms of respect, with ambiguous intent to harm, and being of generally low intensity (Andersson & Pearson, 1999). Gossiping, ostracizing, passing blame, taking credit inappropriately, ignoring, and teasing are all forms of disrespectful workplace behaviors that can grow rapidly or spiral into more serious forms of aggression (i.e., intentional harm-doing short of physical violence) and physical violence (Andersson & Pearson, 1999; Fox & Stallworth, 2010; Lim et al., 2008). Thus, leaders and managers should be concerned about workplace incivility because it can lead to more aggressive forms of behavior (Fox & Stallworth, 2010). In May, 2010, for example, a Transportation Security Administration worker at Miami International Airport was arrested for allegedly assaulting a coworker with a police baton who had had been teasing him about the highly personal results of an inadvertent full body scan at the airport (Hunter, 2010). This incident is emblematic of how seemingly harmless behaviors with ambiguous intent to harm can spiral out of control to produce acts of physical violence. Physical violence refers to more severe forms of workplace aggression, such as physical assault (Neuman & Baron, 1998). Although we cannot claim that every instance of workplace aggression has its roots in being treated uncivilly by a coworker or supervisor, instances of uncivil behavior leading to actual physical violence in workplaces such as airports and schools are all too common (Fox & Stallworth, 2010; Waggoner, 2003).

Alarmingly, there were 97,830 aggravated assaults committed in US workplaces in 2007 (National Center for Victims of Crime, 2010). The same report noted that female workers were victims in 61 percent of the workplace assault cases. Further, twelve percent of the victims sustained injuries, with less than half receiving medical care. Thus, physically violent acts like assault occur frequently in US workplaces; yet, such behavior is not limited to the US. Comparable to the US, for example, one in twenty workers in the European Union reported having experienced physical violence in the past 12 months. Exposure to physical violence was higher among women, particularly younger ones (European Foundation for the Improvement of Living and Working Conditions, 2010). A key finding too was that the level of physical violence was relatively high in the health, public administration, and education sectors. Being harassed/bullied by their colleagues (a more persistent form of incivility), a potent predictor of aggression and physical violence (Hogh, Henriksson, & Burr, 2005), was reported by almost seven percent of the EU teachers. Approximately twelve percent were threatened with physical violence (EU average for all occupational types was six percent), with roughly five percent of teachers actually suffering physical violence from colleagues. In addition, five percent of teachers experienced physical violence from non-colleagues. Thus, even in workplaces like schools, uncivil behaviors and its negative consequences occur all too often.

Situational, social, and personal factors contribute to workplace incivility, aggression, and physical violence (Neuman & Baron, 1998). Situ-ational factors might include school change (e.g., an unpopular new federal or state mandate) and the nature of the work environment. At schools where the work environment affords little control over one's work (e.g., having an authoritarian principal), accompanied by high intensity levels and conflict (e.g., with students, parents, coworkers, or supervisors), the likelihood of uncivil behavior and aggression increases (Neuman & Baron, 1998; Steffgen & Ewen, 2007). Examples of social factors would be teachers' perceptions of being treated unfairly by principals and district personnel, frustration-interference with on-going goal-directed behavior by parents or students, and school workplace norms that support uncivil and aggressive behavior (Fox & Stallworth, 2010; Waggoner, 2003). Personal factors relate to personality traits, in that certain individuals have a greater propensity to tease and agitate, aggress, and become physically violent than others (e.g., Type A Behavior Pattern, obstructionist, hostile attribution bias). Likewise, some individuals may also be more prone to reacting strongly to even mild provocation or vice versa. Overall, the combination of social and situational factors may affect individuals differently depending on their interaction with a possible range number of personal factors.

OUTCOMES OF INCIVILITY

What happens to employees who perceive they have been treated uncivilly where they work? First, being the target, observer, or instigator of uncivil behavior can have important implications for teachers' health (Hogh et al., 2005; Vartia, 2001). Stress, sleeplessness, depression, anxiety and frustration, and irritability are common reported short- and long-term health-related symptoms (Lim et al., 2008; Lim & Teo, 2009). Such symptoms, in turn, have been associated with increased burnout, absenteeism, and voluntary turnover, and reduced productivity (Fox

& Stallworth, 2010). For instance, in a study of 779 teachers, Fox and Stallworth found a positive link between physical health symptoms (e.g., headaches, fatigue, sleep problems, and stomach upset) that required a doctor's office visit and being the target of uncivil behavior. Likewise, in a study of 1158 US Circuit Court workers (Lim et al., 2008), increased personal incivility was associated with decreased physical health. Gender differences were not found (Lim et al., 2008). Likewise, Reio and Ghosh (2009) found that even among instigators of incivility ($N=402$), being the instigator of uncivil behavior negatively predicted the instigators' physical health.

Describing a line of research extending 10 years, Porath and Pearson (2010) reported significant losses associated with being treated uncivilly in the workplace. For example, 48% intentionally decreased work effort, 47% decreased time at work, 38% decreased work quality, 66% claimed their performance declined, 78% indicated their organizational commitment had declined, and 12% said they left the organization as a result of their poor treatment. Turnover was highlighted as being particularly damaging financially in that it might cost anywhere from 30-50%, for instance, of a low-level employee's salary for replacement (e.g., a novice teacher). For supervisors (e.g., a principal), replacement cost is roughly 150% of their salary.

Mirroring Porath and Pearson's (2010) research, Hutton and Gates (2008) found a negative link between supervisor incivility and direct health care staff productivity. Incivility from supervisors and patients and not physicians or other direct care staff members were significant predictors of decreased productivity. The annual costs associated with the decreased productivity were $1235 per nursing assistant and $1484 per RN. Further, in a Canadian nursing study ($N = 612$), Laschinger et al. (2009) examined the association between workplace empowerment, incivility, and burnout, and three dependent variables: job satisfaction, organizational commitment, and

turnover intentions. Supervisor incivility was a powerful predictor of each dependent variable, and coworker incivility was less so.

Demonstrating that uncivil behavior exists in not only face-to-face interactions, Lim and Teo (2009) estimated that rude emails generated roughly $5 billion in health-related costs to organizations due to targets' stress-related illnesses. The authors also ascertained that exposure to cyber incivility predicted less job satisfaction and organizational commitment, and greater turnover intent among banking and financial service employees in Hong Kong. Male supervisors engaged in more active forms of cyber incivility like saying something hurtful through email; females tended to engage in more passive forms such as not replying to an email.

Issues, Controversies, and Problems

School researchers can play a vital role in revealing the insidious nature of workplace incivility and its consequences. Despite evidence that workplace incivility can have important organizational consequences, little empirical research has examined workplace incivility among teachers and their coworkers and supervisors in the context K-12 schools. If educational leaders and researchers hope to increase teacher commitment to their school and decrease turnover intent, we need more information about the degree to which supervisory and coworker incivility is associated with teacher commitment and turnover intentions. Lack of teacher commitment can lead to less productivity (Porath & Pearson, 2010) with its accompanying negative ramifications for student learning. Turnover intent has been shown to be one of the strongest predictors of actual turnover (Porath & Pearson, 2010); again, the costs associated with replacing a teacher are simply too high. Principals and human resource practitioners may be able to apply this new knowledge into devising zero-tolerance policies toward uncivil face-to-face and online behavior and designing training interventions that can effectively reduce the frequency and severity of uncivil behavior, which ultimately can benefit the school (Reio & Ghosh, 2009).

CONCEPTUAL MODEL TESTED IN THE STUDY

Drawing from the extant theoretical and research literature linking workplace incivility to organizational outcomes (Cortina et al., 2001; Fox & Stallworth, 2010; Lim et al., 2008; Neuman & Baron, 1998; Porath & Pearson, 2010; Vartia, 2001; Waggoner, 2003), we propose a conceptual model where coworker and supervisory incivility are associated with teachers' organizational commitment and turnover intention (see Figure 1). First, we hypothesized that both coworker and supervisory incivility are negatively associated with teacher commitment to the school. Second, we hypothesized that coworker and supervisor incivility are positively associated with teacher turnover intention.

METHOD

This research is part of a larger workplace learning study. Sections describing the sample and data collection protocol, and research measures follow below:

- ***Participants and Data Collection Protocol.*** Teachers (N = 94) completed the survey that measured their commitment to the school, turnover intent, frequency of being the target of supervisor or coworker incivility, and certain demographics (i.e., age, gender, ethnicity, hours worked per week, length of employment at current school, and length of overall teacher experience). Four middle schools from an urban school district in the US Midwest participated in this research. The teachers received the survey through the school mail system. To assure teachers of complete anonymity, a sealed collection box was set up in the school's main office. After two weeks, the data were collected by the lead researcher where the overall response rate was 33.9%. The participants were largely female (n = 57; male: n = 37), with an average age of 39.6 years (SD = 11.9). As for ethnicity, 4.3% (n = 4) identified themselves as Asian, 18.3% (n = 17) African-American, 17.2% (n = 16) Hispanic, 54.8% (n = 51) Caucasian, and 5.3% (n = 5) as "Other," with one not responding. Average length of time teaching at their current school was 6.7 years (SD = 3.8), while average length of overall teaching experience was 9.3 years (SD = 4.5). Finally, average hours worked per week was 40.5 (SD = 12.2).
- ***Research Measures.*** In this section, we describe the research measures employed

Figure 1. Hypothesized model of association between workplace incivility and organizational outcomes

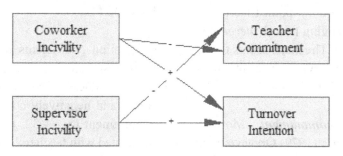

in this study. Each is a self-report measure based upon the respondent's perceptions, not actual behaviors. The independent variables (coworker and supervisor incivility), are presented first, followed by the dependent variables (organizational commitment and intent to turnover).

- *Workplace Incivility.* Coworker and supervisor incivility were measured by modified versions of Cortina, Magley, Williams, and Langhout's (2001) 7-item Workplace Incivility Scale (WIS). The WIS asked the respondent to think about being exposed to supervisor or coworker incivility over the past five years; we reduced the time period to the past year to reduce the likelihood of recall-related issues. Instead of one instrument to measure a combination of supervisor or coworker incivility, we decided to modify the measure by splitting it into two separate scales: one measuring supervisor incivility and one measuring coworker incivility. We also introduced new items from the literature; the teacher's coworker and teachers' supervisor incivility scales now included 15 (α =.94) and 12 items (α =.96), respectively. The frequency of being the target of coworker incivility over the past year was specified through statements such as coworkers "Snapped at you" or "Talked about you behind your back." The frequency of being the target of supervisor incivility over the past year was specified through statements such as supervisors "Gave you the silent treatment" or "Did not give credit where credit was due." The items were rated on a 5-point Likert scale with responses ranging from 1 (*never*) to 5 (*most of the time*). The mean scores for the coworker and supervisor incivility measures were 18.2 (SD = 7.5) and 24.1 (SD = 9.6), respectively.

- *Organizational commitment.* Mowday, Steers, and Porter's (1979) Organizational Commitment Questionnaire (OCQ) was used to measure teachers' commitment to one's school. The OCQ is a summative 15-item, 7-point Likert scale (1 = *strongly disagree* to 7 = *strongly agree*). Six items were reverse scored. Sample items included "I really care about the fate of this organization" and "I talk up this organization to my friends as a great organization to work for." The mean score for the measure was 47.6 (SD = 4.7); the Cronbach's alpha in this study was.90.

- *Turnover intent.* Participants' turnover intent was measured with the 3-item scale from Singh, Verbeke, and Rhoads (1996). The three items assessed the teachers' overall intent of leaving their jobs in their current organizations. The items were rated on a 5-point Likert-type scale with responses ranging from 1 (*strongly disagree*) to 5 (*strongly agree*). A sample item from the scale is "I often think about quitting." The mean score for the measure was 7.0 (SD = 3.0); the Cronbach's alpha in the present study was.78.

- *Control variables.* Because there is research evidence indicating that gender (coded 0 = male; 1 = female), years teaching at current school, and hours worked per week might influence the dependent variables (e.g., Cortina et al., 2001; Mowday et al., 1979; Pearson et al., 2000; Reio & Ghosh, 2009), they were used as statistical controls in our two regression models.

RESULTS

Correlation coefficients between the variables of interest were determined and investigated for meaningfulness. Coworker incivility was significantly and negatively correlated with teachers' commitment (r = -.32, p <.01) and positively associated with teachers' turnover intent (r =.29, *p* <.01). Likewise, supervisor incivility was negatively correlated with commitment (*r* = -.55, *p* <.001), but associated positively with turnover intent (*r* =.40, *p* <.001). Finally, commitment and turnover intent were negatively related (*r* = -.69, *p* <.001), indicating logically that greater commitment to the school was associated with less turnover intent. What these results suggest is that increased levels of being the target of either coworker or supervisor incivility decreased teachers' commitment to the school and increased their turnover intent. Supervisor incivility was the strongest predictor of the two dependent variables (large effect size; Cohen, 1988).

MANOVA results. Before testing the regression models, we ran a 2 (gender) X 5 (ethnicity) X 2 (coworker incivility and supervisor incivility) MANOVA to investigate the possibility of group mean differences in the dependent variables. Box's Test indicated that equal variances could be assumed (*p* =.44). Wilks's criterion suggested the absence of a multivariate effect; thus, there were no statistically significant differences by gender (Wilks's Λ =.93, $F(4, 140) = 1.14$, *p* =.34, η^2 =.03) or ethnicity (Wilks's Λ =.80, $F(8, 140) = 1.88$, *p* =.08, η^2 =.09) with respect to the combination of dependent variables. There was an absence of an interaction effect as well (Wilks's Λ =.94, $F(6, 140) =.69$, *p* =.66, η^2 =.03). Thus, no group mean differences were found by gender or ethnicity. However, because a number of studies have demonstrated gender differences in uncivil behavior (e.g., Reio & Ghosh, 2009), we retained the variable for our regression analyses.

Regression analyses. To test the first hypothesis where coworker and supervisor incivility negatively predicted commitment to the school, a hierarchical regression was run. In the first step of the regression equation, the demographic variables were entered as control variables; the variance explained was R^2 =.03, *p* >.05. Gender (β = -.11, *p* >.05) and time teaching at current school (β =.12, *p* >.05) did not make statistically significant contributions to the regression equation, while hours

worked weekly (β =.30, *p* <.01) was a significant predictor of teachers' school commitment. In essence, the analyses suggested that greater hours worked was positively associated with teacher school commitment. After controlling for the block of demographic variables, we entered both incivility variables into the regression equation (Block 2; ΔR^2 =.34, *p* <.001). The supervisor (β = -.68, *p* <.001) but not coworker incivility (β =.07, *p* >.05) variable was a significant negative predictor of teacher commitment. In other words, those who experienced supervisor incivility more frequently were less committed to their school. The third step, interaction terms (cross-products of three demographic variables and the two incivility variables) were entered (Block 3; ΔR^2 =.007, *p* >.05). None of the six interactions added significant variance to the regression equation. Overall, 38.0% of the variance (adjusted R^2) in teachers' school commitment was explained by the model. Hypothesis one was partially supported in that supervisor incivility significantly and negatively predicted commitment to the school. A summary of regression results are detailed in Table 1.

To test the second hypothesis where coworker and supervisor incivility positively predicted teachers' turnover intent, a second hierarchical regression analysis was run. In the first step of the regression equation, the demographic variables were entered as control variables; the variance explained was R^2 =.04, *p* >.05. None of the demographic variables made statistically significant contributions to the regression equation: gender (β =.24, *p* >.05), hours worked weekly (β = -.41, *p* >.05), time teaching at current school (β = -.19, *p* >.05). After controlling for the block of demographic variables, we entered the two incivility variables into the regression equation (Block 2; ΔR^2 =.16, *p* <.001). The supervisor (β =.39, *p* <.01) but not coworker incivility (β =.03, *p* >.05) variable was a significant positive predictor of turnover intent. Thus, being the target more frequently of supervisor incivility was associated with a greater likelihood of turnover intention

Table 1. Summary hierarchical regressions with demographic and incivility variables predicting teacher commitment and turnover intent

Variable	Commitment and Turnover Intent Models	
	Commitment	Turnover Intent
	β ΔR²	β ΔR²
Step 1		
Demographic		
Gender	-.11	.24
Hours	.30**	-.41
Experience	.12	-.19
Block	.03	.04
Step 2		
Incivility		
Supervisor	-.68***	.39**
Coworker	-.07	.03
Block	.34***	.16***
Step 3		
Interactions (Supervisor)		
Gender X Incivility	.44	.14
Hours X Incivility	.35	.01
Experience X Incivility	.27	.19
Interactions (Coworker)		
Gender X Incivility	.23	-.11
Hours X Incivility	-.22	.18
Experience X Incivility	.05	.08
Block	.007	.003
Total adjusted R²	.38***	.20***

Note: N = 94. **p <.01; *** p <.001.

among the teachers. In the third step, interaction terms were entered (Block 3; ΔR^2 =.003, p >.05). None of the six interactions added significant variance to the regression equation. Hypothesis two was partially supported in that supervisor incivility positively predicted teacher turnover intent. Overall, 20.1% of the variance (adjusted

R^2) in teacher turnover intent was explained by the regression model (see Table 1).

DISCUSSION AND IMPLICATIONS OF INCIVILITY FOR ORGANIZATIONAL OUTCOMES: FUTURE TRENDS AND CONCLUSIONS

Little research has investigated the link between workplace incivility, organizational commitment (teachers' commitment to the school), and turnover intent among K-12 teachers. Results from this exploratory study demonstrated that the majority of teachers had been the target of coworker and supervisor incivility over the past year. In the regression models, supervisor incivility was the most powerful predictor of both commitment and turnover intent.

Frequency of workplace incivility. Almost 85% of this sample of teachers reported being the target of some form of coworker incivility in the past year. Likewise, 71% indicated they were the target of supervisor incivility as well. Slightly over 50% experienced coworker incivility at the "from time to time" to "always" levels; similarly, 33% experienced supervisor incivility from time to time to always. This result compares with Laschinger et al.'s (2009) hospital worker study where 68% of nurses reported experiencing supervisor incivility and 78% experienced coworker incivility. These findings are also in line with Cortina et al.'s (2001) research where 76% of the US Circuit Court participants experienced acts of uncivil behavior. The most frequent coworker uncivil acts in this research were leaving a jammed copier or printer for the next person to handle, snapping at you, showing little interest in your opinion, talking about you behind your back, and giving you dirty looks. Supervisor incivility exhibited itself most frequently as not being paid attention to, having your judgment doubted, not giving credit where credit was due, being putting down, and being cut off in the middle of a conversation without regard for your feelings.

Consistent with the prior literature (European Foundation for the Improvement of Living and Working Conditions, 2010; Fox & Stallworth, 2010; Waggoner, 2003) then, the results of this study suggest that the majority of teachers reported being the targets of coworker and supervisor uncivil behavior over the past year. Although we did not find gender or ethnic differences in being the target of uncivil coworker of supervisor behaviors, the frequency of being the target of uncivil incivility should be a cause for concern because such behavior, albeit ambiguous in intent, has been shown to spiral into patterns of repeated incivility (i.e., bullying) and "tit for tat" responses from targets, to aggression and finally physical violence (Andersson & Pearson, 1999; Porath & Pearson, 2010) across a broad range of occupations. Not only can uncivil behavior escalate into more severe forms of problematic interactions among coworkers and supervisors, there are concomitant decreases in target work engagement and commitment to the school, and turnover becomes more likely (Porath & Pearson, 2010).

Correlation results: Target incivility and organizational outcomes. The correlational analyses revealed that coworker and supervisor incivility were associated with less commitment to the school and greater intent to turnover. The effect sizes demonstrated ranged from moderate to large (Cohen, 1988). For each dependent variable, the relation to supervisor incivility demonstrated the largest effect. The correlation results mirror the bulk of the literature in that being the target of coworker and supervisor incivilities is associated with important organizational outcomes (Fox & Stallworth, 2010; Porath & Andersson, 2010; Waggoner, 2003); in this case, less commitment to the school organization and greater intent to depart the school.

Regression results. Before running the regression analyses, we ran a MANOVA to examine possible group mean differences in the incivility variables by gender and ethnicity. No statistically significant differences were found in being the target of uncivil behavior by gender or ethnicity. This finding is in contrast to other studies where females were found to be more likely than males to be targets of incivility (Cortina et al., 2001). Then again, Porath and Pearson (2000) established that women were no more likely to be targets of incivility than men. Perhaps the difference lies in the types of organizations represented in the two studies. Cortina et al. (2001) surveyed US Circuit Court workers, excluding judges, while this study dealt specifically with teachers.

The regression analyses involved examining the predictive relationships between the demographic variables of gender, length of time teaching at the school, and hours worked weekly, coworker and supervisor incivility, and the two dependent variables. First, neither being female nor being employed longer at the school made a statistically significant contribution to predicting commitment to the school and turnover intent. However, working more hours weekly was positively associated with commitment, but not significantly with turnover intent. This finding may be a reflection that the hours worked by the teachers (40.5 hours weekly) were sufficiently consistent with norms in other professions to not be a factor in this study.

Supervisor incivility predicted commitment and turnover intent, but coworker incivility did not. This is in contrast to Laschinger et al.'s (2009) research with nurses, after controlling for perceived empowerment, that both supervisor and coworker incivility negatively predicted commitment, and positively predicted turnover intent. This inconsistency may be more of a reflection of the large sample ($N = 612$) examined because the reported beta weights are very small but similar to those found in this study for the coworker incivility variables. The results of this study do parallel Hutton and Gates' (2008) findings that supervisor, but not coworker incivility was linked with another important organizational outcome, that is, productivity. As was the case in this study, supervisor incivility was the strongest predictor of organizational outcomes in the research informing this investigation.

Limitations and recommendations for future research. There are several limitations in this study. The response rate was relatively low, but consistent with other social science research of this type where response rates can range from as low as 8% and as high as 75% (Dillman, 2000). Still, we must be very cautious in generalizing the results. The use of single-source, self-report data also raises concerns of potential common method variance bias because it has been shown to either inflate or deflate correlations among variables (Burton-Jones, 2009). However, as Lim et al. (2008) suggested, properly developed and standardized instruments like the ones employed in this research can reduce the likelihood of introducing common method variance bias into a study. All the scales used in this study have been tested previously and thus provide validity and reliability evidence. Although the sample size for this research was appropriate for running the statistical analyses (Tabachnick & Fidell, 2001), future larger studies with proportional ethnic and gender representation of the link between incivility and other vital organizational outcomes could incorporate different sources of objective data, for example, organizational records pertaining to absenteeism to substantiate turnover intent, or corroborating data from supervisors or coworkers in regard to job performance, worker adaptation, and uncivil behaviors. Cyber or online incivility could be investigated as well for evidence of uncivil behavior (Lim & Teo, 2009).

Because the data were collected at a single point in time, this precludes making causal inferences. Longitudinal research is recommended to overcome this limitation. Examining the behaviors and responses of teachers over time would add to the emerging base of research suggesting that uncivil behavior impacts both short- and long-term work outcomes at schools.

Implications for Future Practice. This study has several practical implications. The relation between coworker and supervisor incivility and teacher commitment to their school and turnover intent has some major implications at both individual and school levels. Consequently, macro- and micro-level strategies are imperative to lessen the likelihood of future problems with uncivil behavior.

At the school level, district leaders and principals may wish to consider macro-level strategies to limit the likelihood of uncivil behavior and diminish its effects by establishing policies and codes of conduct aimed specifically at encouraging respect and discouraging incivility (Pearson et al., 2000; Reio & Ghosh, 2009). As the school's environment may perpetuate or inhibit incivility through workplace norms (Pearson et al., 2000), principals and other school leaders must model and promote appropriate behavioral standards. Modeling appropriate behavior must not only include face-to-face interactions, but in the online context as well (Lim & Teo, 2009). Rude, snippy emails and any other type of uncivil online communication should not be tolerated. Indeed, standards of civility should be positively reinforced to perpetuate norms of civility at the school (Porath & Pearson, 2010; Reio & Ghosh, 2009). However, we must remember that individuals can communicate online through more than exchanging email; the availability of a wide variety of Web 2.0 supported technologies like blogs, wikis, podcasts, and social-networking sites (e.g., Facebook) have increased opportunities for communicating uncivilly. At the micro-level, professional development opportunities might help address individual and group interpersonal skill gaps. Human resource professionals could help schools focus on training interventions to improve interpersonal skills. Training interventions could also include mediation or conflict management trainings for principals, assistant principals and other school leaders. This may be considered a preventative strategy because school leaders, once equipped, can identify and manage uncivil behaviors before they escalate.

CONCLUSION AND FUTURE NEEDS

Educational leaders and researchers need to know that teachers were the target of frequent uncivil behavior from coworkers and supervisors in the four middle schools examined in this study. Although the frequency of incivility found was consistent with prior empirical research, these findings warrant considerable concern because as Neuman and Baron's (1998) and Andersson and Pearson's (1999) theoretical notions suggest, uncivil behavior, unchecked, can escalate into aggression and physical violence. Teachers work daily with children and the stakes seem so much higher; more must be done to reduce its likelihood in schools. This research also indicates that incivility can diminish teacher commitment and promote turnover intent. Clearly, we need more research to find productive ways for dealing with the insidious problem of workplace incivility at both the school and individual level.

REFERENCES

Andersson, L. M., & Pearson, C. M. (1999). Tit for tat? The spiraling effect of incivility in the workplace. *Academy of Management Review*, *24*, 452–471. doi:10.2307/259136

Baron, R. A., & Neuman, J. H. (1996). Workplace violence and workplace aggression: Evidence on their relative frequency and potential clauses. *Aggressive Behavior*, *22*, 161–173. doi:10.1002/(SICI)1098-2337(1996)22:3<161::AID-AB1>3.0.CO;2-Q

Burton-Jones, A. (2009). Minimizing method bias through programmatic research. *Management Information Systems Quarterly*, *33*, 445–471.

Chen, C. C., & Eastman, W. (1997). Toward a civic culture for multicultural organizations. *The Journal of Applied Behavioral Science*, *33*, 454–470. doi:10.1177/0021886397334003

Cohen, J. (1988). *Statistical power for the behavioral sciences* (2nd ed.). Hillsdale, NJ: Erlbaum.

Cortina, L. M., Magley, V. J., Williams, J. H., & Langhout, R. D. (2001). Incivility in the workplace: Incidence and impact. *Journal of Occupational Health Psychology*, *6*, 64–80. doi:10.1037/1076-8998.6.1.64

Dillman, D. A. (2000). *Mail and internet surveys: The tailored design method* (2nd ed.). New York: Wiley.

European Foundation for the Improvement of Living and Working Conditions. (2010). *Physical and psychological violence at the workplace*. Dublin, Ireland: Author.

Fox, S., & Stallworth, L. E. (2010). The battered apple: An application of stress-emotion-control/support theory to teachers' experience of violence and bullying. *Human Relations*, *63*, 927–954. doi:10.1177/0018726709349518

Hogh, A., Henriksson, M. E., & Burr, H. (2005). A 5-year follow-up study of aggression at work and psychological health. *International Journal of Behavioral Medicine*, *12*, 256–265. doi:10.1207/s15327558ijbm1204_6

Hunter, M. (2010, May 7). Anatomical ridicule raises body-scanning concerns. *CNN Travel*, p. A2.

Hutton, S., & Gates, D. (2008). Workplace incivility and productivity losses among direct care staff. *AAOHN Journal*, *56*, 168–175. doi:10.3928/08910162-20080401-01

Laschinger, H. K., Leiter, M., Day, A., & Gilin, D. (2009). Workplace empowerment, incivility, and burnout: Impact on staff nurse recruitment and retention outcomes. *Journal of Nursing Management*, *17*, 309–311.

Lim, S., Cortina, L. M., & Magley, V. J. (2008). Personal and workgroup incivility: Impact on work and health outcomes. *The Journal of Applied Psychology*, *93*, 95–107. doi:10.1037/0021-9010.93.1.95

Lim, V. K., & Teo, T. S. H. (2009). Mind your e-manners: Impact of cyber incivility on employees' work attitude and behavior. *Information & Management*, *46*, 419–425. doi:10.1016/j.im.2009.06.006

Mowday, R. T., Steers, R. M., & Porter, L. W. (1979). The measurement of organizational commitment. *Journal of Vocational Behavior*, *14*, 224–247. doi:10.1016/0001-8791(79)90072-1

National Center for Victims of Crime. (2010). *Workplace violence*. Retrieved October 16, 2010, from http://www.ncvc.org/ncvc/Print.aspx

Neuman, J. H., & Baron, R. A. (1998). Workplace violence and aggression: Evidence concerning specific forms, potential causes, and preferred targets. *Journal of Management*, *24*, 391–419. doi:10.1016/S0149-2063(99)80066-X

Pearson, C. M., Andersson, L. M., & Porath, C. L. (2000). Assessing and attacking workplace incivility. *Organizational Dynamics*, *29*, 123–137. doi:10.1016/S0090-2616(00)00019-X

Porath, C. L., & Pearson, C. M. (2010). The cost of bad behavior. *Organizational Dynamics*, *39*, 64–71. doi:10.1016/j.orgdyn.2009.10.006

Reio, T. G. Jr, & Ghosh, R. (2009). Antecedents and outcomes of workplace incivility: Implications for human resource development and practice. *Human Resource Development Quarterly*, *20*, 237–264. doi:10.1002/hrdq.20020

Singh, J., Verbeke, W., & Rhoads, G. K. (1996). Do organizational practices matter in role stress processes? A study of direct and moderating effects for marketing oriented boundary spanners. *Journal of Marketing*, *60*, 69–86. doi:10.2307/1251842

Steffgen, G., & Ewen, N. (2007). Teachers as victims of school violence-The influence of strain and school culture. *International Journal of Violence and Schools*, *3*, 81–93.

Tabachnick, B. G., & Fidell, L. S. (2001). *Using multivariate statistics* (4th ed.). Boston: Allyn & Bacon.

Vartia, M. A. (2001). Consequences of workplace bullying with respect to the well-being of its targets and the observers of bullying. *Scandinavian Journal of Work, Environment & Health*, *27*, 63–69.

Waggoner, C. (2003). Teachers behaving badly. *The American School Board Journal*, *90*(8), 29–31.

Chapter 6
Literacy Level and Vocational Training for Substance-Using Hispanic Adults

Michele M. Wood
California State University, Fullerton, USA

Dennis G. Fisher
California State University, Long Beach, USA

Grace L. Reynolds
California State University, Long Beach, USA

Yesenia Guzman
California State University, Long Beach, USA

William C. Pedersen
California State University, Long Beach, USA

ABSTRACT

The Hispanic population has become the largest ethnic minority group in the United States. To successfully incorporate this population in adult vocational training, social service, and health programs, it is essential that programs design and implement materials at a reading level appropriate for the population served. This study determines the reading level in a population of Hispanic adult substance users receiving HIV prevention services in Long Beach, California. One hundred seven Spanish speakers were administered the Spanish Reading Comprehension Test. Spanish reading ability was determined to be at the third grade level for this sample. Results suggest that substance-using subpopulations of Spanish speakers in the Southwest United States face considerable language and literacy barriers. Findings have implications for adult vocational training as well as social service and health programs that include Hispanic subpopulations, and highlight the importance of designing materials that do not exceed the reading abilities of target populations.

DOI: 10.4018/978-1-4666-2062-9.ch006

INTRODUCTION

In recent years, the Hispanic population in the United States has grown rapidly compared to other minority ethnic groups, increasing by 57.9%, from 22.4 million in 1990, to 35.3 million in 2000 (U.S. Census Bureau, 2001). By contrast, the U.S. population as a whole increased by only 13.2% during the same time period. In 2002, more than one in eight people in the United States were of Hispanic origin (Ramirez & Cruz, 2003). In 2009, the number of U.S. Hispanics increased to 48.4 million, constituting the nation's largest ethnic minority group at 16% of the nation's total population (U.S. Census Bureau, 2010). Moreover, it is estimated that during the next 40 years, Hispanics will contribute more people to the overall U.S. population than any other racial/ethnic group, increasing to 25% of the overall population (U.S. Census Bureau, 1996). Of the 35.3 million Hispanics living in the United States at the turn of the Century, 4.2 million lived in Los Angeles County, California—the largest county in the nation (Guzman, 2001). Since July 2008, Los Angeles County has had the greatest numerical increase in Hispanic residents (78,000) nationwide (U.S. Census Bureau, 2010). In 2009, the number of Hispanics living in Los Angeles County reached 4.7 million (U.S. Census Bureau, 2010). These demographic trends have important implications for adult vocation, social service, and health programs serving members of this expanding population.

Low literacy is a substantial and understudied problem in the U.S. (Miller, McCardle, & Hernandez, 2010). In 2003, the National Assessment for Adult Literacy (NAAL) assessed English literacy in a nationally representative sample of U.S. adults (National Center for Education Statistics, 2003) and found that 30 million Americans were assessed at a "Below Basic" level for prose literacy, indicating "no more than the most simple and concrete literacy skills" (Kutner, Greenberg, & Baer, 2005). An additional 11 million were assessed as "non-literate." Hispanics were overrepresented among those with poor prose literacy, with 36% of all Hispanics, and 61% of those Hispanics who spoke only Spanish before beginning school, scoring in the "Below Basic" group (Kutner et al., 2005).

Nationwide, Los Angeles County has the highest percentage of individuals with low literacy. Half (53%) of the county's working age population has low literacy skills (The United Way of Greater Los Angeles, 2004). Of these, approximately 2.3 million are categorized at literacy level 1, the lowest of five literacy levels measured. People at this level typically are unable to locate an intersection on a street map. The city of Long Beach, which is part of Los Angeles County, ranks second highest out of five other southern California cities having the largest low literacy numbers (Los Angeles, Long Beach, Pomona, Glendale and El Monte), with 166,000 individuals who fall into literacy levels one and two. Limited education and minimal English language skills are major contributing factors. In Los Angeles County, 31% of the working age population has limited English skills, including more than 360,000 who report not speaking English at all (The United Way of Greater Los Angeles, 2004). More than half of the Hispanic population in the southwest United States lack basic English-language skills.

The level of education attained by a substantial number of Hispanics in the U.S educational system is quite limited. A 2002 report by the U.S. Department of Commerce (Ramirez & Cruz, 2003) found that Hispanics aged 25 years and older were less likely to have graduated from high school than were their non-Hispanic White counterparts. In addition, about 27% of Hispanics had less than a ninth-grade education (Ramirez & Cruz, 2003). The report also found that in 2002, 40.2% of the U.S. Hispanic population was foreign born. This figure is noteworthy because a large portion of the foreign-born population may be proficient only in their native language, Spanish. Thus, literacy rates in both English and Spanish are a concern for this population.

Literacy performance influences a number of life skills, including access to and comprehension of adult vocational training, as well as social and health services (Berkman et al., 2004; U.S. Department of Health and Human Services, 2004). Educational materials used within various public health domains have been assessed at reading levels that exceed the ability of their intended populations (Freimuth, 1979; Johnson, Mailloux, & Fisher, 1997; Streiff, 1986). Research (Cotugna, Vickery, & Carpenter-Haefele, 2005) has shown that the average reading level of 31% of the patients in a Veterans Administration Arthritis Center was below the 7th grade level, yet materials designed for these individuals were assessed at grade levels 8 to 13. Johnson and colleagues (Johnson, Fisher, Davis, & Cagle, 1995; 1996) found that the average reading ability of substance users receiving HIV and AIDS prevention services in Anchorage, Alaska was between 8.5 and 8.7 grade reading levels, making the average study participant's reading level lower than approximately 76% of the general population; Native and White participants had significantly higher reading levels than Hispanic and Black participants. The National Work Group on Cancer and Health recommends that written materials for health communications be at a 5th grade level or lower (Cotugna et al., 2005).

The challenges associated with delivery of adult education and social services are compounded in communities where English language skills are minimal. Vocational skill acquisition and workplace opportunities for adult learners can be limited by low literacy. Studies that have examined literacy among Hispanic AIDS patients have found that patients with low literacy skills report low medication adherence, feelings of shame, avoiding disclosure of their inability to read, and low utilization of health care services (Murphy, Roberts, Hoffman, Molina, & Lu, 2003; Servellen, Brown, Lombardi, & Herrera, 2003; Servellen et al., 2003). Language can be a salient barrier to the delivery of high quality programs for adults, especially for members of first- and second-generation migrant families. Language barriers affect the likelihood that individuals will participate in adult training and other programs, as well as their understanding of the information and services provided.

Acculturation

Acculturation has been defined as an explanation of how and why experiences vary among ethnic and cultural minorities as international migration, economic globalization, and political conflicts have led to increasingly multicultural societies (Trimble, 2002). Changes that constitute acculturation include those at the individual psychological level as well as at the sociocultural level.

Acculturation can bring about positive or negative changes. *Acculturative disorganization* (Chance, 1965) refers to negative, disruptive, and stressful circumstances that result from acculturation. Berry (1980) pioneered a *psychological acculturation* perspective involving intergroup contact, conflict, and adaptation. Berry and Annis (1974) developed an *ecological-cultural-behavioral* model, which proposes that acculturation behavior varies as a function of ecocultural setting. This model focuses on behavioral shift that occurs prior to and during contact and stress, and on disruptive behaviors that emerge because of contributions from the dominant culture.

The relationship between acculturation and mental health in Hispanics has been studied more than in any other racial/ethnic group since about 1970 (Organista, Organista, & Kurasaki, 2002). A seminal review of the literature (Rogler, Cortés, & Malgady, 1991) determined that findings could not be integrated across the research because of pervasive inconsistencies in methods and measurement. In fact, studies showed conflicting results, with roughly half indicating a positive relationship between acculturation and mental health, and half indicating a negative relationship. A noteworthy exception is the consistently positive relationship between acculturation and alcohol and substance abuse, which persists even when controlling for age, sex, and marital status. For example, in one study, U.S. born Mexican Americans, who had higher acculturation scores, also had higher rates of all mental health issues measured, including alcohol and substance abuse and dependence (Burnham, Hough, Karno, Escobar, & Telles, 1987). Furthermore, immigrant Mexican Americans had lower lifetime prevalence of alcohol and substance abuse problems than did non-Hispanic White individuals, while US-born Mexican Americans had a higher prevalence.

Rogler et al. (1991) noted that although new immigrants may feel optimistic about their economic prospects relative to others from their country of origin, Hispanics from second and later generations may feel pessimism when comparing their futures to those of mainstream American society because of the effects of prejudice, discrimination, and a devalued status as an ethnic minority. Portes and Rumbaut (2001) studied the education, employment, and health experiences of second generation immigrants in the US. In their study, Mexican parents did not gain increased income with increased years of US residence, and acquiring English language skills provided a smaller financial reward for Hispanic immigrants than for immigrants from other countries. The researchers describe the difficult process of adaptation that Mexican Americans experience when they confront lowered aspirations, expectations, and self-esteem in light of economic disadvantages and language barriers. The researchers note that *downward assimilation* oftentimes occurs as a result of the cumulative effect of these and other challenges that Hispanic second generation immigrants face.

Adult Basic Education and Vocational Training

The large number of adults in the US who perform below a basic literacy level, particularly among Hispanic and other racial/ethnic groups, has led to

funding of adult basic education (ABE) programs by the US Department of Education (MacArthur, Konold, Glutting, & Alamprese, 2010). Data from the National Assessment of Adult Literacy (NAAL) indicate that of the 2.5 million adults served in the 2004-2005 program year, 22% attended these programs to improve their English language skills; Hispanics represented 43% of all ABE program enrollees (Kutner, et al., 2005).

Research has found that literacy level (Kutner et al., 2007) and earning a GED (Rivera-Batiz, 1995) are positively associated with labor force participation. The National Adult Literacy Survey (NALS) (Rivera-Batiz, 1995) found that among Hispanics, employment increased in 1992 from 76.8% among dropouts to 93.3% among those who had earned a GED, with women experiencing the strongest effect. GED graduates, both men and women alike, had literacy scores that were higher than those of high school dropouts, but roughly equivalent to those of high school graduates (Rivera-Batiz, 1995). More recent data also has found that earning a GED or high school diploma was associated with higher earnings (Liming & Wolf, 2008).

It has been argued that bilingual instruction is a critical means to attaining adult career and technical education equity for non-English speakers (Huerta-Macias, 2003). In support of this notion, Huerta-Macias has identified four factors that bear on adult education in the United States: (1) demographics, (2) high school drop-out rates, (3) demand for English as a second language (ESL) classes, and (4) the worker population. First, the Hispanic population is growing 53% faster than the population as a whole (U.S. Census Bureau, 2001). Second, Hispanics have the highest public school dropout rate relative to every other racial/ethnic group, with 27.8% of Hispanics dropping out in 2000 (versus 10.9% overall) and 22.4% in 2005 (versus 9.4% overall) (National Center for Education Statistics, 2010). Third, enrollment in tuition-based ESL programs and waiting lists for free programs remain high; in 2000, the waiting list for ESOL (English for Speakers of Other Languages) programs in Los Angeles included 50,000 adults. The 2003 NAAL Prison Survey found that although more than a quarter (29%) of prison inmates had participated in some sort of vocational training, a larger number were on waiting lists than actually were enrolled (Greenberg, Dunleavy, & Kutner, 2008). Fourth, a large proportion of the US Hispanic population is limited to low-wage jobs because of limitations in skills such as reading, writing, and computation; effective communication; and basic technology (Imel, 1999; Liming & Wolf, 2008; Miller et al., 2010). Given this population's limited access to ESL classes (because demand greatly exceeds supply) and adult education (because classes are typically offered in English), these four factors create a pressing need for bilingual adult education with the dual purpose of developing English language and literacy in addition to providing career and technical training.

Lewis (1997) has argued that although economic and productivity concerns have highlighted the extent of low literacy in the U.S., vocational training programs rooted solely in economics cannot sufficiently address the problem. Typically, employers narrowly focus vocation-related training on productivity rather than on literacy. Workplaces do not and will not seek to promote empowerment and critical consciousness through literacy, but instead will focus their efforts on activities that can, first and foremost, improve the bottom line. Such activities include acquiring new technology, downsizing operations, and other means of reengineering productivity. Lewis goes on to argue that if the motivation underlying provision of adult literacy and vocational training programs is tied *exclusively* to economics, and if literacy is viewed *entirely* in a workplace context, then the problem of illiteracy will persist, if not fester, as businesses implement alternative solutions to address competition. Thus, it is argued that adult education and vocational training should be embedded in broader efforts to remedy societal inequity.

Purpose

The purpose of this study was to determine the literacy level in a social service population of Hispanic substance users in Long Beach, California. The confluence of increasing prevalence of low literacy skills, workplace literacy demands, and competition for jobs creates greater need for adult basic skill education programs. It is important to understand language and literacy barriers faced by Hispanic subpopulations in order to design effective education, vocational training, social service, and other programs for this growing segment of the population.

METHOD

Participants

The sample was recruited from a pool of substance users participating in ongoing HIV prevention programs operated by the Center for Behavioral Research and Services (CBRS) at California State University, Long Beach. Eligibility criteria included: reporting Hispanic ethnicity, being proficient in speaking and reading Spanish, and reporting current substance use (alcohol or drug use within the prior 30 days). Participants received a $5 monetary incentive for their participation in the study. In addition, a bag of groceries and HIV-related services and prevention supplies (condoms and lubricants) were provided to further encourage participation.

A total of 107 Spanish-speaking alcohol and drug users participated in the study ($N = 107$). Participants were either monolingual Spanish speakers or bilingual in English and Spanish, with their primary language being Spanish. All were of Hispanic ethnicity, except for one participant who self-identified as "other" because of mixed ethnicity (Hispanic and Persian). Two-thirds of the sample identified their Hispanic family origin as Mexican or Mexican American, with 37% Mexican (40/107), 28% Mexican American (30/107), 20% Central/South American (22/107), 5% Puerto Rican (5/107), 5% Cuban (5/107), and 5% other (5/107) (Table 1). Among participants whose families hailed from Central/South American, thirteen different countries of origin were reported, with Guatemala (27%, 6/22) and El Salvador (17%, 4/22) being the most frequent for this sample. A complete breakdown of country of family origin for those who self identified as Central/South American is included in Table 2.

Participant gender, education, and income are presented in Table 3. Sixty-six percent were men (71/107). The mean age was 39.87 years (*SD*=13.27), with participant's ages ranging from 18 to 81 years. Five percent had graduated from college (graduado de la universidad) (5/107), 19% had some college education (algo de ensenanza universitaria o preparatoria) (20/107), 1% had

trade/technical training (entrenamiento tecnico) (1/107), 18% had a high school education (graduado del colegio/gaduado escuela secundaria) (19/107), 6% had obtained a GED (un GED, certificado equivalente de la secundaria) (7/107), 34% had less than a high school education (no es graduado del colegio o escuela secundaria superior) (37/107), 14% had an 8th grade education or less (octavo grado o menos) (15/107), and 3% had no formal education (no tiene educacion formal) (3/107). More than half (55%) had an income of less than $500 a month.

Materials

For the present study, program staff conducted structured interviews with participants using the following two instruments—the Spanish Reading Comprehension Test (Moreno, 1993) and the Risk Behavior Assessment (National Institute on Drug Abuse, 1993).

Spanish Reading Comprehension Test

The Spanish Reading Comprehension Test (Moreno, 1993) was developed, standardized, and normed in Mexico; however, it was devel-

Table 1. Hispanic family origin (N = 107)

Ethnicity	*n* (%)
Mexican	40 (37.38)
Mexican American	30 (28.05)
Central/South American	22 (20.56)
Puerto Rican	5 (4.67)
Cuban	5 (4.67)
Other	5 (4.67)

Table 2. Central/South American and other country of origin (N = 22)

Country of Origin	*n* (%)
Guatemala	6 (27.27)
El Salvador	4 (18.18)
Honduras	3 (13.63)
Argentina	2 (9.09)
Chile	1 (4.54)
Panama	1 (4.54)
Peru	1 (4.54)
Colombia/Peru	1 (4.54)
Columbia/Guatemala	1 (4.54)
Honduras/Puerto Rico	1 (4.54)
Mexico/ Brazil	1 (4.54)

Table 3. Demographic information (N = 107)

Variable	n (%)
Gender	
Men	71 (66.35)
Women	36 (33.65)
Education	
College graduate	5 (4.68)
Some college	20 (18.69)
Trade/technical training	1 (.93)
HS graduation	19 (17.75)
GED (HS equivalence)	7 (6.54)
Less than HS graduation	37 (34.58)
8th grade or less	15 (14.02)
No formal schooling	3 (2.80)
Monthly Income	
Less than $500	59 (55.14)
$500 - $999	26 (24.29)
$1,000 - $1,999	17 (15.89)
$2,000 - $3,999	5 (4.68)

oped and designed for use in the United States. The Spanish Reading Comprehension Test was designed to determine the level of Spanish reading achievement compared with Mexican norms (Moreno, 1993). The instrument also can be used for determining adult Spanish reading level. The test is administered to determine adult functional reading level, either for further instruction in Spanish or in another language (Moreno, 1993). The test is made up of 73 items, and is administered within a 30-minute time limit. The 73 items are stories that were obtained from textbooks used in grades 1-6 in Mexico. The stories were arranged in order of difficulty beginning with the first grade story, then the middle grade story, and so forth. Questions were then written for each of the stories. The questions were designed to reflect the order of difficulty, with the easiest items being first (Moreno, 1993). The results determine Spanish reading comprehension level for grades 1-6 in the Mexican educational system.

Risk Behavior Assessment

The Community Research Branch of the National Institute on Drug Abuse (NIDA) in collaboration with grantees involved with the Cooperative Agreement for AIDS Community-Based Outreach/Intervention Research program developed the Risk Behavior Assessment (RBA) questionnaire (National Institute on Drug Abuse, 1993). The RBA is a 20-40 minute structured interview that includes items on demographics, drug use, needle sharing, sexual behaviors, drug treatment history, health history, work status, and income. The English version of the RBA has been found to have good reliability and validity (Dowling-Guyer et al., 1994; Fisher, Kuhrt-Hunstiger, Orr, & Davis, 1999; Schlicting et al., 2003). The Spanish version of the RBA was used to collect demographic information from all participants.

Design and Procedure

Each participant met individually with a peer health educator. The peer health educator read a script to the participant describing eligibility requirements and the voluntary nature of the study. After confirming interest in continuing, the peer health educator obtained informed consent for study participation. A copy of the consent form (approved by the California State University, Long Beach Institutional Review Board) was provided to the participant to review. The peer health educator carefully read and discussed the consent form with the participant, and answered any questions or concerns regarding the study. Once the participant and the peer health educator signed the consent form, the peer health educator offered the participant a copy to keep.

Next, the participant completed a client locator form, which included the client's name, contact information, date of birth, and other identifying information. This information was entered into the encrypted CBRS client database system, and a client identification number was assigned to each participant.

Following informed consent procedures, the peer health educator administered the Spanish Reading Comprehension test and the Risk Behavior Assessment. Finally, the peer health educator thanked the participant for completing the interviews, provided the participation incentives, and scheduled a return visit for participation in other program and research activities.

RESULTS: SPANISH READING LEVEL

Average reading level by education is presented in Figure 1. The sample's overall mean score on the Spanish Reading Comprehension Test was a 30.65, which is equivalent to a 3.9 grade level. Individual scores ranged from 0 to 60, which is equivalent to grade levels of less than the first

Figure 1. Mean reading level score by educational attainment (N = 107); overall mean=30.65; possible range of scores: 1-60

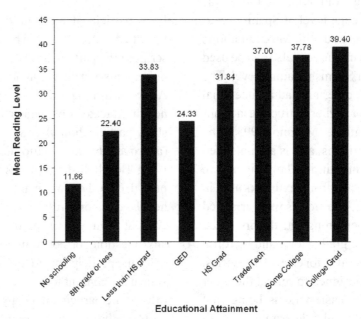

grade to beyond sixth grade. Of 73 possible points, the mean score was: 11.66 for those with no formal schooling, 22.40 for those with 8th grade education or less, 33.83 for those with less than a high school education, 24.33 for those who had obtained a GED, 31.84 for those who had graduated from high school, 37.00 for those with trade or technical training, 37.78 for those with some college, and 39.40 for college graduates.

DISCUSSION

The very low reading level obtained for this sample can be explained in several ways. First, the sample consisted of a majority of low-income individuals with 58.31% having less than a high school education. Most participants, because of their limited experience in the educational system, had difficulty understanding the concept of a multiple-choice test. All participants were given a thorough explanation of how to take the test and performed four practice questions with the health educator. However, some participants were still unable to follow the multiple-

choice instructions because of their unfamiliarity with the test format. This difficulty could have resulted in a slower pace, and hence, failure to complete the exam within the allotted time frame or in answering questions incorrectly. Substance use, either alone or in combination with unfamiliar test conditions, also could have contributed to low scores. Moreover, the literacy level in Los Angeles County has been reported as very low, with 53% of the working-age population being unable to properly read a bus schedule (The United Way of Greater Los Angeles, 2004). Therefore, a third grade reading level in this sample of Hispanic substance users is not entirely surprising.

To examine the distribution of the Spanish reading comprehension scores, the mean Spanish Reading Comprehension Test score was calculated separately for each level of educational attainment (Figure 1). As expected, reading level roughly correlated with educational attainment. The educational attainment category with the lowest mean score (11.66) was "no formal schooling"; the category with the highest mean score (39.40) was "college graduate" (Figure 1).

Careful examination of the Spanish version of the educational attainment question provides further context for interpreting the results of this study. The educational attainment question was translated as a literal translation from English into Spanish, and did not take into consideration that the education system in Latin American countries is not equivalent to the educational system of the United States. For example, in Mexico, unlike in the United States, trade technical training is known as "Educacion Media Superior." This level of education usually takes place at the age of 16 and is three years in length (World Education Services, 2006). "Educacion Media Superior" is therefore equivalent to a 10th through 12th grade education in the United States. According to Education Profiles (2006), higher education in Mexico is classified as a Bachillerato (Trade/technical training), Licenciatura (undergraduate), Maestria (Masters degree), and a Doctorado (Doctorate degree). In other Latin American Countries, such as El Salvador and Columbia, a college education is similarly classified as in Mexico; however, students as young as 15 may begin a Bachillerato degree. When the educational attainment for the study sample was obtained this fact was not taken into account.

The number of years of education a child receives in a Latin American Country is not equivalent to the number of years of education a child receives in the United States (Table 4). Consequently, it may be that the actual educational attainment of this sample is even lower than indicated. For those who reported some college education or college graduation, this may repre-sent completion of a Bachillerato in their country of origin, which is equivalent to a high school education or less in the U.S. educational system. Future studies assessing educational attainment of individuals should clarify where the education was received and the equivalence in the United States. An alternative solution is to create an educational attainment question that is more culturally specific to Latin American Countries. This change would improve assessment of educational attainment in future studies.

This research was conducted in hope that similar research will follow. Unfortunately, it is not uncommon for questionnaires, informational pamphlets, and other documents to be created without consideration of the challenges faced by those for whom the documents are created. Further research is needed in this area to ensure that literacy among Spanish speakers is properly assessed and that materials for Spanish-speaking populations are appropriately designed based on documented reading level.

Implications

In this sample, the native Spanish language reading level was very low—a fact that should be taken into account in future work with this population. Thus, readability is not only a concern for materials printed in English, but also for those translated to Spanish. Efforts to assess native language reading level are critical in order to ensure that intended content is accessible. Training materials as well as data collection and test instruments created specifically for Hispanic substance users should

Table 4. Higher educational systems for the United States and Mexico

US Educational System	Typical Age of Student	Mexico Educational System	Typical Age of Student
High School	15-18	Bachillerato	15-18
Undergraduate	18-22	Licenciatura	18+
Master's	Unknown	Maestria	Unknown
Doctoral	Unknown	Doctorado	Unknown

be assessed and adjusted to ensure that the reading level is appropriate. Training adaptations may require incorporating pictorial information, assistive technology, as well as other strategies to help communicate key concepts. Assistive technology using text-to-speech and speech-recognition software has been shown to help improve literacy among adults with learning disabilities when used as a supplement to adult basic education classes (Silver-Pacuilla, 2006). Language- and literacy-appropriate training adaptations are critical because the quality and relevance of instructional materials are directly related to learner outcomes.

The particular method used to assess readability of text materials is important. A study conducted by Mailloux, Johnson, Fisher, and Pettibone (1995) found that the Microsoft Word program provided significantly lower grade levels than other approaches and was more inconsistent in the scores it provided when assessing the readability level of 28 pieces of printed educational materials on HIV and the Gettysburg address. More robust methods of measuring readability should be used. Future research should seek to identify a workable Spanish language readability program to help measure readability and assess the appropriateness of Spanish translations.

Moreover, future research must seek to identify the critical features of adult instruction that are associated with greatest improvements in adult literacy skills. As assistive technology continues to expand and improve, new approaches must be evaluated. Identifying the particular program components and instruction strategies that result in literacy level gains can lead to greater use of evidence-based programs, and consequently, greater program success. Learner characteristics that may be associated with greater success as a result of participating in different types of programs also should be identified. Such information can be used to help match learners to the most appropriate program approaches based on their individual needs.

Research has found that literacy in one's native language helps adults who are learning to read in English through the transfer of basic reading skills from one language to another (Wagner & Venezky, 1999). Thus, Hispanic adult subpopulations with particularly low Spanish reading skills, such as our sample, can be expected to face greater challenges in learning English compared to Hispanic adults who have greater Spanish literacy skills.

Lastly, we hope that the results from this study highlight the language and literacy barriers faced by many Hispanic adults, as well as the critical importance of assessing, documenting, and responding to reading level within the adult learner population when designing training materials. Literacy and the challenges it poses are critical issues to address in planning for the success of Hispanic adult learners and consumers of social and health services. By assessing and documenting the literacy level of Spanish-speaking subpopulations within Los Angeles County, it is hoped that better, more accessible materials can be developed for individuals who face language and literacy barriers to adult education and vocational training in an increasingly competitive global economy.

ACKNOWLEDGMENT

The project described was supported by Award Number P20MD003942 from the National Center on Minority Health and Health Disparities. The content is solely the responsibility of the authors and does not necessarily represent the official views of the National Center on Minority Health and Health Disparities or the National Institutes of Health.

REFERENCES

Berkman, N., DeWalt, D., Pignone, M., Sheridan, S., Lohr, K., & Lux, L. (2004). *Literacy and health outcomes (Tech. Rep. No. AHRQ 04-E007-2)*. Rockville, MD: Agency for Healthcare Research and Quality.

Berry, J. W. (1980). Acculturation as varieties of adaptation. In Padilla, A. (Ed.), *Acculturation: Theory, models and some new findings* (pp. 9–25). Boulder, CO: Westview.

Berry, J. W., & Annis, R. C. (1974). Accultruative stress: The role of ecology, culture and differentiation. *Journal of Cross-Cultural Psychology, 5*, 382–405. doi:10.1177/002202217400500402

Burnham, M. A., Hough, R. L., Karno, M., Escobar, J. I., & Telles, C. A. (1987). Acculturation and lifetime prevalence of psychiatric disorders among Mexican Americans in Los Angeles. *Journal of Health and Social Behavior, 28*, 59–102.

Chance, N. A. (1965). Acculturation, self-identification and personality adjustment. *American Anthropologist, 67*, 372–393. doi:10.1525/aa.1965.67.2.02a00050

Cotugna, N., Vickery, C. E., & Carpenter-Haefele, K. M. (2005). Evaluation of literacy level of patient education pages in health-related journals. *Journal of Community Health, 30*(3), 213–219. doi:10.1007/s10900-004-1959-x

Dowling-Guyer, S., Johnson, M. E., Fisher, D. G., Needle, R., Watters, J., & Anderson, M. (1994). Reliability of drug users' self-reported HIV risk behaviors and validity of self-reported recent drug use. *Assessment, 1*, 383–392.

Fisher, D. G., Kuhrt-Hunstiger, T. I., Orr, S., & Davis, D. C. (1999). Hepatitis B validity of drug users' self-report. *Psychology of Addictive Behaviors, 13*(1), 33–38. doi:10.1037/0893-164X.13.1.33

Freimuth, V. S. (1979). Assessing the readability of health education messages. *Public Health Reports, 94*(6), 568–570.

Greenberg, E., Dunleavy, E., & Kutner, M. (2008). Literacy behind bars: Results from the 2003 national assessment of adult literacy prison survey, executive summary. *Journal for Vocational Special Needs Education, 30*(2), 16–19.

Guzman, B. (2001). *The Hispanic population*. Washington, DC: U.S. Department of Commerce.

Huerta-Macias, A. G. (2003). Meeting the challenge of adult education: A bilingual approach to literacy and career development. *Journal of Adolescent & Adult Literacy, 47*(3), 218–226.

Imel, S. (1999). *Work force education: Beyond technical skills (Trends and issues alert no. 1)*. Columbus, OH: ERIC Clearinghouse on Adult, Career, and Vocational Education.

Johnson, M. E., Fisher, D. G., Davis, D. C., & Cagle, H. H. (1995). Reading abilities of drug users in Anchorage, Alaska. *Journal of Drug Education, 25*(1), 73–80. doi:10.2190/0314-YCWJ-LX7T-HWL3

Johnson, M. E., Fisher, D. G., Davis, D. C., Cagle, H. H., Rhodes, F., & Booth, R. (1996). Assessing reading level of drug users for HIV and AIDS prevention purposes. *AIDS Education and Prevention, 8*, 323–334.

Johnson, M. E., Mailloux, S. L., & Fisher, D. G. (1997). The readability of HIV/AIDS educational materials targeted to drug users. *American Journal of Public Health, 87*(1), 112–113. doi:10.2105/AJPH.87.1.112

Kutner, M., Greenberg, E., & Baer, J. (2005). *National assessment of adult literacy (NAAL): A first look at the literacy of America's adults in the 21st century (Tech. Rep. No. NCES 2006-470)*. Washington, DC: U.S. Department of Education.

Kutner, M., Greenberg, E., Jin, Y., Boyle, B., Hsu, Y., & Dunleavy, E. (2007). *Literacy in everyday life: Results from the 2003 national assessment of adult literacy*. Washington, DC: U.S. Department of Education.

Lewis, T. (1997). America's choice: Literacy or productivity? *Curriculum Inquiry, 27*(4), 391–421. doi:10.1111/0362-6784.00062

Liming, D., & Wolf, M. (2008). *Job outlook by education, 2006-16*. Retrieved from http://www.bls.gov/opub/ooq/2008/fall/art01.pdf

MacArthur, C. A., Konold, T. R., Glutting, J. J., & Alamprese, J. A. (2010). Reading component skills of learners in adult basic education. *Journal of Learning Disabilities, 43*(2), 108–121. doi:10.1177/0022219409359342

Mailloux, S. L., Johnson, M. E., Fisher, D. G., & Pettibone, T. J. (1995). How reliable is computerized assessment of readability. *Computers in Nursing, 13*(5), 221–225.

Miller, B., McCardle, P., & Hernandez, R. (2010). Advances and remaining challenges in adult literacy research. *Journal of Learning Disabilities, 43*(2), 101–107. doi:10.1177/0022219409359341

Moreno, S. (1993). *Spanish reading comprehension test*. San Diego, CA: Moreno Educational Co.

Murphy, D. A., Roberts, K. J., Hoffman, D., Molina, A., & Lu, M. C. (2003). Barriers and successful strategies to antiretroviral adherence among HIV-infected monolingual Spanish-speaking patients. *AIDS Care, 15*(2), 217–230. doi:10.1080/0954012031000068362

National Center for Education Statistics. (2003). *National assessment of adult literacy*. Washington, DC: U.S. Department of Education.

National Center for Education Statistics. (2010). *The condition of education 2010*. Washington, DC: U.S. Department of Education.

National Institute on Drug Abuse. (1993). *Risk behavior assessment questionnaire*. Rockville, MD: National Institute on Drug Abuse.

Organista, P. B., Organista, K. C., & Kurasaki, K. (2002). The relationship betwen acculturation and ethnic minority mental health. In Chun, K. M., Organista, P. B., & Marín, G. (Eds.), *Acculturation: Advances in theory, measurement, and applied research* (pp. 139–161). Washington, DC: American Psychological Association.

Portes, A., & Rumbaut, R. G. (2001). *Legacies: The story of the immigrant second generation*. Berkeley, CA: Unversity of California Press.

Ramirez, R. R., & Cruz, P. D. l. (2003). *The Hispanic population in the United States: March 2002*. Washington, DC: U.S. Department of Commerce.

Rivera-Batiz, F. L. (1995). *The impact of vocational education on racial and ethnic minorities*. New York, NY: ERIC Clearinghouse on Urban Education.

Rogler, L. H., Cortés, D., & Malgady, R. G. (1991). Acculturation and mental health status among Hispanics: Convergence and new directions for research. *The American Psychologist, 46*, 585–597. doi:10.1037/0003-066X.46.6.585

Schlicting, E. G., Johnson, M. E., Brems, C., Wells, R., Fisher, D. G., & Reynolds, G. L. (2003). Validity of injecting drug users' self report of Hepatitis A, B, and C. *Clinical Laboratory Science, 16*(2), 99–106.

Servellen, G. V., Brown, J. S., Lombardi, E., & Herrera, G. (2003). Health literacy in low-income Latin men and women receiving antiretroviral therapy in community-based treatment centers. *AIDS Patient Care and STDs, 17*(6), 283–298. doi:10.1089/108729103322108166

Servellen, G. V., Carpio, F., Lopez, M., Garcia-Teague, L., Herrera, G., & Monterrosa, F. (2003). Program to enhance health literacy and treatment adherence in low-income HIV infected Latino men and women. *AIDS Patient Care and STDs, 17*(11), 581–594. doi:10.1089/108729103322555971

Silver-Pacuilla, H. (2006). Access and benefits: Assistive technology in adult literacy. *Journal of Adolescent & Adult Literacy, 50*(2), 114–125. doi:10.1598/JAAL.50.2.4

Streiff, L. D. (1986). Can clients understand our instructions? *Journal of Nursing Scholarship, 18*(2), 48–52. doi:10.1111/j.1547-5069.1986.tb00542.x

The United Way of Greater Los Angeles. (2004). *Literacy at work: The L.A workforce literacy project*. Los Angeles, CA: Literacy Network of Greater Los Angeles.

Trimble, J. (2002). Introduction: Social change and acculturation. In Chun, K. M., Organista, P. B., & Marín, G. (Eds.), *Acculturation: Advances in theory, measurement, and applied research* (pp. 3–13). Washington, DC: American Psychological Association.

U.S. Census Bureau. (1996). *Population projections of the United States by age, sex, race, and Hispanic origin: 1995 to 2050*. Washington, DC: U.S. Department of Commerce.

U.S. Census Bureau. (2001). *The Hispanic population 2000* (Tech. Rep. No. C2KBR/01-3). Washington, DC: U.S. Department of Commerce.

U.S. Census Bureau. (2010). *Hispanic heritage month 2010: Sept. 15 - Oct. 15*. Retrieved from http://www.census.gov/newsroom/releases/pdf/cb10ff-17_hispanic.pdf

U.S. Department of Health and Human Services. (2004). *Adult and family literacy: Current and future research directions—a workshop summary*. Washington, DC: U.S. Department of Health and Human Services.

Wagner, D. A., & Venezky, R. L. (1999). Adult literacy: The next generation. *Educational Researcher, 28*(1), 21–29.

World Education Services. (2006). *WES grade conversion guide*. Toronto, ON, Canada: World Education Services.

This work was previously published in the International Journal of Adult Vocational Education and Technology, Volume 2, Issue 2, edited by Victor C.X. Wang, pp. 42-54, copyright 2011 by IGI Publishing (an imprint of IGI Global).

Chapter 7
Educational Leadership and Ralph Tyler

Victor C. X. Wang
California State University at Long Beach, USA

Judith Parker
Columbia University, USA

ABSTRACT

This article addresses the traditional instructional leadership (characterized with Tyler's four questions; teachers prescribe a curriculum; learners assume a submissive role of following instructors) in comparison with the andragogical or innovative instructional leadership. As more and more scholars cast their doubt on this particular instructional mode (traditional instructional leadership), especially when compared with the innovative instructional leadership, this article seeks to draw on traditional instructional leadership that revolves around Ralph Tyler's model. In doing so, instructors and practitioners will see clearly what the traditional instructional leadership may bring to most education settings and above all, they may rely on a ready-made formula when planning curriculums, instruction, program planning, or evaluation. While traditional instructional leadership may have come under much criticism, there is much to learn from it.

INTRODUCTION

Educational leadership can be divided into two areas: administrative leadership and instructional leadership. Administrative leadership deals with administrators leading followers in a certain organization or institution of learning whereas instructional leadership deals with teachers helping learners in classroom settings. In actuality, scholars tend to focus more on instructional leadership than administrative leadership because the majority of educators, teachers, or trainers serve as instructors or teachers in the classroom or in the virtual environment. A small number of educators are chosen as administrative leaders, such as university presidents, school principals,

DOI: 10.4018/978-1-4666-2062-9.ch007

superintendents or staff development managers. Researchers spend years trying to discover the most effective forms of instructional leadership, and the answer changes with the context. This should not be surprising considering the fuzziness that surrounds the notion of leadership itself. Schein (2010) notes that while the literature has increased with writings about leadership in the past 25 years, most people are not any clearer today about "what is a good leader and what a leader should be doing" (p. x). Wheatly (1999) describes leadership as "an amorphous phenomenon that has intrigued us since people began organizing" (p. 13). Lojewski and Reilly (2008) apply descriptive labels such as charismatic, transformational or ambassadorial to leaders but none of these gets to the essence of the term. Wiseman and McKeown (2010) might offer a description of a leader that is particularly applicable to instructional leadership. They suggest that "some leaders make us better and smarter. They bring out our intelligence" (p. 4). They continue that these leaders "access and revitalize the intelligence in the people around them. We call them Multipliers" (p. 4). Becoming a "multiplier" might be the perfect goal for the instructional leader.

Researchers have been innovative, trying to determine what prescribed instructional leadership may lead to the desired learning outcomes, or student performance objectives as termed by some scholars and educators in some organizational settings. Indeed, teachers are classroom leaders. They are just like drivers of cars or busses. Learners are, in a way, passengers. They do not know where to go until their teachers tell them where to go. This is especially true when learners are traditional age students or children. Teachers provide the direction and structure regarding how learners can embark on their learning journeys. Teachers prescribe curriculums, and they know what ought to happen in their classroom settings, given their prescribed curriculum's approval by experts in their field and stakeholders in their community. Teachers conform to their school's or organization's mission and goals which give them a clear idea of what is expected of them. Once a curriculum is prescribed, they will go about selecting the means for attaining the school's or organization's mission and goals. Then, teachers select the specific instructional methods that will work for a particular class. Finally, teachers have the responsibility of choosing methods to evaluate student learning. Teachers are driving the bus; they know where they need to go and when they should arrive. However, while the route the bus takes to arrive at the final destination is flexible, the driver, or teacher, needs to assess which route is the best and why.

In recent years, this traditional model of the teacher as the bus driver has come under criticism. Some scholars argue that traditional instructional leadership may lead to docile learners, learners who are high in scores and low in abilities (Ross, 1992). In the Western Hemisphere, researchers focus on critical thinking skills or problem solving skills rather than on rote learning or how much learners can regurgitate information or knowledge (Mezirow, 1991, 2000). Some scholars focus on learners' "cognitive metamorphosis" rather than on psychomotor skills when the majority of their learners are adult learners. Another movement is that scholars focus more on higher order thinking skills than on the lower order thinking skills based on Bloom's Taxonomy (1956).

Regardless of the movements or debate regarding what instructional leadership may result in the right learning outcomes, all instructional leadership has three kinds of educational objectives. In other words, instructional leadership is bound to change learners in three domains of educational objectives: cognitive domain, psychomotor domain and affective domain. In plain language, educators and teachers are concerned with whether their learners will be able to think, act, and feel differently at the end of their instruction in a classroom setting or in a virtual classroom environment (Wang, 2008). Clearly, being able to think, act, and feel differently by the end of a teacher's instruction indicates that learners have achieved cognitive change not only through instruction by also via their own learning or efforts. Several authors have expressed similar ideas about the multidimentional aspect of learning. Illeris (2004) describes a model that proposes three dimensions of learning: cognitive, emotional and social and positions them at the three corners of a triangle. Merriam (2008) describes a shift in the twenty-first century from previously describing learning as a purely cognitive activity to a more holistic, multidimensional phenomenon. She considers that "learning is construed as a much broader activity involving the body, the emotions, and the spirit as well as the mind" (p. 95). As researchers and scholars focus on the aforementioned movements or debate around educational objectives, less attention has been paid to the differences between traditional instructional leadership and innovative instructional leadership. Because more attention has been given to innovative instructional leadership, such as higher order thinking skills (Wang & Farmer, 2008) or transformative learning, some instructors may not even know the theories behind traditional instructional leadership.

Traditional instructional leadership is more akin to pedagogy, which deals with the art and science of teaching children whereas innovative instructional leadership is more akin to andragogy, which deals with the art and science of helping adult learn (Knowles, 1970, 1975, 1986). For example, andragogical instructors are learning facilitators, linking learners to learning resources. While this may be their primary role, the andragogical instructor may also be responsible for imparting new knowledge especially if the instructor is the subject matter expert in a field. Pedagogical instructors may be classroom information presenters, focusing more on pattern drills and evaluation of learning of any kind. Prominent educators point out that the whole educational enterprise has been frozen to the pedagogical model, which means all learners, young or old, have been educated or trained by conforming to the art and science

of teaching children. The question remains, is traditional instructional leadership more effective than innovative instructional leadership such as the art and science of helping adults learn? The answer can be yes and no.

There is no question that those master teachers have played a major role in helping students achieve changes in those three domains of educational objectives. These master teachers are knowledge dictators, not learning facilitators. Above all, these teachers conform to the traditional instructional leadership, such as prescribing a certain curriculum, selecting the means for attaining a school's or organization's purposes, organizing effectively those educational activities, and evaluating students' learning outcomes or their achievement of the performance objectives. These instructors believe that learning can be measured and observed. When this type of teaching is not resulting in learning, the instructors may need to switch to innovative instructional leadership, which means that they do not believe that learners can be taught directly. Learning has to be facilitated. These instructors will play a secondary role of trying to link students to learning resources because learners may be self-directed in learning.

The intent of this article is not to argue that traditional instructional leadership has more advantages over innovative instructional leadership or vice versa. Rather, it is intended is to give the readers a better idea of what traditional instructional leadership is and how this pedagogical model can be used effectively in a classroom setting or in a virtual environment since the whole educational enterprise has been frozen into the pedagogical model (Knowles, Holton, & Swanson, 1998, 2005), which is the so-called traditional instructional leadership. Indeed, traditional instructional leadership is closely linked to accountability. Since accreditation agencies as well as state and national mandates require accountability and quantitative measurement of improvement, traditional instructional leadership is often preferred. The Ralph Tyler Model will be the focus of this article, one of many forms of traditional instructional leadership, but one that innovative instructional leaders can learn from.

OVERVIEW OF TRADITIONAL INSTRUCTIONAL LEADERSHIP

Many examples of traditional instructional leadership exist throughout history. In fact, traditional instructional leadership traces back more than 6000 years ago when unorganized training existed when fathers had to teach their sons a trade (Wang & King, 2008, 2009). By way of teaching another person, there must be those essential elements in pedagogy such as a curriculum, instructional methods, and evaluation methods. Or traditional instructional leadership traces back 6000 years ago in Egypt where scribes were formally trained in order to copy documentation from documentation. Some scholars argue that traditional instructional leadership occurred in the 7th and 12th century in Europe where young boys were trained to be clergymen or national leaders. "Vocational focused programs such as the Workers Education Movement in Great Britain and the apprenticeships and Agricultural Societies in the U.S. emerged in the post-Renaissance era" (Parker, 2009, p. 215). Knowles (1989) notes that the institutionalization of education for children began during the period between the fall of Rome and the Renaissance. Others argue that traditional instructional leadership occurred when Confucius started to use a variety of pedagogical methods to educate and train adults and children 2500 years ago in China (Wang & King, 2006). Yet, others argue that traditional instructional leadership emerged when Socrates and Plato started to teach children and adults in Europe. Regardless of the debate, traditional instructional leadership has a long history and has come a long way. Numerous articles, books and chapters have been written about instructional strategies initiated by Confucius, Socrates, Plato and many prominent educators.

What is truly revolutionary is the book written and published by Ralph Tyler. This is not to say that other prominent educators have contributed less to traditional instructional leadership. Ralph Tyler's book on curriculum development has dominated traditional instructional leadership since the first publication of his book in 1949. The book is still in print and is being used by various educational programs.

Most current theoretical formulations of program planning in education are borrowed from Tyler's seminal work in curriculum development (Pennington & Green, 1976, p. 14). Although the critiques of the Tylerian rationale or model do exist, these critiques seem to be invalid as those who created those critiques may not know how to apply the Tylerian model to practice. For example, some scholars claim that the Tylerian model is lacking in attention to context, neutral with regard to social stratification, vague and too technical-rational (Jarvis, 2004; Slattery, 1995; Sork, 2000). First of all, this could be justified by remembering that Tyler was born and raised in a capitalist country. Why would he focus on a social context that is different than the context in which he was familiar? Tyler was interested in curriculums that would work for all. Why would he be concerned with social stratification? The next section will illustrate how clear Tyler's model is and how it has contributed to traditional instructional leadership. Indeed, Tyler's model has influenced educators and learners with its essential feature of its practicality.

A DISCUSSION OF RALPH TYLER'S FOUR QUESTIONS

The center of Tyler's model is essentially four questions, the heart and soul of traditional instructional leadership. Traditional instructional leadership does not deviate from Tyler's four fundamental questions. Without asking these questions, teachers or educators are not teaching, using the pedagogical instructional principles. However, asking the four questions is not enough. Only when instructors implement the four questions do they conform to traditional instructional leadership. The first question is *what educational purposes should the school seek to attain?* Schools have learning objectives; departments have learning objectives; classroom teachers have learning objectives for their specific classes. This is such a crucial step in traditional instructional leadership that Tyler dedicates almost half of his book to explaining this step. Instructors are considered content experts, and they should be able to formulate learning objectives. Instructors are also encouraged to take into consideration the needs of learners and the needs of society when formulating learning objectives. In some countries, learning objectives are prescribed by higher authorities such as ministry of education (Cochran, 2007; Wang, 2007). The heart and soul of learning objectives must be started or written in quantifiable, behavioral terms. In other words, learning objectives must be measurable and observable. Piskurich (2006) among others has expanded this advice by suggesting that these objectives must be SMART: specific, measureable, achievable, realistic, and time bound. These learning objectives in turn provide a guide for instructors to select teaching and evaluation methods.

An example of a well written learning objective can be as follows:

In a computer laboratory situation, given a simple set of specifications for a data table [situation], the student will demonstrate [learned capability verb] the construction of a database table in Microsoft Access [object] by typing it into the computer [action verbs], using the appropriate data types, and selecting an appropriate key [tools, constraints and/or special conditions] (Gagne, 2005, p. 134).

Also worthy of note is that schools may select their educational purposes based on their leaders' educational philosophies (Elias & Merriam,

2005). To date, there are seven teaching philosophies that educators may be equipped with (Lee, 2011). Depending on where the school leaders are educated, they may prescribe a totally different educational purpose. For example, if some school leaders are educated in adult education programs, lifelong learning may be their school's educational purpose. Likewise, if those leaders are educated in a liberal arts college, their school's purpose may lay in this arena. Instructors must align their educational objectives with their school's purposes if there teaching is to be effective. In other words, their learning objectives cannot deviate too much from their school's educational purposes. Learning objectives should serve to support the school's educational purposes.

What Educational Experiences can be Provided that are Likely to Attain these Purposes?

Traditional instructional leadership specifies that teachers prescribe educational experiences or learning activities. This is the second question of the Tylerian model. Instructors believe that certain educational experiences or learning activities will lead to achievement of the learning objectives. For example, if instructors want learners to retain as much information as possible, they may provide opportunities to practice behavior implied by the learning objectives. An ESL instructor may specify that by the end of his/her class, all learners should have memorized 30 new English words and be able to utilize them in meaningful sentences. To practice using the 30 English words in meaningful sentences, opportunities to practice using sentence structures or verb patterns should be provided so that learners can practice using these words again and again in order to memorize these words. These educational experiences must be closely linked to learning objectives. While some experiences may be engaging for learners, if they are not linked to the learning objectives, they are not an effective use of time. Instructors can provide learning tools, instructional materials, instructional aides, and even their own learning experiences to help learners attain these educational purposes or learning objectives. Above all, there is an essential role that instructors can play in order to help learners attain their learning objectives. If the learners' objective is for "cognitive metamorphosis," then, instructors are required to rely more on guided lecture, storytelling, or symposiums. If learners are predominantly from adult education programs or workforce education programs such as nursing, instructors are required to provide more hands-on educational experiences in order for learners to achieve a change in psychomotor and affective domains. This essential role on the part of instructors cannot be underestimated. Without taking into consideration educational objectives, instructors will fail to provide meaningful educational experiences that are likely to help attain these purposes or objectives. In a nutshell, providing educational experiences to help attain educational purposes involves selecting the means. The means could mean the right instructional methods or strategies. The means could mean providing the right educational opportunities. The means could also mean maximizing the instructors' teaching styles. The increased use of technology has increased the choices of means even more. Many factors need to be taken into consideration when trying to select the means. Once the means is successfully selected, teachers come to the third question of the Tylerian model.

How can these Educational Experiences be Effectively Organized?

The third question addresses the criteria for organizing learning experiences including continuity, sequence, and organization. Educational experiences can be learning activities designed by instructors. This question really addresses the instructional strategies or teaching methodologies. The goal here is to achieve effective instruction.

In order to make instruction work in a classroom setting or in a virtual environment, educational experiences should be organized according to the principles of instruction for pedagogy or andragogy.

The most used and most abused method of instruction is the lecture. When learners are inexperienced with a subject matter, instructors should conform to the use of lecture so that learners can be given enough information about a certain subject. Brookfield (2006) devotes an entire chapter of his book to methods for the effective lecture including innovative ideas for engaging students in a lecture situation. When learners are experienced with a subject matter, instructors should conform to guided discussions in order to link students to learning resources. In order to effectively organize any educational experiences, instructors need to study their learners, their characteristics, and their learning styles. If learners are predominantly children, instructors need to be pedagogical instructors, which means they must provide direction and structure so that learning can occur. If learners are predominantly adult learners, instructors may become learning facilitators, which means adult students are capable of teaching themselves. Their need for instructional assistance may be minimal. However, this dichotomy should be tempered by the student's background in the subject. As mentioned earlier, an adult learner embarking in a new, unfamiliar area may be in need of the direction and structure of the more pedagogical instructor.

There are many ways to effectively organize these educational experiences but many factors need to be taken into consideration. There are societal needs, institutional needs and individual needs as well as subject matter differences. These factors must be given enough consideration when trying to organize effective learning activities. Effective learning activities simply mean that they work for learners. Brookfield (2006) gets to the essence of this issue by describing the skillful teacher as one that uses whatever methods help the student learn.

Learners engage in these learning activities and they will lead to the desired learning outcomes so that educators and instructors will be able to observe and measure those learning outcomes in quantifiable or behaviorist terms.

Educational leaders in adult education offer a unique model that instructors of adults can rely on. Of course, the heart and soul of this model revolve around the core adult learning principles articulated by Malcolm Knowles. However, educational leaders in this particular field remind all instructors to take into consideration other factors they term as the goals and purposes for learning, societal growth, institutional growth, individual growth and subject matter differences. It is true that these factors significantly influence the implementation of the core principles of adult learning. Based on the core principles of adult learning and the other highly relevant factors, adult educators can organize effective educational experiences such as giving out learning contracts, negotiating the syllabi at the first classes of a semester or encouraging learner self-evaluation etc. This is just one example to illustrate that organizing effective educational experiences depend on principles of learning. To effectively organize effective learning activities, instructors must rely on other principles of learning such as behaviorism, Piaget's (1967) developmental theory.

Figure 1 is a borrowed figure designed by Knowles, Holton, and Swanson in 1998 to illustrate that adult educators do depend on these factors in the figure to organize effective educational experiences. Instructors of children should learn from this model. Clearly andragogy and pedagogy present two different approaches to the education of children and adults. Dewey (1961, p. 255) called these two approaches traditional and progressive. Indeed, as noted by Knowles (1980), "I don't see andragogy as ideology at all but as a system of assumptions about adult learners that needs to be tested out for different learners in different situations" (p. 59). Here, one can assume that different learners must include children. See Figure 1 to see how effective educational experiences can be organized.

How Can We Determine Whether These Purposes Are Being Attained?

The final question addresses evaluation. As noted by Tyler himself (1949, p. 106), "The process of evaluation is essentially the process of determining to what extent the educational objectives are actually being realized by the program of curriculum and instruction." If those educational objectives are not realized, this means learners have not learned what was intended. Once again, there are many ways to evaluate educational objectives. Observation and interview can be an informal method. Learners may learn in a classroom or a lab setting. Instructors can choose to observe their learning or to interview them to see whether learning by those learning standards has occurred. Learning is all about changes in the three domains of educational objectives: cognitive domain, psychomotor domain and affective domain. If learners can demonstrate that they can think, act, and feel differently by the end of a class or a learning module, this indicates that they have realized the educational objectives prescribed to them by their course instructors. Another information evaluation method can be learner self-evaluation. Some scholars are convinced that self-evaluation remains the goal of adult education, including career and technical education (Cranton, 2010). Then the formal evaluation methods can include both objectively-scored assessments and subjectively-rated assessments.

Depending on pedagogy and andragogy, instructors can use different approaches of assessments. For example, in andragogy, instructors depend more on learner self-evaluation or learning contracts. In pedagogy, instructors may conform to those objectively-scored assessments such as tests, exams, and quizzes. As argued by Cranton (2010), in most formal education settings, total teacher control over evaluation is the norm. But

Figure 1. Andragogy in Practice (adapted from Knowles, Holton, & Swanson, 1998)

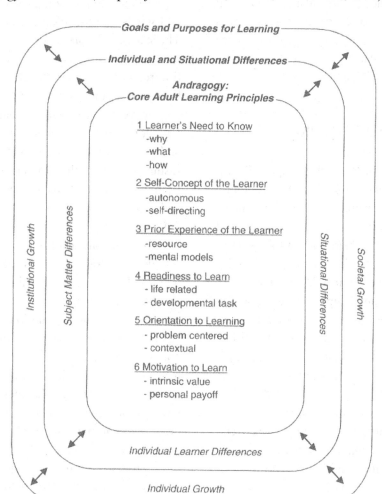

Figure 2. Movement towards learner self-evaluation

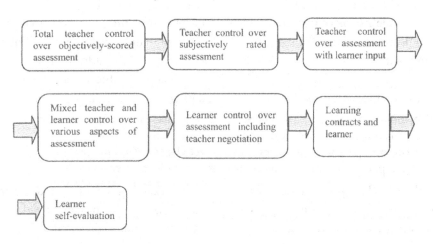

in more informal and non formal adult education settings, there seems to be the movement towards learner self-evaluation again based on the core principles of adult learning. Figure 2 created by Cranton (2010, p. 10) illustrates such a movement.

LOOKING TO THE FUTURE

Traditional education leadership, especially instructional leadership, has been in place for many centuries and has inspired teachers for generations. Teachers continue to delve into traditional instructional leadership, learning new things about this instructional mode. Scholars in teacher education and instructor training keep on studying this particular area and keep on generating new knowledge. There is one thing that most scholars would agree on, that is, traditional instructional leadership does work in most education settings. The methods, strategies, techniques and instructional ideas passed onto us by our predecessors have guided instructors in their classroom settings and even in their virtual environment. One trend in the future is that scholars will continue to study those prominent figures in history. The work of Confucius, Socrates, Plato, Dewey, Knowles and many others will continue to be tested out for different learners in different situations. Greene (2001) continues with the challenge to see the future as an opportunity for "thinking of things as if they could be otherwise" (p. 127).

The debate on which educational approach will better help learners achieve changes in the three domains will be another trend. While Western educators argue that educators should emphasize higher order thinking skills such as analysis, synthesis, and evaluation as revealed by Bloom's Taxonomy, educators in some Asian countries indicated that lower order thinking skills characterized by knowledge, comprehension and application should precede higher order thinking skills. Therefore, these lower order thinking skills must be taught first. Parker's (2010) description of

a good educator providing the student with "roots and wings" might bring the two ideas together. The instructor's role is to provide the foundational knowledge necessary for the roots and the inspiration required to guide the choices of wings and the direction they will take the learner (p. 14).

Ten years ago, some researchers in United Kingdom showed their fondness for rote learning and memorization, claiming that their research results indicated that for critical thinking and problem solving skills to occur, rote learning and memorization should be taught first (Jarvis, 2002). Rote learning and memorization are just parts of traditional instructional leadership. Their fondness for traditional instructional leadership may spark more research in this area. As far as the innovative instructional leadership goes, it cannot replace traditional instructional leadership as it has been used in most education settings. It will continue to exist hand in hand with traditional instructional leadership. Perhaps the best way to describe its existence is that these two approaches will continue to supplement and complement each other. Scholars will definitely delve into the innovative instructional leadership. But there is no question that traditional instructional leadership will remain dominant for many years to come. As far as Tylerian model goes, it will remain the predominant model among many other models as the model focuses more on individual and instrumental focus (Faillos, 2006). Tyler's rationale has really formed the foundation for curriculum, and program planning. As time goes on, researchers may come up with different critiques of this particular model. But as the foundation for curriculum and instruction, the Tyler's rationale will remain a pillar of the educational community.

CONCLUSION

This article has demonstrated that traditional instructional leadership advanced many centuries ago still remains the predominant instructional mode in the education and training of a nation's workforce as compared with the innovative instructional leadership characterized by andragogy. There are some misconceptions associated with the use of the traditional instructional leadership. This article has clarified those misconceptions via robust discussions. It seems that there has been a movement in North America to launch educational leadership programs. As these programs in educational leadership are launched, this article with its pertinent discussion on traditional instructional leadership can serve as the best resource for learning. Of course, the other part of educational leadership concerns administrative leadership. While that is beyond the scope of the discussion in this article it is important to acknowledge its significance in providing an organizational climate in which the instructional leader can succeed.

This article particularly talks about traditional instructional leadership revolving around Ralph Tyler's four questions. The four questions can be treated as a formula that may guide instructors' curriculum development and program planning. The four questions can be treated as a model as well. They can also be treated as Tyler's rationale. While the innovative instructional leadership is not the focus of the article, it is addressed in comparison to the traditional instructional leadership so that readers will see traditional instructional leadership more objectively. Without a doubt, traditional instructional leadership has many advantages in many venues. Among many, it can help instructors plan their programs in a linear manner or step by step. Above all, instructors know in advance how to measure and observe student learning. For those instructors who need to control assessment, traditional instructional leadership serves as an excellent model. Even those andragogical leaders such as Knowles borrow the concepts of curriculum development from Ralph Tyler. The four components of Tyler's model seem to be such essential parts that no educators can remove them if they are engaged in curriculum

development and program planning. What they can do is perhaps to add more components. For example, Knowles added a component such as needs assessment to Tyler's model. This article is by no means indicative of the fact that the traditional instructional leadership is superior to the innovative instructional leadership characterized by andragogy. Rather, it was written in an attempt to show when and how it should be most used, but should not be most abused. Like the lecture, it has many advantages and many disadvantages. Keeping all the advantages while trying to add more innovative methods will definitely revitalize this traditional instructional leadership as used and desired in most education settings.

REFERENCES

Bloom, B. S. (Ed.). (1956). *Taxonomy of educational objectives*. London, UK: Longman.

Brookfield, S. (2006). *The skillful teacher*. New York, NY: John Wiley & Sons.

Cochran, J. (2007). Reactions to Western educational practice: Adult education in Egypt. In King, K. P., & Wang, V. C. X. (Eds.), *Comparative adult education around the globe* (pp. 85–111). Hangzhou, China: Zhejiang University Press.

Cranton, P. (2010). Working toward self-evaluation. In Wang, V. C. X. (Ed.), *Assessing and evaluating adult learning in career and technical education* (pp. 1–11). Hershey, PA: IGI Global. doi:10.4018/978-1-61520-745-9.ch001

Dewey, J. (1961). *Democracy and education*. New York, NY: Macmillan.

Elias, J. L., & Merriam, S. B. (2005). *Philosophical foundations of adult education* (3rd ed.). Malabar, FL: Krieger Publishing.

Faillos, C. A. (2006). Adult education and the empowerment of the individual in a global society. In Merriam, S. B., Courtney, B. C., & Cervero, R. M. (Eds.), *Global issues and adult education: Perspectives from Latin America, Southern Africa, and the United States* (pp. 15–29). San Francisco, CA: Jossey-Bass.

Gagne, R. M., Wager, W. W., Golas, K. C., & Keller, J. M. (2005). *Principles of instructional design* (5th ed.). Stamford, CT: Thomson Learning.

Greene, M. (2001). *Variations on a blue guitar.* New York, NY: Teachers College Press.

Illeris, K. (2004). *The three dimensions of learning.* Malabar, FL: Krieger Publishing.

Jarvis, P. (2002). *The theory & practice of teaching.* London, UK: Kogan Page.

Jarvis, P. (2004). *Adult education and lifelong learning: Theory and practice* (3rd ed.). London, UK: Routledge.

Knowles, M. S. (1970). *The modern practice of adult education: Andragogy versus pedagogy.* New York, NY: Association Press.

Knowles, M. S. (1975). *Self-directed learning: A guide for learners and teachers.* New York, NY: Association Press.

Knowles, M. S. (1980). *The modern practice of adult education* (Rev. ed.). New York, NY: Cambridge Book Company.

Knowles, M. S. (1986). *Using learning contracts.* San Francisco, CA: Jossey-Bass.

Knowles, M. S. (1989). *The making of an adult educator.* San Francisco, CA: Jossey-Bass.

Knowles, M. S., Holton, E., & Swanson, A. (1998). *The adult learner.* Houston, TX: Gulf Publishing.

Knowles, M. S., Holton, E., & Swanson, A. (2005). *The adult learner* (6th ed.). Oxford, UK: Butterworth-Heinemann/Elsevier.

Lee, K. (2011). Philosopher or philistine? In Wang, V. C. X. (Ed.), *Assessing and evaluating adult learning in career and technical education* (pp. 23–43). Hershey, PA: IGI Global.

Merriam, S. B. (2008). Adult learning theory for the twenty-first century. *New Directions for Adult and Continuing Education, 119,* 93–98. doi:10.1002/ace.309

Mezirow, J. (1991). *Transformative dimensions of adult learning.* San Francisco, CA: Jossey-Bass.

Mezirow, J. (Ed.). (2000). *Learning as transformation: Critical perspectives on a theory in progress.* San Francisco, CA: Jossey-Bass.

Parker, J. (2009). Adult learning and CTE: A shared history influenced by technology. In Wang, V. C. X. (Ed.), *Definitive readings in the history, philosophy, practice and theories of career and technical education* (pp. 215–234). Hershey, PA: IGI Global.

Parker, J. (2010). Technology as integral to a new paradigm of adult education. *International Journal of Adult Vocational Education and Technology, 1*(2), 10–18. doi:10.4018/javet.2010040102

Pennington, F., & Green, J. (1976). A comparative analysis of program development processes in six professions. *Adult Education, 27*(1), 13–23. doi:10.1177/074171367602700102

Piaget, J. (1967). The mental development of the child. In Elkind, D. (Ed.), *Six psychological studies by Piaget.* New York, NY: Random House.

Piskurich, G. (2006). *Rapid instructional design.* New York, NY: John Wiley & Sons.

Ross, H. (1992). Foreign languages education as a barometer of modernization. In Hayhoe, R. (Ed.), *Education and modernization: The Chinese experience* (pp. 239–254). New York, NY: Pergamon Press.

Schein, E. (2010). *Organizational culture and leadership* (4th ed.). San Francisco, CA: Jossey-Bass.

Slattery, P. (1995). *Curriculum development in the postmodern era.* New York, NY: Garland Reference Library of Social Science.

Sork, T. J. (2000). Planning educational programs. In Wilson, A. L., & Hayes, E. R. (Eds.), *Handbook of adult and continuing education* (pp. 171–190). San Francisco, CA: Jossey-Bass.

Tyler, R. W. (1949). *Basic principles of curriculum and instruction.* Chicago, IL: University of Chicago Press.

Wang, V. C. X. (2007). Chinese knowledge transmitters or western learning facilitators adult teaching methods compared. In King, K. P., & Wang, V. C. X. (Eds.), *Comparative adult education around the globe* (pp. 113–1370). Hangzhou, China: Zhejiang University Press.

Wang, V. C. X. (2008). *Facilitating adult learning: A comprehensive guide for successful instruction.* Boston, MA: Pearson Education.

Wang, V. C. X., & Farmer, L. (2008). Adult teaching methods in China and Bloom's taxonomy. *International Journal for the Scholarship of Teaching and Learning, 2*(2), 1–15.

Wang, V. C. X., & King, K. (2006). Understanding Mezirow's theory of reflectivity from Confucian perspectives: A model and perspective. *Journal of Radical Pedagogy, 8*(1).

Wang, V. C. X., & King, K. (Eds.). (2008). *Innovations in career and technical education: Strategic approaches towards workforce competencies around the globe.* Charlotte, NC: Information Age Publishing.

Wang, V. C. X., & King, K. (2009). *Building workforce competencies in career and technical education.* Charlotte, NC: Information Age Publishing.

Wheatley, M. (1999). *Leadership and the new science: Discovering order in a chaotic World* (2nd ed.). San Francisco, CA: Berrett-Koehler Publishers.

Wiseman, L., & McKeown, G. (2010). *Multipliers: How the best leaders make everyone smarter.* New York, NY: HarperCollins.

This work was previously published in the International Journal of Adult Vocational Education and Technology, Volume 2, Issue 3, edited by Victor C.X. Wang, pp. 48-59, copyright 2011 by IGI Publishing (an imprint of IGI Global).

Chapter 8
Promoting Team Learning in the Classroom

Lila Holt
University of Tennessee, USA

Mary Ziegler
University of Tennessee, USA

ABSTRACT

The new workplace is a key arena for learning in today's society. The spiraling demand for knowledge in the workplace has increased interest in learning, especially team learning. Team learning can be viewed from multiple perspectives, making it difficult for career and technical educators (CTEs) to know how to prepare students for a team-based work environment, especially one that includes virtual teams. In addition, emerging technology adds to the confusion about how to provide effective learning experiences that mirror what is occurring in the workplace. To prepare the workforce of tomorrow, CTE instructors can become facilitators of team learning by providing ample opportunity for learners to practice team skills in a low-risk learning environment. By providing the exposure and practice to team learning skills and technology tools, CTEs may help equip students with added skills in entering a global workplace.

INTRODUCTION

The new workplace is a key arena for learning in today's society. Because of the rapid pace of change brought about by new forms of work, globalization, and technological advances, learning the need for learning is pervasive in all types of organizations. The speed of change influences workplaces whether they are businesses, governmental agencies, health care organizations, not-for-profit groups, or educational institutions. The spiraling demand for knowledge in the workplace has increased interest in learning, especially team learning. Fenwick (2008) notes that prior to 1990 most of the literature viewed learning in the workplace as an individual experience. Since then, concepts such as the "learning organiza-

DOI: 10.4018/978-1-4666-2062-9.ch008

tion" (Senge, 1990), Total Quality Management (Deming, 2000) and criteria for "high-performing teams" (Dyer, W & Dyer, J, 1987) have shifted the focus from the individual as the learner to the team as the learner. "Twenty-first century organizations will need to be highly nimble, capable of deploying spontaneous teams of employees within ever-changing organizational configurations in response to shifting market conditions" (Raelin, 2008, p. 11). In instances where individuals do not have sufficient knowledge to solve problems teams outperform the individual (Scholtes, Joiner, & Streibel, 2003). Not only is team learning prevalent in most workplaces, workers are now required to be on teams with members in other states or even countries. Yet team learning can be viewed from multiple perspectives making it difficult for career and technical educators (CTEs) to know how to prepare students for a team-based work environment, especially one that includes virtual teams. In addition, emerging technology adds to the confusion about how to provide effective learning experiences that mirror what is occurring in the workplace.

"Career and technical education is about preparing people, young and old, for the world of work" (Wang, 2010, p. 72). The world of work requires not only traditional skills, but also includes the ability to learn in teams. Although most areas of curriculum in career and technical education focus on individual achievement, increasingly learning as a team has become a foundational skill. How do teams learn and how can technology help instructors integrate team learning into the CTE curriculum? We propose to address these questions by reviewing the concept of team learning, identifying research that contributes to understanding team learning from multiple perspectives, describing recent technological advances that have the potential to enhance team learning, and providing implications and recommendations for the encouragement of team learning by CTEs.

DESCRIBING TEAM LEARNING

As learning shifts from the individual to the collective, using research to describe team learning provides multiple lenses from which to understand how learning in groups is different from learning on one's own. How does a team learn? Some authors contend that team learning differs from individual learning and goes beyond team development. For example, Kasl, Marsick, and Dechant (1997) note that although teams might work their way through Tuckman's (1965) stages of forming, norming, storming, and performing they may not create the new knowledge of collective learning. In another example, Pawlowsky (2001) suggests that team learning occurs in four phases information generation, diffusion, integration, and action. In the first phase, participants identify and generate information about a common goal. At this point, only individual learning is occurring. Second is diffusion or the exchange of information from individuals to the team. This phase is like a conversation where individual team members voice their ideas and better understand the ideas of others. Third is the integration and modification of the information. In this phase, isolated bits of information are integrated into the knowledge of the group as a whole, different from the information contributed by any one individual. Similar to a conversation, this phase is somewhat unpredictable as team members build on one another's ideas. And fourth is the action that results from applying the knowledge. This action may cause the team to reevaluate what it knows if the application is different from what they thought it would be. These stages are not necessarily sequential but provide insight into how individual contributions contribute to team learning. Likewise, McCarthy and Garavan (2008) agree with Pawlowsky (2001) saying that even when an individual learns on a team, that learning must be transferred to the group. This transfer or diffusion is an essential aspect of team learning. This is the step where learning as a team begins.

Remembering what is learned presents a challenge when it is a team memory rather than an individual memory.

Wenger (1987) introduced the term *transactive memory system* as the team's memory that they achieve by documenting their interaction and their decisions. The transactive memory system includes encoding, storage and retrieval processes that can be both individual, which is within the individual memory, and external that can be retrieved from books, data, or in the case of the team, other team members. A transactive system occurs when team members document what they learned so they can share it with others and learn others' areas of expertise.

The four processes that Pawlowsky (2001) describes, exchange of information, interaction, integration, and modification that address how teams learn together to create new knowledge is supported in the literature (Kasl, Marsick, & Dechant, 1997; Poell, Yorks, & Marsick, 2009). In addition, Watkins and Marsick (1990) add that teams integrate and modify what they learn through reflection on previous actions. Reflection is an essential step in the integration stage of the team learning process because it gives a team the opportunity to question its often taken-for-granted assumptions about common beliefs or the way things should be done. In order for groups to learn, their reflection must be collective; each member of the team contributes to the reflective process. According to Senge (1990) reflection enables a team to align what its learning toward a common goal. When knowledge is aligned, actions and subsequent results are greater than could be achieved by one individual (London & Sessa, 2007; Von Krogh, Nonaka, & Ichijo, 2000)

The literature has contributed to the start of a definition for team learning:

Team learning is a process engaged in by a group of people who have a common goal, where individual perspectives contribute to collective knowledge that is greater than that of any one individual, and the team as a learning unit can reflect on and question its assumptions as a part of the learning process.

Researchers have studied the characteristics and factors that embody team learning. In this paper, we are reviewing a brief set of studies from the fields of education, human resource development, and organization management in order to amplify our understanding of team learning so we can better relate it to classroom activities. While most of the research has a tendency to be self-referential by field (Fenwick, 2008), the following section presents an selection of studies across the three fields to gain a broader insight into which aspects of team learning are measured and how these aspects relate to the team learning definition.

TEAM LEARNING RESEARCH

Team learning research confirms the value of effective team learning. London and Sessa (2007) see team learning as a process or resulting in a product such as performance improvement. Others see team learning resulting in a group product such as performance improvement and mastering new tasks (Edmondson, Dillon, & Roloff, 2007). Whether product or process, studies show that team learning increases outcomes for the organization. Research supports Raelin's (2008) contention that organizations need teams of people who can respond with speed to changes in market conditions. Lynn, Skov, and Abel (1999) conducted a study of team learning to determine how long it took a product from development and its speed to the market. Technical mangers who were members of the American Society for Engineering Management were surveyed concerning recent new product development teams (N=95). An analysis of the surveys showed a correlation between team learning, the impact on speed to market, and new product success. The results indicated that team learning can have positive outcomes for an organization.

Team learning occurs when teams view their mistakes as opportunities to learn by turning the mistake into a problem to be solved. Tjosvold, Yu, and Hui (2004) studied 107 teams from transportation, manufacturing, and finance in Shanghi. Team managers rated the teams on learning from mistakes while the team members rated how their goals related to problem solving, Results showed that when teams view mistakes as problems to be solved their learning as a team increases.

Instruments that Measure Team Learning

As well as showing the importance of team learning in the market, research into the factors that comprise team learning is ongoing. A key aspect of this research is the development of instruments that attempt to measure the different factors of team learning and knowledge. To develop these instruments, researchers examine the literature for aspects of learning that seem relevant for teams. For example, the *Team Learning Questionnaire* (Bresó, Gracia, Latorre, & Peiró, 2008) was developed from a sample of 566 workers from one nuclear power plant. The questionnaire was designed to measure behaviors in four team learning dimensions: continued improvement, dialogue and open communication, collaborative learning, and strategic and proactive leadership that promote learning. Although the goal was to develop and validate a team learning scale, the authors identified four behaviors that they believed comprised team learning. Three of these behaviors are not new based on other research we have reviewed, however *leadership* has not been mentioned before. Lack of noting leadership previously may be because many teams do not have a specific leader. However, if the leader is considered to be the instructor or the supervisor, then leadership is an important part of team learning.

Another instrument designed to measure behaviors associated with team learning was developed by Savelsbergh, van der Hejden, and Poell (2009). This instrument focused on the behaviors of teams that indicated learning. These included co-constructing of meaning, collective reflection, error management, feedback, and experimenting. Researchers developed the instrument by working with 19 service teams in the Dutch banking industry. In the initial study, a positive relationship was found between team learning behaviors and team performance. However, the authors note that the results are suggestive only as the sample size was too limited to draw any conclusions from the study. Further research is needed to test this questionnaire.

What is important to note about these instruments is the identification of the behaviors that the authors consider relevant to team learning. They reinforce the four processes found by Pawlowsky (2001) of information, exchange & integration, modification, and action. Dialogue and open communication are particularly prominent and these would fit into what Pawlowsky (2001) calls exchange and integration. Open dialogue has been measured in the Teal Learning Questionnaire (Dori et al., 2003). Other studies on dialogue have identified the effects of social and political influences that can detract from open communication (McAvoy & Butler, 2007; McCarthy & Garavan, 2008). Open dialogue, according to Senge (1990) means recognizing and trying to put aside one's viewpoint while being open to the viewpoints of others. This does not mean, however, that people should always agree with one another. For example, McAvoy and Butler (2007) investigated learning failures in a software team. The investigation showed the group conformed to ideas of the leader of the group for "political correctness" as opposed to risking disagreement with the more "powerful" team member. Differences in power can impact how the team learns. If team members are reluctant to voice their views, especially if they are in opposition to the views of a more prominent member of the group, then team learning does not occur. Edmondson and Nembhard (2009) in an extensive literature review and field study agree that knowledge-based risks interfere with learning. Although the art of dialogue may appear contradictory, for learning to occur, team members must be free to state their views without fear of political and social influences, while at the same time, mastering the skills of putting aside their own views to fully attend to others in the team in order to understand their meaning. Dialogue (Isaac, 1997) fundamentally means that authenticity is a norm, otherwise, errors in thinking can go unspoken.

Along with behaviors identified above, studies have focused on collective efficacy and group cohesion. This type of efficacy is distinct from what other studies have found. Some authors refer to collaboration, but collective-efficacy is the team's belief about its ability to complete a task. The collective efficacy of a team has been found to have an effect on team learning. For example Little and Madigan (1997) conducted a field study of team efficacy and performance in an automotive manufacturing plant. Efficacy for an individual is the ability to create a desired result. In team efficacy, the focus shifts to the team as a whole and its collective ability as shown in the team's level of confidence to complete a particular task (Knight, Durham, & Locke, 2001). After analyzing in-depth interviews of 88 team participants of 13 teams, the result was a positive correlation between the efficacy of the team and the team performance. More recently, Hsu, Chen, Chiu, and Ju (2007) conducted a longitudinal field study of 604 university students divided into 188 teams. Teams' members reported on their perceived capabilities to complete a task on an unknown software package. After completing the tasks using the software, instructors rated the team's performance. The result was a positive correlation between team efficacy and performance. "A team who perceives a high level of collective efficacy may therefore activate a more positive thought process, which

results in positive outcome expectations, which in turn leads to better performance" (Hsu et al., 2007, p. 712). Collective efficacy is a relatively new term that describes the perceived ability to complete a task, not by an individual, but by the group as a whole. This research suggests that teams be given tasks or take on tasks that they believe that they can do.

In another study of socio and cognitive factors (Van den Bossche, Gijselaers, Segers, & Kirschner, 2006) researchers investigated whether task cohesion and interdependence influenced the learning process. Results showed that there was a positive influence and that task cohesion and interdependence contributed to collective learning. According to the authors, these findings support allocation for group development time as an enhancement to team learning. Prichard and Ashleigh (2007) corroborate that team skills development increases team performance. In a study with 16 teams, 8 of the teams received team training in the skills that would help them develop transactive memory where 8 did not receive the training. Teams that received team skill-training training showed a significantly increased rating over those who did not receive team-skill training. These findings agree with Senge's (1990) suggestion that groups need time to "practice" group skills as a strategy for team learning.

In addition to the importance of identifying factors integral to team learning, transferring knowledge from one group to another has been identified as influencing performance (Argote & Ingram, 2000). New studies are being conducted into how team knowledge is transferred at the team level as opposed to the individual level. Studies show that social relationships among members affect knowledge transfer. For example, a study to search for determinants of knowledge-based transfer was conducted in the travel industry (Wu, Hsu, & Yeh, 2007). The focus of this study was to find the relationship between affect-based trust and social interaction on knowledge sharing and learning intensity where affect-based trust occurs when people help others - not out of obligation or gain but rather simply because help is needed. Knowledge sharing requires the willingness to share knowledge with others while learning intensity is the ability to absorb the knowledge that was shared. Through interviews and questionnaires of managers in the industry, the findings showed a positive relationship between affect-based trust with both knowledge sharing and learning intensity. That is, when affect-based trust was fostered, both knowledge sharing and learning intensity increased. When social interaction was increased there was an increase in learning intensity; however, there was no positive impact on knowledge sharing by increasing social interaction. Kozlowski and Ilgen (2007) noted that the longer teams stay together and create relational bonds they become more productive. It is also noted that allowing teams to learn the interactive skills promotes positive results in group efforts and Kozlowski and Ilgen (2007) suggest these team skills should be part of today's learning curriculum.

In summary, even this brief look at the research suggests that team learning is a valuable asset in the workplace. Relating this result to an educational setting, in team learning, a) information is circulated through discussion and dialogue, b) the information is interpreted and leads to the construction of new knowledge by the team, c) the new knowledge leads to action and reflection, d) reflection leads to questioning assumptions and new action. New knowledge is stored in the minds of the team members, in their documents, and other archives that provide the team with an integral team memory. Factors that affect the effectiveness of team learning are issues of power, collective efficacy, group cohesion, commitment, and shared responsibility. These factors play an integral role in supporting team learning.

The research makes it clear that team learning is not as straight forward as individual learning, or even individuals learning together in a group. The team itself learns. The only way to improve the skills needed for team learning is to engage in the process. Research implies that team learning takes time. This presents a challenge for CTE educators. With all that students are expected to learn in a typical curriculum, how can students gain skills in team learning?

TECHNOLOGY FOR PROMOTING TEAM LEARNING

One way to benefit from the time it takes to conduct team learning activities is to simultaneously introduce technology so that students become familiar with technology while they are building their skills to work effectively as a team. Building on the behaviors identified in the research, we are going to show how the use of technology can stimulate learning at multiple levels. Recent changes in technology and the ubiquitous presence of the Internet in most educational institutions makes it possible to introduce team learning in a variety of ways. An advantage in using Web-based technology is that students can access it wherever they have a connection to the Internet. Most of the technology that is suitable for teaching is generally available without purchasing new, expensive software. We are going to discuss how technology can enhance opportunities for students to engage in team learning as we draw from our own experience and Ubell's (2010) work on virtual teams.

Information Distribution

The most prevalent information technologies are those available for information distribution. Information distribution is only one step in team learning, but a prominent one, that enables all members of the team to access the same information. Dissemination technologies distribute information one-way – similar to receiving an office memorandum. There is no opportunity to respond to the text other than reading it. While dissemination technologies can be used for training and other purposes, they are most commonly used to transmit up-to-date, general information to specific individuals and/or groups of individuals. Email is one of the most common forms of information dissemination. Most students are not only familiar with email but have an email account of their own. Similarly, a Website generally provides information for a reader but does not necessarily enable the reader to give a response. Another common dissemination device is an electronic newsletter. All of these types of technologies are one-way, the information goes to the reader or viewer. What has changed as technology has evolved is what is generally referred to as Web 2.0. This type of technology allows for two-way communication, a move that raises the educational value of technology, particularly for team learning. Taking the example of the electronic newsletter, we will show how the different two-way technologies can enhance a team's capability to learn as a unit.

Collaboration Technologies

As the popularity of the Internet has increased, so has the development of collaboration tools using the Internet. Collaboration technologies enable peer-to-peer learning. One simple tool that can enable a group to see how they can share information is an electronic schedule that resides on the Web; both the instructor and each team member can contribute information to it. This is the simplest form of collaboration, but it provides a glimpse into other possibilities. In discussion boards, for example, team members can interact with each other to solve a problem or accomplish a task. What makes these technologies different from discussion in a classroom is that they can be done two ways, real-time interaction as well as asynchronous interaction. Asynchronous interactions make it possible for students to engage in a project at a time and place of their choosing. Asynchronous collaboration enables students, especially those who are hesitant to contribute in class, time to think about their responses. Its use can improve many types of skills including the

ability to state one's ideas to a group and write clearly with a keyboard. A popular evolutionary advance of the discussion list is a blog. *Blog,* a blend of Web and Log, is an electronic journal that is often interactive, meaning that individuals can post comments to one another. This interactivity is what distinguishes these types of technologies from those that we have called *information distribution.*

Considering the application of an electronic newsletter, a team could start a blog where it can share ideas about how to compile a newsletter, be reporters or photographers, and most importantly learn how to be comfortable writing what others will read. The blog itself could become a living newsletter. This form of a project engages a variety of the team skills we have identified in the research including dialogue, interpretation, action, reflection, and questioning assumptions. The instructor can be as involved as he or she wants to be in the project after students are comfortable using the technology.

Text-based technology applications can be supplemented with audio, video, or any combination of the three. These applications provide a written record of a team's work and they can also be distributed to others. Project-based work has been shown to increase knowledge retention (McInerney & Fink, 2009). Rather than an electronic newsletter, students may prefer distributing their creative activity through a podcast. A podcast consists of audio or video files that can be downloaded from the Internet to a client device of choice. The name itself was derived from Webcasting where the files were made accessible to be played on a portable iPod as opposed to having to be played on a computer. Podcasts are usually small files that are released in a series much as a newsletter; and a person can set up an automatic download of these files as they become available, that is subscribe to the podcast.

What makes these technologies (often called learning tools or Web 2.0) particularly useful for team learning is that they are available on the Web. Students can access the same Website, add their contribution, and respond to the next student's contribution. Because these sites are interactive, they are especially useful for team learning including creating shared knowledge. Research suggests that students learn more from and with one another while they are engaged in a project than they can from a lecture (Hsieh & Knight, 2008).

An incentive for using these new technologies, especially for those entering or improving their skills, is the growing interest that workplaces have in using these technologies for team learning. Interestingly, students are interested in how these new technologies work also, and in fact, may be using them in their social lives.

Audio technologies range from audio conference calls that may be performed over traditional phone technology, Compressed Interactive TV (CIV or ITV) to Voice Over Internet Protocol (VoIP) that incorporates both video and audio computer transmission over the Internet. In addition, the VoIP and web conferencing may now include video components as well. The video components may include the use of cameras to see participants, the sharing of computer screens and/ or files, and the use of shared online whiteboards where all participants have access to write and draw diagrams. Newer on the horizon for workplace collaboration are social interaction sites. In these sites, participants can post text, audio and video information and provide for response by other members participating in an asynchronous format. Use of these technologies can also be set up to perform anonymous communications that may reduce unequal power distribution among group members during dialogue and discussions.

Reflection and Action

As team members work together to make meaning from shared experiences, they build their investment in the work they are doing. The technologies we have described are different because they are shared. For example, if a team was working on a project to identify work behaviors by evaluating employer Websites, they could write their findings in two ways. One way would be to use a word processor, a tool that many students are comfortable using. If a group is using a word processor, then a document must be sent via email or file (exchange with other students) sharing to another student for his or her input. This process can be cumbersome when working in a group because the document can only be sent one way – on to the next person. Newer technologies such as wikis, Websites where groups can work collaboratively, are different because the group's document resides in one place, on a Website. Each group member can go to that document and add his or her contribution to the problem they are solving. Content of the wiki may also be controlled through permissions granted by the wiki manager. The group literally creates a group document. In this process, they can reflect on one another's posts and question each other for meaning. Whatever tools groups use should enhance sharing ideas and constructing new shared knowledge.

Memory

Use of technology provides another benefit for teams and instructor Web 2.0 tools create artifacts that may be saved and thus contribute to a team memory. Team members who miss a meeting can see a record of that meeting. When instructors want to monitor team work, they can peruse the group discussion lists or blogs. What is essential is that work is saved and can be accessed by the team, another team, or the instructor. Thus, the knowledge does not reside in the head of a single individual.

Technology and Factors That Can Inhibit and Foster Team Learning

Team politics: Technology can be used to help promote dialogue and discussion when there is a strong political figure in the mix with which group members do not want to disagree. Anonymous instant messaging, social software, or web conferencing may be utilized to reduce fear of disagreement.

Team cohesion: Team cohesion may be aided with interactions of social media. Social media can provide a means of asynchronous communication that is ongoing as opposed to set meeting times. This increased interaction may aid group cohesion.

Team efficacy: Team efficacy or team members believing in themselves to accomplish the task may also be impacted by the use of technology. Team members' lack of comfort with technology may in turn inhibit team efficacy and over all confidence in completing their goal.

TEAM LEARNING, TECHNOLOGY AND CTEs: PUTTING IT ALL TOGETHER

So how can CTE's aid in preparing today's students for the workplace in which they will soon embark? Cranton (1996) suggests the role of the educator may be troublesome in team learning because it takes judgment when to provide instruction and when to let the team struggle to gain the knowledge they seek. In this way, the CTE is a facilitator who supports learning. In addition, much like the ways group leaders can facilitate team learning (London & Disessa, 2007), CTE's can be a catalyst for team learning by being a training and resource provider for technology tools that aid in team learning.

In transforming the CTE into a facilitator of team learning CTE's can:

- Create a climate that is supportive of risks
- Have fun with the technology until everyone is comfortable using it

- Provide projects where teams can develop their collective efficacy and gain from their successes in meeting the next challenge
- Assure that team roles are clear so that unequal power relationships do not develop
- Provide students with experience in leading a team
- Give student teams with opportunities for social interaction and knowledge sharing among teams
- Help students in reflecting as a team on actions taken
- Discuss assumptions, what they are, and how they can help teams break through barriers
- Allow teams time to practice

Each of these actions becomes a model for learners, not only on how they can participate on a team, but also how to facilitate and help others become productive members in team learning.

As Pawlowsky (2001) suggests, team learning occurs in four phases: information generation, diffusion, integration, and action. Providing professional development for instructors on the use of technology tools to support team learning gives instructors the confidence they need to integrate these technologies into teaching and learning, a necessary element for the CTE.

- Information generation: Web pages, books, instructor-developed projects, learner-developed projects, or any source that disseminates information.
- Diffusion: Shared Web documents, discussion threads, blogs, and email.
- Integration through collaboration: Web conferencing, VoIP packages, instant messaging and chat, discussion threads, social software, web shared documents, and email.
- Action or sharing what was learned: Presentation software, electronic newsletters, and podcasts

• Software that will create a team memory that will outlast any one individual's memory.

FURTHER RESEARCH

As interest in learning in the workplace grows to keep up with dynamic markets, research on best practices will need expansion. Also with the plethora of technology tools available today, a challenge for future research for team learning will be how to best channel these technologies to enable nimble and productive teams. For example, what elements of team development and skills promote effective team learning, especially in CTE? How do team learning skills taught in the classroom successfully carry over into the workplace? Which technologies best aid team learning dynamics? What team learning skills and technologies contribute to learning in virtual teams? In addition, the cross-cultural and social skills needed to succeed in virtual, global teams need to be addressed in both the classroom and in industry itself. These questions will just begin to explore team learning in the business environments and technologies that impact the workplace. From the perspective of the business world, a prevalent question will be what impact will team learning and hiring individuals who possess team skills have within the organization?

CONCLUSION

Teams and team learning are integral in the workplace today. Decisions are made in teams in a dynamic environment that requires organizations to adapt quickly and efficiently. Team learning encompasses interaction, sharing information, and creating memory artifacts. Research supports the value of effective team learning and practicing team skills have also been shown to increase team learning. Technology facilitates teams as they interact, record information and create new knowledge. Use of Web 2.0 tools as well as other technologies may influence team politics, cohesion, and efficacy which, in turn, may impact team learning. The technology tools employed to disseminate information and to collaborate create a team memory beyond the memory of any one team member. These same memory artifacts also offer team members a chance to reflect on previous team interactions and actions for learning. To prepare the workforce of tomorrow, the CTE instructor can become facilitators of team learning by providing ample opportunity for learners to practice team skills in a low-risk learning environment. By creating opportunities for exposure and practice with team learning skills and technology tools, CTEs may help provide the students with added confidence in entering a global workplace. Furthermore, this added confidence coupled with the skills to interact and learn in teams may help undergird business and industry survival in the dynamic global workplace in which we live.

REFERENCES

Argote, L., & Ingram, P. (2000). Knowledge transfer: A basis for competitive advantage in firms. *Organizational Behavior and Human Decision Processes*, *82*(1), 150–169. doi:10.1006/obhd.2000.2893

Bresó, I., Gracia, F. J., Latorre, F., & Peiró, J. M. (2008). Development and validation of the team learning questionnaire. *Organizational Behavior and Management*, *14*(2), 145–160.

Deming, W. E. (2000). *The new economics: For industry, government, education*. Cambridge, MA: MIT Press.

Dori, Y. J., Belcher, J., Bessette, M., Danziger, M., McKinney, A., & Hult, E. (2003). Technology for active learning. *Materials Today*, *6*(12), 44–49. doi:10.1016/S1369-7021(03)01225-2

Dyer, W. G., & Dyer, J. H. (1987). *Team building*. Reading, MA: Addison-Wesley.

Edmondson, A. C., Dillon, J. R., & Roloff, K. S. (2007). Three perspectives on team learning: Outcome improvement, task mastery, and group process. *Academy of Management Annals, 1*, 269–314. doi:10.1080/078559811

Edmondson, A. C., & Nembhard, I. M. (2009). Product development and learning in project teams: The challenges are the benefits. *Journal of Product Innovation Management, 26*(2), 123–138. doi:10.1111/j.1540-5885.2009.00341.x

Fenwick, T. (2008). Understanding relations of individual--collective learning in work: A review of research. *Management Learning, 39*(3), 227. doi:10.1177/1350507608090875

Hsieh, C., & Knight, L. (2008). Problem-based learning for engineering students: An evidence-based comparative study. *Journal of Academic Librarianship, 34*(1), 25–30. doi:10.1016/j.acalib.2007.11.007

Hsu, M. H., Chen, I. Y. L., Chiu, C. M., & Ju, T. L. (2007). Exploring the antecedents of team performance in collaborative learning of computer software. *Computers & Education, 48*(4), 700–718. doi:10.1016/j.compedu.2005.04.018

Isaacs, W. (1997). *Dialogue and the art of thinking together: A pioneering approach to communicating in business and in life*. New York, NY: Doubleday.

Kasl, E., Marsick, V. J., & Dechant, K. (1997). Teams as learners: A research-based model of team learning. *The Journal of Applied Behavioral Science, 33*(2), 227. doi:10.1177/0021886397332010

Knight, D., Durham, C. C., & Locke, E. A. (2001). The relationship of team goals, incentives, and efficacy to strategic risk, tactical implementation, and performance. *Academy of Management Journal, 44*(2), 326–338. doi:10.2307/3069459

Kozlowski, S., & Ilgen, D. (2007). The science of team success. *Scientific American Mind, 18*(3), 54–61. doi:10.1038/scientificamericanmind0607-54

Little, B. L., & Madigan, R. M. (1997). The relationship between collective efficacy and performance in manufacturing work teams. *Small Group Research, 28*(4), 517. doi:10.1177/1046496497284003

London, M., & Sessa, V. I. (2007). How groups learn, continuously. *Human Resource Management, 46*(4), 651–670. doi:10.1002/hrm.20186

Lynn, G. S., Skov, R. B., & Abel, K. D. (1999). Practices that support team learning and their impact on speed to market and new product success. *Journal of Product Innovation Management, 16*(5), 439–454. doi:10.1016/S0737-6782(98)00071-X

McAvoy, J., & Butler, T. (2007). The impact of the Abilene Paradox on double-loop learning in an agile team. *Information and Software Technology, 49*(6), 552–563. doi:10.1016/j.infsof.2007.02.012

McCarthy, A., & Garavan, T. N. (2008). Team learning and metacognition: A neglected area of HRD research and practice. *Advances in Developing Human Resources, 10*(4), 509–524. doi:10.1177/1523422308320496

McInerney, M. J., & Fink, L. D. (2009). Team-based learning enhances long-term retention and critical thinking in an undergraduate microbial physiology course. *Journal of Microbiology & Biology Education, 4*(1).

Pawlowsky, P. (2001). The treatment of organizational learning in management science. *Handbook of Organizational Learning and Knowledge*, 61-88.

Poell, R. F., Yorks, L., & Marsick, V. J. (2009). Organizing project-based learning in work contexts: A cross-cultural cross analysis of data from two projects. *Adult Education Quarterly, 60*(1), 77. doi:10.1177/0741713609334138

Prichard, J. S., & Ashleigh, M. J. (2007). The effects of team-skills training on transactive memory and performance. *Small Group Research, 38*(6), 696. doi:10.1177/1046496407304923

Raelin, J. A. (2008). *Work-based learning: Bridging knowledge and action in the workplace.* San Francisco, CA: Jossey-Bass.

Savelsbergh, C., van der Heijden, B., & Poell, R. F. (2009). The development and empirical validation of a multidimensional measurement instrument for team learning behaviors. *Small Group Research, 40*(5), 578. doi:10.1177/1046496409340055

Scholtes, P. R., Joiner, B. L., & Streibel, B. J. (2003). *The team handbook* (3rd ed.). Madison, WI: Oriel Incorporated.

Senge, P. M. (1990). *The fifth discipline: The art and practice of the learning organization.* New York, NY: Doubleday.

Tjosvold, D., Yu, Z., & Hui, C. (2004). Team learning from mistakes: The contribution of cooperative goals and problem-solving. *Journal of Management Studies, 41*(7), 1223–1245. doi:10.1111/j.1467-6486.2004.00473.x

Tuckman, B. W. (1965). Developmental sequences in small groups. *Psychological Bulletin, 63,* 348–399. doi:10.1037/h0022100

Ubell, R. (2010). *Virtual teamwork: Mastering the art and practice of online learning and corporate collaboration.* Hoboken, NJ: John Wiley & Sons. doi:10.1002/9780470615782

Van den Bossche, P., Gijselaers, W. H., Segers, M., & Kirschner, P. A. (2006). Social and cognitive factors driving teamwork in collaborative learning environments: Team learning beliefs and behaviors. *Small Group Research, 37*(5), 490. doi:10.1177/1046496406292938

Von Krogh, G., Nonaka, I., & Ichijo, K. (2000). *Enabling knowledge creation: New tools for unlocking the mysteries of tacit understanding.* New York, NY: Oxford University Press.

Wang, V. C. (2010). Critical components of curriculum development for career and technical education instructors in the United States. *International Journal of Adult Education and Technology, 1*(1), 72–89. doi:10.4018/javet.2010100905

Watkins, K., & Marsick, V. (1990). *Informal and incidental learning in the workplace.* London, UK: Routledge.

Wenger, D. M. (1987). Transactive memory: A contemporary analysis of the group mind. *Theories of Group Behavior,* 185-208.

Wu, W. L., Hsu, B. F., & Yeh, R. S. (2007). Fostering the determinants of knowledge transfer: A team-level analysis. *Journal of Information Science, 33*(3), 326–339. doi:10.1177/0165551506070733

This work was previously published in the International Journal of Adult Vocational Education and Technology, Volume 2, Issue 3, edited by Victor C.X. Wang, pp. 1-11, copyright 2011 by IGI Publishing (an imprint of IGI Global).

Chapter 9
Identifying Predictors of Academic Success for Part-Time Students at Polytechnic Institutes in Malaysia

Norhayati Ibrahim
Iowa State University, USA

Steven A. Freeman
Iowa State University, USA

Mack C. Shelley
Iowa State University, USA

ABSTRACT

A central challenge for higher education today is to understand the diversity and complexity of non-traditional students' life experiences and how these factors influence their academic success. To better understand these issues, this study explored the role of demographic characteristics and employment variables in predicting the academic success of part-time students at four polytechnic institutes in Malaysia. Demographic characteristics studied included respondent's age, gender, marital status, number of children, parent's educational level, and financial resources. Employment variables assessed were number of years working, job relatedness to the program, job satisfaction, and monthly salary. A total of 614 part-time students completed the survey. Results indicated that being an older student, being female, paying for their own education, and having high job satisfaction were statistically significant predictors of part-time students' academic success. Understanding the effects of demographic characteristics and employment variables on students' academic success might help administrators and educators to develop teaching and learning processes, support services, and policies to enhance part-time students' academic success.

DOI: 10.4018/978-1-4666-2062-9.ch009

INTRODUCTION

To remain competitive in a rapidly changing economy, many adults are continuously acquiring new knowledge and skills to improve their competencies in their workplace (Desjardin, Rubenson, & Milana, 2006; UNESCO, 2009). Ritt (2008) emphasized that the fastest growing jobs require a postsecondary qualification. In addition, possessing postsecondary credentials enables adults to gain broader economic and social benefits such as higher income over a lifetime (Brennan, Mills, Shah, & Woodley, 1999; Ritt, 2008). An increasing number of adults participating in higher education has led to greater attention focused on understanding the diversified needs of adults in higher education.

Malaysia, one of the developing countries in Asia, has placed an emphasis on providing wider opportunities for adults to continue their education in such higher education institutions as public and private universities, polytechnics, and community colleges (National Higher Education Research Institute [NHERI], 2007). In 2010, the working-age population (15–64 years) in Malaysia was expected to increase to 65.7% with the median age of 26.7 years (Bax & Hassan, 2003). Only 14% of the labor force in Malaysia, however, possess tertiary education qualifications (Bax & Hassan, 2003). This implies a need for more opportunities for adult learners to improve their education and training to meet the challenges of a knowledge-based economy.

To facilitate adults' participation, higher education institutions in Malaysia offer full-time and part-time enrollment with a broad range of e-learning instructional settings that offer learners more flexibility and greater autonomy (NHERI, 2007). Part-time enrollment seems to be the most preferred program in higher education, particularly for working adults because they can seek higher qualifications while still maintaining their jobs as well as their earnings (Chen & Carroll, 2007; Tuttle, 2005).

Polytechnic institutions are one segment in the Malaysian higher education system that provides tertiary level technical education and training. In 2000, these institutions began to offer part-time programs to adults to upgrade their academic qualifications (Bax & Hassan, 2003). These part-time programs adopt similar courses and the same assessment methods used for traditional full-time students, except that classes and practical activities in the workshop are held on weekends. The duration for the part-time diploma program is two years, compared to one year for full-time students (Bax & Hassan, 2003). From 2000 to 2009, a dramatic increase of part-time enrollment occurred. The part-time student population grew from 171 to 2,972 students (Department of Polytechnic and Community College Education [DPCCE], 2009).

As adult learners, part-time students may have different expectations of their learning and different needs due to their maturity and the complexity of their daily lives (Graham, Donaldson, Kasworm, & Dirx, 2000; Kasworm, Polson, & Fishback, 2002). Treating them like traditional students, who enter higher education immediately after finishing high school, means that educators often neglect to take into account the influence of their diverse needs and life experiences on their academic learning and success.

The purpose of this quantitative study, therefore, was to examine whether demographic characteristics and employment variables predict academic success of students in a part-time weekend program at four Malaysian polytechnic institutes. Previous research has shown that the diversity and complexity of adult learners' life experiences have a considerable impact on their academic success in higher education (Cantwell, Archer, & Bourke, 2001; Graham et al., 2000; Rogers, 2002; UNESCO, 2009). This area remains largely unexamined, particularly in the context of the polytechnic educational system in Malaysia.

LITERATURE REVIEW

Definitions of Adult Learners in Postsecondary Education

Adult learners in higher education are commonly referred to by various terms such as adult students (Richardson & King, 1998), nontraditional students (Bean & Metzner, 1985; Horn & Carroll, 1996; King, 2003; Spitzer, 2000; Taniguchi & Kaufman, 2005), and mature students (Richardson, 1994, 1995; Trueman & Hartley, 1996). Focusing on the different purposes and contexts of studies, some researchers define adult learners based on characteristics such as age, social roles, and traits (Darkenwald & Merriam, 1982; Kim, 2002; Rogers, 2002).

Age is extensively used as a definition of adult learners due to biological changes (English, 2009) and psychological development (Cranton, 1992; Rogers, 2002). Based on biological aspects, Bromley (as cited in English, 2009) stated that adulthood occurs between the ages of 16 to 20. Furthermore, Cranton (1992) concluded that an individual could be considered an adult learner between the ages of 18 to 29. Other studies, however, defined adult learners by different minimum ages such as age 16 (Kim, Hagedorn, & Williamson, 2004), age 21 (Taniguchi & Kaufman, 2005), and age 25 (Spitzer, 2000; UNESCO, 2009).

On the other hand, Darkenwald and Merriam (1982) argued that age alone is not a good indicator to describe adult learners; independence and social roles also should be used. They defined adult learners as "those who have responsibilities for managing their lives" (1982, p. 77) and who have "left the role of full-time students and assumed the role of worker, spouse, and/or parents, voter, and citizen, which denote independence characteristics of adults" (p. 8).

Horn and Carroll (1996) expanded the definition of adult learners (also referred to as nontraditional students) to include those who possess at least one of the following traits: work full-time, enroll in a part-time program, experience delayed enrollment, are financially independent, have dependents other than a spouse, are a single parent, and lack a high school diploma. These characteristics are consistent with almost 80% of the part-time students in polytechnic institutions (personal communication, December 3, 2008). Due to these similarities in characteristics, this study adopts the definition of adult learners as defined by Horn and Carroll. The term *adult learner* is also used interchangeably with *adult student* and *nontraditional student*.

Demographic Predictors of Academic Success

Demographic characteristics of nontraditional students have been widely discussed to explain their academic performance. For example, previous researchers have examined the effect of age (Cantwell et al., 2001; Hoskins & Newstead, 1997; Kasworm, 1990; Richardson, 1995; Spitzer, 2000); gender (Cantwell et al., 2001; Hoskins & Newstead, 1997; Spitzer, 2000); family responsibilities such as marital status (Reay, 1998) and number of children (Choy, 2002; Horn & Carroll, 1996; Kember, 1999; Taniguchi & Kaufman, 2005); generation status (Bui, 2002; Education Resource Institute [ERI] & Institute for Higher Education Policy [IHEP], 1997); and financial support (Fenske, Porter, & Dubrock, 2000; McGivney, 2004) on students' academic success.

Age has been identified as being positively associated with grades at tertiary levels (Hoskins & Newstead, 1997; Kasworm, 1990; Richardson, 1994; Spitzer, 2000). Richardson (1995) found that mature students achieved slightly higher grades than nonmature students. Hoskins and Newstead (1997) indicated that age was a strong predictor of academic success for nontraditional entry students as compared to gender and type of qualifications.

In relation to gender differences, Cantwell et al. (2001) compared traditional and nontraditional students' academic achievement and found females performed better than males. Nontraditional and female students also achieved higher grades than traditional and male students (Spitzer, 2000). Nontraditional female students performed academically better than traditional female students (Carney-Crampton & Tan, 2002). Robertson (1991) revealed that female students were more likely to exhibit greater study skills including interest, motivation, and time management.

Family responsibilities, such as married life and childcare, often appear to affect adult students' academic performance, particularly for females (Fairchild, 2003; Johnson, Schwartz, & Bower, 2000; Reay, 1998). Reay (1998) revealed, however, that married life is more supportive for females as compared to males. Furthermore, childcare concerns were often reported to be a priority over education (Fairchild, 2003). In fact, having children was found to be negatively associated with degree completion and persistence (Choy, 2002; Horn & Carroll, 1996; Kember, 1999; Taniguchi & Kaufman, 2005). Regardless of studies indicating the struggles to balance academic demands and family responsibilities (Home, 1998; Padula, 1994), nontraditional female students achieved higher grades than males (Spitzer, 2000) and traditional female students (Carney-Crampton & Tan, 2002).

Researchers have noted differences between first- and continuing-generation students in academic achievement. First-generation students are defined as students whose parents had no college education (Ishtani, 2006; National Center for Educational Statistics [NCES], 1998; Terenzini, Springer, Yaeger, Pascarella, & Nora, 1996). Compared with continuing-generation students, first-generation students are more likely to have low family income with more dependents (Inman & Mayes, 1999; NCES, 1998; Terenzini et al., 1996). Thus, they are more likely to seek part-time enrollment and work full-time (NCES, 1998). These students are often associated with low achievement and being psychologically unprepared (Bui, 2002; ERI & IHEP, 1997), with less family and peer support (ERI & IHEP, 1997;

Hsaio, 1992; Terenzini et al., 1996). They are also found to be at higher risk of having lower grades or not completing their studies (Ishtani, 2006; Terenzini et al., 1996).

Financial resources were one of the most often stated factors determining adults' persistence and success in higher education (Community College Survey of Student Engagement Report [CCSSE], 2008). Many students decided to further their studies through a part-time program because of financial obligations. CCSSE reported that almost 45% of the participants responded *likely* and *very likely* to the statement that lack of finances caused them to withdraw from class or college. McGivney (2004) found those with high financial difficulties tended to have low retention or achievement. Fenske et al. (2000) found that students who paid their own tuition tended to have the lowest retention rates after the first year of enrollment, compared to those who received financial aid.

Employment Factors

Employment is one of the main factors that differentiate part-time students from full-time students. Work experiences of part-time students are typically viewed as continually enriching and contributing to their learning process. Bourner et al. (as cited in Brennan et al., 1999) argued that part-time students could concurrently relate their work experience to their academic learning. Therefore, they could constructively apply their job knowledge and skills to their learning, or vice versa. This advantage could reinforce their academic understanding as well as enhance their academic success as suggested by Rogers (2002, p. 63):

... the development of intelligence seems to be dependent more on the amount of educational experience one has received and on the subsequent use of learning skills in one's occupations than on any basic learning ability inherited or developed when young.

Because most adults indicate that job-related reasons led to their participation in education (Desjardins et al., 2006; UNESCO, 2009), they should have clear career goals. Consequently, they are more prepared and motivated to learn, particularly if the program is related to their occupational field.

Furthermore, Dreher and Ryan (2000) argued the possibility of students with work experience having a better chance to succeed in their studies. Challenges and problems faced in the workplace make them able to more easily link and make connection between their academic learning and their job knowledge and skills as compared to students with no work experience. On the other hand, Dreher and Ryan also suggested that having work experience not related to the studies may not be beneficial to students' academic achievement.

In the model of Adult Learners' College Outcome, Donaldson and Graham (1999) also emphasized the potential role of prior experiences to affect the academic outcomes of adult students. Prior experiences were defined as previous academic experiences as well as life experiences from their work, family, and other social roles. The model included prior experiences and personal biographies such as external factors that influence four other variables—psycho-social and value orientation, adult cognition, life-world environment, and connecting classroom. Consequently, three factors (adult cognition, life-world environment, and connecting classroom) directly affected the college outcome. This model clearly demonstrated that adults' prior experiences influence their classroom learning and academic success. Graham et al. (2000) tested the model and emphasized the importance of prior experiences to adult students' academic success and persistence.

RESEARCH QUESTIONS

The importance of demographic characteristics and employment variables in predicting academic success is supported by the literature. Hence, examining the effects of these factors is pertinent to assisting adult learners in acquiring new skills, knowledge, attitudes, and behaviors that facilitate their success in higher education.

Thus, this study sought to explore the predictive power of demographic characteristics and employment variables on part-time students' academic success.

METHODOLOGY

Population

The study population consisted of 1,054 part-time diploma students enrolled in second- to final-semester, who enrolled for the July 2009 session (July–December) at four polytechnic institutions in Malaysia. For a diploma program, the applicant must have a polytechnic certificate with at least six months working experience. This population was selected because, by being in a part-time program, it met at least one criterion of nontraditional students defined previously. These students were also diversified in work sectors such as manufacturing, private, and civil service.

A total of 614 students (58% response rate) from five part-time programs in technical education (electrical engineering, mechanical engineering, civil engineering, information technology, and commerce) completed the questionnaire. The sample consisted of 437 (71.5%) males and 174 (28.5%) females. The respondents' ages ranged from 20 to 49 years (mean=25.5).

Design and Procedure

This study investigated the effect of demographic characteristics and employment variables on part-time students' academic success. Quantitative data collection was employed, using survey methodologies which allowed the data to be quantified and analyzed using statistical analysis (Gliner & Morgan, 2000).

Independent variables. There were six demographic variables—gender, age, marital status, number of children, financial resources, and generation status. Gender was coded with 1 for male and 0 for female. Age was measured in years. Marital status was assessed as single, married, or divorced. Number of children was determined using four categories from no children to more than four. Generation status was identified using parents' educational level consisting of six levels: from did not complete high school to completed a doctoral program. Financial support was assessed using five categories: support from parents, spouse, and relatives; loan from financial institution; loan from government; loan from employer; and employment earnings.

The employment variables included salary information based on the response to four categories of monthly income level ranging from below Malaysian Ringgit (MYR) 1,000 to above 3,000; number of years working with four categories from none to more than 10 years. Job relatedness to program was determined by comparing the job designation and program enrolled. The judgment of relatedness was based on the researcher's previous experience of teaching and managing part-time programs. For example, job designations such

as technician, machinist, chargeman, mechanic, fitter, and welder were labeled as job-related to the respective engineering programs. Similarly, those who worked as clerks or were involved in administrative and business work were designated in a job-related category to the commerce program.

Dependent Variable. Academic success was measured using the student's cumulative grade point average (CGPA) extracted from the student's official academic report. A complete listing of variables used in the study is presented in Table 1.

The questionnaire used dual languages, English and Malay, to increase clarity during the collection of data. The translation was completed by a native speaker, who is a graduate student from Iowa State University, and a lecturer from one of the polytechnic institutions in Malaysia. Formal approval from both the Iowa State University Human Subject Institutional Review Board (IRB) and the Director of the Department of Polytechnic and Community College Education was obtained prior to conducting this study.

Questionnaires were personally hand-delivered to each part-time student enrolled in second- to final-semester at the four selected polytechnics during 30 minutes of his/her scheduled class by this researcher or the student's academic advisor. Hand-delivered distribution was chosen to increase the response rate. Surveys were completed

Table 1. Description of variables

Variables	Description
Demographic Variables	
Gender	Male, Female
Age	18–24, 25–34, 35–44, 45–54, 55–64, 65 years and older
Marital status	Single, Married, Divorced
Number of children	No children, 1–2, 3–4, more than 4
Types of financial resources	Financial support from parents, spouse, other relatives, not to be repaid; loans from financial institutions or government; financial assistance from your employer; earnings from employment
Generation status	First-generation; Continuing-generation
Employment Variables	
Number of years working	None, 1–3; 4–6; 7–10; more than 10 years
Monthly salary	More than MYR 3000; MYR 2001 to MYR 3000; MYR1001 to MYR 2000; MYR 1000 and below
Job satisfaction	*Rating scale of 1-4 (1=very dissatisfied, 4=very satisfied)*
Job relatedness to program	Related, Not related
Academic Success	
	Student's Cumulative Grade Point Average (CGPA) extracted official student's academic report.

during the first and second weeks of the July 2009 academic session.

A letter of introduction was attached to each questionnaire to explain the purpose and the importance of this study and to assure confidentiality of the responses. The letter also noted that the participants were free to not participate and could discontinue the survey at any time. The participants were requested to write their identification numbers on the questionnaire to access their cumulative grade point averages from the official academic records. The participants were given time to read the letter of introduction before they responded to the questionnaires. Consent was implied if the participants returned the questionnaires.

The official database of the students' academic reports was obtained from the examination unit at each polytechnic. To ensure participants' confidentiality and anonymity, the names of the students were eliminated from their academic reports.

Data Analysis

A standard multiple regression was conducted using demographic and employment variables as predictors and academic success as the outcome variable. Analysis was performed using SPSS version 17.0. The block regression analysis was conducted on two models. Model 1 included all the demographic variables (age, gender, number of children, marital status, financial resources, and generation status). Model 2 added the employment variables to Model 1 (number of years working, job relatedness to the program, salary, and job satisfaction). Finally, all significant predictors in Model 2 were regressed on academic success. The equation of academic success was determined based on the final regression. The level of significance for all analyses was set at .05.

RESULTS

From the 614 collected surveys, four respondents were excluded from the dataset because their questionnaires had more than 30% nonresponse variables (Tabachnick & Fidell, 2007). The remaining 610 respondents were used for the analysis. Descriptive statistics for demographic and employment predictors as well as outcome variables are presented in Tables 2 and 3. In general, most of the part-time students had work experience of less than 3 years (55.3%), were first generation students (88.2%), were single or married with no children (78.6%), were enrolled in a program related to their job (75.7%), had a salary between MYR 1000 and 2000 (71.0%), and relied on earnings from employment to support their studies (63.3%). Therefore, the categories for demographic and employment variables used for further analysis were reduced to two or three categories as shown in Tables 2 and 3. All missing values for categorical variables were assigned to an additional category labeled as *Unknown*. The mean series procedure was used to replace missing values for continuous data.

Before performing any analysis, the continuous data were screened with the SPSS program for univariate outliers using histograms of standardized dependent variables. One extreme outlier was found in the CGPA variable and deleted. The descriptive statistics for all the variables did not show severe violation of normality. The skewness and kurtosis of all variables, except age, were within a tolerable range of ±2 for assuming a normal distribution (Tabachnick & Fidell, 2007). Similarly, the examination of the histograms suggested that the distributions of all variables, except age, were approximately normal. Thus, it was reasonable to assume the assumption of normality is not violated for multiple regression analysis. A curvilinear relationship between age and CGPA was observed from the scatter-plot. Because of this quadratic relationship, age-squared was used for further analysis. Residual scatter-plots showed

Table 2. Summary of respondents' demographic characteristics (N=614)

Demographic Characteristics	Frequency	Percentage (%)
Gender		
Male	440	71.7
Female	174	28.3
Program[a]		
Civil Engineering	190	31.0
Electrical Engineering	171	27.9
Mechanical Engineering	161	26.3
Commerce	75	12.2
Information Technology	16	2.6
Age[a,b]		
18 – 24 years	319	52.2
25 – 34 years	257	42.1
35 – 44 years	31	3.3
45 – 54 years	4	.7
Mean	25.5	
Standard Deviation	3.969	
Marital Status[b]		
Single	432	70.7
Married and Divorced	179	28.7
Number of Children[b]		
None	480	78.6
Have children	131	21.4
Financial Resources[b]		
Earnings only	386	63.3
Other sources (Parents, spouse, relatives, financial institution, or government)	198	32.5
Unknown	26	4.3
Generation Status[b]		
First-generation	538	88.2
Continuing-generation	47	7.7
Unknown	25	3.9

Note: [a]Categories were used *for descriptive purposes only.*
[b]Frequency and percentage may not equal to total N=614 or 100% due to nonresponse to questions.

Table 3. Summary of respondents' employment and academic success variables (N=614)

Variables	Frequency	Percentage (%)
Employment		
Job Satisfaction[a]		
Very dissatisfied	11	1.8
Somewhat dissatisfied	76	12.7
Somewhat satisfied	393	65.7
Very satisfied	118	19.7
Monthly Basic Salary[a]		
MYR (Malaysian Ringgit) 1000 and below	61	10.3
MYR 1001 – MYR 2000	422	71.0
Above MYR 2000	86	14.5
Unknown	25	4.2
Occupation[a]		
Related	463	75.8
Not related	116	19.2
Unknown	32	5.2
Academic Success		
Cumulative Grade Point Average (CGPA)[a,b]		
3.75 – 4.00 (mostly A's)	31	5.1
3.25 – 3.74 (about half A's and half B's)	220	36.0
2.75 – 3.24 (mostly B's)	258	42.4
2.25 – 2.74 (about half B's and half C's)	89	14.6
1.75 – 2.24 (mostly C's)	9	1.5
1.25 – 1.74 (about half C's and half D's)	1	2.0
Less than 1.25 (mostly D's or below)	1	2.0
Mean	3.13	
Standard deviation	0.43	

Note: [a]categories were used *for descriptive purposes only.*
[b]Frequency and percentage may not equal to total N or 100% due to non-response to questions.

that assumptions of normality, linearity, and homoscedasticity between predicted scores and errors of predictions were met.

In the first analysis of Model 1, marital status was omitted from the model due to a high correlation with the number of children. The number of children variable was used for further analysis as it represented an increase in responsibilities for taking care of dependents better than marital status. The results of the multiple regression analysis are presented in Table 4. Results indicated Model 1

was statistically significant ($F(7,609)=8.452$, $p <0.001$) and accounted for .090 total variance (R^2) in academic success. The results indicated that age-squared ($\beta=2.78E\text{-}4$, $p=.001$), male ($\beta=-.094$, $p=.009$), childless ($\beta=.117$, $p=.013$), and financing education from other sources ($\beta =-.102$, $p =.003$) were significant demographic predictors for academic success. The first-generation variable was not significant ($\beta =-.053$, $p=.387$). The effects of interactions were analyzed between all possible pairs of demographic characteristics. None of the interactions showed significant effects. Thus, the analysis continued with no interaction effects.

In Model 2, R^2 increased to .119 (F (15,609)=5.310, $p<.001$), indicating that employment variables accounted for 2.9% of the total variance in academic success after controlling for demographic characteristics. Three employment variables—work experience more than 3 years ($\beta=.051$, $p=.221$), job relatedness to the program ($\beta=.059$, $p=.158$), and salary below MYR1000 ($\beta=-.091$, $p=.448$)—were not significant employment predictors. Job satisfaction, the only employ-

ment variable, was marginally positively related to academic success ($\beta=.050$, $p=.054$). Adding employment variables did reduce the effect of significant demographic variables (Table 4) age-squared ($\beta=.1.94E-4$, $p=.030$), educational funding from other sources ($\beta=-.084$, $p=.016$), and male ($\beta=-.112$, $p=.002$). The childless variable was not a significant predictor ($\beta=.083$, $p=.093$). The increase of the adjusted R^2 (.096) value from Model 1 showed the addition of more variables improved the prediction model. The interaction effects among demographic characteristics and

Table 4. Academic success (CGPA) regressed on demographic and employment variables (N=609)

Variables	Model 1		Model 2	
	B	Std error	B	Std error
Age-squared	2.78E-4***	8.137E-5	1.94E-4*	8.893E-5
Gender (Male = 1)	-.094**	.036	-.112**	.036
Number of Child (None = 1)	.117**	.047	.083	.050
Financial Resources Other Sources Unknown Earnings	-.102** -.143 0ᵃ	.035 .111	-.084* -.103 0ᵃ	.035 .115
Generation Status First-generation Unknown Continuing-generation	.053 .156 0ᵃ	.061 .122	035 .182 0ᵃ	.061 .126
Job Satisfaction			.050	.026
Number of years working More than 3 years Unknown 3 years and below			.051 -.057 0ᵃ	.042 .140
Job relatedness to program Related Unknown Not related			.059 -.008 0ᵃ	.042 .082
Salary Below RM1000 RM 1000-2000 Above RM2000 Unknown			-.091 .030 .063 0ᵃ	.120 .112 .118
Intercept R-Squared Adjusted R-Squared F df	2.977*** .090*** .079 8.452 7		2.822*** .119*** .096 5.310 15	

Note: *$p<.05$, **$p<.01$, ***$p<.001$; a = reference group

employment variables indicated no significant effects. Therefore, the overall model only measured the main effects.

The equation for the overall model that includes all significant predictors was:

CGPA = 2.782 -.095Male + 3.74E-4Age-squared -.100Financial from other sources +.066Job satisfaction

This equation implied that with each additional year of age-squared, 3.74E-4 unit cumulative grade point average would increase up to a certain age-point and then decrease. On average, males have a CGPA about .095 points lower than females, after controlling for other variables in the model. After controlling all other variables, on average students who rely solely on their earnings to support their education have a CGPA of .100 units higher than those with other sources of financial resources. After controlling all other variables, the increase of each unit of job satisfaction would increase .066 unit of CGPA. In the overall model, R^2 was .087 ($F(5,609)=11.60$, $p<0.001$) for the variation in academic success of part-time students.

DISCUSSION

This study demonstrated the importance of demographic characteristics and employment variables for understanding part-time students' academic success in Malaysian polytechnic institutes. Demographic characteristics ($R^2 =.09$) were determined more reliable predictors of part-time students' academic success as compared to variables of employment ($R^2 =.029$). Four demographic variables—age, gender, number of children, and financial resources—demonstrated significant relationships on students' CGPAs. Specifically, students who were older, female, childless, and financed their own education were more likely to score higher grades.

Age played a significantly positive role in predicting students' academic success. This finding supports previous studies conducted by Hoskins and Newstead (1997), Kasworm (1990), Richardson (1994), and Spitzer (2000). Other researchers argued older students were committed to their studies because they exhibited greater learning goals (Grimes, 1995), self-regulation, and intrinsic motivation (Spitzer, 2000). Presumably older students possess characteristics such as independence more towards problem-centeredness and internal motivation, which is consistent with the self-directed learning concept introduced by Knowles (1980).

Consistent with the findings of previous studies, females were determined to have significantly higher CGPA than males (Cantwell et al., 2001; Carney-Crampton & Tan, 2000; Spitzer, 2000). Perhaps, the greater self-regulation for females in this technology field explained their higher achievement in academics. In contrast with Fairchild (2003) and Johnson et al.'s (2000) studies, family responsibilities appeared not to affect females' academic achievement.

Students with no children were discovered to have the strongest significant association with academic success. These findings demonstrated the likelihood that caring for dependents limited students' time for studying and affected their academic success. This finding is in agreement with previous studies (Choy, 2002; Horn & Carroll, 1996; Kember, 1999; Taniguchi & Kaufman, 2005).

Financial sources appeared to influence students' academic success. In contrast with Fenske et al.'s (2000) study related to retention rates among adult learners, this study showed that students who financed their education from their earnings tended to have higher grades than those who received financial support from other sources, such as relatives, employers, or loans. It is likely that students who financed their own education were more committed in their studies.

This study suggested that, in general, work experience had significant predictability of students' academic success. This finding indicated that the overall employment variables (number of years working, job relatedness to the enrolled program, job satisfaction, and monthly salary) contributed significantly (R^2=.029) to students' academic success. Individual employment variables, however, were not significant except job satisfaction. Hence, the relationship between work experiences and academic success is complicated and requires further research.

One plausible explanation for this significant predictability of overall employment predictors was job-related reasons that could be students' main motives to enter higher education. This assumption was made for two reasons: (a) the sample age ranged from 20 to 49, which falls within career-oriented learners as found by Morstain and Smart (1977) and (b) the higher percentage of participants was enrolled in programs related to their occupational field. Job satisfaction was determined marginally significant to predict students' academic success. Perhaps students who were more satisfied with their jobs tended to apply their job's knowledge in their academic learning and were more engaged in their studies.

Adding employment variables to the demographic characteristics reduced the effects of demographic variables and their significant predictability of students' academic performance. This result indicates the potential of significant interactions among employment and demographic variables, which require further investigation.

This research contributes to a better understanding of the effects of the selected demographic and employment variables on part-time students' academic success in Malaysian polytechnic institutes. UNESCO (2009) also supported that each country needs to understand its own characteristics of adult learners to address their needs in developing appropriate policies and programs. The overall factors explained a considerable amount of the variation in students' academic achievement, even though only four variables had significant predictability. These findings provide valuable information to administrators and educators of part-time students to develop policies, teaching and learning processes, and support services to enhance students' performances in their studies. For instance, in the effort to improve students' performances, educators and administrators may design effective motivation programs for younger students, males, and those who receive other types of support to finance their education. Furthermore, these findings indicate females perform better than males academically. This finding may be used to recruit more females to enroll in part-time programs. In addition, providing a support system such as childcare may also assist to improve students' academic success.

With the obvious limitation of examining only the direct effects of demographic characteristics and employment variables on students' academic success, this study suggests further investigation of the relationships between these factors and how they affect students' academic success. Investigating these relationships could explain what drives them to become successful based on their demographic and employment information.

Another extension for future research might be to include other potential predictors of academic success, such as previous academic achievement, learning approach, and students' motivation to fully explore the relationships among demographic, employment, and part-time students' academic success. In addition, a more comprehensive assessment of employment variables, such as attitudinal aspects related to how students' perceived the influence of their work experiences on their academic learning, would be beneficial. Furthermore, conducting this same study with a broader group of part-time students could enhance the generalization of the findings in the Malaysian context and allow researchers to investigate potential differences due to academic discipline among these part-time students.

In conclusion, providing wider access for adult learners in higher education may not ensure their success in academia. To help them succeed in their academic pursuits, administrators and educators could use this study's findings to effectively develop intervention programs, policies, and teaching and learning processes that suit students.

CONCLUSION

The following conclusions are based upon the findings of this study:

- Demographic characteristics and employment variables were significant in predicting part-time students' academic success at polytechnic institutions in Malaysia.
- Demographic characteristics—gender, age-squared, number of children, and financial support—were determined significant predictors of students' academic success.
- Employment variables—after controlling demographic characteristics and other employment variables, job satisfaction exhibited significant predictability of students' academic achievement.
- Gender, age-squared, financial support, and job satisfaction were significant predictors in the overall model that included demographic characteristics and employment variables.

Recommendations for Future Research and for Administrators

Based on this study's discussions and conclusions, the following recommendations are generated:

- Examine the relationships among demographic characteristics and employment variables to better understand how these factors affect students' academic success.

- Include other potential predictors of academic success, such as learning approach and students' motivations, to fully explore the relationships among demographic, employment, and students' academic success.
- Develop a more comprehensive assessment of employment variables, such as attitudinal aspects related to how students' perceive the influence of their work experiences on their academic learning.
- Conduct this same study to a broader group of part-time students in higher education in Malaysia to enhance the generalization of the findings in a Malaysian context and investigate potential differences due to academic discipline among these part-time students.
- Develop effective intervention programs, policies, and teaching and learning processes based on students' gender, age, financial resources, and job satisfaction. For instance, motivational program for younger and male students could improve their academic achievement.

ACKNOWLEDGMENT

The researcher would like to express her gratitude to the Malaysian Government, Ministry of Higher Education, and Department of Polytechnic Education for their support in funding this project and their cooperation during data collection process.

REFERENCES

Bax, M. R. N., & Hassan, M. N. (2003). *Lifelong learning in Malaysia*. Paper presented at the IIEP/UNESCO KRIVET International Policy Seminar, Seoul, Korea.

Bean, J. P., & Metzner, B. S. (1985). A conceptual model of nontraditional undergraduate student attrition. *Review of Educational Research, 55*(4), 485–540.

Brennan, J., Mills, J., Shah, T., & Woodley, A. (1999). *Part-time students and employment: Report of a survey of students, graduates and diplomats.* London, UK: Centre for Higher Education Research & Information, Open University Quality Support Centre.

Bui, K. V. T. (2002). First-generation college students at a four-year university: Background characteristics, reasons for pursuing higher education, and first-year experiences. *College Student Journal, 36*(1), 3–11.

Cantwell, R., Archer, J., & Bourke, S. (2001). A comparison of the academic experiences and achievement of university students entering by traditional and nontraditional means. *Assessment & Evaluation in Higher Education, 26*(3), 221–234. doi:10.1080/02602930120052387

Carney-Crompton, S., & Tan, J. (2002). Support systems, psychological functioning, and academic performance of nontraditional female students. *Adult Education Quarterly, 52*(2), 140–154. doi:10.1177/0741713602052002005

Chen, X., & Carroll, C. D. (2007). *Part-time undergraduates in postsecondary education: 2003-04.* Washington, DC: National Center for Education Statistics.

Choy, S. (2002). *Nontraditional undergraduates: Findings from the condition of education, 2002.* Washington, DC: U.S. Department of Education, National Center for Education Statistics.

Community College Survey of Student Engagement (CCSSE). (2008). *High expectations and high support.* Austin, TX: The University of Texas at Austin.

Cranton, P. (1992). *Working with adult learners.* Middletown, OH: Wall & Emerson.

Darkenwald, G., & Merriam, S. (1982). *Adult education: Foundations of practice.* New York, NY: Harper Collins.

Department of Polytechnic and Community College Education. (2009). *Quick facts.* Retrieved from http://www.portal.mohe.gov.my/portal/page/portal/ExtPortal/IPT/POLITEKNIK/files/QuickfactApril09.pdf

Desjardins, R., Rubenson, K., & Milana, M. (2006). *Unequal chances to participate in adult learning: International perspectives.* Paris, France: UNESCO Institute for Educational Planning.

Donaldson, J. E., & Graham, S. (1999). A model of college outcomes for adults. *Adult Education Quarterly, 50*(1), 24–40.

Dreher, G. F., & Ryan, K. C. (2000). Prior work experience and academic achievement among first-year MBA students. *Research in Higher Education, 41*(4), 505–525. doi:10.1023/A:1007036626439

Education Resources Institute & Institute for Higher Education Policy. (1997). *Missed opportunities: A new look at disadvantaged college aspirants.* Washington, DC: Education Resources Institute & Institute for Higher Education Policy.

English, L. M. (2009). *International encyclopedia of adult education.* Adelaide, Australia: National Centre for Vocational Education Research (NCVER).

Fairchild, E. E. (2003). Multiple roles of adult learners. *New Directions for Student Services, 102*, 11–16. doi:10.1002/ss.84

Fenske, R. H., Porter, J. D., & Dubrock, C. P. (2000). Tracking financial aid and persistence of women, minority, and needy students in science, engineering, and mathematics. *Research in Higher Education, 41*(1), 67–94. doi:10.1023/A:1007042413040

Gliner, J. A., & Morgan, G. A. (2000). *Research methods in applied settings: An integrated approach to design and analysis*. Mahwah, NJ: Lawrence Erlbaum.

Graham, S. W., Donaldson, J. F., Kasworm, C., & Dirkx, J. (2000). *The experiences of adult undergraduate students—what shapes their learning?* Retrieved from http://www.eric.ed.gov/ERICWebPortal/ search/ detailmini.jsp? _nfpb= true&_ &ERICExtSearch_ SearchValue_0= ED440275&ERICExtSearch_ SearchType_0= no&accno= ED440275

Grimes, S. K. (1995). Targeting academic program to student diversity utilizing learning styles and learning-study strategies. *Journal of College Student Development, 36*, 422–430.

Home, A. M. (1998). Predicting role conflict, overload and contagion in adult women university students with families and jobs. *Adult Education Quarterly, 48*(2), 85–97. doi:10.1177/074171369804800204

Horn, L. J., & Carroll, C. D. (1996). *Nontraditional undergraduates: Trends in enrollment from 1986 to 1992 and persistence and attainment among 1989-90 beginning postsecondary students. Postsecondary Education Descriptive Analysis Reports: Statistical Analysis Report*. Washington, DC: U.S. Government Printing Office.

Hoskins, S. L., & Newstead, S. E. (1997). Degree performance as a function of age, gender, prior qualifications and discipline studied. *Assessment & Evaluation in Higher Education, 22*(3), 317. doi:10.1080/0260293970220305

Hsaio, K. P. (1992). *First-generation college students*. Los Angeles, CA: ERIC Clearinghouse for Junior Colleges.

Inman, W. E., & Mayes, L. D. (1999). The importance of being first: Unique characteristics of first-generation community college students. *Community College Review, 26*(4), 3–22. doi:10.1177/009155219902600402

Ishitani, T. T. (2006). Studying attrition and degree completion behavior among first-generation college students in the United States. *The Journal of Higher Education, 77*(5), 861–885. doi:10.1353/jhe.2006.0042

Johnson, L. G., Schwartz, R. A., & Bower, B. L. (2000). Managing stress among adult women students in community colleges. *Community College Journal of Research and Practice, 24*, 289–300. doi:10.1080/106689200264079

Kasworm, C. (1990). Adult undergraduates in higher education: A review of past research perspectives. *Review of Educational Research, 60*(3), 345–375.

Kasworm, C., Polson, C., & Fishback, S. (2002). *Responding to adult learners in higher education*. Malabar, FL: Krieger.

Kember, D. (1999). Integrating part-time study with family, work and social obligations. *Studies in Higher Education, 24*, 109–124. doi:10.1080/03075079912331380178

Kim, K. A. (2002). Exploring the meaning of "nontraditional" at the community college. *Community College Review, 30*(1), 74–89. doi:10.1177/009155210203000104

Kim, K. A., Hagedorn, M., & Williamson, J. (2004). *Participation in adult education and lifelong learning 2000-01 (Tech. Rep. No. NCES 2004-50)*. Washington, DC: U.S. Government Printing Office.

King, J. E. (2003). Nontraditional attendance and persistence: The cost of students' choices. *New Directions for Higher Education*, (121): 69–84. doi:10.1002/he.102

Knowles, M. S. (1980). *The modern practice of adult education: From pedagogy to andragogy* (2nd ed.). New York, NY: Cambridge Books.

McGivney, V. (2004). Understanding persistence in adult learning. *Journal of Open and Distance Learning, 19*(1), 33–46. doi:10.1080/0268051042000177836

Merriam, S. B. (2005). How adult life transitions foster learning and development. *New Directions for Adult and Continuing Education, 108*, 3–13. doi:10.1002/ace.193

Morstain, B., & Smart, J. (1977). A motivational typology of adult learners. *The Journal of Higher Education, 48*(6), 665–679. doi:10.2307/1979011

National Center for Educational Statistics. (1998). *First-generation students: Undergraduates whose parents never enrolled in postsecondary education.* Washington, DC: U.S. Department of Education.

National Higher Education Research Institute (NHERI). (2007). *The effectiveness of academic programmes at higher educational institutions (HEIs) towards lifelong learning.* Retrieved from http://www.usm.my/ipptn/fileup/ Lifelong%20 Learning.pdf

Padula, M. A. (1994). Reentry women: A literature review with recommendations for counseling and research. *Journal of Counseling and Development, 73*, 10–16.

Pascarella, E., & Terenzini, P. (1991). *How college affects students.* San Francisco, CA: Jossey-Bass.

Reay, D. (1998). 'Always knowing' or 'never being sure': Institutional and familial habituses and higher education choice. *Journal of Education Policy, 13*, 519–529. doi:10.1080/0268093980130405

Reay, D. (2002). Class, authenticity and the transition to higher education for mature students. *The Sociological Review, 50*(3), 398–418. doi:10.1111/1467-954X.00389

Richardson, J. T. E. (1994). Mature students in higher education: I. A literature survey on approaches to studying. *Studies in Higher Education, 19*(3), 309–323. doi:10.1080/0307507941 2331381900

Richardson, J. T. E. (1995). Mature students in higher education: II. An investigation of approaches to studying and academic performance. *Studies in Higher Education, 20*(1), 5–17. doi:10 .1080/03075079512331381760

Richardson, J. T. E., & King, E. (1998). Adult students in higher education: Burden or boon? *The Journal of Higher Education, 69*(1), 65–89. doi:10.2307/2649182

Ritt, E. (2008). *Redefining tradition: Adult learners and higher education.* Retrieved from http://eric.ed.gov/ERICWebPortal/ recordDetail?accno=EJ860772

Robertson, D. L. (1991). Gender differences in the academic progress of adult undergraduates: Patterns and policy implications. *Journal of College Student Development, 32*, 490–496.

Rogers, A. (2002). *Teaching adults.* Berkshire, UK: Open University Press.

Spitzer, T. M. (2000). Predictors of college success: A comparison of traditional and nontraditional age students. *NASPA Journal, 38*(1), 82–98.

Tabachnick, B. G., & Fidell, L. S. (2007). *Using multivariate statistics* (5th ed.). Boston, MA: Allyn & Bacon.

Taniguchi, H., & Kaufman, G. (2005). Degree completion among nontraditional college students. *Social Science Quarterly, 86*(4), 912–927. doi:10.1111/j.0038-4941.2005.00363.x

Terenzini, P. T., Springer, L., Yaeger, P. M., Pascarella, E. T., & Nora, P. M. (1996). First-generation college students: Characteristics, experiences, and cognitive development. *Research in Higher Education, 37*(1), 1–22. doi:10.1007/ BF01680039

Truemen, M., & Hartley, J. (1996). A comparison between the time-management skills and academic performance of mature and traditional-entry university students. *Higher Education*, *32*(2), 199–215. doi:10.1007/BF00138396

Tuttle, T. (2005). *Part-time students: Enrollment and persistence in state of Indiana*. Bloomington, IN: Indiana Project on Academic Success (IPAS).

UNESCO Institute for Lifelong Learning (UIL). (2009). *Global report on adult learning and education*. Hamburg, Germany: UNESCO Institute for Lifelong Learning.

This work was previously published in the International Journal of Adult Vocational Education and Technology, Volume 2, Issue 4, edited by Victor C.X. Wang, pp. 1-16, copyright 2011 by IGI Publishing (an imprint of IGI Global).

Chapter 10
E–Leadership in the New Century

Victor C. X. Wang
California State University - Long Beach, USA

ABSTRACT

This article argues that E-leadership emerged out of technological development among all other major developments in our society. In the virtual environment, leaders are required to lead followers by using different approaches. This is not to say that traditional leadership has no place in the new virtual environment characterized by the constant use of technology. Rather, traditional leadership and leadership style studied and conceptualized by researchers and scholars enhance E-leadership supported by Rogers' facilitative leadership. Leadership theories are meant to be applied to practice. Further, leadership theories can be applied in part or in whole. They are not ideologies that must be followed to the letter.

INTRODUCTION

About 40 percent of the workforce in the United States telecommute from home to their workplaces (Chafkin, 2010), slightly more than 2% of the U.S. employee workforce (2.8 million people, not including the self employed or unpaid volunteers) considers home their primary place of work (Lister, 2010) and roughly one in six students enrolled in higher education — about 3.2 million people —

took at least one online course last fall of 2005, a sharp increase defying predictions that online learning growth is leveling off (Pope, 2006). What are the implications of these numbers? They make E-leadership important and necessary in the new century. They prompt researchers and scholars reexamine leadership and leadership styles in relation to E-leadership.

The literature about leadership and leadership styles has not changed much in the 21st century. Researchers and scholars have studied leadership and leadership styles for years. Leadership theories

DOI: 10.4018/978-1-4666-2062-9.ch010

have been tested in varying situations in different countries. For example, leadership theories by Karl Marx have been applied to countries such as the former Soviet Union, China, North Korea, and Cuba. Have these leadership theories worked for these countries? The answer is to a certain degree, yes. The answer can also be leadership theories are not ideologies that must be applied to the letter. Leadership theories can be applied in part or in whole, or they can be modified based on differing situations. Speaking of situations and circumstances, major economic developments from newly emerged nations and technological breakthroughs coupled with the most recent wars in West Asia and in the Middle East have reshaped the world. They have changed the way people work, think, and, above all, react to leadership theories.

The situations and circumstances surrounding leadership and leadership styles have drastically changed in recent years. The business world has become more competitive and volatile, influenced by such factors as faster technology change, greater international competition, the deregulation of markets, overcapacity in capital-intensive industries, an unstable oil cartel, raiders with junk bonds, and the changing demographics of the work force (Kotter, 1998, p. 40). Due to the changes in situations and circumstances, nowadays, there is downsizing, merging, restructuring and even more laying off of current employees if their leaders consider the skills of the employees as being obsolete. Most job descriptions for leaders specify that leaders must possess skills in the use of technology. Without the skills in the use of technology, leaders are not hired, or employees are not promoted to leadership positions.

Without a doubt, among all those other developments in the new century, technology has played a major role in reshaping the world. Technology has permeated society in general, and major government and economic stakeholders have recognized the importance of incorporating technology throughout education in order to prepare a competitive workforce in a global economy

(Farmer, 2011, p. 230). The United States used to have the largest number of Internet users. To date, the number of Internet users (179.7 million) in China has surpassed that of the United States (163.3 million) now (Schonfeld, 2009). What are the implications for the leadership and leadership styles? Should leaders change the way they see themselves, others, and everything (Cramer & Wasiak, 2006)? Leaders in the past did not depend on technology. Their secretaries may have done everything related to the use of technology. Now leaders are required to do everything themselves related to the use of technology. Does this shift require further changes in leadership and leadership styles? Although the basic tenets of leadership and leadership styles remain the same, regardless of the changes through the ages, our changing environment requires further examination of today's leadership and leadership styles. Nowadays, the term E-leadership has emerged in both business world and in higher education. In K-12 education, E-leadership has also emerged. The purpose of this article is to discuss what constitutes E-leadership in the new century and to reveal its far reaching implications in this fast changing environment.

BACKGROUND

There are many studies associated with leadership style. Most people are familiar with the Ohio State University study on leadership style (Northouse, 2007). Less attention has been paid to a class study by Lippit and White (1958) who examined the leadership styles of youth leaders. According to Jarvis (2002), Lippit and White (1958) highlighted a threefold typology: authoritarian, laissez-faire, and democratic. They found the following:

- Authoritarian leaders create a sense of group dependence on the leader. Their presence holds the group together, and no work was done in their absence;

- Laissez-faire leaders achieve little work whether they were present or absent;
- Democratic leaders achieve group cohesion and harmonious working relationships whether they were present or not.

Since then, their finding has been applied to the business world, higher education etc. The threefold typology regarding leadership style seems to exist in every country as long as there are leaders and followers in any organizations. Authoritarian leaders exist in both authoritarian countries and democratic countries. It would be a mistake to claim that this kind of leadership style exists only in communist countries. Many leaders in democratic countries are more authoritarian than leaders in communist countries. Likewise, it is commonly argued that laissez-faire leaders are everywhere as long as we know their human nature. These leaders do not seem to make each day "count." Perhaps, these leaders are not internally motivated to achieve much. Democratic leaders do strive to achieve group cohesion. Based on this leadership style, new terms have been created in especially higher education. Shared governance, transparency, job rotations are just a few terms to show that these terms have been derived from this particular leadership style.

Later, other studies broke down the three leadership styles and divided them into more detailed categories. Numerous studies (Badaracco, 1998; Farkas & Wetlaufer, 1998; Heifetz & Laurie, 1998; Mintzberg, 1998; Nohria & Berkley, 1998; Teal, 1998; Zaleznik, 1998) indicated that leadership should be viewed dialectically. On the one hand, it should be leader-centered. This is the so-called "follow me" approach. No diversity is encouraged in this kind of leadership. The advantage of this leadership is that it is an easier form of leadership because no novel ideas or innovations are required on the part of the followers. The disadvantage of this kind of leadership is that emergence of leadership from followers is not encouraged. Whatever goals leaders have, followers do not buy into them.

The follow me approach is prone to creating dictatorship in any organizations. Because emergence of leadership from followers is not encouraged, hard feelings may be created between leaders and followers. Turn-over rate among employees may be high. This type of leader may eventually alienate themselves from their followers. In reality, it is not surprising that followers may rise up against these leaders and cause these leaders to be removed from their positions. These leaders tend to hire followers that share the same philosophies with them. The followers may come from the same race as their leaders. Diversity to these leaders is not something that is on their priority list.

On the other hand, there is other-centered leadership. The obvious advantage of this kind of leadership is that people buy into something leaders try to promote. For example, leaders may help set goals collaboratively with their followers. Leaders involve followers in every step of their planning process. People take ownership. People assume responsibility for all their actions. Leaders help people get involved in tasks. Based on this kind of leadership style, leaders do their best to motivate their followers, align them and even set the direction and structure for their followers. This is not to say that leaders are "hands-off" type of leaders. Rather, their goal is to encourage change among followers by motivating followers to do a good job. The disadvantage of this kind of leadership is that it is not an easier form of leadership. For example, aligning followers may be the most difficult to accomplish because people do have differences, philosophies etc.

Starting in the 1960s and 1970s, people grew disillusioned with this dichotomy of leadership: leader-centered versus other-centered. They developed a new kind of leadership, facilitative leadership, from Rogers's (1951, 1961, 1969, 1980) facilitative approach to teaching:

- Facilitative leadership allows for continuity of operation;

- Facilitative leadership recognizes that all people possess different values and beliefs;
- Facilitative leadership encourages objectivity in program evaluation;
- Facilitative leadership leads to shared leadership, and the effect of shared leadership do have the potential to exceed the sum of effects generated by individual members with one status leader. (this is called synergism)

Facilitative leadership became popular simply because people began to recognize humanism (Wang & King, 2006) where every one has unlimited potential for learning. People have a propensity to become self-directed in learning (Knowles, Holton, & Swanson, 1998, 2005). Although this type of leadership is not the same as other-centered leadership, there are similarities between the two types of leadership. Regarding facilitative leadership, people are capable of taking control of their own learning. Above all, people are responsible for their own actions and are responsible for making decisions. A leader is not synonymous with a dictator. The role of a leader is that of a helper, a facilitator who makes things easier for their followers. It is this type of leadership that can be easily translated into E-leadership in the new century. Adult learning theory is firmly based on facilitative leadership. In every educational leadership program, a course titled Adult Learning Theory is taught simply to show that E-leadership is derived from facilitative leadership and that E-leadership will remain popular in the virtual teaching and learning environment as long as technology is used to achieve desired student learning outcomes.

One of the most authoritative studies was conducted by Hersey and Blanchard (1969) regarding leadership quadrants (as cited in Wang, 2006, p. 49). From Hersey and Blanchard's (1969) study, Ohio State University, USA developed the leadership quadrants seen in Figure 1 that have

Figure 1. Leadership quadrants

	Structure	
Consideration	High consideration Low structure	High consideration High structure
	Low consideration Low structure	High structure Low consideration

been widely applied in the business world and higher education.

Other scholars refer to structure as "task" and consideration as "relationship." Some leaders prefer high structure and high consideration. Once they focus on task instead of relationship, their leadership styles can be summarized as the following:

- They are autocratic;
- They are authoritarian;
- They are production-oriented;
- They prefer goal achievement;
- They apply a theory X-hard approach to leadership.

Other leaders prefer high consideration and low structure. Once they focus on relationship, their leadership styles can be summarized as the following:

- They are democratic;
- They are equalitarian;
- They are employee-oriented;
- They enjoy group maintenance;
- Their leadership approach is considered soft.

The most recent research regarding leadership was conducted by Warren Bennis. He argued that transformational leadership is characterized by the ability of a person to reach the souls of others in a fashion, which raises human consciousness, builds meanings, and inspires human intent that is the source of power (Bennis, 1989; Bennis & Nanus, 1997). Bennis (1989, 1997) defined leadership as being capable of achieving the following:

- Building a vision;
- Establishing goals;
- Providing intellectual stimulation;
- Offering individualized support;
- Modeling best practices and important organizational values;
- Demonstrating high performance expectations;
- Creating a productive organizational culture;
- Developing structures to foster participation in organizational decisions.

A closer examination of Bennis's definition of leadership reveals that his definition does not deviate much from structure (task) and consideration (relationship). What leaders do constantly revolves around these two basic factors. The current research focuses more on the effective leadership. Numerous studies show that the effective leader:

- Should provide direction and structure to the group;
- Should be a good planner;
- Should organize the task/organize the group;
- Should use an agenda;
- Should be a skillful communicator;
- Have a tendency to talk more than the average member of a group does;
- Should be able to adapt leadership styles to meet the needs of the group;
- Should be sensitive to the group's current situation and adapt to meet changing needs of followers. (as cited in Wang, 2006, p. 126)

Will the historical research about leadership and leadership styles apply to the new situations and circumstances in new century? What are their educational implications? The following section addresses these questions in more detail.

ELECTRONIC LEADERSHIP IN THE NEW CENTURY

The situation in the new century is such that "you think you understand the situation, but what you don't understand is that the situation just changed" (Toffler, 1971, 1980, 1990). Leadership (Kotter, 1998) is about coping with change (p. 40). Although the situations in the new information age change faster than people can think, the basic tenets of leadership may take on some new meanings but basically remain the same. Scholars and researchers still research E-leadership revolving around the historical issues.

Leaders in the new information age are still required to lead an organization to constructive change by setting a direction. Setting the direction is the leader's responsibility. Leaders are supposed to be more knowledgeable in a certain field. Leaders are supposed to have more technical skills in a certain field. Leaders are supposed to be more ethical. Leaders are supposed to have more human skills. Above all, leaders are supposed to have more conceptual skills. Followers are basically dependent in nature, although some followers perform much better without being told what to do. Leaders in any organization need to set the direction and structure to ensure that followers will perform based on their direction and structure. In other words, leaders set the parameters, and followers should not cross the parameters. In the virtual environment, leaders apply facilitative leadership because leaders cannot "watch" their followers perform. This does not mean giving up the responsibility of setting the direction and structure. After setting the direction and structure, then leaders need to change their leadership roles from being directive to being facilitative due to the virtual environment. This is where E-leadership is needed, and E-leadership means a totally different leadership style needed in the virtual environment.

Leaders are supposed to develop a vision of the future along with strategies for producing the changes needed to achieve that vision. This is only a beginning for leaders. Then they need to communicate the new direction to those who can create coalitions that understand the vision and are committed to its achievement. In other words, a vision has to be realistic. If it is beyond the followers, there is no way to achieve it. To communicate a vision to followers requires motivating and inspiring. Motivating and inspiring can keep followers moving in the right direction, despite obstacles to change, by appealing to basic but often untapped human needs, values, and emotions (Kotter, 1998). If leaders choose to control followers, they do not lead, they manage.

Effective leaders are not synonymous with effective managers. Managers cope with day-to-day tasks, not change. Simple planning is a management process. Leaders use more data and look for patterns and themes and relationships and then create a vision and strategies. To motivate and inspire followers, E-leadership skills are needed. Again, facilitative leadership as emphasized by Rogers (1951, 1961, 1969, 1980) are useful and helpful. Leaders should forget about subjectivity in program evaluation. Instead, objectivity in program evaluation is stressed. Leaders are committed to shared leadership, which means leaders must delegate power to followers. Followers may be experts in the virtual environment. Followers may have prior experience. Leaders must tap into followers' prior experience. Every follower should be allowed to voice his/her opinion and above all, leaders should respect and value different values and beliefs. In other words, leaders should serve as "honest brokers" and allow for continuity of operation. The leader's vision should be communicated constantly among followers via technological means such as the Internet.

People work in systems or hierarchies. Trying to get people to comprehend a vision of an alternative future is a communications challenge. Those who can motivate rather than control people are considered effective leaders. There is a variety of ways to motivate people. Articulating the organization's vision is of course number one. More importantly, the effective leaders involve people in deciding how to achieve the organization's vision. Certainly, this gives people a sense of control so that people can take ownership of leadership. This is not to say that the effective leaders never coach, provide feedback, or model. Rather, people need leaders to do these when followers are dependent and do not have the expertise to achieve a goal. Finally, the effective leaders recognize and reward success. A simple paragraph via the Internet technology may mean a great deal to followers.

Effective leaders recognize and reward success by writing and posting accurate stories about employee success on the Internet. Email communication should not be one way communication. In most organizations, leaders can email all followers, and followers are not supposed to write back if they have different opinions. These leaders do not possess E-leadership skills. The new century E-leadership requires leaders to allow followers to write back to them to voice their opinions and concerns. And these opinions and concerns should be addressed in a timely manner before they are escalated into big issues. Email communication system should be used as a multiple-way communication between leaders and followers.

Kotter (1998) pointed out that creating a culture of leadership can make people value strong leadership and strive to create it. In some authoritarian cultures, people may fear leadership. However, leadership is inherent in all social systems and in all human relationships. It is an aspect of any and all relationships among people. Hence, it is inescapable and neutral, neither good nor bad. No wonder some scholars argue that creating a culture of leadership is the ultimate act of leadership. Creating a culture of leadership does not mean that leaders bombard followers with their constant email messages. It is not surprising that employees receive multiple messages via email or other electronic means per day. All these messages may mean more or less the same things. When this happens, E-leadership may annoy employees more than motivate them to work harder. Being accurate and flexible in the virtual environment is more crucial to creating a culture of leadership. Followers need to change their view about leadership since it is inherent in all human relationships. It is neither good nor bad. There is nothing to fear about leadership. E-leadership requires leaders to possess not only facilitative leadership, but also a lot more other skills such as communication skills, writing skills, work ethics and working philosophies.

FUTURE TRENDS

Some people fear leadership while others think it is mystical and mysterious. Still others think that leadership has to do with charisma or other exotic personality traits. Really, leadership emerges out of a culture of leadership. This is not to say that leadership cannot emerge out of dismal environment. Rather, great leadership has arisen out of extremely bad conditions. For example, the brilliant leadership by Winston Churchill arose in the United Kingdom after Britain was heavily bombed by Hitler. Mao developed highly successful guerrilla tactics after his army was repeatedly cornered by his chief opponent, Jiang.

This information age is characterized by high speed development of technology. The internet provides fertile ground for creativity. Human beings' potential is extended beyond people's imagination. Global economy is a given. In such an environment, will traditional leadership and leadership styles work for today's organizations? The answer is yes and no. For the information age, traditional leadership does provide answers while

in extreme circumstances, it does not. When it does not, we have to turn to future research for help.

One obvious future trend will be to examine what effective leaders really do in order to determine whether they help achieve an organization's vision. Common sense tells us that when leaders do not do their homework, an organization will collapse sooner rather than later. What leaders say may not have as much an impact as what they really do on today's organizations.

Although ample research has been conducted, many people still confuse management with leadership. Some people think managers are leaders and leaders are managers. In fact, they are totally different. They have different roles. What managers and leaders do have different impacts on today's organizations. While management is about coping with complexity, leadership is about coping with change. They are two distinctive and complementary systems of action. Both are important and necessary in today's information age and business environment. One area of research in the future can be will technology make a leader's job easy or a manager's job easy? Profound comparison may be needed in order to determine whose job would be easier.

The same old argument regarding whether leadership emerges naturally or leadership can be taught will surface again in the new era. This has been an unsettling question for scholars and researchers. More research in this area will be conducted in the future. One enhancing research question can be will technology facilitate the emergence of E-leadership in the new century?

CONCLUSION

This article examined some of the old issues and some new issues regarding leadership and leadership styles. E-leadership did not grow out of vacuum. Instead, it emerged out of a totally new environment, the virtual environment which is characterized by faster technology change (King,

2005), greater international competition (Petty & Brewer, 2005), the deregulation of markets, overcapacity in capital-intensive industries, an unstable oil cartel, raiders with junk bonds, and the changing demographics of the work force. Leadership is geared to help an organization achieve its vision. Even though the times have changed, Bennis's transformational leadership and Hersey and Blanchard's situational leadership are not outmoded. In fact, both Bennis and Hersey and Blanchard addressed the same type of leadership. They just did it from different angles. The most successful leaders in today's organizations are those who truly adapt to the current needs and future needs of their followers. The most successful leaders are those who change their roles according to different situations that may arise out of this virtual environment. No leadership is deemed successful unless it works for an organization. Numerous studies indicate that the best leadership is the one that can cope with change by changing its roles according to its relationship with followers and environments. In the new century, almost all leaders and followers are required to depend on technology for work. The implication may mean that leaders are required to apply E-leadership to practice in the virtual environment. Although the roles of today's e-leadership go beyond the four roles specified in the quadrants seen in Figure 2, the quadrants are illustrative of what today's leaders really need to do, depending on their followers' need for direction and need for support. In fact, the best leaders are those who are able to go in and out of those quadrants freely (Hersey & Blanchard, 1969; Wang, 2006).

This article also demonstrated that E-leadership is derived from the adult learning theory, which is derived from Rogers' facilitative leadership. In the virtual environment, facilitative leadership is the best approach to leading followers. Is this approach different from the leadership quadrants? They support each other.

Figure 2. Leadership roles

REFERENCES

Badaracco, J. L. (1998). The discipline of building character. In *Harvard business review on leadership* (pp. 89–114). Boston: Harvard Business School Publishing.

Bennis, W. (1989). *On becoming a leader*. Wilmington, MA: Addison-Wesley Publishing Company.

Bennis, W., & Nanus, B. (1997). *Leaders' strategies for taking charge* (2nd ed.). New York: Harper Collins Publishers.

Chafkin, M. (2010). *Telecommuting by the numbers*. Retrieved from http://www.inc.com/magazine/20100401/telecommuting-by-the-numbers.html

Cramer, K. D., & Wasiak, H. (2006). *Change the way you see everything: Through asset-based thinking*. Philadelphia: Running Press.

Farkas, C. M., & Wetlaufer, S. (1998). The ways executive officers lead. In *Harvard business review on leadership* (pp. 115–146). Boston: Harvard Business School Publishing.

Farmer, L. (2011). Career and technical education technology: Three decades in review and technological trends in the future. In Wang, V. C. X. (Ed.), *Definitive readings in the history, philosophy, practice and theories of career and technical education* (pp. 216–231). Hershey, PA; Hangzhou, China: Information Science Reference and Zhejiang University Press.

Heifetz, R. A., & Laurie, D. L. (1998). The work of leadership. In *Harvard Business Review on Leadership* (pp. 171–198). Boston, MA: Harvard Business School Publishing.

Hersey, P., & Blanchard, K. (1969). *Management of organizational behavior: Utilizing human resources*. Englewood Cliffs, NJ: Prentice-Hall.

Jarvis, P. (2002). Teaching styles and teaching methods. In *The theory & practice of teaching* (pp. 22–30). London: Kogan Page.

King, K. P. (2005). *Bringing transformative learning to life*. Malabar, FL: Krieger.

Knowles, M. S., Holton, E., & Swanson, A. (1998). *The adult learner*. Houston, TX: Gulf Publishing Company.

Knowles, M. S., Holton, E., & Swanson, A. (2005). *The adult learner* (6th ed.). Boston: Elsevier Butterworth Heinemann.

Kotter, J. P. (1998). What leaders really do. In *Harvard Business Review on Leadership* (pp. 37–60). Boston: Harvard Business School Publishing.

Lippit, R., & White, R. K. (1958). An experimental study of leadership and group life. In Maccoby, E. E., (Eds.), *Readings in Social Psychology* (3rd ed.). New York: Holt.

Lister, K. (2010). *Telework research network*. Retrieved from http://undress4success.com/research/people-telecommute/

Mintzberg, H. (1998). The manager's job: Folklore and fact. In *Harvard Business Review on Leadership* (pp. 1–36). Boston: Harvard Business School Publishing.

Nohria, N., & Berkley, J. D. (1998). Whatever happened to the take-charge manager? In *Harvard Business Review on Leadership* (pp. 199–222). Boston: Harvard Business School Publishing.

Northouse, P. G. (2007). *Leadership theory and practice* (4th ed.). Thousand Oaks, CA: Sage.

Petty, G. C., & Brewer, E. W. (2005). Perspectives of a healthy work ethic in a 21st-century international community. *International Journal of Vocational Education and Training, 13*(1), 93–104.

Pope, J. (2006). *Number of students taking online courses rises*. Retrieved from http://www.usatoday.com/tech/news/2006-11-09-online-learning_x.htm

Rogers, C. R. (1951). *Client-centered therapy*. Boston: Houghton-Mifflin.

Rogers, C. R. (1961). *On become a person*. Boston: Houghton-Mifflin.

Rogers, C. R. (1969). *Freedom to learn*. Columbus, OH: Merrill.

Rogers, C. R. (1980). *A way of being*. Boston: Houghton Mifflin.

Schonfeld, E. (2009). *Techcrunch*. Retrieved from http://techcrunch.com/ 2009/01/23/ comscore-internet- population- passes- one- billion- top-15- countries/

Teal, T. (1998). The human side of management. In *Harvard Business Review on Leadership* (pp. 147–170). Boston: Harvard Business School Publishing.

Toffler, A. (1971). *Future shock*. New York: Bantam Books.

Toffler, A. (1980). *The third wave*. New York: Morrow.

Toffler, A. (1990). *Powershift: Knowledge, wealth, and violence at the edge of the 21ˢᵗ century*. New York: Bantam Books.

Wang, V. C. X. (2005). Perceptions of the teaching preferences of online instructors. *Journal on Excellence in College Teaching, 16*(3), 33–53.

Wang, V. C. X. (2006). *Essential elements for andragogical styles and methods: How to create andragogical modes in adult education*. Boston: Pearson Education.

Wang, V. C. X., & King, K. P. (2006). *Understanding Mezirow's theory of reflectivity from Confucian perspectives: A model and perspective*. Retrieved from http://radicalpedagogy.icaap.org/content/issue8_1/wang.html

Zaleznik, A. (1998). Managers and leaders: Are they different? In *Harvard Business Review on Leadership* (pp. 61–88). Boston: Harvard Business School Publishing.

This work was previously published in the International Journal of Adult Vocational Education and Technology, Volume 2, Issue 1, edited by Victor C.X. Wang, pp. 50-59, copyright 2011 by IGI Publishing (an imprint of IGI Global).

Chapter 11
A Case Study of an Intervention to Support Ed.D. Students in Dissertation Writing

Beth Kania-Gosche
Lindenwood University, USA

Lynda Leavitt
Lindenwood University, USA

ABSTRACT

Dissertation writing is often the most challenging aspect of the doctoral program. In an effort to raise completion rates and lower time-to-degree as well as increase student satisfaction with the program, professors in an Ed.D. program developed a semester-long course to support students writing their dissertations. This case study describes the development of the course and the implementation of the first semester. The course consisted of a series of workshops on various aspects of dissertation writing as well as various other activities such as peer review. The students did not receive a grade for the course. After reviewing data, students in the course were classified by their productivity that semester and engagement in the course. Students who were highly engaged but not highly productive were the most prevalent group. In this article, the authors also provide follow-up, including changes made the next semester and data on student completion.

INTRODUCTION

While most high schools and undergraduate programs in the United States intensely focus on graduation rates, the spotlight is only recently beginning to shift to this issue for graduate programs.

As enrollment in graduate programs increase and jobs require more education, graduate programs must begin to examine their own completion data in detail (Wendler et al., 2010). Doctoral programs are notorious for their attrition rates, which are even worse than medical or law schools (Lovitts & Nelson, 2000). Attrition from doctoral programs

DOI: 10.4018/978-1-4666-2062-9.ch011

is rarely calculated on a program or institutional level, and Lovitts and Nelson (2000) call it a "national crisis." While not every student who enrolls in a doctoral program should necessarily graduate, universities and departments should investigate the reasons students fail to complete the program, like Golde (2000) did in his four case studies of students who left their programs. Often, faculty or administrators believe that students fail to graduate because of their own shortcomings rather than because of the program (Lovitts & Nelson, 2000). If the reasons can be traced to university or department policy, lack of writing or research skills, or the dissertation process itself, then supports or professional development could be offered to the students and faculty in these area.

The Council of Graduate Schools (CGS) (2010) made many such recommendations after conducting a seven year study on Ph.D. Completion. "There is widespread recognition that students at the dissertation stage feel isolated and vulnerable and universities are putting into place a number of efforts to help students overcome these feelings and remain on track" (CGS, 2010, p. 57). While the three part monograph detailing the Ph.D. Completion Project provided brief descriptions of some of the interventions different programs are utilizing, longitudinal data is still being collected on the effectiveness of the interventions. Other studies have been conducted detailing specific interventions at specific institutions such as Nerad and Miller's (1997) description of one university's efforts to increase the doctoral graduation rates in the humanities and social sciences, which at the time had the longest time to completion and lowest completion rates. They also conducted a qualitative study to verify the quantitative completion information. From this information, they created "an intellectual support structure to help students at the dissertation-writing stage of the doctoral program break the isolation, establish intellectual communities, overcome their anxieties about the dissertation's scope and character, and make the transition from 'book reading' to 'book writing'"

(p. 81). Their interventions, including a series of interdisciplinary dissertation writing workshops, were successful in increasing completion in these fields by 11%. Other universities must follow this example. The authors of this case study will examine not only the content and development of one such intervention but data evaluating its immediate effectiveness. Data are still being collected on if the intervention has any impact on completion rates and time-to-degree longitudinally.

LITERATURE OF BEST PRACTICES FOR DISSERTATION WRITING

For most new faculty, their only experience with dissertation supervision was their own as a student. Thus, they may mentor doctoral students as they were mentored, with little knowledge of what is actually effective or how to meet the needs of different doctoral students. "The traditional model of graduate student supervision can no longer work. It is simply inadequate to the demands of a situation where many supervisors are barely socialized into the demands and rigours of an academic scholarly and research culture" (Yeatman, 1995, p. 9). Kluever (1997) compared responses of doctoral graduates and ABD students in the field of education, finding "regularly scheduled meetings with an advisor, seminars on approaching the dissertation, and a thorough understanding of college and university dissertation guidelines were rated most highly" by completers (p. 52). Similarly, De Valero (2001) examined departmental factors and their influence on doctoral student time-to-degree, making recommendations such as orientations and dissertation workshops, but not implementing any such programs. While articles have been published describing the different responsibilities of a dissertation supervisor, such as "Cheerleader, Coach, Counselor, Critic: Support and Challenge Roles of the Dissertation Advisor" (Spilleti & Moisiewicz, 2004), few have examined best practices in the field (Creighton, Parks, & Creighton, 2008; Mullen, 2007; Yeatman, 1995).

Although the completion of the dissertation is undoubtedly of importance to graduate students, the broader issue for faculty is that doctoral students are prepared to conduct quality research. The dissertation, for many doctoral students, is their first experience with academic culture and writing. In their large-scale study of doctoral students, Nettles and Millett (2006, p. 44) wrote, "An important area of the doctoral experience needing more focused attention is the dissertation process. The variability of this document, depending on institution, department, and individual committee members, seem to constitute a research project in and of itself." Thus, it may take dissertation supervisors years to even learn the procedures and processes of the department, and these will probably be different than the university where they themselves graduated.

Faculty's expectations of the dissertation are rarely articulated beyond formatting requirements. Lovitts' (2007) book *Making the Implicit Explicit* examined the expectations of experienced dissertation supervisors in various disciplines, resulting in rubrics. She noted, "virtually no research exists in the United States on the standards used by faculty to judge dissertations, most likely because dissertation assessment is viewed as a private affair" (p. 4). Dissertation supervision is also often viewed as a personal preference rather than a skill, like teaching, that could be enhanced by examining one's own practice and that of others.

More specifically, in the field of education, little research has been written on dissertation research and writing for Ed.D. students, except Butin's (2010) *The Education Dissertation* which is an advice book. In this book, he articulated the differences between "traditional" doctoral students in Ph.D. programs and the typical Ed.D. student. These students often work a demanding full time job as a school leader, and they may have spouses and families, a sentiment echoed in other literature about the Ed.D. (Goldring & Shuerman, 2009).

Nettles and Millett (2006) noted that education doctoral students had on average 12 years between completion of a bachelor's degree and enrollment in a doctoral program, while most traditional Ph.D. students progress through their masters and continue immediately with a doctorate.

In addition, Ed.D. programs are also notoriously larger than traditional Ph.D. programs. In the introduction to a themed issue of the *Peabody Journal of Education* on the Ed.D., Guthrie and Marsh (2009) noted, "Literally hundreds of colleges and universities offer the doctor of education degree (Ed.D.), and annually issue hundreds of thousands of degrees" (p. 1). The course described in this case study is one way to reach a large number of students with helpful information and support about dissertation writing, while requiring little time from faculty.

Little research has examined the effectiveness of specific strategies to facilitate dissertation completion in *any* discipline, and the intervention described here has only been implemented for two semesters. This article will examine an intervention of a dissertation writing course, based on dissertation completion research as well as literature in other fields, since so few best practices have been established in this area. Even if a solid link between interventions and increased completion rates cannot be established, the relationship between satisfaction and persistence in a program is well established (e.g., Nettles & Millett, 2006). If faculty can increase doctoral student satisfaction with the program and with the dissertation writing process, everyone benefits.

DEVELOPMENT OF THE DISSERTATION WRITING COURSE

The organization of the dissertation writing hours in this program was different than most traditional Ph.D. programs, using a concurrent approach to the dissertation (Willis, Inman, & Valenti, 2010). Rather than 12 credit hours of dissertation writing, which essentially was independent study supervised by the student's dissertation chair, this program embedded the dissertation writing hours throughout the program to encourage students to select a topic and develop their research skills. The last course was called Dissertation Writing. This was the last official course in the program, although students had to pay a continuous enrollment fee for subsequent semesters until they defended their dissertations. In the Spring of 2010, the Dissertation Writing was completely redesigned based on doctoral student and faculty feedback and data from an anonymous, electronic student satisfaction survey. The course was redesigned in response to concerns about the program's completion rate and time-to-degree.

The instructor of this course, sought to clarify specific issues that applied to majority of the students, so that chairs could focus on the specifics of each individual student's research and results. The instructor was a former high school English teacher, so she drew on her own experience and knowledge of teaching writing. The instructor's goal was also to create a supportive community of students who were all working toward the same objective of dissertation completion. This particular institution did not have the cohort system that is common in other Ed.D. programs, and the instructor did not want students to feel isolated during the most challenging time in their program, a common feeling (CGS, 2010). In addition, many doctoral faculty served on a large number of dissertation committees. The instructor wanted to make their role about the research and content of the dissertation rather than APA or grammar.

Following the advice of Butin (2010), the instructor incorporated detailed and concrete strategies to support our students' ultimate success (e.g., clarifying theoretical frameworks and research designs, discussing the minutiae of APA style and bibliographic reference tools, strategizing library research skills and the most effective means by which to do a literature review) (p. 7).

Rather than defining the dissertation as a journey, Butin (2010) referred to it as a process. It is this practical approach that was the driving force behind the Dissertation Writing course. The instructor could help students improve the organization and flow of their writing, no matter the topic or methodology, with her training as a writing teacher. Butin also emphasized the importance of treating doctoral students as the accomplished professionals they are, as adults.

The program at this institution had large numbers, but the graduation rate was about 42%. Time-to-degree was a concern, particularly the amount of time students took to progress through the editing process before official submission of their dissertation to the library. In the Spring of 2010, the first semester of implementation, 36 students were enrolled in the dissertation writing course with the same number the following fall. At the same time, over 70 additional students were continuously enrolled, at the infamous all but dissertation or ABD stage. The instructor of the Dissertation Writing course invited these students to attend the parts of the course they needed, even if they were not officially on the roster for that semester. In short, a way was needed for a large number of doctoral students to receive the same information and apply it to their own dissertation writing. Faculty often had students soliciting them for writing help, but they needed strategies to evaluate and correct their own writing rather than relying on faculty members to give them individual feedback on elements such as organization, grammar, and APA citations, a process which could take weeks or even months with the large numbers of students with which we worked.

The instructor with colleagues and doctoral students developed a list of specific areas where students struggled when writing the dissertation. Rather a traditional course schedule, students had the option of attendance at class when the topic was an area of weakness. From this list, the instructor created a schedule of workshops covering these different areas. Each workshop was taught by one of the instructors or by a guest speaker. Guest speakers included librarians, alumni of the program, and other doctoral faculty with specific expertise particularly quantitative and qualitative research. Students had to attend eight of the 16 workshops.

The first class students created a learning contract based on the work of Malcolm Knowles (Knowles, Holton, & Swanson, 1998). In this contract, students wrote their own goals and deadlines. They selected which workshops and other campus resources they would utilize to meet each of their goals. However, this document and its goals and deadlines was intended only to foster self-directedness. The professors of the course did not actually give the students a grade. Students received a grade of "Incomplete" until they defended their dissertation. In this way, the course was truly about achieving the objective of dissertation completion rather than earning a grade. So, while the instructor recommended students attend eight workshops, they, in all reality, did not have to attend any.

While the content of the workshops was somewhat similar to Nerad and Miller's (1997) descriptions of UC Berkley's "Practical Strategies for Dissertation Writing" and the CGS accounting of other university's similar interventions, the organization and availability was very different in this study. The workshops were designed not only to increase student satisfaction with the dissertation writing process but also to foster self-directedness in dissertation writing through the incorporation of the principles of andragogy (Knowles, Holton, & Swanson, 1998). In alignment with these principles, I invited all ABD students to attend any workshop they thought would benefit them. This also enabled current students in the class to know they could attend a workshop the next semester if they were not ready. In addition, all materials from the workshops were available online, so students could access the materials at any point, even months before the workshop was officially scheduled. The class met in a computer lab, so students could open their own dissertation drafts and make changes on the spot. Workshops were held from 5:00-6:30 Mondays and Tuesdays.

METHODOLOGY

For the initial pilot of the course, the instructor gathered multiple forms of data to describe the intervention and evaluate its effectiveness. This data was later used to make modifications to subsequent offerings of the course; analysis did not occur until after the course was complete. The authors of this article continue to examine the completion and time-to-degree data from students who have experienced the new format of the Dissertation Writing course. The instructor of the course collected quantitative data including number of workshops attended, number of pages added, number of references added, and activity on the course WebCT site. While number of pages or references added is not necessarily a sign of quality, it is a quantifiable, verifiable piece of data that could be collected easily. This data was used to measure student engagement (attendance and website activity) and student productivity (number of pages and references). In addition, the instructor used the learning contract, written reflections students completed at the end of every workshop, students' dissertation drafts, observations of the course, and her own reflective journaling to further describe and evaluate the course.

Data analysis led to categorizing the students in a matrix of their productivity and engagement as displayed in Table 1. High Engagement High Productivity (HEHP) students responded well to the new format of the course. They attended more than eight workshops and made clear progress by adding pages, obtaining IRB approval, extensively revising previous drafts, and collecting and analyzing data. High Engagement Low Productivity (HELP) students attended more than eight workshops but did not add much to their dissertation in the course of the semester. Low Engagement

Table 1. Quadrants of Ed.D. student productivity and engagement

Low Engagement, High Productivity (LEHP)	High Engagement, High Productivity (HEHP)
Low Engagement, Low Productivity (LELP)	High Engagement, Low Productivity (HELP)

Low Productivity (LELP) students attended less than eight workshops and made little progress in their writing during the course. Low Engagement High Productivity students (LEHP) followed the traditional model of dissertation writing. Doctoral candidates are often expected to be highly engaged in dissertation writing without the regular meetings and deadlines of coursework. These students were highly self-directed and attended less than eight workshops, perhaps because they did not feel the need.

DESCRIPTION OF THE DISSERTATION WRITING COURSE

The computer lab where the workshops took place was reserved for the class from 4:30 until 9:30 in the evening on Mondays and Tuesdays. At times the computer lab was beneficial because students could open their dissertation document and make changes. Yet, at other times, students had to be reminded to turn off their screens so they would focus on the guest speaker. Especially at the beginning of the semester, a handful of students stayed and worked in the lab after every workshop. The instructor utilized this time to meet one on one with students. There were several workshops where students had to stand in the back because every one of the 30 seats were full. This was in part because the workshops were open to any ABD student as well. all dissertation committee chairs were also invited, but none of them ever attended, probably because of an already overwhelming workload.

In Spring of 2010, the class consisted of 36 students. One student had her dissertation essentially completed before the class began, so she did not attend any workshops. Fourteen of the students in this class were male (39%), and 22 were female (61%). Twenty of these students were Caucasian (55%), and 16 were African American (44%). An overwhelming majority of students worked in K-12 public schools, some of them in struggling urban schools. These students held a variety of jobs within public schools including teachers, principals, special education coordinators, or assistant superintendents. Three students worked in higher education, and three other students held jobs in other fields. The demographics of this group were consistent with the Ed.D. program's enrollment overall.

As much as possible, the workshops were designed to be interactive. The instructor gave many examples, either from published journal articles or from her own work, including a draft of this article. Students wrote in their reflections at the end of the workshops comments such as "having a successful example of a finished product was helpful" and "I think I that I will go back through your sample paper and highlight items I need to include in my paper" (Kania-Gosche, 2010). In several workshops the instructor gave students a few pages from her own dissertation and asked them to make suggested corrections in groups. The class then discussed the strengths and weaknesses, and most students were shocked to learn that the writing they had so heavily criticized was the instructor's own.

The class climate of these workshops was important, consistent with the principles of adult learning (Knowles et al., 1998). The instructor encouraged students to stop with questions at any point. "The conversation made a comfortable climate, in turn my volunteers shared much more info!" one student wrote in a workshop reflection. "Love the openness to ask questions when we have them, and love that you even see when we have confused looks!" wrote another.

At the end of every workshop, students wrote a reflection, responding to several questions that changed depending on the workshop. This was how the instructors kept track of attendance. This was data was used to improve subsequent workshops. These reflections were almost all positive, and the last question for the reflection asked students how they were going to apply what they learned to their own dissertation. In the grammar workshop, almost every student wrote he or she had learned the difference between parentheses and brackets. only spent about two minutes on this topic, but apparently, it was the most memorable.

One workshop that focused more on motivation and inspiration rather than writing skills was the alumni panel. The instructor invited three students who had completed or nearly completed their dissertation in the Fall of 2009. One student summarized what he had learned in that workshop, "I learned that the dissertation process is difficult but attainable. There are no right or wrong answers. Things change and situations change. You have to be able to take constructive suggestions and use the information wisely." Another student wrote "[The workshop] validated how I am approaching this process-giving up weekends; just do it, revise, rewrite, get critical feedback, then rewrite some more. I feel good about where I am because this weekend I did not want to stop working." *Validating* was a word that appeared in several of the reflections for this workshop. Although the content of this workshop was not a specific dissertation writing skill, it was one of the most valuable for the students, demonstrating how the course was also about emotional support not just writing skills.

The three instructors of the course provided feedback on student writing in regard to APA, format, and grammar. The focus of the actual research methodology was left to the chairs, but the instructors could help with creating tables and figures, organizing the literature review, etc. Any feedback was copied to the chair of the student's dissertation committee. Most of the feedback was electronic using the comments and track changes on Microsoft Word 2007.

The course culminated with student presentations in preparation for their dissertation defenses. The students themselves created the scoring guide for this activity in groups. This activity benefitted some students more than others. For those who had collected data, the presentation was a positive experience for both the audience and the presenter. For those who had made little progress, the presentations only emphasized how far behind they were. Students in the HEHP group expressed their surprise to the instructor after the presentations. They assumed that everyone in the course was making the same progress they were.

EVALUATION OF THE DISSERTATION WRITING COURSE

Regarding the objective of improving student satisfaction with the dissertation experience, the workshops were a success. Students indicated they felt more comfortable with the expectations of a dissertation as well as having specific strategies to improve their writing. "I think this format is very beneficial and supportive. The guidance is really giving me tools to make meaningful progress," one student wrote. The reflection/evaluation that students completed at the end of each workshop were almost all positive. The average number of workshops attended was 8.44, with a low of 4 and a high of 15. Of the 36 students in the class, 24 (67%) attended eight or more workshops, and 11 (30%) students attended ten or more. These workshops were also open to students who had completed all coursework (including the previous format of the Dissertation Writing course) but not the dissertation. Twelve of these students attended throughout the semester.

However, almost none of the students achieved the learning objectives of their contract. However, perhaps this is because students had unrealistic expectations for dissertation completion at the beginning of the class, and the instructor also probably had unrealistic expectations for their accomplishments in one semester. The instructor asked students to email their working draft the first night of class, at midterm, and at the end of the course, so their progress could be tracked. Some students made great progress, while others stalled. Also, the learning contracts were somewhat forgotten by the end of class, partially because students did not receive a grade in the class. The instructor did not specifically ask students to reevaluate their goals halfway through the semester and write a reflection or evaluate at the end of the course. As the workshops progressed, some students told me, "I am a little overwhelmed at the pace. I don't have time to apply all I've learned."

True learning contracts would not have dictated a number of workshops that students attend (Knowles et al., 1998). Students would have chosen the topics that applied most to them, in consultation with the instructor. Unfortunately, due to the large number in the class, the instructor was unable to assess their work before the workshops started, so she relied on their own perceptions of their needs. Doctoral faculty also felt there needed to be a minimum number to conform to the course's six credit hours. This had pros and cons. "I do like this format a lot, but do not like the requirement that we attend 8 of them. There are not 8 that I felt would be beneficial to me, just because I was already further along than a lot of other people in the class," one student wrote. By offering similar workshops in the fall, students could attend when they were ready, in theory. Even if students were not ready for later chapters, they noted in their evaluations how it was helpful to know what was expected.

This course was also implemented in the Fall of 2010 with modifications. The final student presentations were eliminated in favor of a poster session. Rather than workshops two days a week, two workshops were offered on Monday nights based on student feedback. One class meeting a month was set aside as work time, where the computer lab and instructors were available for questions. This was in response to student feed-back that they needed more time to process the information from the workshops. The workshop topics remained the same, although some instructional strategies and guest speakers were changed. While the class size for the second cohort remained consistent (36), seven of these students graduated the following semester. However, more data is needed to conclude the longitudinal effect of the new course format, as each cohort is different and the course was modified each semester to better meet student needs.

DISCUSSION OF STUDENT ENGAGEMENT AND PRODUCTIVITY

Students came into the Dissertation Writing course in varying places in the dissertation process. Some added as many as 50 pages to their dissertation, while others seemed to write nothing or at least failed to share any writing with the instructors. The demographics of each group are consistent with the overall completion rates in the program. White females in this Ed.D. program have higher completion rates than any other group. One of the reasons for implementing the pilot of the Dissertation Writing course was the low graduation rate of African American students in the program, but these results indicate the pilot did little to improve that. While these categories only represent one semester's experience, the authors discuss the number of students who graduated from each group a year later, at the time of this writing.

Only one student made progress without attending the workshops (LEHP); however, she had several deaths in the family that semester and found it difficult to physically come to the workshops. She did indicate that she accessed the course website, but she did not share her writing with the instructors. However, a year later, this student has still made little progress toward completion.

Students who seemed to benefit most from the Dissertation Writing course were those who came into the course with IRB approval to col-

Table 2. Engagement and productivity of Ed.D. students in dissertation writing course

Student Category	Number and % of Total	Female White African American	Male White African American
HEHP	10 (28%)	7 1	1 1
HELP	14 (39%)	2 5	5 2
LELP	11 (31%)	1 5	3 2
LEHP	1	1 0	1 0

lect data. This was a hurdle for many students in the class, some of whom struggled to gain access to collect data in a school setting. Of the HEHP group, seven of those students already had IRB approval to collect data before the course began, and the other three obtained approval during the semester of the course. Table 2 displays the number and demographics of the students in each of the four quadrants.

HEHP students made clear progress throughout the semester, and they responded well to deadlines. When turning in writing to the instructors, these students were often apologetic, "Sorry if it does not appear polished." One semester after the pilot of the Dissertation Writing course, three of the students from the course had completed, all of them HEHP. One year after the pilot of the course, eight of the ten HEHP had graduated. These students probably would have graduated even without the Dissertation Writing course; however, these students indicated that the course had made the dissertation expectations clear to them. The dissertations of these students had few issues during the program's final read for APA, format, etc. because of the course.

Most concerning to the instructor was the high percentage of HELP students, most of whom (nine out of 14) did not have an approved IRB. These students wrote positively about the workshops in their reflections, yet they did not seem to apply the knowledge to their own writing. They participated in the workshops and seemed to enjoy the social

element of the class, often staying to chat with other students but not to work on their papers. If the students were attending the workshops but not writing, the instructor perceived that the course was not effective. However, since most students in the class were working adults, they may simply not have had the time to dedicate to writing. Two students from this group (both African American) went on to graduate a year later, and one other HELP student left the program with a specialist (Ed.S.) degree. Several of these students struggled with a job change or other barrier that semester which prevented them from moving forward. However, a year later, most of these students have made little progress. Although they are invited to return to any of the workshops when they are ABD, few have.

Unfortunately, LELP students outnumbered the HEHP. In class, these students did not hesitate to offer a complain about the program or the dissertation process. Their reflections indicated that they resented the requirement to attend eight of the 16 workshops and they felt the reflections and assignments of the course took time away from their writing. None of these students shared their writing with an instructor and in fact, several of them told instructors that they were good writers and did not need help. Interestingly, four of these students had an approved IRB before the class started. Predictably, none of these students have graduated at the time of this writing.

CONCLUSION

The dissertation workshop model is one approach programs can implement at a relatively low cost. These workshops are especially helpful for students who are ABD who may be forced to pay a fee to the university for continuous enrollment. The workshops provide a place for peer support and social interaction similar to coursework. Dissertation writing is often a solitary activity. The social learning that occurs in coursework is missing if a student's only official contact is with his or her dissertation committee chair. The content of the workshops should derive from both faculty's expertise with supervising dissertations and students' perceived needs. Alumni may be another source to present at workshops or to generate workshop content. Since they have successfully completed the process, their insight is valuable. However, the workshops themselves are not enough. The students must be self-directed and motivated to complete work on their own, as the graduation rates for each group of students indicates. While the dissertation workshops may not necessarily directly impact graduation rates, they do impact student satisfaction with the program, especially the dissertation process. The program faculty need to continue to explore ways to increase the graduation rate, especially for African American students.

Improving the dissertation process benefits not only students but also faculty. Research indicates that a high student attrition rate is linked to faculty turnover (Lovitts & Nelson, 2000). The student-dissertation chair relationship should focus on the research rather than policies, citation style, organization, or grammar. Every university has a wealth of resources available for doctoral students, but not all students are aware of these services or know how to access them, despite having progressed successfully through coursework. Time may be another issue; such interventions must be scheduled to be accommodating for the typical student in the program. No intervention described here or in other literature should be replicated exactly; faculty in each doctoral program must examine their own data to best support their students. Often the quantitative data is difficult to find or calculate, and the qualitative data is, at best, based on anecdotal conversations or complaints from students. As doctoral faculty, we must do better than this. At the very least, we could each examine our own practices when working with doctoral students and determine their effectiveness.

REFERENCES

Atler, C., & Adkins, C. (2001). Improving the writing skills of social work students. *Journal of Social Work, 37*(3), 493–505.

Belcher, W. L. (2009). Reflections on ten years of teaching writing for publication to graduate students and junior faculty. *Journal of Scholarly Publication, 40*(2), 184–200. doi:10.3138/jsp.40.2.184

Butin, D. W. (2010). *The education dissertation.* Thousand Oaks, CA: Corwin.

Council of Graduate Schools. (2010). *Ph.D. completion and attrition: Policies and procedures to promote student success.* Washington, DC: Council of Graduate Schools.

Creighton, C., Parks, D., & Creighton, L. (2008). *Mentoring doctoral students: The need for pedagogy.* Retrieved from http://cnx.org/content/m14516/1.3/

De Valero, Y. R. (2001). Departmental factors affecting time-to-degree and completion rates at one land grant institution. *The Journal of Higher Education, 72*(3), 341–367. doi:10.2307/2649335

Golde, C. M. (2000). Should I stay or should I go? Student descriptions of the doctoral attrition process. *Review of Higher Education, 23*(2), 199–227.

Guthrie, J. W., & Marsh, D. D. (2009). Introduction to the special issue on the education doctorate. *Peabody Journal of Education, 84*, 1–2. doi:10.1080/01619560802679518

Kamler, B., & Thomson, P. (2008). The failure of dissertation advice books: Toward alternative pedagogies for doctoral writing. *Educational Researcher, 37*(8), 507-514.

Kania-Gosche, B. (2010, September). Using the principles of adult learning to facilitate self-directed dissertation writing. In *Proceedings of the 29ᵗʰ Annual Mid West Research to Practice Conference on Adult, Continuing, Community, and Extension Education*, East Lansing, MI.

Kluever, R. C. (1997). Students' attitudes toward the responsibilities and barriers of doctoral study. *New Directions for Higher Education, 99*, 47–56. doi:10.1002/he.9904

Knowles, M. S., Holton, E. F., & Swanson, R. A. (1998). *The adult learner* (5th ed.). Houston, TX: Gulf Publishing.

Lovitts, B. E. (2007). *Making the implicit explicit: Creating performance expectations for the dissertation.* Sterling, VA: Stylus.

Mullen, C. (2006). *Best writing practices for graduate students: Reducing the discomfort of the blank screen.* Retrieved from http://cnx.org/content/m14054/1.2/

Nerad, M., & Miller, D. S. (1997). The institution cares: Berkley's efforts to support dissertation writing in the humanities and social sciences. *New Directions for Higher Education, 99*, 75-90.

Nettles, M. T., & Millett, C. M. (2006). *Three magic letters: Getting to Ph.D.* Baltimore, MD: Johns Hopkins University Press.

Rose, M., & McClafferty, K. A. (2001). A call for the teaching of writing in graduate education. *Educational Researcher, 30*(2), 27–33. doi:10.3102/0013189X030002027

Spillett, M. A., & Moisiewicz, K. A. (2004). Cheerleader, coach, counselor, critic: Support and challenge roles of the dissertation adviser. *College Student Journal, 38*(2), 246-256.

Wendler, C., Bridgeman, B., Cline, F., Millett, C., Rock, J., Bell, N., & McAllister, P. (2010). *The path forward: The future of graduate education in the United States.* Princeton, NJ: Educational Testing Service.

Yeatman, A. (1995). Making supervision relationships accountable: Graduate student logs. *Australian Universities'. RE:view, 2*, 9–11.

This work was previously published in the International Journal of Adult Vocational Education and Technology, Volume 2, Issue 4, edited by Victor C.X. Wang, pp. 17-27, copyright 2011 by IGI Publishing (an imprint of IGI Global).

Chapter 12

Vocational Interests and Needs of Unemployed, Low-Education Adults with Severe Substance Abuse Problems in Anchorage, Alaska

Mark E. Johnson
University of Alaska Anchorage, USA

Grace Reynolds
California State University Long Beach, USA

Dennis G. Fisher
California State University Long Beach, USA

Colin R. Harbke
Western Illinois University, USA

ABSTRACT

Vocational assessment data were collected from 94 low-education adults with severe substance abuse problems not currently in treatment. Participants completed the My Vocational Situation (MVS), Self-Directed Search (SDS), and Reading-Free Vocational Interest Inventory (R-FVII). Lower scores than the normative sample were revealed on all MVS scales, with scores for men being significantly lower than the normative sample. These findings indicate that these participants, particularly the men, lack a clear and stable view of their occupational future, need information to clarify their occupational options and goals, and perceive multiple barriers in attaining employment. SDS and R-FVII results provide detailed information about these participants' occupational interests and vocational likes and dislikes. These findings highlight vocational counseling and guidance as critical needs for individuals with severe substance abuse problems who are unable or unwilling to seek treatment. Providing vocational services to this out-of-treatment population may be an essential pathway for their long-term recovery.

DOI: 10.4018/978-1-4666-2062-9.ch012

INTRODUCTION

Within the substance abuse treatment community, gaining and maintaining gainful employment is recognized as a critical component of successful treatment and long-term recovery. For example, Lamb et al. (1996) found that stability of one's occupational role before entering treatment was strongly related to retention in substance abuse treatment. Conversely, Milby et al. (2010) found that longer abstinence <u>after</u> treatment was associated with increased likelihood of stable employment. Given this relationship between employment and long-term treatment outcomes, considerable research has been conducted into the effects of adding vocational rehabilitation services into substance abuse treatment programs (Platt, 1995). What has drawn less research attention is the provision of such services to individuals with severe substance abuse problems who are unable or unwilling to seek treatment. Following, we review the research literature on the effects of providing vocational rehabilitation services within substance abuse treatment. This literature review provides the basis for this study's focus on the vocational needs of individuals who have serious substance abuse problems but are not currently in treatment.

LITERATURE REVIEW

Research into the effects of providing vocational rehabilitation in substance abuse treatment has followed three main lines of inquiry. The first type of research has focused on identifying external barriers to employment in drug users, including the lack of jobs due to local economic environments, or a scarcity of jobs that are structured in such a way that recovering individuals can perform them. Two examples of this research include the evaluation of the Wildcat experiment (Friedman, 1978) and the National Supported Work Demonstration Project (Dickinson, 1981). These programs included intensive case management and supportive services in addition to providing subsidized employment. Successful outcomes of these projects included longer length of participation in treatment programs and movement from subsidized to unsubsidized jobs.

Platt, Widman, Lidz, Rubenstein, and Thompson (1998) and Vines and Mandell (1999) focused on the assessment of external barriers to employment among individuals with substance addictions and ways in which treatment programs can reduce the barriers through collaborative relationships with other service providers. Schottenfeld, Pantalon, Chawarski, and Pakes (2000) found that a community reinforcement approach to drug treatment that included engagement in alternative activities (such as work and family activities) for opiate and cocaine addicts was effective. This research attempted to quantify the amount of time spent on various activities to understand the impact of positive and negative uses of time on recovery from addiction, and to provide external community support to the individual in spending time on positive activities. French, Dennis, McDougal, Karuntzos, and Hubbard (1992), conducted a large effort to assess the need for and efficacy of training and employment programs in methadone maintenance. These researchers found that the participants had a strong interest in such services but had somewhat unrealistic expectations about their value.

The second type of research has focused on addressing individual or personal barriers that people with severe substance abuse problems experience with respect to employment. Programs to address these barriers have attempted to increase personal skills to enhance the prospects for gainful employment. An example of this type of program was developed by Loeb, LeVois, and Copper (1981). Designated the Job Seeker's Workshop, the content of this program involved three components: job interviewing skills, instruction in the completion of application forms, and job search procedures. The intent of these skill building components was to increase the likelihood that participants could find gainful employment. Platt, Husband, Hermalin, Cater, and Metzger (1993) developed an intervention for methadone maintenance clients that focused on problem-solving skills and interpersonal skills as a way to facilitate employment among this group.

The third line of inquiry of researchers has investigated differences in underlying psychological symptomatology between employed and unemployed drug users. Szirony (1997) found that MMPI-2 Work Interference Scale differences among incarcerated substance abusers were statistically significant between those who were employed and those who were not employed before incarceration. Higher scores on this scale were associated with low self-esteem, anxiety, and depression. Johnson, Reynolds, and Fisher (2001) found differences between out-of-treatment drug users reporting employment and those reporting unemployment on several domains of psychological functioning captured by the Symptom Checklist 90 (SCL-90), with unemployed individuals presenting more evidence of psychopathology. Reynolds et al. (1999) found that unemployed out-of-treatment drug users exhibited greater levels of depression than employed out-of-treatment drug users on three different scales of depression, including the Center for Epidemiological Studies-Depression Scale (CES-D), the Beck Depression Inventory (BDI) and the Brief Symptom Inventory (BSI).

Virtually all of the research that has explored the effects of providing vocational rehabilitation to individuals with severe substance abuse problems has included participants drawn from substance abuse treatment programs. Although this research has contributed great insights into the importance of vocational rehabilitation for this population, it has overlooked individuals with severe substance abuse problems who are either unable or unwilling to obtain substance abuse treatment. Further, most of the research to date has not used standardized assessment tools to measure vocational-related variables, but rather has considered variables such as post-treatment employment status. To begin to fill these gaps in the research, the purpose of this study was to examine the vocational profiles of unemployed, low-education individuals with severe

substance abuse problems who are not currently in substance abuse treatment. To do so, we used three well-validated vocational assessment tools, namely, My Vocational Situation, Self-Directed Search, and Reading-Free Vocational Interest Inventory.

METHOD

Participants

Data were gathered from participants in the National Institute on Drug Abuse-funded study, "Interventions to Reduce Hepatitis B, Hepatitis C & HIV in IDUs." The purpose of this study implemented in Anchorage, Alaska was to compare a needle exchange and pharmacy needle sales on the incidence of various blood-borne diseases, use of needles, and substance use. Eligibility to participate in the study included being at least 18 years of age, reporting current injection as determined by presentation of track marks (Cagle, Fisher, Senter, Thurmond, & Kastar, 2002), and positive urinalysis for cocaine metabolites, morphine or amphetamine. A detailed description of this study can be found in Fisher et al. (2002).

As part of their involvement in this study, participants completed the Risk Behavior Assessment (RBA) (National Institute on Drug Abuse, 1991), a structured interview that includes questions about demographics, including current employment status. The items regarding employment status and other economic issues were found to be reliable (Johnson, Fisher, & Reynolds, 1999). Participants who reported being unemployed ($n=94$) completed additional vocational assessment tools. This sample included 78 (83%) men and 16 (17%) women, with an average age of 40.3 ($SD=7.5$). Relative to cultural heritage, 51 (57%) were Caucasian, 17 (19%) African American, and 21 (24%) Alaska Native. The majority ($n=70$; 74%) reported having a high school equivalency or less, with only 26% reporting any education beyond high school. Table 1 provides participants' substance abuse history.

Table 1. Participants' substance use history

Drug use	last 48 hours	last 30 days	lifetime
Alcohol	59.2%	81.7%	96.8%
Marijuana/Hashish	18.3%	51.4%	94.0%
Crack	33.5%	53.2%	75.2%
Cocaine	40.4%	65.1%	89.4%
Heroin	46.8%	64.7%	85.8%
Speedball	16.1%	46.8%	72.9%
Methadone	5.5%	9.6%	29.8%
Other opiates	3.7%	13.8%	45.9%
Amphetamines	2.3%	3.2%	47.7%
Other drugs	2.8%	3.2%	23.9%

Instrumentation

As part of their involvement in this study, participants completed the following three vocational assessment tools: My Vocational Situation, Self-Directed Search, and Reading-Free Vocational Interest Inventory.

My Vocational Situation (MVS) (Holland, Daiger, & Power, 1980) was designed to provide an evaluation of several issues addressed in career counseling. It includes the following three scales: 1) Vocational Identity (VI), 18 items that assess the degree to which respondents have a "clear and stable picture of one's goals, interests, personality, and talents: (Holland et al., 1980, p. 1); 2) Occupational Information (OI), 4 items that assesses respondents' expressed need for additional occupational information; and 3) Barriers (B), four items that assess respondents' perceived obstacles that limit their occupational pursuits. Each item is responded to with either yes or no, and scale scores are calculated by summing the number of positive responses. Higher scores on all scales indicate the more positive direction; for example, lower scores on the VI category indicate participants do not have a definite idea of their occupational goals. The instrument developers (Holland, Gottfredson, & Power, 1980; Holland et al., 1980) and

other researchers (Fuqua & Newman, 1989; Lucas, Gysbers, Buescher, & Heppner, 1988) have found the MVS to have adequate reliability and validity.

Self-Directed Search (SDS) (Holland, Fritzsche, & Powell, 1994) is a self-administered instrument designed to yield career guidance. Results of the SDS include a two-letter summary code that represent the first letter of one of the following six interest groups: Realistic (e.g., skilled trades, labor, technical, some helping jobs), Investigative (e.g., scientific, some technical jobs), Artistic (e.g., musical, some writing jobs), Social (e.g., teaching, helping jobs), Enterprising (e.g., sales, supervisory jobs), and Conventional (e.g., office, clerical jobs) (Holland, 1996). Different types of jobs correspond to different summary codes. For example, an individual with the summary code RE might be interested in Realistic-Enterprising jobs (e.g., Rug Cleaner, Forest-Fire Fighter, or Lumber Sorter).

Reading-Free Vocational Interest Inventory (R-FVII) (Becker, 1981) was designed to assess respondents' vocational likes and dislikes. The R-FVII includes trios of drawings depicting a wide range of job activities, including the setting and tools used in each job. Participants respond by choosing which of the three jobs depicted in each set they would prefer to have. Scores are obtained for each of 11 general job categories: Automotive, Building or Construction, Clerical, Animal Care, Food Service, Patient Care, Horticulture, Housekeeping, Personal Services, Laundry Service, and Materials Handling.

Procedures

Informed consent was obtained using an informed consent form approved by the University of Alaska Anchorage Institutional Review Board. These vocational assessment tools were administered to unemployed participants as part of their regular involvement in the NIDA-funded project. The order of the instruments was held constant across all participants, namely, My Vocational Situation,

Self-Directed Search, and Reading-Free Vocational Interest Inventory.

Statistical Analysis

For the MVS, mean scores of men ($n = 66$) and women ($n = 14$) who completed the instrument were compared to the mean normative scores provided in the MVS manual (Holland et al., 1980). One-tailed z-tests were performed using an alpha level of .05 to determine whether differences were statistically significant between the current sample and the normative group. The SDS was scored to summary codes for vocational interest. Participants' scores on The Reading-Free Vocational Interest Inventory were compared to the normative data provided in the R-FVII manual (Becker, 1981) for economically and environmentally-disadvantaged adults. Scores above the 75th percentile for a specific interest area suggest the participant a strong vocational interest. Analyses for all assessment tools were conducted separately by sex.

RESULTS

My Vocational Situation

Table 2 provides MVS scale scores for the current sample and normative scores, separately by sex. As indicated in the table, male and female participants had lower mean scores on all three scales than the normative group. Lower scores on the Vocational Identity (VI) scale indicate that these individuals do not possess a well-established picture of their occupational goals; lower scores on the Occupational Information (OI) scale indicate a strong need for additional occupational information; and lower scores on the Barriers (B) scale indicate these individuals perceive significant external obstacles to achieving their occupational goals. For the men, all comparisons between the current and normative samples were statistically significant. For the women, although sample means were all lower than the normative means, these differences were not statistically significant, due, at least in part, to the small number of women in the sample

Self-Directed Search

Table 3 provides the SDS summary codes, separately for men and women. For men, the most common single code was R (realistic) with 79% of the men's results yielding codes that included S. This suggests that occupations that include contact with other people would be the most rewarding. Relative to the most common two-codes, 26% of the men had the summary code RS (realistic-social); sample occupations in this category include truck or bus driver, firefighter, and police officer. An additional 17% of the men had a summary code of

Table 2. My vocational situation questionnaire, mean scores, by sex

	Men ($n = 66$)						Women ($n = 14$)					
	Current Sample		Normative Sample		Sample Comparison		Current Sample		Normative Sample		Sample Comparison	
MVS Scale	M	SD	M	*SD*	*Z-test*		M	SD	M	*SD*	*Z-test*	
Vocational Identity	11.35	4.29	12.28	4.28	1.76*		9.60	4.38	11.08	4.12	1.37	
Occupational Information	2.44	1.49	2.87	1.35	2.58**		1.93	1.90	2.24	1.51	0.77	
Barriers	2.48	1.30	3.37	0.90	8.03***		2.71	1.20	3.10	1.18	1.24	

* $p < .05$, ** $p < .01$, *** $p < .001$.

Table 3. Self-directed search summary codes, by sex

Summary Code	Men (*n* = 67)		Women (*n* = 14)	
	N	%	N	%
Realistic-Social	20	26%	2	14%
Enterprising-Realistic	13	17%	0	--
Artstic-Realistic	6	8%	2	14%
Investigative-Realistic	6	8%	1	7%
Reaistic-Conventional	5	7%	1	7%
Entrprising-Investigative	4	5%	0	--
Artstic-Enterprising	3	4%	0	--
Entrprising-Social	3	4%	1	7%
Artstic-Social	2	3%	2	14%
Conventional-Social	2	3%	4	29%
Investigative-Social	2	3%	0	--
Artstic-Investigative	1	1%	0	--
Artstic-Conventional	0	--	1	7%

ER (enterprising-realistic), a code that includes jobs such as construction worker, chef, and salesperson.

For women, the most common SDS single code was S (social) with 64% of the women's results yielding codes that included S. This suggests that occupations that include contact with other people would be the most rewarding. Relative to two-codes, 29% of the women had the summary code CS (conventional-social); sample occupations in this category include clerk, telephone operator, and fast food worker. An additional 14% of women participants had a summary code of AR (artistic-realistic), a code that includes jobs such as cook, floral designer, and photographer; 14% a code of AS (Artistic-Social) that includes jobs such as teacher and writers; and 14% a code of RS (Realistic-Social) that includes jobs such as truck or bus driver, firefighter, and police officer.

Reading-Free Vocational Interest Inventory

Table 4 provides percentages of male and female participants who scored greater than the 75th per-

centile for each of the 11 R-FVII vocational interest areas. For men, horticulture was the most endorsed area, men, followed by housekeeping, patient care, and animal care. For women, housekeeping and automotive were the most endorsed areas, followed by personal service, clerical, and building trades.

DISCUSSION

The research findings indicate that unemployed, low-education individuals who experience severe substance abuse problems and are not currently receiving treatment for these problems evidence serious challenges to gaining and maintaining gainful employment. More specifically, based on the My Vocational Situation, these individuals lack a clear and stable view of their occupational future, need information to clarify their occupational options and goals, and perceive multiple barriers in attain-

Table 4. Participants who scored above the 75th percentile by vocational interest area on the R-FVII, by sex

	Men (*n* = 57)		Women (*n* = 12)		Both (*n* = 69)	
	N	%	N	%	N	%
Animal Care	13	23%	0	0%	13	19%
Automotive	11	19%	4	33%	15	22%
Building Trades	9	16%	3	25%	12	17%
Clerical	9	16%	3	25%	12	17%
Food Service	6	11%	2	17%	8	12%
Horticulture	26	46%	2	17%	28	41%
Housekeeping	18	32%	4	33%	22	32%
Laundry Service	4	7%	1	8%	5	7%
Materials Handling	5	9%	1	8%	6	9%
Patient Care	13	23%	2	17%	15	22%
Personal Service	8	14%	3	25%	11	16%

ing employment. These challenges are particularly heightened for the men in the current sample.

Findings from the Self-Directed Search and Reading-Free Interest Inventory suggest that valuable information regarding this sample's occupational interests is attainable through the use of standardized instruments. Although these instruments provided no profound findings, their successful administration suggests that standardized instruments are a viable avenue through which to gain a starting basis for vocational rehabilitation and counseling with these individuals.

The MVS findings are consistent with regard to the lack of occupational goals among these individuals with substance abuse problems prior to obtaining treatment. For example, Hermalin, Steer, Platt, and Metzger (1990) noted that previous employment or higher levels of education prior to substance abuse treatment predicted employment after treatment initiation. Combining the experiencing of substance abuse problems with low levels of education creates a situation that may seem insurmountable to these individuals.

More research is needed to understand the perceived barriers to employment in among men with severe substance abuse problems not currently in treatment. Much work has been done on perceived barriers for women due to the recent legislation concerning welfare to work. Programs that attempt to reduce barriers for women with minimal education and job skills have focused on the need for childcare, transportation, and additional training (Vines & Mandell, 1999), and have become the subject of research assessing the impact of changes to the welfare system brought about the federal legislation concerning Temporary Assistance for Needy Families (TANF). Much less emphasis has been placed on identifying, understanding, or reducing barriers to vocational success among low-educated, unemployed men with severe substance abuse problems.

Another challenge that individuals with substance abuse problems face is the increased use of drug screening in the workplace, particularly in settings in which the minimally educated seek jobs. For example, many employers that operate warehouses routinely screen new applicants for drug use if the position requires the operation of forklifts or other equipment. Although such screening makes sense from the employers' point of view for liability reasons, it creates another obstacle to gaining employment for individuals with substance abuse problems.

CONCLUSION

The findings of occupational challenges among this sample are consistent with and similar to the occupational challenges experienced by individuals receiving substance abuse treatment. However, a major difference between these two groups is that individuals in substance abuse treatment often have the opportunity to receive vocational rehabilitation whereas such services are not as readily available, if at all, for individuals not currently in treatment. It should be noted that despite the oft-cited relationship between vocational rehabilitation and positive treatment outcomes, calls for the offering of such services in all substance abuse treatment programs have not been met with universal acceptance. For example, West (2008) surveyed 159 substance abuse treatment facilities and found nearly three-quarters did not offer vocational assessments or counseling and fewer than one-third provided any job skills training at all.

Nevertheless, individuals in substance abuse treatment are more likely to be able to access vocational rehabilitation than individuals not currently in treatment. Such lack of access may have unforeseen consequences. That is, given the established relationship reported between gainful employment and attaining and maintaining sobriety, the provision of vocational rehabilitation to an out-of-treatment population may be enough, for at least some individuals, to attain sobriety and avoid costly substance abuse treatment. The possibility that vocational rehabilitation for individuals with severe substance abuse problems not currently in treatment may lead to positive outcomes beyond just employment is an important issue to address in future research.

In summary, these results indicate that individuals with severe substance abuse problems not currently in treatment face occupational obstacles to gainful employment. By neglecting the vocational needs of these individuals, our society may be missing an opportunity to facilitate positive outcomes that would benefit both the individuals and society as a whole. For individuals in substance abuse treatment, Shepard and Reif (2004) found vocational rehabilitation to be associated with increased probability of abstinence and to be a cost effective part of substance abuse treatment. Although conducting a cost analysis was beyond the scope of this study, just as with individuals in treatment, it is likely that the expense of providing vocational services to this out-of-treatment population would be exceeded by savings attained through the avoidance of costly substance abuse treatment not to mention other reduced societal costs.

REFERENCES

Becker, R. L. (1981). *Reading-free vocational interest inventory: Manual.* Columbus, OH: Elbern.

Cagle, H. H., Fisher, D. G., Senter, T. P., Thurmond, R. D., & Kastar, A. J. (2002). *Classifying skin lesions of injection drug users: A method for corroborating disease risk.* Rockville, MD: Center for Substance Abuse Treatment, Substance Abuse and Mental Health Services Administration.

Dickinson, K., & Maynard, E. S. (1981). *The impact of supported work on ex-addicts (Vol. 4).* New York, NY: Manpower Demonstration Research Corporation.

French, M. T., Dennis, M. T., McDougal, G. L., Karuntzos, G. T., & Hubbard, R. L. (1992). Training and employment programs in methadone treatment: Client needs and desires. *Journal of Substance Abuse Treatment, 9,* 293–303. doi:10.1016/0740-5472(92)90022-G

Friedman, L. N. (1978). *The Wildcat experiment: An early test of supported work in drug abuse rehabilitation.* Washington, DC: U. S. Government Printing Office.

Fuqua, D. R., & Newman, J. L. (1989). An examination of the relation between career subscales. *Journal of Counseling Psychology, 36,* 487–491. doi:10.1037/0022-0167.36.4.487

Hermalin, J. A., Steer, R. A., Platt, J. J., & Metzger, D. S. (1990). Risk characteristics associated with chronic unemployment in methadone clients. *Drug and Alcohol Dependence, 26,* 117–125. doi:10.1016/0376-8716(90)90118-X

Holland, J. L. (1996). *Self-directed search: Job finder.* Odessa, FL: Psychological Assessment Resources.

Holland, J. L., Daiger, D. C., & Power, P. G. (1980). *My vocational situation: Description of an experimental diagnostic form for the selection of vocational assistance.* Palo Alto, CA: Consulting Psychologist Press.

Holland, J. L., Fritzsche, B. A., & Powell, A. B. (1994). *Self-directed search, technical manual.* Odessa, FL: Psychological Assessment Resources.

Holland, J. L., Gottfredson, D. C., & Power, P. G. (1980). Some diagnostic scales for research in decision making and personality: Identity, information, and barriers. *Journal of Personality and Social Psychology, 39,* 1191–1200. doi:10.1037/h0077731

Johnson, M. E., Fisher, D. G., & Reynolds, G. L. (1999). Reliability of drug users' self-report of economic variables. *Addiction Research, 7,* 227–238. doi:10.3109/16066359909004385

Johnson, M. E., Reynolds, G. L., & Fisher, D. G. (2001). Employment status and psychological symptomatology among drug users not currently in treatment. *Evaluation and Program Planning, 24,* 215–220. doi:10.1016/S0149-7189(01)00011-8

Loeb, P., LeVois, M., & Cooper, J. (1981). Increasing employment in ex-heroin addicts II: Methadone maintenance sample. *Behavior Therapy, 12,* 453–460. doi:10.1016/S0005-7894(81)80083-4

Lucas, E. B., Gysbers, N. C., Buescher, K. L., & Heppner, P. P. (1988). My vocational situation: Normative, psychometric, and comparative data. *Measurement & Evaluation in Counseling & Development, 20,* 162–170.

Milby, J. B., Schumacher, J. E., Wallace, D., Vuchinich, R., Mennemeyer, S. T., & Kertesz, S. G. (2010). Effects of sustained abstinence among treated substance-abusing homeless persons on housing and employment. *American Journal of Public Health, 100,* 913–918. doi:10.2105/AJPH.2008.152975

National Institute on Drug Abuse. (1991). *Risk behavior assessment.* Rockville, MD: National Institute on Drug Abuse (Community Research Branch).

Platt, J. J. (1995). Vocational rehabilitation of drug abusers. *Psychological Bulletin, 117,* 416–433. doi:10.1037/0033-2909.117.3.416

Platt, J. J., Husband, S. D., Hermalin, J., Cater, J., & Metzger, D. (1993). A cognitive problem-solving employment readiness intervention for methadone clients. *Journal of Cognitive Psychotherapy, 7,* 21–33.

Platt, J. J., Widman, M., Lidz, V., Rubenstein, D., & Thompson, R. (1998). The case for support services in substance abuse treatment. *The American Behavioral Scientist, 41,* 1050–1062. doi:10.1177/0002764298041008003

Reynolds, G. L., Theno, S. A., Fisher, D. G., Fenaughty, A. M., Johnson, M. E., & Schlicting, E. G. (1999, November). *Depression and unemployment among Alaskan drug users.* Paper presented at the 127th Annual Meeting of the American Public Health Association, Chicago, IL.

Schottenfeld, R. S., Pantalon, M. V., Chawarski, M. C., & Pakes, J. (2000). Community reinforcement approach for combined opioid and cocaine dependence: Patterns of engagement in alternative activities. *Journal of Substance Abuse Treatment, 18,* 255–261. doi:10.1016/S0740-5472(99)00062-8

Shepard, D. S., & Reif, S. (2004). The value of vocational rehabilitation in substance user treatment: A cost-effectiveness framework. *Substance Use & Misuse, 39,* 2581–2609. doi:10.1081/JA-200034732

Szirony, G. M. (1997). *MMPI-2 work interference difference among incarcerated substance abusers.* Unpublished doctoral dissertation, Kent State University, Kent, OH.

Vines, J. A., & Mandell, C. J. (1999). Characteristics of female alcohol and drug substance users engaged in treatment programs. *Journal of Applied Rehabilitation Counseling, 30,* 35–43.

West, S. (2008). The utilization of vocational rehabilitation services in substance abuse treatment facilities in the U.S. *Journal of Vocational Rehabilitation, 29,* 71–75.

This work was previously published in the International Journal of Adult Vocational Education and Technology, Volume 2, Issue 2, edited by Victor C.X. Wang, pp. 1-10, copyright 2011 by IGI Publishing (an imprint of IGI Global).

Chapter 13

The Scenario of a Learning Society Model toward Promoting a Positive Paradigm Shift for Communities

Suwithida Charungkaittikul
Chulalongkorn University, Thailand

ABSTRACT

This study uses a prospective qualitative approach. The Ethnographic Delphi Futures Research (EDFR) technique is used to propose a learning society model. The data include a review of peer-reviewed literature, a field study visit and observation of five best practices communities in Thailand, in-depth interviews to gain experts' perspectives, mini-Delphi techniques questionnaires, focus group discussions, and model evaluation. Qualitative data were transcribed and analyzed using content-analysis. Policy makers, practitioners from public and private agencies, educational personnel, and community leaders were among the 42 individuals involved in the data collection effort. Results revealed essential elements for development of a learning society including, principles, developmental processes, strategies, and key success factors to enhance a positive paradigm shift for communities. It is anticipated that the findings will (1) add meaningful information and practical guidelines for developing a learning society, (2) contribute to ensuring the quality of citizen participation and ensure balanced and sustainable development of communities and societies, and (3) serve as a basis for further research.

INTRODUCTION

Today's world may be characterized as the dawn of the new millennium of the learning society, where knowledge is a society's most valuable asset, a country's primary source of power (Knight, 1995)

and one which needs to be efficiently and effectively managed. A society thrives and survives on the foundation laid by its wealth of knowledge. Previous research (Sibmuenpiam, 2003; Sangsri, 2005; Knight, 1995; Malone & Yohe, 2002; Carrillo, 2002, 2004; Choi, 2003, Ergazakis et al., 2004; Lantz & Brage, 2006; Casey, 2006) clearly

DOI: 10.4018/978-1-4666-2062-9.ch013

indicated that issues of knowledge play a major role in development of communities, cities, societies, and nations. As knowledge is gained through learning, the current development initiative is geared toward transforming the society into a learning society (Office of the Education Council, 2008) which is defined as one engaged in a sustainable development strategy that promotes the unending learning of individuals –the smallest unit of the society (Holden & Connelly, 2004). At the heart of the learning society is the commitment of all members to a set of values and the system of lifelong learning, and sharing knowledge with its members and others on a regular lifelong basis that enhances the opportunity of all community members to develop their full capacity of knowledge, skills, and attitude. In such a society education is interwoven with the social, political, and economic (Senesh, 1991).

The increasingly intense competition among the international community in all regards include the Constitution of the Royal Kingdom of Thailand 2007 (B.E. 2550), the Tenth National Economic and Social Development Plan 2007-2011 (B.E. 2550-2554), the National Education Act 1999 (B.E. 2542) and its amendment the National Education Act Amendment (Issue 2) 2002 (B.E. 2545), and the Non-Formal Education and Informal Education Act 2008 (B.E. 2551). All of these carry stipulations concerning lifelong learning, educational enhancement and global competitiveness with the aim of developing the society toward sustainable happiness. It also emphasizes the balance among all aspects: economy, society, natural resources and environment; and, transforming the Thai people into knowledge citizens and knowledge workers (Dulayakasem, 2005). This leads to an appropriate development of manpower and a learning society for sustainable development.

Thailand is in transition from a rural to an urban society. As a result of the compartmentalized development of urban and rural areas, there is imbalance in the development of rural communities. The society is plagued with several obstacles to lifelong learning. For instance, there is an unequal opportunity to access: knowledge and learning resources, infrastructure, exclusive public services, economic background, and information technology system. Computer networks used for the transfer of knowledge do not cover all parts of the country. There remain a great number of Thai people who are not appropriately educated and are without means to pursue knowledge (Pongpaiboon, 2007). Although it is true that the national development strategies have provided a foundation on which Thailand can become a learning society, private and public agencies (e.g., Knowledge Management Institute, Thailand Productivity Institute, Office of Non-Formal Education and Informal Education Promotion) at the policy and implementation levels, as well as the communities, are actively and successfully pursuing study of the concept to establish measures for transforming the Thai society into a learning society. Their shared missions are to achieve tangible results. Several communities have been officially recognized as model learning societies by the Office of the Education Council (2008) for their successful implementation.

The studies of Sibmuenpiam (2003), and Sangsri (2005) revealed that Thai public and private agencies remain without an appropriate learning society model that is developed from the synthesis of knowledge appropriate to the social contexts and aimed at achieving an actual positive paradigm shift for communities in a structured and procedural manner. Similarity, those studies from foreign countries (Longworth & Osborne, 2010; Cisco, 2010; Su, 2007; Laszlo & Laszlo, 2007; Lantz & Brage, 2006; Casey, 2006; Faris, 1998, 2006; UNESCO, 2005; Longworth, 2006; Carrillo, 2004; Faris & Peterson, 2000; Keating & Hertzman 1999; Yarnit, 1998) showed that there is a growing interest of the knowledge cities and societies but the field still lacks a consensus regarding description or clarification, appropriate conceptual and methodological frameworks.

The lack of research regarding a learning society model applicable to the Thai context, limited diffusion of the lifelong learning research developed within worldwide countries. Additionally, the 2005 UNESCO World Report *Towards Knowledge Societies* emphasized the need to: clarify the aims of knowledge societies, align them with paradigms of growth and development, guide them with ethics such as freedom and responsibility, and include within them the means for all to share knowledge (UNESCO, 2005). Therefore, it is the intention of the researcher to conduct an in-depth study of the learning society concept to develop a practical learning society model toward promoting a positive paradigm shift for communities. New knowledge will help reinforce positive thinking, and action for individuals, communities and the society at large, thereby contributing to the potential of a society to become a learning society. It is hoped that the knowledge obtained through this study can effectively and valuably propose the guideline for the countries to start moving national development towards learning society status, sound equilibrium, fairness and sustainability, and to pave the way toward *a Learning Society: Society of Happy Coexistence* that may enhance the wellness of all people.

THEORETICAL/ CONCEPTUAL FRAMEWORK

The framework of this study is the learning society. According to the 21st century global demands for economic competitiveness and social cohesion, application of information technologies for interactive communications and associated learning, and growing awareness of the need for lifelong learning strategies to ensure sustainable economic and community development. The idea of developing *Lifelong Learning Communities/ Cities/Towns/Regions* was a watershed in global thought about moving toward a knowledge-based economy and society, where economic benefits and the creation of wealth are directly based on the production, distribution and use of knowledge and information. It also includes business performance based on intellectual capital and the capacity for innovation and collaboration. The society needs to reengineer a comprehensive approach to learning and development that benefits all of society. Since the Organization for Economic Cooperation and Development (OECD) funded a project to create the *Educating Cities* in the 1970s (IAEC, 2009; Longworth, 2006), the idea of developing Lifelong Learning Cities has expanded throughout the world. According to the International Association of Educating Cities (IAEC), 335 cities in 36 countries have organized around the concept (Kwon & Schied, 2009). A list of learning cities includes Barcelona, Spain; Stockholm, Sweden; Munich, Germany; Montreal, Canada; Dublin, Ireland; Delft, Netherlands; Birmingham, the United Kingdom; Edinburgh, Scotland; Victoria, Australia; Espoo, Finland, and countries in the Asia-Pacific Region such as Singapore, China, Japan, and Korea (Cisco, 2010; Faris, 1998, 2006; Kwon & Schied, 2009; Ergazakis et al., 2006). These cities influenced the development of the learning society. Even though the concept of the leaning society is a relatively new one, progress is underway, perhaps spurred by international positions and policies, such as the World Development Report on Knowledge for Development (World Bank, 1998), UNESCO's World Report, Toward Knowledge Societies (UNESCO, 2005), and a wide range of European Union activities (Morris & Cranford, 2007). A number of countries (e.g., New Zealand, Ireland, Poland, and China) have strategies to build knowledge societies.

Learning society characteristics generally include the nature of a group of individuals residing within one locality, an agency or a community engaged in single or multiple matters simultaneously. It involves preservation, nourishment, rehabilitation, protection, promotion, assistance, development, and distribution through information technology, learning resources, local wisdoms and knowledge that allow members of the society to create, share, and use knowledge, common skills, and opinions with fellow members of the same and other communities on a regular lifelong basis. They generate new knowledge and appropriate knowledge management systems, as well as making the best life decisions for the prosperity and well-being of its people. A learning society comprises of learners, learning providers, learning resources, knowledge/wisdom, lifelong learning activities, learning climates, learning networks, knowledge management, and learning organizations.

Building the learning society means assembling a new coalition that can make innovations from all sectors of society and response to the long-term drivers of change for the benefit of learners. It needs to be organized on a different set of principles requiring values and creation of a new learning culture and system. It also needs to mobilize new structures, new approaches, and new technology to deliver a new balance of skills to a lifelong population. It is a way of organizing learning that deals with these new realities and better meets our global and local needs for learning. A learning society model is the visualization of components of a learning society, learning society principles, learning society developmental processes, strategies for the development of learning society, key success factors, and, the coordination among such components. A learning society model toward promoting a positive paradigm shift for communities ensures balanced and sustainable development of a society.

RESEARCH OBJECTIVES

Research objectives for this study are as follows:

1. To analyze and synthesize learning society concepts from both local and global literatures;

2. To explore the experts' perspectives on a learning society development and developmental strategies;

3. To develop the tentative and preliminary learning society model toward promoting a positive paradigm shift for communities; and,

4. To propose the learning society model toward promoting a positive paradigm shift for communities.

METHODOLOGY

Participants

The participants are comprised of forty-two experts in the field from relevant public and private agencies in Thailand: Executives of the Office of Non-Formal Education and Informal Education Promotion, directors of community or society development departments, human resource development managers, educational institution directors/teachers, educational personnel, practitioners who are the Directors of Non-Formal and Informal Education Center in provincial and district levels, local government administrators, community leaders, and local wisdom teachers.

Instruments

Five different research instruments used include: (1) an analysis form, (2) an in-depth interview question guide, (3) a mini-Delphi Techniques questionnaire, (4) a focus group discussion guide, and (5) a model evaluation form. By these means this study employed a qualitative method using the EDFR (Ethnographic Delphi Futures Research) technique.

RESEARCH DEFINITIONS

These research definitions are used in this study:

- **Learning society**: The nature of an agency, a city/town, a community engaged in single or multiple matters simultaneously on the local and national level. It involves preservation, nourishment, rehabilitation, protection, promotion, assistance, development, and distribution through lifelong learning, information technology, learning resources, local wisdoms and knowledge. A learning society is comprised of learners, learning providers, learning resources, knowledge/wisdom, lifelong learning activities, learning climates, learning networks, knowledge management, and learning organizations.

- **Learning society model**: The visualization of a learning society model includes the learning society components, principles, developmental processes, strategies, key success factors and the coordination among such components. A learning society model ensures balanced and sustainable development of a society.

- **Local wisdom:** Local wisdom means the body of community's knowledge, ability, outstanding value and skills of the Thais which is inherited from experiences that are respectively preserved and transmitted through generations. Nine local wisdoms include: (1) agriculture, (2) handicraft, and cottage industry, (3) traditional medicine/herbal doctors, (4) management and conservation of natural resources, (5) funding, and community business/economics, (6) fine arts, (7) languages and literatures, (8) philosophy, religion, and tradition, (9) food and nutrition. The local wisdom has long been recognized from the past to present time, both at local and national levels as a common asset of the nation to help younger generations improving their quality of lives. A person who possesses this knowledge is called a local wisdom holder.

- **Local wisdom teachers:** Local wisdom teachers also known as the Thai local wisdom holders are apprised and honored by the Office of National Education Commission, Ministry of Education. The wisdom teacher is regarded as an important teacher who is eligible to teach at both formal and non-formal institutions.

- **Positive paradigm shift**: The change of concepts, perceptions, practices, valuations and way of life of the people in a positive and creative manner as generally accepted by the majority. It leads to balanced and sustainable resolution of issues faced by individuals, communities and societies; and, propels the societies forward in the appropriate direction for the benefit of all members.

- **Community**: A group of individuals residing within one locality. These members are interested in incidents occurring among themselves, meeting and exchanging opinions, and, sharing common behaviors. They are able to achieve basic requirements and resolve the majority of issues faced by their own community.

RESEARCH PROCEDURES

The study is a prospective qualitative research where the EDFR (Ethnographic Delphi Futures Research) technique is used. The research procedures comprised of four stages. Figure 1 was developed by the researcher and it depicts all of the research procedure stages. Three of these stages have been conducted as of this writing. The fourth stage will be conducted in the future during 2011.

Stage 1: Researcher analyzed and synthesized learning society models in Thailand and

Figure 1. The conceptual framework based on research procedures

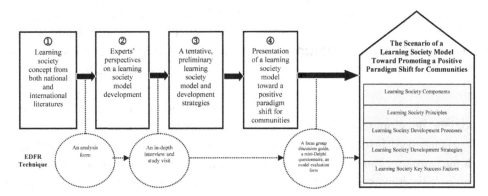

foreign countries from 2003 to present with respect to: (1) social contexts, (2) development direction and policies, (3) components of learning society, (4) relevant individuals and networks, (5) procedures or nature of activities, (6) lifelong learning activities, (7) success factors, (8) principle of practicing community, (9) problems and obstacles, (10) factors leading to the successful implementation of learning society, (11) paradigm and positive paradigm shift for communities, and (12) strategies for the development of learning society.

Stage 2: Researcher explored forty-two experts' perspectives on a learning society development using in-depth interview and study visit.

Stage 3: Researcher developed the tentative and preliminary learning society model toward promoting a positive paradigm shift for communities based on the gathered data from stage 1 and 2, as well as learning society development strategies.

Stage 4: Researcher will propose a learning society model to a focus group. They are encouraged to discuss about particular aspects, enrich and extend the findings, and give their feedback and comments for a clearer explanation of the learning society. To evaluate the developed model for future implementation, the mini-Delphi Techniques questionnaires were distributed to those experts to evaluate the overall model in five major dimensions: (1) the model structure, (2) the model components, (3) the developmental process, (4) the strategic plan, and (5) the administrative management; and, in six sub major dimensions: (a) the correctness, (b) the effectiveness, (c) the implementation plausibility, (d) the coordination with the contexts, (e) the value and benefit, and (f) the sustainability.

Data Analysis

In each research procedure stage, the data were analyzed using content analysis by the researcher. It must be noted that the fourth stage will be conducted at a future time and it is anticipated that any possible changes will be minimal. Thus, this article is written with only the results from the first three stages leaving open whatever changes that may occur in stage four.

RESULTS AND DISCUSSION

To be in line with major changes that Thailand may need to make in this future, and to progress towards the desired learning society, both local and national development shall pursue the following aspects. The results showed that to develop a learning society, it is important to consider the learning society components, principles, developmental processes, strategies, and key success factors.

1. Learning Society Components

Results

Learning society development comprised of both social structure and institutional structure toward lifelong learning. The individual learning communities/cities/towns all operate in their own locally appropriate ways but there nine common themes: *(1) Learners, (2) Learning Providers, (3) Learning Resources/ Institutions, (4) Knowledge/Wisdom, (5) Lifelong Learning Activities, (6) Learning Climate, (7) Learning Network, (8) Knowledge Management, and (9) Learning Groups/Organizations*. In addition, the extra elements that are required for the learning society included community size, community culture and tradition, sharing culture, various groups of people living together, close relationship and socialization, communication network, warm family and strong community, high quality of natural resources and environment, definite development plans and strategies, highly respect the essential of knowledge and lifelong learning, the development of infrastructure, appropriate community design, IT network system, creation of community learning innovation, assurance of knowledge society right of citizens, active support of government and agencies, and setting-up of specific agencies.

Discussion

Learning society, information society, learning city, intelligence city, learning region, technopolis, and knowledge-economy are the common concepts. The common features of the successful cities such as Barcelona, Stockholm, Munich, Montreal, Dublin, Delft as the advantages of the knowledge-based development included: the design and development process including political

and societal will is indispensable; strong dynamics of innovation across all sectors of economic and social activity; strategic vision and development plan is crucial; financial support and strong investment are necessary for setting-up of agencies to promote the development; international, multi-ethnic character of the city is necessary; metropolitan web site is very important; value creation to citizens is indispensable; creation of urban innovation engines is significant; assurance of knowledge society right of citizens is substantial; operation process such as low cost access to communication networks is imperative; citizens are actively involved in their city's development, identity, and character; more sustainable economy; and, creation of a tolerant environment toward minorities and immigrants (Carrillo, 2002, 2006; Malone & Yohe, 2002). The widespread emphasis on ICT infrastructure and education means such as re-structured educational system, better educational services; existence of public libraries' network is necessary; strengthen R&D collaboration between research institutes, universities, and industry that the city has scored high in knowledge dissemination capability. A report of a 1998 high-level OECD seminar on *Competitive Strength and Social Cohesion Through Learning Cities and Regions* summarized their characteristics: (1) a clear and sustained commitment to set learning at the heart of the city/region's development through partnerships; (2) a development strategy encompassing the whole range of learning; (3) creating globally competitive knowledge-intensive production and service activities; (4) improving human and organizational capacities and creating environments conducive to learning, innovation, creativity and change; (5) a specific purpose and identity implying shared values and networks; and (6) social cohesion and environmental issues are an integrated part of the development (Faris, 1998). Moreover, an advisory board and strategic plan, learning towns staff, resourcing and commitment, engagement of local government and the declaration of a community as a learning community, town, city, and region, projects and innovation, networks, partners, flexibility and opportunity in approach and operation, overcoming barriers-a safe neutral space for developing networking skills, new partnerships, learning, increased awareness in the value of learning, promotion and publicity of communities as learning societies, cities, towns, and regions, mentors and models of learning communities are important (McCullough et al., 2003). Additionally, Walters (2005) underlined that "… building a learning region requires a new understanding of the centrality for economic and social development based on lifelong learning process, prioritize excellent education and training systems at all levels, provide frequently update, easily accessible information and counseling services to enable citizens to maximize their learning opportunities and have integrated systems, and the creation of social capital through partnerships and networks" (p. 360).

Therefore, several major concerns for learning society development include the development of lifelong learners, learning providers or groups, community learning resources, community knowledge/ local wisdom, various learning activities, learning environment, learning network, knowledge management, and many learning groups/ organizations.

2. Learning Society Development Principles

Results

The principles that characterize the learning society are informed by the demands of the 21st century, by emergent innovations at the very leading edge, and by what we now know about how learning happens. The learning society principles included the concept of: *(1) Partnership, (2) Participation and Collaboration, (3) Monitoring and Evaluation Process, (4) Lifelong Learning Needs, (5) Community-Based Development, (6)*

Knowledge-Based Community Development, (7) Variety of Lifelong Learning Activities/ Knowledge-Related Activities, (8) Learning Related to Life and Lifelong Learning, (9) Equity Process, and (10) Proactive and Continuous Process.

Discussion

Many empirical studies (Knight, 1995; Carrillo, 2002; Ergazakis et al., 2004; Flores, 2006; Chatzkel, 2006) considered the importance of knowledge as a primary source of power that drives community, city, and society development. The goal of a learning society is to bring out the community's own internal value, direction, character, and energy as recognized by learning communities and community of practice, learning/ knowledge cities, and knowledge organizations. Senesh (1991) indicated that the heart of the learning society is the commitment to a set of values and to a system of education that affords all members of the community the opportunity to stretch their minds to full capacity from early childhood to adulthood. In such a society, lifelong learning is important not only for what it contributes to one's career, but also for the value it adds to the general quality of individuals' lives as well as society at large. Similarly, the key to survival in today's world is lifelong learning, the foundation of learning organizations, a learning society, and a learning culture (Fryer, 1997; Hake, 1999). Moreover, Cisco (2010) pointed out the set of principles designed to meet society's new demands for learning and to realize the learning potential of every part of society and every part of the globe including that it engenders a culture of learning throughout life; aims to develop motivated and engaged learners; takes learning to the learner; believes that learning is for all; recognizes that people learn differently; cultivates and embraces new learning providers; develops new relationships and new networks between learners, providers, funders, and innovators; provides the universal infrastructure they need to succeed-still physical but increasingly virtual; and supports systems of continuous innovation and feedback, and noting "the principles that characterize the Learning Society are informed by the demands of the 21st century, by emergent innovations at the very leading edge, and by what we now know about how learning happens" (pp. 4-5).

Implementing a lifelong learning society is not an option for communities but rather a core way of operating and providing the basis for generating new wealth, stable, and sustainable local, national, and global development at the end. Lifelong learning is the creation of the learning environment and the building of learning societies that are committed to social justice and general well-being (UNESCO, 1997). In connection, to provide education throughout life, it must be organized around six fundamental types of learning or pillars of knowledge: learning to know, that is acquiring the instruments of understanding; learning to do, so as to be able to act creatively on one's environment; learning to live together, so as to participate and co-operate with other people in all human activities; learning to be, an essential progression which proceeds from the previous three (Delors, 1998); learning to change, encourages changes in behavior to create a more viable and fairer society for everyone (UNESCO, 2003); and at last learning for sustainability, efforts towards sustainability in any field are build on processes for communicating, learning, and sharing knowledge, engaging people in their multiple roles as individuals, and as members of communities and organizations. Such a vision should inform and guide the future educational reforms and policy in order to form the learning citizens, and build the learning societies. Flores (2006, p. 76) stated that "the foundation of a society is supported by forms of knowledge, such as culture, value, and participation."

Further, the development of learning society is also based on the proactive *partnership* of various networks, *participation* of all members, practitioners/ stakeholders, and networks, and

performance of well-developed programs and activities (Office of Educational Council, 2004). The development of communication or learning networks within schools, families, business, labor, government, organizations, and the community at large is recognized as another important principle of the learning society. This network is the citizens' alliance (Senesh, 1991).

The learning society provides the opportunity to enable all members to actively contribute to the development process and to share equitably in the fruits of development (United Nations, 1981). Finally, the best way to develop a learning society is through the knowledge-based community development (inside out approach) using community resources and knowledge to drive the lifelong learning activities with support from partnerships. Without strong community member's involvement, communities will be unable to build on their strengths as knowledge centers (Knight, 1995).

3. Learning Society Development Processes

Results

The steps for developing and transforming a community into a learning society can be well-developed by both national and local level, including (*1*) *Embracing Learning Society, (2) Setting Up 'Learning Society Development Committee', (3) Diagnosing of Current Community's Status, (4) Developing Learning Society Vision and Strategies, (5) Designing of Detailed Action Plan, (6) Integrating of Partnerships Collaboration, (7) Implementation the Developed Programs and Activities, (8) Carrying Out Monitoring and Evaluation System, (9) Sharing Knowledge/Lesson Learned, and (10) Promoting and Publishing of Communities.* At the national level, the government should support and promote a better grasp of knowledge and understanding of the learning society by coaching community leaders and staff as well as staging an awareness campaign and identification benefits of the learning society to its people. Each community needs to embrace the learning society as a value/conceptual framework among its members. In this study, the learning society integrated the *'bottom-up approach'* to strengthen community's capacity to determine their values and priorities, and to act on these. Meanwhile other external agencies and organizations can be seen as being a partner and facilitator in the developmental processes. In implementing this process, community core groups and members may need to identify the learning society vision and strategies that are appropriate to the community development planning, the local government's administrative system, and recognize the needs and interests of different target groups. Consequently, any effort to develop a learning society should have assured the active support and interactive commitment of all sectors in the society. The process needs to engage these five main actors: (a) key individual; (b) key institutions; (c) core groups; (d) wider interests; and (e) key employers.

Discussion

The projects and activities investigated from various research studies tend to differ according to different context, perception, situation, and objectives. The major projects undertaken by the Victorian Learning Towns include the learning festivals, leadership projects, ICT projects, outreach to potential learners projects, environmental projects, learning plan projects (McCullough et al., 2003). The Lifelong Learning City in South Korea (Choi, 2003) implemented different projects and programs related to lifelong learning such as the annual lifelong learning festival, award ceremony to award outstanding lifelong learning city among the local government, etc. European Learning Cities services often include local economic and community development; educational provision; parks, recreation and informal services; policing and public safety; community health services;

libraries and museums; environmental/waste services; and housing (Faris, 1998). However some communities are beginning to focus the lens of lifelong learning on a range of their services such as Books for Babies family literacy campaign. The processes of monitoring, assessment and evaluation are needed to determine the performance of the community as a learning society and improve the quality and effectiveness of the implemented programs, including the use of informal and formal evaluation opportunities, and authentic assessment throughout the knowledge gathering and lessons sharing among key actors, related groups, and other community members for further recommendation of the current and/or future programming directions. Similarly, a study of development of learning communities in Australia distilled three key findings: local community involvement; networks and partnerships; and learning. The report identified four community development steps: identifying a need; planning; action; and reflection/evaluation (Australia National Training Authority, 2000). At each phase and the end of the process, it is needed for sharing knowledge/ lesson learned among communities' members, other communities nationally and internationally using both formal and informal methods. A primary target of knowledge cities or communities is to reassure that the knowledge management processes (creation, storage, sharing, evaluation, and use of knowledge) at each stage is complete (Ergazakis et al., 2004). Promoting and publicity of the outstanding communities that provided full concepts of learning societies (or towns, cities, and regions) and continuing improvement, including various lifelong learning projects and activities to develop active citizenship and building of social capital, as well as promoting a positive paradigm shift for communities, are also important.

At the end, to transform the community into the learning society, a continuous improvement process is needed. That includes the participatory planning, designing, implementation, and evaluation of various lifelong learning activities based on the community members' needs and interests. The process of developing a learning society is neither quick nor simple (Ergazakis et al., 2004). It is ongoing and dynamic, as well as sustainable. To emphasize, the analysis of the current situation, formulation of a clear and definite learning society plan, vision, and strategy, implementation of the knowledge-based development and lifelong learning programs and activities, and evaluation, the results of the successful processed in developing learning communities in Thailand depend on the participation of key actors in the communities such as community leaders, local authorities, vocational groups leaders, well-respected monks, Thai wisdom teachers, senior teachers, and well-known older adults.

4. Learning Society Development Strategies

Results

To progress towards the desired long-term vision according to the Tenth National Economic and Social Development Plan (2001-2011) "people will have integrity and knowledge of world standard; families are warm; communities are strong; society is peaceful; economy is sufficient, stable, and equitable; environment is of high quality; natural resources are sustainable; administration follows good governance under the system of democracy with the king as head of state; and the country is a respected member of the world community" (National Economic and Social Development Board, 2007, p. 8). Learning society development under the Philosophy of a Sufficiency Economy is the key to pursue those national goals in development and administration from the family level to the community and government levels. Development of a learning society shall pursue the following strategies: *Strategy 1: Development of Lifelong Learners; Strategy 2: Development of Learning Resources; Strategy 3: Development of Knowledge and Wisdom; Strategy 4: Development of Appropriate Community/City Design; Strategy 5: Development of Learning Community and Organization; Strategy 6: Development of Knowledge Management; Strategy 7: Development of Learning Climate and Knowledge Sharing Culture; Strategy 8: Development of Process Improvement; Strategy 9: Development of Infrastructure and Learning Facilities; and Strategy 10: Development of Network Competencies.*

Discussion

Relevant to several successful learning cities and communities, in planning for the future learning societies and communities, it is important to develop: lifelong learning system, formation of a virtuous circle system of individual development, local economic development, social cohesion, policies aimed at partnership, participation and performance, learning liaison related to local innovative projects, development of models incorporating local characteristics and vision, improvement and expansion of learning community driving structure, construction of monitoring and evaluation system, co-operative and collaborative relationships, action involving networks, strategies for future, support for innovation, and adequate infrastructure to support the movement (Carrillo, 2006; Choi, 2003; McCullough et al., 2003). Moreover, to carry out knowledge-based development strategies for the cities (e.g., Buenos Aires, Andalusia cities, Bibao, Birmingham, Barcelona, Sao Paulo, Boston, Edinburgh, Korea, London, Manchester, Munich, Malaga, and Mataro), requires resources, work plan, key success and failure factors, and quality assurance procedures as the main important strategies (Martinez, 2006). Whereas Faris (1998) showed earlier OECD analysis that had emphasized three strengths of the community as a setting for active learning: humans relate their learning to their immediate environment; cities can provide a framework to give coherence to, and enable collaboration among fragmented and diverse education and training providers; and, cities can provide a focus for community led learning and action.

Therefore, developing a learning society is a whole-society endeavor. It demands full participation from all sectors (Cisco, 2010).

5. Key Success Factors

Results

Through an analysis of successful learning society and in-depth interview of experts in the field, as well as the review of several international and national literatures, the following fourteen requisites were revealed as the key success factors: *(1) Community Leaders, (2) Active Funds Support, (3) Various Learning Networks and Partnerships, (4) Appropriate Community Size, (5) Definite Policy, Structure, and Direction, (6) Construction of Strategies and the Implementation, (7) Appropriate Community Design, (8) Community Members/ Volunteer Groups, (9) Knowledge Sharing Culture, (10) Close Relationship among Community Members, (11) a Variety of Learning Activities, (12) Infrastructure System, (13) Appropriate IT Networks System, and (14) Learning Insurance System*

Discussion

Several empirical studies (Martinez, 2006; Knight, 1992, 1989; Drewett et al., 1992) indicated other influential factors for developing a successful learning society. For instance, personal internal factors such as the learning motivation, public and volunteer mind, social responsibility and caring, eager to learn, risk taking, active commitment to participation and collaboration of all agents involved, the definite planning strategies that build on the strengths of communities' knowledge and resources, a desire for continuous improvement, and maintaining a balance between global and local forces are considered as main factors for innovation and competitiveness. Correspondingly,

Carrillo (2003) pointed out that "the opportunity that each city, region, country engages in this new development dynamics and gets measured with this new global yardstick vanishes every day that it procrastinates the decision. Even trying, the evidence suggests that it takes a lot more than good will to succeed" (p. 5). The key conditions underlying the successful knowledge cities, knowledge regions, knowledge world: urban (Singapore, Barcelona), regional (Veneto Valley, Basque Country), national (Denmark, New Zealand), and supranational (European Union) included a leadership committed to the sustainable wellbeing of its community; a critical mass of change agents having a sufficient understanding of the qualitative differences of knowledge-based development; a conceptual and technical capacity to articulate and develop the social system of capitals; a rigorous and transparent state of knowledge-based social capital; a series of strategic initiatives to reach an optimal capital balance, feeding on best global practices; and an international network of relationships with leading entities in knowledge-based innovation (Carrillo, 2003).

In the context of Thai society, most of the initiatives are led by local government. According to the National Economic and Social Development Board (2007), there are 1.7 million development leaders, including community leaders and keepers of local wisdom (or Thai wisdom teachers), who play important roles as the driving force in community development. Although, local government administrators, and community committee, as well as stakeholders play crucial roles in community development, once the learning society structure is relatively developed and implemented, the role of community members will greatly influence continued and sustainable development. When such results are evident, other related organizations will naturally take active interest and seek to successfully promote the communities.

Certainly, different types of change exist. Hohn (1998) identifies four: change by exception, incremental change, pendulum change, and paradigm change. Paradigm change involves a fundamental rethinking of premises and assumptions, and both individuals and communities can experience it. Paradigm change involves a changing of assumptions, beliefs, and values about how the world works. Hence, to develop the learning society model that promotes a positive paradigm shift for communities, it is essential for the communities to prepare for future changes. This will happen by putting greater attention on how to develop the learning society that maintains a balance between global and local forces, integrates various local wisdom and knowledge producing cultures, encourages the collaboration among social networks, and awakens individual learning in order to achieve sustainable development and the well-being of people. Further, it is believed that positive paradigm shifts can lead to resolution of social problems and crises. Past paradigms have led to more positive changes and improved quality of life.

The structure of essential elements of a learning society model toward promoting a positive paradigm shift for communities was developed by the researcher in a capsule form as illustrated in Figure 2, which depicts the findings of the study. A learning society model comprised of the learning society components, learning society principles, learning society development processes, learning society development strategies, and learning society key success factors.

RECOMMENDATIONS

Recommendations for Further Development

Building the Learning Society needs to mobilize new structures, new approaches, and new technology to deliver a new balance of skills to a lifelong learning population. All groups in the society: government, local agencies, private organizations,

NGOs, and communities should be involved in the learning society development as follow:

1. The government should set a national workshop and conference for developing a national learning society driving structure, as well as propose the learning society as the *National Agenda* for the preparation of the country to become the complete learning society toward the cooperation among social networks, and the support in policy administrative management and budget.

2. The government, related organizations and communities should implement the learning society development strategies based on the results including the development of lifelong learners, learning resources, knowledge and wisdom, the community/city learning environment, learning infrastructure and learning facilities, learning community and organization, knowledge management, learning climate and knowledge sharing culture, and network competencies.

3. The government should promote and support communities, learning providers, and individuals to be able to develop their own learning materials, facilities, and lifelong learning activities to enhance community lifelong learning based on community-based development.

4. Local agencies, government, private organizations, NGOs, and communities should develop the learning society network parties as a partnership for community learning development and learning society, and enhance network's capabilities in conducting lifelong learning programs and activities that serve the needs and interests of the target groups focusing on the proactive participation and continuing process.

5. Local agencies should set the learning society development plan for their own communities within the local government's administrative system by involving community

Figure 2. A learning society model toward promoting a positive paradigm shift for communities

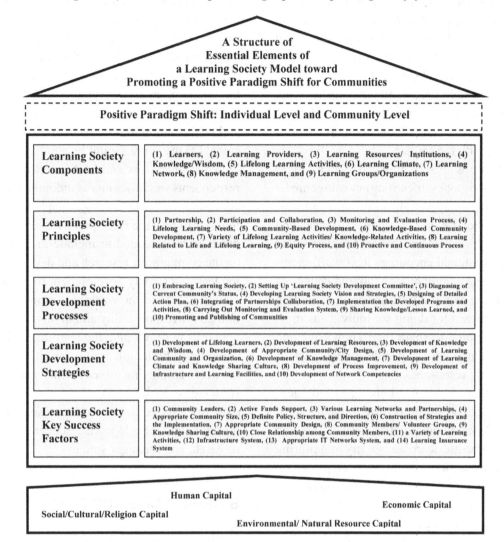

members, the government and other related organizations.

6. The government should develop a national learning society data base to provide the opportunity for people and organizations within the country and other countries to be able to access and acquire the essential fundamental knowledge and practices of learning society.

7. The local and national educational institutions and communities should collaboratively conduct the new knowledge and innovation, research and development on the learning society development in different community contexts.

8. Community committee, local authority, and community members should form a learning society development committee in generating a learning society system by involving community members, the government and other related organizations.

9. The Office of the Non-Formal and Informal Education, Ministry of Education should be the main organization responsible for developing the extensive learning society, promote a value framework and increase

awareness of learning society value, and enhance the potential of the educational personnel, teachers, adult educators, and network parties in particular areas: learning society development, knowledge-based development, community lifelong learning, program development, etc., to create new ways of managing lifelong support relationships with the learner.

10. All groups must be prepared to invest more time and money in learning innovative media development, provide more learning areas, organize lifelong learning programs and activities in the communities. Employers and unions should encourage their staff, members, and communities to take advantage of learning opportunities, and provide funding and reward for doing so. Individuals must be prepared to share their knowledge and experience among people though various learning resources.

11. The related organizations e.g., local agencies, government, private organizations, NGOs, and communities should construct an authentic learning society monitoring and evaluation system, with emphasis on an authentic assessment and evaluation in their real life situations and contexts.

12. International organizations and social investors should lead governments and businesses in a long-term process to develop legitimate, standard credentialing systems that offer the prospect of portable qualifications that are recognized around the world.

Recommendations for Future Research

It is recommended that further studies should focus on (1) the implementation of the learning society developmental processes in various communities toward in-depth investigation on the validation, effectiveness, plausibility, coordination and connection, value, and sustainability of the structure and components, developmental processes, strategic planning and evaluation by inviting different levels of participation and focus on the holistic community knowledge-based development. Besides, once the learning society has been outlined, researchers should be able to explore specific aspects of the overall process and help communities make their own best decisions; (2) the study should be administered with larger sample sizes and best practices and that respondents are chosen more randomly from wider contexts as well as different geographical locations in order to provide more precise knowledge; (3) needs to be extended to include in-depth study on the comparative research and development of the learning society development from different countries around the world; (4) more investigation on the responsibility and involvement of the networks in developing the learning society and community lifelong learning activities development; (5) employing mixed methods and various strategies to look for more fundamental and true data (e.g. participatory action research study, research and development, scenario planning research, and foresight studies).

SIGNIFICANCE AND CONCLUSION

As yet the challenges of globalization do not have the same influence on all countries, and the countermeasures for them differ respectively as well. Thus the focus for learning society development will differ according to the challenges faced by the nation and local communities. Therefore, it is needed for communities to examine their contexts and develop the appropriate planning and implementation of the learning society based on the above mentioned knowledge at various levels from communities, organizations, cities, regions, and the world society. People and systems must be fully prepared to adapt to future changes and reap future benefits by keeping up with globalization, building resilience, and developing learning societies to enhance the wellness of individuals and society.

Although it remains to be seen, future progress needs focus group discussion and implementation of the developed model in the real community contexts for the future implementation. The study aims to contribute to the shaping of the emerging field of learning societies by collecting data from both primary and secondary sources, using various methods to: propose a feasible learning society model that promotes the positive paradigm shift for communities; raise local and global citizens awareness with respect to the transformation of communities, cities and regions into learning societies where knowledge is considered one of the most valued assets in country development; promote lifelong learning in all sectors of the society; transform the communities into ones of the learning society; provide guidance for those who pursued lifelong learning environment and climate; guide the establishment of learning society development strategies of the stakeholders from both public and private agencies and communities; benefit individuals interested; and, serve as a basis for conducting further research on the subject.

ACKNOWLEDGMENT

With the utmost gratitude, the author would like to deeply thank Dr. Archanya Ratana-Ubol, Dr. Pan Kimpee, the Non-Formal Education Division, the Department of Educational Policy, Management, and Leadership, and the Faculty of Education at Chulalongkorn University. Many thanks are extended to family and friends for valuable support, guidance, and encouragement. And finally, the author wishes to acknowledge and thank Dr. John A. Henschke for his insightful comments on this paper.

REFERENCES

Australian National Training Authority. (2000). *Turning on learning communities*. Canberra, Australia: Australian National Training Authority.

Carrillo, F. J. (2002). Capital systems: Implications for global knowledge agenda. *Journal of Knowledge Management*, 6(4), 379–399. doi:10.1108/13673270210440884

Carrillo, F. J. (2003). *A note on knowledge- based development* (Tech. Rep. No. CSC2003-07). Monterrey, Mexico: The World Capital Institute.

Carrillo, F. J. (2004). Capital cities: A taxonomy of capital accounts for knowledge cities. *Journal of Knowledge Management*, 8(5), 28–46. doi:10.1108/1367327041058738

Carrillo, F. J. (Ed.). (2006). *Knowledge cities: Approaches, experiences and perspectives*. Oxford, UK: Butterworth- Heinemann/Elsevier.

Casey, C. (2006). A knowledge economy and a learning society: A comparative analysis of New Zealand and Australian experiences. *British Journal of Comparative Education*, 36(3), 343–357.

Chatzkel, J. (2006). Greater phoenix as a knowledge capital. In Carrillo, F. J. (Ed.), *Knowledge cities: Approaches, experiences and perspectives* (pp. 135–144). Oxford, UK: Butterworth- Heinemann/Elsevier.

Choi, S. D. (2003). *Changing skills formation and lifelong learning in South Korea*. Unpublished doctoral dissertation, University of London, London, UK.

Cisco. (2010). *The learning society*. Retrieved from http://tools.cisco.com/search/JSP/search-results.get?strQueryText=the+learning+society+& Search+All+cisco.com= cisco.com&language= en&country= US&thissection= f&accessLevel= Guest

Delors, J. (1998). *Learning the treasure within.* Paris, France: UNESCO.

Drewett, R., Knight, R., & Schubert, U. (1992). *The future of European cities: The role of science and technology.* Brussels, Belgium: European Commission.

Dulayakasem, U. (2005). *Past/future of non-formal education management.* Bangkok, Thailand: Monitoring and Evaluation Group, The Office of Non-formal Education Administration.

Ergazakis, K., Karnezis, K., Metaxiotis, K., & Psarras, J. (2004). Towards knowledge cities conceptual analysis and success stories. *Journal of Knowledge Management, 8*(5), 5–15. doi:10.1108/13673270410558747

Ergazakis, K., Metaxiotis, K., Psarras, J., & Askounis, D. (2006). An emerging pattern of successful knowledge cities' main features. In Carrillo, F. J. (Ed.), *Knowledge cities: Approaches, experiences and perspectives* (pp. 3–16). Oxford, UK: Butterworth- Heinemann/Elsevier.

Faris, J., & Peterson, W. (2000). *Learning-based community development: Lessons learned for British Columbia.* Victoria, BC, Canada: Ministry of Community Development, Cooperatives and Volunteers.

Faris, R. (1998). *Learning communities: Cities, towns and villages preparing for a 21st century knowledge-based economy.* Retrieved from http://members.shaw.ca/rfaris/LC.htm

Faris, R. (2006). *Learning cities: Lessons learned.* Retrieved from http://members.shaw.ca/rfaris/docs/VLC%20Lessons%20Learned.pdf

Flores, P. (2006). Implementation of the capital system for a knowledge city. In Carrillo, F. J. (Ed.), *Knowledge cities: Approaches, experiences and perspectives* (pp. 75–84). Oxford, UK: Butterworth- Heinemann/Elsevier.

Fryer, R. H. (1997). *Learning for the twenty first century (the Fryer report).* London, UK: DFEE.

Hake, B. (1999). *Learning to survive in late modernity: From emancipation to employability in the learning society.* International Jahrbuch der Erwachsenenbildung.

Hohn, M. D. (1998). Why is change so hard? Theories and thoughts about the organizational change process. *Focus on Basics, 2,* 1–8.

Holden, M., & Connelly, S. (2004). The learning city: Urban sustainability education and building toward WUF legacy. In Oberlander, H. P. (Ed.), *The Vancouver working group discussion papers for the world urban forum on sustainability* (pp. 1–54). Ottawa, ON, Canada: The Canadian Institute of Planners, Government of Canada.

International Association of Education Cities. (2009). *Members cities of the IAEC.* Retrieved from http://www.bcn.es/edcities/aice/estatiques/angels/sec_iaec.html

Keating, D. P., & Hertzman, C. (1999). *Developmental health and the wealth of nations: Social, biological and educational dynamics.* New York, NY: Guildford Press.

Knight, R. V. (1989). City development and urbanization: Building the knowledge-based city. *Urban Affairs Annual Reviews, 35,* 223–242.

Knight, R. V. (1992). *The future of European cities: The role of science and technology, part IV: Cities as Loci of knowledge-based development (Tech. Rep. No. FOP 379).* Brussels, Belgium: European Commission.

Knight, R. V. (1995). Knowledge-based development: Policy and planning implications for cities. *Urban Studies (Edinburgh, Scotland), 32*(2), 225–260. doi:10.1080/00420989550013068

Kwon, I. T., & Schied, F. M. (2009). *Building communities into lifelong learning cities: The case of the Republic of Korea.* Retrieved from http://www.adulterc.org/Proceedings/2009/proceedings/kwon_schied.pdf

Lantz, A., & Brage, C. (2006). *A learning society/ learning organization.* Paris, France: UNESCO.

Laszlo, K. C., & Laszlo, A. (2007). Fostering a sustainable learning society through knowledge-based development. In *Proceedings of the 50th Annual Meeting of the ISSS.*

Longworth, N. (2006). *Learning cities, learning regions, learning communities: Lifelong learning and government.* London, UK: Routledge.

Longworth, N., & Osborne, M. (2010). *Perspectives on learning cities and regions.* Leicester, UK: NIACE.

Malone, T. F., & Yohe, G. W. (2002). Knowledge partnership for sustainable, equitable, and stable society. *Journal of Knowledge Management, 6*(4), 368–378. doi:10.1108/13673270210440875

Martinez, A. (2006). A comparative framework for knowledge cities. In Carrillo, F. J. (Ed.), *Knowledge cities: Approaches, experiences and perspectives* (pp. 17–30). Oxford, UK: Butterworth-Heinemann/Elsevier.

McCullough, M., Carolane, R., & Hetherington, B. (2003). The experience so far. In *Proceedings of the 43rd Annual National Conference Adult Learning Australia*, Canberra, Australia (pp. 297-311).

Morris, L., & Cranford, S. (2007). Toward a knowledge society in the context of a knowledge economy: Where will we go and how we get there? A global perspective. In *Proceedings of the Commission on International Adult Education and the American Association for Adult and Continuing Education Conference*, Norfolk, VA (pp. 137-149).

National Economic and Social Development Board, Office of the Prime Minister. (2007). *The tenth national economic and social development plan 2007-2011* (pp. 1–18). Bangkok, Thailand: National Economic and Social Development Board.

OECD. (1998). *High level seminar on competitive strength and social cohesion through learning cities and regions: Concepts, developments, evaluation.* Paris, France: Center for Research and Innovation.

Office of the Education Council. (2004). *Learning city.* Bangkok, Thailand: Educational Standards and Learning Development Bureau.

Office of the Education Council. (2008). *Research study on evaluation process of education for learning society promotion.* Bangkok, Thailand: Ministry of Education.

Pongpaiboon, P. (2007). *Learning society.* Retrieved from http://learners.in.th/blog/yardnapa2/15632

Sangsri, S. (2005). *The development of learning communities/ cities for Thai society. Bangkok: Learning policy development group in local wisdom and traveling.* Bangkok, Thailand: Standards and Learning Bureau.

Senesh, L. (1991). *Building a learning society.* Retrieved from http://www.ERIC.org

Sibmuenpiam, N. (2003). *The development of learning city model: Local administrative organization, Chonburi Province.* Bangkok, Thailand: Chulalongkorn University.

Su, Y. H. (2007). *The learning society as itself: Lifelong learning, individualization of learning, and beyond education.* Retrieved from http://www.ERIC.org

UNESCO. (1997). *The Hamburg declaration on adult learning.* Paper presented at the Fifth International Conference on Adult Education.

UNESCO. (2003). *Nurturing the treasure - vision and strategy of the UNESCO institute for education 2002-2007*. Retrieved from http://www.unesco.org/education/uie/pdf/MTS.pdf

UNESCO. (2005). *Towards knowledge societies*. Retrieved from http://www.unesco.org/en/worldreport

United Nations. (1981). *Popular participation as a strategy for planning community level action and national development*. New York, NY: United Nations.

Walters, S. (2005). Learning region. In English, L. M. (Ed.), *International encyclopedia of adult education* (pp. 360–362). Hampshire, UK: Palgrave Macmillan.

World Bank. (1998). *Knowledge for development*. Retrieved from http://www.worldbank.org/wdr/wdr98

Yarnit, M. (1998). *Learning towns and cities-survey*. Hershey, PA: IGI Global.

This work was previously published in the International Journal of Adult Vocational Education and Technology, Volume 2, Issue 3, edited by Victor C.X. Wang, pp. 30-47, copyright 2011 by IGI Publishing (an imprint of IGI Global).

Chapter 14
Exploring the Preparedness of Business Education Teacher Candidates for their Internships:
The Perspectives of Mentor Teachers

Edward C. Fletcher Jr.
University of South Florida, USA

Kathy Mountjoy
Illinois State University, USA

Glenn Bailey
Illinois State University, USA

ABSTRACT

Applying a modified-Delphi technique, this research study sought consensus from business educa-tion mentor teachers regarding the top three areas in which business education student teachers were prepared as well as underprepared for their roles as teachers. Further, the mentor teachers provided recommendations for business education teacher preparation programs to implement to better prepare their teacher candidates for the student teaching internship. To that end, the mentor teachers did not gain consensus on the top three areas their student teachers were most prepared. However, they did agree classroom management and working with special needs' students were among the top three areas their student teachers were least prepared. The mentor teachers agreed business education teacher preparation programs could provide more experiences with classroom management in public schools and provide their teacher candidates with more information about the workload and commitment needed to be effective teachers.

DOI: 10.4018/978-1-4666-2062-9.ch014

INTRODUCTION

The student teaching internship is the final preparatory experience, and has been cited as the most vital, exciting, and problematic time for teacher candidates (Conderman, Morin, & Stephens, 2005; Fives, Hamman, & Olivarez, 2007; Grossman, Schoenfeld, & Lee, 2005; Pena & Almaguer, 2007). Moreover, the result of the experience is one of the best indicators predicting teacher candidates' likelihood to pursue a teaching career (Conderman et al., 2005). To better prepare teacher candidates for their internships, it is critical to understand the issues and challenges which occur throughout their student teaching experiences.

The majority of studies investigating the student teaching experience have examined the perspectives of student teachers in terms of their issues and challenges (Fletcher, Mountjoy, & Bailey, in press); however, little research has investigated the perspectives of their mentor teachers (commonly referred to as cooperating teachers Crews & Bodenhamer, 2009). Furthermore, very little research has been conducted examining the possible unique issues of business education student teachers (Fletcher et al., in press). Instead, the research which has ensued on this topic has largely left out the business education discipline.

PURPOSE AND RESEARCH QUESTIONS

To that end, the purpose of this research study was to explore the perspectives of mentor teachers regarding issues, challenges, and barriers they encountered when mentoring their student teachers. More specifically, this study examined which areas business education student teachers were prepared as well as underprepared for their roles as teachers as well as initiatives business education teacher preparation programs could implement to better prepare their teacher candidates for the student teaching internship. The research questions guiding this study were as follows:

1. What are the top three areas which mentor teachers believed their student teachers were most prepared?
2. What are the top three areas which mentor teachers believed their student teachers were least prepared?
3. What initiatives might business teacher preparation programs implement to better prepare their student teachers?

REVIEW OF THE LITERATURE

The two most important considerations in individuals' abilities to successfully develop competencies include the process of learning and the transfer of learning (Bransford, Brown, & Cocking, 1999). Learning experiences which support transfer include, but are not limited to, the following: (a) the mastery of foundational concepts which are germane to the subject; (b) the focus on understanding instead of mere memorization; (c) an adequate investment of time to gain sufficient knowledge; (d) the level of engagement in intentional practice with continuous monitoring and feedback; and, (e) the context in which the initial learning takes place: "people can learn in one context, yet fail to transfer to other contexts" (Bransford et al., 1999). All of these factors are perennial challenges for teacher preparation programs. In the context of teacher preparation, the ability of teacher candidates to transfer and apply knowledge gained from coursework and prior field experiences to clinical practice is oftentimes a difficult and problematic process. As such, this puts a lot of pressure and dependence on the triad relationship (university supervisor, mentor teacher, and student teacher), in clinical practice, in terms of developing teacher candidates and helping them bridge the gap between theory and practice.

Extensive research has been conducted in the field of teacher education regarding the quintessential student teaching experience (Hamman et al., 2006; Kent, 2001). Given the importance of this experience for student teachers' probabilities of entering into the teaching profession (Conderman et al., 2005), this vast investment in better understanding how to construct and facilitate effective clinical experiences is well warranted. According to Dever, Hager, and Klein (2003), "a partnership in which university and public school faculties work in concert to connect academic learning and practical experience is optimal for student teachers as well as beneficial to the work of the university and public school partners" (p. 246).

Based on the findings of studies on the nature of the triad relationship in clinical practice, research has suggested the mentor teacher plays a pivotal and leading role in the development of their future teachers (Dever et al., 2003; Killian & Wilkins, 2009). The roles and responsibilities of mentor teachers include, but certainly are not limited to, modeling best practices, co-planning lessons, providing continuous and frequent feedback and practice, co-reflecting, and assisting in the development of pedagogical content knowledge (knowledge of how to teach the content) while the student teacher progressively gains more accountability for the classroom (Darling-Hammond, Hammerness, Grossman, Rust, & Shulman, 2005; Goodnough, Osmond, Dibbon, Glassman, & Stevens, 2009; Nilsson & van Driel, 2010). Parker-Katz and Bay (2008) described the mentoring process by stating: "for in mentoring we recognize a teacher's role, wisdom, and ability to link kinds of knowledge into a fabric to guide, support, and direct novices as they advance their understandings of teaching and pupils' learning" (p. 1260). Further, Dever et al. (2003) indicated the relationship between mentor teachers and student teachers should emphasize the need to analyze, evaluate, and identify ways in which student teachers might change their future instructional practices to help promote a positive

learning environment and enhance student learning. However, most mentor teachers never receive any formal training for their critical roles. This practice is quite problematic because they have such influence over the long-term practices of their student teachers (Dever et al., 2003).

Moreover, this practice of collaborative reflection and co-construction of lessons also contributes to the professional development of the mentor teacher as well (Dever et al, 2003). In fact, in a qualitative research study utilizing a case study method, Nilsson and van Driel (2010) examined two pairs of science student teachers and their mentor teachers to explore what learning took place among both student teachers and their mentor teachers. They found collaborative reflections and co-construction of lessons enabled the mentor teachers to build on their own instructional practices and allowed them to reflect on their student teachers' instructional practices. These two events were mutually advantageous for both parties involved.

CONCEPTUAL FRAMEWORK

During their professional careers, teachers will experience an array of frustrations and concerns related to teaching. The most intense time teachers encounter these issues is during student teaching and throughout the first years of their careers (Fritz & Miller, 2003). The concerns of practicing teachers and teacher candidates are important because it usually embodies their professional development needs, indicates what issues are most relevant, and points to areas they are most motivated to learn. These individuals are also less likely to be motivated to learn about topics which are not within their immediate scope of concerns (Fuller, Parsons, & Watkins, 1974).

Teacher candidates and beginning teachers tend to be particularly preoccupied with their own performances and success with teaching, in contrast to being focused on their students' well-being and performance. The most perennial concerns for teacher candidates are oftentimes their abilities to manage the classroom, their content knowledge, their evaluations from university supervisors and mentor teachers, and whether they are fond of their students (Fuller et al., 1974).

These phenomena have been explainable through Fuller et al.'s (1974) teaching concerns model, which categorized them based on three stages: (a) pre-teaching-typified by survival or concerns with individual performances; (b) early teaching-characterized by task concerns; and, (c) late concerns-illustrated by concerns with student learning and achievement. Pre-teaching concerns, which mostly plague teacher candidates, are connected to a fixation with one's own self-adequacy and survival in the classroom. The early teaching stage is frequently experienced by beginning teachers and is usually manifested with concerns about instruction, workload, the perceptions of students, and evaluating students' learning. The late concerns stage is emblematic of fixation with student achievement and the holistic development of students. This stage is an ideal one because it puts the focus on where it should be-the students.

METHODS

Research Design

To address the research questions, a modified-Delphi technique (a mixed methods approach) was implemented for the purpose of gaining a consensus among business education mentor teachers around the competencies which business student teachers were most and least prepared as well as forming a consensus around the areas which business teacher preparation programs could reform their curricula to better prepare business education student teachers for their internships. The modified-Delphi design differs slightly from a typical Delphi study as it begins with a list of items, developed from the literature, in which

respondents rank. The Delphi approach consisted of three rounds of data collection.

The Delphi technique is valuable in terms of encapsulating areas of evidence or understandings which are not often publicized, but are domains of collective knowledge (Stitt-Gohdes & Crews, 2004), and for determining a consensus opinion concerning an area which does not lend itself to exact quantification (Dalkey, Rourke, Lewis & Snyder, 1972; Ludwig, 1994). This technique permits panel members to unreservedly articulate their individual points of views, while still developing agreement among the group to gain expert opinions on the topic of interest (Clayton, 1997).

In this study, the researchers sought to extend beyond merely identifying a list of competencies and areas of needed development of the business teachers; instead, the intent of this research study was to identify a sense of priorities or importance to the needs articulated by the business education mentor teachers as well as to offer recommendations for business education teacher preparation programs to enhance the preparation of their student teachers. The researchers chose the Delphi method because it enabled business education mentor teachers to evaluate their subjective experiences, establish priorities in terms of their student teachers' professional development needs, and allowed them to come to a consensus in terms of their issues and challenges in working with business education student teachers without being influenced by group dynamics in a focus group situation. This consensus assisted the researchers in better understanding the entire group's experiences and enabled the researchers to examine ways in which programs might be re-structured and transformed to better meet the needs of their business education student teachers as well as their mentor teachers.

Panel Selection

The participants of this study included recent business education mentor teachers from one

Midwestern teacher preparation program using purposive sampling. To be included in this study, the mentor teachers were required to have mentored business education student teachers within the last year, were considered to have deep knowledge and experience in the topic, and had important information to share. Participants were recruited from a list of business education mentor teachers ($n = 67$) compiled from a business education student teaching internship course.

Participants

From the 67 potential participants, 32 mentor teachers confirmed their willingness to participate as members of the panel of experts, providing a 48% response rate. All 32 participants were from one Midwestern state. The number of participants appropriate for Delphi studies tends to be from 10 to 30, since the goal of this type of research is to gain consensus (Delbecq, Van de Ven, & Gustafson, 1975). All participants included in this study were current practicing teachers and were licensed to teach business, marketing, or computer education in K-12 school settings. Only business education mentor teachers which have mentored student teachers within the last year were selected to participate in this study for the primary reason they would have better recollections of their challenges and issues with regard to mentoring business education student teachers. The researchers determined recent experience in mentoring a business education student teacher was most appropriate in order to truly reflect on their experiences in working with a business education student teacher from a contemporary teacher preparation program. These mentor teachers were deemed to be experts in knowing and understanding the mentoring process for business education student teachers. Further, these teachers were identified as being effective teachers and mentors.

The expert panel widely ranged in ages from 25 to 63 years old. In terms of gender, 12 (37.5%) were male and 20 (62.5%) were female. In regard to ethnicity, the participants were rather monolithic with 31 (96.9%) participants being Caucasian and one participant being Asian. The mentor teachers were comprised of three (10.7%) elementary teachers, six (18.8%) middle school teachers, 21 (65.6%) high school teachers, one (3%) mentor teacher which taught both at the middle and high school levels, and one (3%) mentor teacher which taught at all grade levels. The school communities in which the mentor teachers taught ranged from nine (28.1%) teaching in a rural (population of < 2,500), 17 (53.1%) teaching in a small urban (2,501 to 50,000), five (15.6%) teaching in a large urban (50,000 to 2 million), and one (3.1%) teaching in a metropolitan (> 2 million) area. All participants taught in a comprehensive school. The number of years of experience of the participants ranged from two to 38, with a mean of 18. The number of student teachers the mentor teachers mentored ranged from one to 24. The highest degree achieved ranged from seven (21.9%) having earned a bachelor's degree, 24 (75%) individuals having earned a master's degree, and one (3.1%) whom earned an educational specialist degree.

Instrumentation

Specialized instruments were created for use with the panelists in this study. Three online questionnaires were developed and sent to the participants through e-mail. The questionnaires consisted of 30 items for the first round, 10 for the second round, and 28 for the third.

Content validity, the determination of whether the items accurately represent the intended domain, was established by a panel of experts in business education. These experts included six business teacher educators. Based on their comments and suggestions, the researchers revised the questionnaires as appropriate. Given the nature of the Delphi study, conventional means of determining reliability are not appropriate (Hughes, 1993). By design, the Delphi technique strives to achieve consistency in responses by gaining consensus with the items of the questionnaire.

Delphi Procedure

Round One: This research study utilized a three-round, iterative multistage modified-Delphi design to seek agreement on the items of the questionnaires; two to three rounds are typically recommended when using the Delphi method (Altschuld, 1993; Cyphert & Gant, 1971; Hasson, Keeney, & McKenna, 2000). The first-round asked the panelists to respond to 12 demographic items and to identify the top three areas in which the mentor teachers believed their student teachers were most and least prepared for their student teaching internships. In addition, they listed initiatives business education teacher preparation programs could implement to better prepare their business education student teachers. The participants were also encouraged to provide rationales for their rankings.

Round Two: The second round asked the respondents to review the statistical summaries and rationales provided from the first round, which was summarized by the researchers, to make the participants aware of the diversity of opinions and rationales underlying them (Altschuld, 1993; Ulshak, 1983). In addition, the mean and frequency were reported for each response for the participants to review (Hasson et al., 2000; Ulschak, 1983; Witkin, 1984). The participants were then asked to re-rank the areas they believed their student teachers were most and least prepared as well as rank the top three initiatives business education teacher preparation programs could implement to better prepare their student teachers.

Round Three: The third and final round provided a summary of statistical results from the second round and asked the respondents to agree or disagree with the rankings for the

purpose of achieving group consensus. In addition, the expert panel rated the level of importance of each item for their student teachers to understand based on a Likert-type scale (1 = *not important* to 5 = *critical*) as well as how much the item impacts K-12 students' learning (1 = *no impact* to 5 = *major impact*).

Data Analysis

An online survey provider, Survey Monkey, was chosen to create the online instruments. Data were aggregated from the group responses with frequencies and means. Consensus of the items were determined when 80% of the respondents agreed, since this criterion is oftentimes preferred in Delphi studies (Ulschak, 1983).

RESULTS

Results from Round One

For round one, the expert panel were asked to rank the top three areas they believed their student teachers were most prepared to confront at the start of their student teaching internships as well as the top three areas they were least prepared to handle. The researchers provided areas which the participants ranked, based on a review of literature as well as based on the researchers' own experiences in working with student teachers. The expert panel were given the opportunity to provide additional areas as they thought appropriate. In addition, the participants suggested the top three areas in which business education teacher preparation programs could implement to better prepare their student teachers. The participants developed their own list of recommendations in response to an item on the questionnaire which asked them to name three areas they believed business education teacher preparation programs should implement to better prepare their student teachers.

Most and least prepared areas (Round One). As illustrated in Table 1, 17 (53.1%) individuals from the expert panel indicated their student teachers were most prepared in the area of integrating technology (53.1%), 14 (43.8%) thought their student teachers had appropriate dispositions (i.e., a belief that all students are able to learn), and 13 (40.6%) believed their student teachers were most prepared in the area of content knowledge. In regard to the areas in which the student teachers were least prepared, 17 (53.1%) individuals from the expert panel selected classroom management, nine (29%) indicated working and accommodating

special needs' students, and eight (25.8%) stated organizational and time management skills.

Recommendations for business education teacher preparation programs (Round One). In round one, the expert panel were able to identify numerous initiatives in which business education teacher preparation programs could implement to better prepare their student teachers. Based on the areas identified, the researchers categorized the responses in round one for the participants to then rank in round two.

Most and least prepared areas (Round Two). For round two, 18 individuals (56.3%) from the expert panel ranked professionalism as the area in which the student teachers were most prepared, 16 (50%) ranked technology integration, and 16 (50%) ranked content knowledge (Table 2). In terms of the areas in which the expert panel believed the student teachers were least prepared, 20 individuals (62.5%) ranked working with special needs' students, 13 (40.6%) ranked classroom management, and 13 (40.6%) ranked organizational and time management skills.

Recommendations for business education teacher preparation programs (Round Two). In regard to recommendations for business education teacher preparation programs, 17 mentor teachers (53.1%) from the panel of experts ranked experiences with classroom management as one of the top three areas to be implemented, 13 (40.6%) ranked information about workload/ commitment, and 11 (34.4%) ranked teaching more about working with diverse learners (Table 3).

Round Three (Final Round) Results. The purpose of the final round was to seek closure and consensus on the top three areas in which the panel of experts believed their student teachers were most and least prepared as well as to finalize recommendations in terms of initiatives business education teacher preparation programs could implement to better prepare their student teachers. In addition, the mentor teachers rated the importance of each area for student teachers to learn as

Table 1. Top three competencies of student teachers in round one

Areas	Most Prepared		Least Prepared	
	f	*M*	*f*	*M*
Appropriate dispositions	14	43.8	1	3.2
Content knowledge	13	40.6	5	16.1
Effective strategies to engage students	2	6.3	7	22.6
Planning for instruction	9	28.1	4	12.9
Classroom management	5	15.6	17	54.8
Establishing rapport with students	9	28.1	2	6.5
Working with special needs' students	3	9.4	9	29.0
Technology integration	17	53.1	5	16.1
Assessment	5	15.6	5	16.1
Obtaining instructional resources	8	25.0	1	3.2
Pedagogical knowledge	6	18.8	0	0
Pedagogical content knowledge	4	12.5	3	9.7
Knowledge of business education as a profession	7	21.9	3	9.7
Knowledge of effective communication to parents	2	6.3	4	12.9
Teaching-related administrative duties	2	6.3	4	12.9
Organization and time management	4	12.5	8	25.8
Professionalism	11	34.4	4	12.9
Other	0	0	2	6.5

Note: f = frequency; *M* = mean; *n* = 32

Table 2. Top Three competencies of student teachers in round two

	Most Prepared		Least Prepared	
Areas	*f*	*M*	*f*	*M*
Appropriate dispositions	14	43.8	1	3.1
Content knowledge	16	50.0	4	12.5
Effective strategies to engage students	4	12.5	10	31.3
Planning for instruction	4	12.5	6	18.8
Classroom management	1	3.1	13	40.6
Establishing rapport with students	8	25.0	3	9.4
Working with special needs' students	0	0	20	62.5
Technology integration	16	50.0	3	9.4
Assessment	0	0	4	12.5
Obtaining instructional resources	3	9.4	2	6.3
Pedagogical knowledge	2	6.3	0	0
Pedagogical content knowledge	3	9.4	1	3.1
Knowledge of business education as a profession	5	15.6	0	0
Knowledge of effective communication to parents	0	0	8	25.0
Teaching-related administrative duties	0	0	7	21.9
Organization and time management	2	6.3	13	40.6
Professionalism	18	56.3	3	9.4

Note: f = frequency; *M* = mean; *n* = 32

Table 3. Recommendations for business teacher preparation programs in Round Two

Recommendations	*f*	*M*
Experiences with classroom management in a public school	17	53.1
Information about workload/commitment needed	13	40.6
Teach more about working with diverse learners	11	34.4
Classroom management courses	6	18.8
Special education courses	6	18.8
Information about the importance of student teaching	5	15.6
Methods courses	5	15.6
Providing competencies the student teacher needs to master	5	15.6
Work on organization/time management skills	5	15.6
Work on organization/time management skills	5	15.6
Providing competencies the student teacher needs to master	5	15.6
Information on professionalism	4	12.5
Broaden the scope of what types of jobs are available	3	9.4
Developing technology skills	3	9.4
Allowing cooperating teacher to meet with student teacher prior to accepting	2	6.3
Information on how to set up gradebook	2	6.3
Information on current licensure requirements	1	3.1
Limiting the class load and allowing to observe other teachers	1	3.1
Providing experiences in middle and high schools	1	3.1
Providing more appropriate placements	1	3.1
Providing teaching experiences with a block schedule	1	3.1

Note: f = frequency; *M* = mean; *n* = 32

well as the impact each area made in regard to K-12 student learning. The participants rated these items on a five-point Likert scale (1 = *not important* and 5 = *critical*; 1 = *no impact* and 5 = *major impact*, respectively). To that end, 25 (78.1%) of the participants perceived technology integration was one of the top three areas in which business education student teachers were most prepared (Table 4). The participants rated this item a 4.06 in terms of importance for student teachers to learn and 4.09 for impact on K-12 student learning. In addition, 22 (68.8%) believed appropriate dispositions were one of the top three areas in which business education student teachers were most prepared. This item rated 4.22 for importance

for student teachers to learn and 4.31 for impact on K-12 student learning. Further, 22 (68.8%) also perceived professionalism was one of the top three areas in which their business education student teachers were most prepared. This item rated 4.44 in terms of importance for student teachers to learn and 4.22 in regard to impact on K-12 student learning.

Table 4. Round three (Final Round) results

Areas	Most Prepared		Least Prepared		Advice for business education programs		Ratings	
							Importance for student teachers to learn	Impact on K-12 student learning
	f	*M*	*f*	*M*	*f*	*M*	*M*	*M*
Technology integration	25	78.1					4.06	4.09
Appropriate dispositions	22	68.8					4.22	4.31
Professionalism	22	68.8					4.44	4.22
Classroom management strategies			30	93.8			4.53	4.69
Working with special needs' students			26	81.3			4.09	4.13
Organization and time management skills			14	75.0			4.16	4.03
More experiences with classroom management in schools					29	90.6		
More information on amount of workload/commitment needed					29	90.6		
Teaching more about working with diverse learners					23	71.9		

Note: f = frequency; *M* = mean; *n* = 32

In terms of areas in which the panel of experts perceived their student teachers were least prepared, 30 (93.8%) agreed classroom management strategies were in the top three areas. The expert panel rated this item as a 4.53 in terms of importance for student teachers to learn and a 4.69 for impact on K-12 student learning. In addition, 26 (81.3%) agreed working with and accommodating special needs' students was one of the top three skills student teachers were least prepared. The mentor teachers rated this item as 4.09 in terms of importance for student teachers and 4.13 for impact on K-12 student learning. Further, 23 (71.9%) believed organizational and time management skills were among the top three areas their student teachers were least prepared. The respondents rated this item a 4.16 in regard to importance for student teachers to learn and 4.03 for impact on K-12 student learning.

In regard to one of the top three initiatives in which the mentor teachers recommended business education teacher preparation programs implement to better prepare their student teachers, 29 (90.6%) of the individuals in the expert panel agreed providing the student teachers with more experiences with classroom management in public school settings would be highly beneficial. In addition, 29 (90.6%) also agreed business education teacher preparation programs could provide more information to their student teachers about the amount of workload and commitment needed to be an effective classroom teacher. Last, 23 (71.9%) individuals in the expert panel believed business education teacher preparation programs could teach student teachers more about working with diverse learners.

CONCLUSION AND DISCUSSION

The 32 members of the expert panel could not reach a consensus on the areas in which their business education student teachers were most prepared. This lack of consensus could be an indication business education student teachers have different and unique strengths each individual brings with them to their internships. To illustrate, one Caucasian, 58 year old, female elementary teacher with 27 years of teaching experience, which we will call Ann, noted in the first round: "This was hard to answer because all three [student teachers] had different strengths. Some came better prepared in some areas over others". A second respondent, Susan, whom was a Caucasian, 40 year-old female with 17 years of experience indicated: "These are difficult to rank, as my two student teachers were completely different. One was an over-achiever, the other was a procrastinator. But one related better to the students than the other. Their strengths were definitely in opposite areas". Another plausible explanation could point to the issue that student teachers might be mentored and assessed in vastly different ways, and the quality of their experiences could be more a result of the placement than a standardized mentoring process. This divergence provides a rationale for recommending more guidance be provided to assist mentor teachers, particularly with specific competencies business education teacher preparation programs are seeking as well as including metrics to evaluate them. Despite the lack of consensus concerning strengths of business education student teachers, the top three areas articulated by the mentor teachers in terms of strengths were student teachers' abilities to integrate technology into their lessons. In addition, appropriate dispositions (such as attitudes or beliefs that all students can learn) as well as professionalism were both areas of strength. The majority of the mentor teachers believed professionalism was very important for student teachers to learn and most believed appropriate dispositions from their student teachers made a large to major impact on K-12 students' learning.

On the other hand, the mentor teachers did indeed reach consensus on two of the three top areas in which their business education student teachers were least prepared. As expected, the expert panel believed classroom management strategies was an area of deficiency for their student teachers. Not only is this finding consistent with a wealth of teacher education research in the

area of student teaching (Gal, 2006; Sadler, 2006), but it also corresponds to research examining the challenges and issues of business education student teachers reported by teacher candidates themselves (Fletcher et al., in press). Fletcher et al. (in press) in a previous study found classroom management was *the* primary concern business education student teachers had during their student teaching internships. The student teachers in their study indicated they were not prepared to handle certain students and problematized it as the inability to deal with defiant and unmotivated K-12 students. Further, this finding is explainable through Fuller et al.'s (1974) teaching concerns model, specifically of those in the pre-teaching concerns stage. The mentor teachers expressed that their student teachers' abilities to control their classrooms was a pertinent issue, which brings added clarity to why student teachers would be so pre-occupied with classroom management issues and explains why they may not be as concerned with K-12 student learning and achievement matters during this stage in their development. Further, the majority of the mentor teachers in this study rated the need for student teachers to develop classroom management strategies as critical for student teacher to learn and a major impact in K-12 students' learning. It is important to note, this area rated the highest in terms of its importance for student teachers as well as its impact on K-12 students.

The other item which reached consensus in regard to the second area the mentor teachers' believed their student teachers were least prepared was with the issue of working with and accommodating special needs students. John, a 63 year-old Caucasian male and high school mentor teacher with 32 years of experience noted:

Student teachers learn quickly that not all students learn at the same pace, but they are usually not sure how to meet the needs of the slower or low motivated student. They need to be better prepared with a variety of strategies to deliver content information to their students. Also, classroom management tends to be a high priority. This is an area that I deal with a lot.

Likewise, Eric, a 25-year old Caucasian male and middle/high school mentor teacher with two years of experience stated:

I felt that my student teacher was ill prepared in the ways to properly deal with a classroom that had students with special needs as well as behavioral issues. I believe this is because he had never been exposed to a public school environment in which students of such varied ability levels were in the same classroom.

This finding was not surprising. Authos et al. (in press) found working with and accommodating special needs' students was the same issue business education student teachers expressed themselves in a previous study, which was articulated as a sub-theme under classroom management issues.

Although organization and time management issues did not reach consensus in terms of one of the top three areas student teachers were least prepared, it was the third highest concern raised by the mentor teachers and was very close to reaching agreement. Nevertheless, this issue did re-appear when the mentor teachers articulated ways in which business education teacher preparation programs could reform their curricula to better meet the needs of their students. In fact, the mentor teachers recommended teacher preparation programs include more information about the overall teaching workload and time commitment needed of business education student teachers. One might argue if student teachers were better organized and had improved time management skills, they would be better able to deal with workload and commitment issues. Ron, a 39-year old Caucasian male mentor teacher with 16 years of experience articulated:

The biggest problem I see is when students simply don't understand the magnitude of the student-

teaching experience. Some do not effectively plan ahead, some do not come truly prepared to facilitate each and every day and rely too much on the cooperating teacher for materials and plans to bail them out when they are not ready. I expect them to be able to run the daily schedule as if I were not here and still meet classroom objectives.

In regard to the same issue, Cynthia, a 34 year-old Caucasian female with 11 years of experience teaching stated: "Just inform them that this process will reflect on them as a future teacher. If they don't take it seriously it does not look good for them if a job should open up in the district". While Julie, a 31 year-old Caucasian female with eight years of experience indicated: "Remind them that the workload of 'good teaching' is intense and their willingness to go above and beyond is ESSENTIAL to becoming successful".

The mentor teachers also gained consensus on the need to provide student teachers with more classroom management experiences in public school settings. Similarly, Crews and Bodenhamer (2009) found business education in-service teachers identified classroom management and discipline skills as critical issues to teach in methods courses (courses which teach instructional strategies for a specific content area). Working with diverse learners did not reach consensus among the expert panel, however, it did rank third in terms of areas the business education teacher preparation programs should emphasize. It was a bit surprising the mentor teachers did not seek agreement on this item; since they did agree working with and accommodating special needs' students was an area their student teachers were least prepared.

Recommendations and Implications for Practice

As a result of this research study, several recommendations and implications for practice surfaced. First, the mentor teachers clearly articulated classroom management and working with special needs' students as areas business education student teachers were in need of improvement. They also indicated business education teacher preparation programs might consider implementing more opportunities for their teacher candidates to practice classroom management strategies and gain valuable experiences in working with special needs' students through more field experiences in public school settings. Crews and Bodenhamer (2009) similarly found in-service business education teachers recommended teacher preparation programs integrate classroom management topics into their Methods courses. Thus, it is recommended teacher preparation programs not only discuss classroom management and special education issues, but also provide experiential learning opportunities for their teacher candidates to explore and examine ways in which they might develop classroom management skills and address special needs' students prior to their student teaching internships. It would also be beneficial to integrate field experience components into Methods courses for teacher candidates to experience the K-12 classroom first-hand and discuss these issues as a class. This would indeed require a partnership with K-12 schools, including teacher candidates, university faculty, mentor teachers, and K-12 school administrators.

Second, this research study found the mentor teachers in this study did not necessarily agree on the ways in which their student teachers were most prepared. As a result, this might signal the need for university faculty to develop specific competencies and evaluation systems to assess critical knowledge, skills, and dispositions needed of effective teachers. Providing more consistency in terms of evaluating student teachers is greatly needed. Student teachers oftentimes have widely varying experiences and are oftentimes graded inconsistently depending on their mentor teachers and the environments in which their student teaching placement occurs. With a well-developed student teacher performance assessment system, this would assist student teachers, university

supervisors, and mentor teachers with a shared vision and common expectations.

Third, from the mentor teachers' perspectives in this study, student teachers frequently come to the classroom with a misconception of the amount of time and effort which is needed to be effective teachers. They oftentimes do not understand what exactly is required of them and what kind of workload teachers carry, particularly for new teachers. As such, it is recommended university faculty provide ample opportunities to have candid discussions regarding the nature of teaching and the workload and commitment which are needed. It also may be highly beneficial for teacher candidates to have dialogue with practicing teachers, particularly recent graduates, to provide opportunities for them to ask questions and discover what their roles and responsibilities are as teachers. This might be facilitated through a panel discussion.

Contribution to the Knowledge Base

The findings of this study help contribute to our understanding of the competencies and areas of opportunity business education student teachers bring to the classroom during their internships. It also provides support to Fuller et al.'s (1974) teaching concern model in terms of significant issues student teachers are challenged with at this stage in their careers. According to the mentor teachers in this study, their concerns were aligned with the pre-concerns phase of Fuller et al.'s (1974) model in which teacher candidates focus on survival concerns and their own teaching performances in contrast to focusing on their students and student learning. Thus, this suggests business education student teachers do not differ extensively from other teacher candidates from other disciplines in terms of their student teaching challenges. Further, this study is consistent with an earlier study by Fletcher et al. (in press) which investigated the issues and concerns of business education student teachers themselves.

This study found the concerns of business education mentor teachers in alignment with the challenges expressed by the business education student teachers themselves. Further, findings are aligned with the perspectives of business education teachers in Crews and Bodenhamer's (2009) study recommended business education student teachers needed more exposure to and practice with classroom management.

Not only do the findings support prior research, this study adds to the business education student teaching knowledge base in terms of the insight the mentor teachers' expressed in regard to the need for business education student teachers to be more knowledgeable about the workload and commitment needed in teaching. In addition, this study found disagreement among the mentor teachers regarding their student teachers' areas of weakness in terms of being prepared to teach. The mentor teachers in this study rationalized this source of disagreement as a function of mentoring vastly different student teachers in terms of their professional development needs.

Future studies might include a national sample of mentor teachers of a variety of racial/ethnic backgrounds. Future studies should also examine the professional development needs of mentor teachers in fulfilling their roles and responsibilities. Although studies have examined the issues and challenges of business education student teachers and their mentor teachers, the researchers have not discovered research which considers the concerns of university supervisors in business education. It might conceivably be argued university supervisors in business education are more adept at knowing the developmental needs of business education student teachers in terms of their preparedness to teach. Since the student teaching experience is so valuable for teacher candidates, more investigations are warranted to better understand the complex dynamics of the relationships between student teachers, mentor teachers, and university supervisors (triad relationship).

REFERENCES

Altschuld, J. W. (1993). *Delphi technique: Lecture, evaluation methods: Principles of needs assessment II*. Columbus, OH: Ohio State University.

Bransford, J., Brown, A., & Cocking, R. (1999). *How people learn: Brain, mind, experience, and school*. Washington, DC: National Academies Press.

Clayton, M. (1997). Delphi: A technique to harness expert opinion for critical decision-making tasks in education. *Educational Psychology*, *17*(4), 373. doi:10.1080/0144341970170401

Conderman, G., Morin, J., & Stephens, T. (2005). Special education student teaching practices. *Preventing School Failure*, *49*(3), 5–10. doi:10.3200/PSFL.49.3.5-10

Crews, T., & Bodenhamer, J. (2009). Preparing student teaching interns: Advice from current business educators. *Delta Pi Epsilon Journal*, *51*(1), 43–55.

Cyphert, F. R., & Gant, W. L. (1971). The delphi technique: A case study. *Phi Delta Kappan*, *52*, 272–273.

Dalkey, N. C., Rourke, D. L., Lewis, R., & Snyder, D. (1972). *Studies in the quality of life*. Lexington, MA: Lexington Books.

Darling-Hammond, L., Hammerness, K., Grossman, P., Rust, F., & Shulman, L. (2005). The design of teacher education programs. In Darling-Hammond, L., & Bransford, J. (Eds.), *Preparing teachers for a changing world: What teachers should learn and be able to do* (pp. 390–441). San Francisco, CA: Jossey-Bass.

Delbecq, A. L., Van de Ven, A. H., & Gustafson, D. H. (1975). *Group techniques for program planning*. Glenview, IL: Scott Foresman.

Dever, M., Hager, K., & Klein, K. (2003). Building the university/public school partnership: A workshop for mentor teachers. *Teacher Educator, 38*(4), 245–255. doi:10.1080/08878730309555321

Fives, H., Hamman, D., & Olivarez, A. (2007). Does burnout begin with student teaching? Analyzing efficacy, burnout, and support during the student-teaching semester. *Teaching and Teacher Education, 23,* 916–934. doi:10.1016/j.tate.2006.03.013

Fletcher, E., Mountjoy, K., & Bailey, G. (in press). Exploring concerns of business student teachers. *Delta Pi Epsilon Journal.*

Fritz, C., & Miller, G. (2003). Concerns expressed by student teachers in agriculture. *Journal of Agricultural Education, 44*(3), 47–53. doi:10.5032/jae.2003.03047

Fuller, F., Parsons, J., & Watkins, J. (1974, April). *Concerns of teachers: Research and reconceptualization.* Paper presented at the Annual Meeting of the American Educational Research Association, Chicago, IL.

Gal, N. (2006). The role of practicum supervisors in behavior management education. *Teaching and Teacher Education, 22,* 377–393. doi:10.1016/j.tate.2005.11.007

Goodnough, K., Osmond, P., Dibbon, D., Glassman, M., & Stevens, K. (2009). Exploring a triad model of student teaching: Pre-service teacher and cooperating teacher perceptions. *Teaching and Teacher Education, 25*(2), 285–296. doi:10.1016/j.tate.2008.10.003

Grossman, P., Schoenfeld, A., & Lee, C. (2005). Teaching subject matter. In Darling-Hammond, L., & Bransford, J. (Eds.), *Preparing teachers for a changing world: What teachers should learn and be able to do* (pp. 201–231). San Francisco, CA: Jossey-Bass.

Hamman, D., Olivarez, A., Lesley, M., Button, K., Chan, Y., Griffith, R., & Elliot, S. (2006). Pedagogical influence of interaction with cooperating teachers on the efficacy beliefs of student teachers. *Teacher Educator, 42*(1), 15–29. doi:10.1080/08878730609555391

Hasson, F., Keeney, S., & McKenna, H. (2000). Research guidelines for the Delphi survey technique. *Journal of Advanced Nursing, 32*(4), 1008–1015.

Hughes, M. (1993). *Career-oriented program activities and learning experiences that promote achievement of middle-grade education goals.* Unpublished doctoral dissertation, Ohio State University, Columbus, OH.

Kent, S. (2001). Supervision of student teachers: Practices of cooperating teachers prepared in a clinical supervision course. *Journal of Curriculum and Supervision, 16*(3), 228–244.

Killian, J., & Wilkins, E. (2009). Characteristics of highly effective cooperating teachers: A study of their backgrounds and preparation. *Action in Teacher Education, 30*(4), 67–83.

Ludwig, B. (1994). *Internationalizing extension: An exploration of the characteristics evident in a state university extension system that achieves internationalization.* Unpublished doctoral dissertation, Ohio State University, Columbus, OH.

Nilsson, P., & van Driel, J. (2010). Teaching together and learning together–Primary science student teachers' and their mentor' joint teaching and learning in the primary classroom. *Teaching and Teacher Education, 26*(6), 1309–1318. doi:10.1016/j.tate.2010.03.009

Parker-Katz, M., & Bay, M. (2008). Conceptualizing mentor knowledge: Learning from the insiders. *Teaching and Teacher Education, 24*(5), 1259–1269. doi:10.1016/j.tate.2007.05.006

Pena, C., & Almaguer, I. (2007). Asking the right questions: Online mentoring of student teachers. *International Journal of Instructional Media, 34*(1), 105–113.

Sadler, T. (2006). "I won't last three weeks": Preservice science teachers reflect on their student-teaching experiences. *Journal of Science Teacher Education, 17*, 217–241. doi:10.1007/s10972-005-9004-1

Stitt-Gohdes, W. L., & Crews, T. B. (2004). The Delphi technique: A research strategy for career and technical education. *Journal of Career and Technical Education, 20*(2), 1–11.

Sutphin, H. (1981). *Positions held by teachers, teacher educators, and state supervisors about selected national issues in agricultural education.* Unpublished doctoral dissertation, Ohio State University, Columbus, OH.

Ulschak, F. L. (1983). *Human resource development: The theory and practice of need assessment* (pp. 111–131). Reston, VA: Reston Publishing.

Weaver, D., & Stanulis, R. (1996). Negotiating preparation and practice: Student teaching in the middle. *Journal of Teacher Education, 47*(1), 27–36. doi:10.1177/0022487196047001006

Witkin, B. R. (1984). *Assessing needs in educational and social programs.* San Francisco, CA: Jossey-Bass.

This work was previously published in the International Journal of Adult Vocational Education and Technology, Volume 2, Issue 4, edited by Victor C.X. Wang, pp. 28-42, copyright 2011 by IGI Publishing (an imprint of IGI Global).

Chapter 15

Collaborative Online Learning in Non–Formal Education Settings in the Developing World:
A Best Practice Framework

Stephen Asunka
Regent University College of Science & Technology, Ghana

ABSTRACT

In the present knowledge economy, individuals, particularly working adults, need to continuously acquire purposeful knowledge and skills so they can better contribute towards addressing society's ever-changing developmental challenges. In the developing world however, few opportunities exist for working adults to acquire such new learning experiences through the formal education sector, and this makes it imperative for organizations to develop non-formal education and training programs to help address this need. With the proliferation of Information and Communication Technologies (ICTs) worldwide, this article recommends the adoption of Collaborative Online Learning (COL) by non-formal learning organizations as a means of helping address the education and training needs of working adults. The article thus provides an overview of COL, and then draws on the research literature on relevant theories to recommend best-practice strategies for designing and delivering effective and workable COL initiatives within non-formal education settings, particularly in the developing world.

INTRODUCTION

With globalization rapidly creating an information and knowledge-based society, addressing societal problems increasingly requires the application of innovative ideas and technologies rather than

physical abilities as pertained in industrial age (Schrum & Levin, 2009). In addition, as Bates (2005) argues, because of these rapid developments in technology, coupled with and increasing job mobility between jobs and between national frontiers, "the idea of being trained as a youth for the same job for life is becoming less and less tenable" (p. 10). To be relevant in this global

DOI: 10.4018/978-1-4666-2062-9.ch015

economy therefore, institutions and organizations, irrespective of their fields of operation, need to evolve into what Gardner (1996) calls 'learning organizations.' These are organizations in which, "new and expansive patterns are permitted" (Gardner, 1996, p. 59), and learning becomes a continuous, strategically used process that is integrated with and running parallel to the work of the organization (Watkins & Marsick, 1993). Learning organizations thus provide learning opportunities outside formal educational institutions, and tend to offer knowledge and skills-based training that complement or supplement the abilities of working adults. This non-formal adult learning, which has long been existence in all parts of the world, offer content and learning experiences that are less structured, more flexible and more responsive to localized needs (Merriam & Brockett, 1997).

In the developing world however, most organizations, especially those in non-education related sectors, cannot currently be described as learning organizations as logistical, financial and personnel constraints all contribute in making them incapable of operating as such. Also, many employees within these organizations benefit little from formal higher education as they cannot find the time to participate in the required "full-time" learning activities and processes. Besides, in some cases, the formal higher education programs might be inappropriate for the peculiar needs of individual employees or the organization as a whole. Investing in customized education and training programs can also be a big financial challenge. Yet these establishments need to become learning organizations if they hope to continuously develop expertise and also remain responsive to societal needs in the current age.

Thankfully, advances in information and communication technologies (ICTs) in recent years, have expanded education and training opportunities dramatically. With the aid of these technologies, not only can educational resources be made flexible enough to meet individual learner requirements, learning can now also take place anytime

and at any place. Indeed, effective integration of ICTs into formal educational curricula, typically implemented as Collaborative Online Learning (COL) has been demonstrated to be as effective as conventional educational programs, and also more cost-effective (Murphy, Anzalone, Bosch, & Moulton, 2002). Organizations and higher educational institutions in the developed countries are therefore increasingly adopting online delivery of instruction especially to non-school based learners (Simmons, 2002). In keeping with this, institutions in the developing world can also now begin working towards becoming learning organizations by developing and implementing their own COL initiatives, or by participating in other non-formal COL activities that are appropriate to their peculiar needs and operational environments.

Presently however, ICT use in non-formal education in the developing world (with its limited technology infrastructure, and other logistical challenges), is in its infancy. It is therefore not certain which technology supported instructional strategies and learning philosophies will be most appropriate in fostering COL within this context. Meanwhile, developing world institutions cannot simply adopt the practices that currently work well in the developed world, not only because this has been shown not to work well even in formal education (Asunka, 2008), but also because the non-indigenous content and contexts of such practices are likely to be inappropriate in the developing world setting. There is therefore the need to evolve COL best-practice strategies, based on sound theories and practitioner experiences, which can help guide organizations to expand their abilities to foster innovation and change through education and training.

This article contributes in that direction by aiming to serve as a reference resource and a practical guide with which non-formal educational institutions in developing countries can use to assist in the development and implementation of effective COL practices within their peculiar environments. Targeted at instructional designers, educational consultants, learning technologists and administrators, the article draws on learning theories including pedagogical, media effects, group interaction/social influence, adult learning, organizational learning, as well as the author's own personal experiences, to conceptualize workable and effective COL strategies and practices within non-formal educational contexts in the developing world.

WHAT IS COLLABORATIVE ONLINE LEARNING (COL)?

Although learning in general has been defined in a variety of ways (Jonassen, Howland, Moore, & Marra, 2003), most contemporary educators have come to accept learning as not just a passive and receptive response to instruction delivery, but as an active, cognitive, constructive and social process where individuals actively engage in authentic (real-life) social activities, creating meaning through their interactions with each other and with the environment they live in (Engvig, 2006; Stacey, 2005).

Undoubtedly, this new approach to learning, also called social constructivism, is being influenced by humanity's rapid progression from the industrial era (where learning was mostly viewed as an end product of instruction), to a global information society and knowledge economy where learning is now expected to be an active, learner-centered, social and lifelong process. The learner should therefore no longer be a passive recipient of information, but must construct knowledge out of the abundant information that is already widely available.

In this context, both formal and non-formal educational institutions and organizations cannot remain focused with the traditional decontextualized content transmission approach to learning, but must modify their structures and processes in ways that will facilitate constructive knowledge and skills acquisition by learners at anytime and anyplace. This is even more imperative in the least developed countries, where, with an average adult literacy rate of 56.6%, compared with 99.3% for developed countries (Unesco Institute for Statistics, 2007), non-formal adult education and training is very much in need to help build competence, foster a sense of community and widen participation at the community level (Franklin & Hosein, 2009).

An important implementation of this constructivist learning approach is collaborative learning, a learning method that evolved from the work of psychologists such as Johnson and Johnson (1975) and Slavin (1987). Collaborative learning is a learner-centered instructional strategy that involves social processes by which small groups of learners work together as teams to complete problem-solving tasks designed to promote learning (Benbunan-Fich, Hiltz, & Harasim, 2005). Examples of collaborative learning thus include authentic learner activities such as seminar-style presentations and discussions, debates, group projects, group problem solving, simulation and role-playing exercises, collaborative composition of essays, websites, stories, or other artifacts that demonstrate the knowledge and skills that are the subject of study (Ally, 2008; Hiltz, Coppola, Rotter, Turoff, & Benbunan-Fich, 2000).

As it engages learners in active knowledge sharing and interdependence, collaborative learning has been demonstrated to be an effective instructional strategy in fostering learners' positive attitudes towards learning and motivation to learn. Such processes also promote good citizenship, and aid learners develop critical thinking and problem solving skills (Barkley, Cross, & Major, 2004). Collaborative learning has however been distinguished from cooperative learning by some authors who refer to the latter as a learning situation where work is split up among group members, as against the case of learner interdependence that occurs in collaborative learning (Bruffee, 1999).

In the non-formal education sector, most knowledge creation and capacity building initiatives often involve some collaborative activities, but these typically happen in the "same place, same time" mode. Naturally, costs, time, space and other logistical issues constrain most establishments, especially the non-profits, from effectively organizing or participating in these capacity building activities alongside executing their core activities.

With ICTs becoming increasingly accessible however, collaborative learning can now take place anytime and at any place with the aid of technologies such as e-mail, discussion boards, learning management systems, social and content sharing software, and other real-time interactive tools such as instant text and video messaging etc. This "collaborative online learning" (COL) has therefore been defined as "the application of a repertoire of cognitively oriented instructional strategies, implemented within a constructivist and collaborative learning environment utilizing the attributes and resources of the World Wide Web" (Relan & Gillani, 1997, p. 43).

COL is thus a form of E-learning or Web-Based Learning, but in practice, particularly in non-formal education, differs from the majority of other internet-enabled or CD-ROM based learning approaches that currently exist. These "e-learning" technologies mainly aim at facilitating individualized, self-directed learning, and so only involve making multimedia learning content accessible to users on CD-ROM or over the web. COL on the other hand involves harnessing the affordances of media and communication technologies to support active and collaborative knowledge creation and capacity building processes among learners with diverse attributes and in different locations. For organizations and institutions in the developing world, the extra challenge in implementing COL is ensuring that the technologies available, though mostly inadequate, are effectively leveraged to support and enhance knowledge co-construction processes. In doing so meanwhile, they must strive to minimize disruptions and distractions due to infrastructural and logistical challenges such as frequent power cuts, inadequate and unreliable telephone and internet services etc.

It is thus clear that several contextual and environmental factors can potentially influence the processes and outcomes of non-formal COL in developing countries. There is therefore no single theory or conceptual framework that can best serve as a guide for implementing such COL practices effectively. Educators wishing to deploy non-formal online learning solutions must therefore have a full appreciation of the salient underlying theories, and be able to apply these in eclectic ways to help develop and implement applications and strategies that can best promote knowledge creation and application.

The rest of this article thus discusses these theories together with findings of research studies pertaining to their practical applications in COL environments within formal and non-formal education settings. Based on the implications of each theory as discussed, recommendations are made on the appropriate media technologies and best practice learning strategies that can best result in effective and positive learning and training outcomes within organizations.

THEORIES OF COLLABORATIVE ONLINE LEARNING AND IMPLICATIONS FOR PRACTICE IN NON-FORMAL EDUCATION IN DEVELOPING COUNTRIES

Several theories can be applied in analyzing the contexts and possibilities for online learning within organizations. With regard to COL in this context however, whilst *adult learning* and *organizational learning* theories provide a general framework, *pedagogical*, *media effects* and *group interaction* theories are directly applicable in whatever resources and strategies are adopted in particular learning situations. These three main groups of theories are therefore the focus of the remainder of this article.

Pedagogical Theories

From pedagogical theory comes two main approaches; the first being objectivism (based on the behaviorist and cognitivist paradigms), which holds that learning involves the direct transfer of existing objective knowledge from instructor or trainer to learner through presentations and explanations (Bernstein, 2008). Learning or training activities that are rooted in this philosophy are instructor led, have predetermined learning content and have outcomes based on front-end analysis. Objectivism also adopts a linear and clearly defined learning path, and assesses learners for complete and correct understanding of content.

The second pedagogical approach is social constructivism, which maintains that meaningful learning occurs when individuals are actively engaged in authentic (real-life) social activities, creating meaning through their interactions with each other and with the environment in which they live (Driscoll & Carliner, 2005; Vygotsky, 1978). Constructivist learning environments are thus learner-centered, encourage learner active participation, focus on real-life problems, include ill-structured activities grounded in the learners' life contexts and experiences, and foster a sense of community among learners (Fosnot, 2005; Schrum & Levin, 2009). Learning content and assessment strategies are also not entirely predetermined, though learner attributes and prevailing cultural values and influences need to be taken into consideration as these can potentially influence learner attitudes and participation

Educators have long believed that the constructivist approach likely leads to more positive learning outcomes, as there is deeper understanding and retention of relevant and applicable knowledge and skills. This approach is thus suited for the current situation of information overload, and also works better for non-formal and need-based education and training.

These two pedagogical approaches, in their strictest sense, represent two extreme ends of a continuum, and most educational and training practices can be seen as falling anywhere along this continuum (Engvig, 2006). Formal school and textbook based education is more oriented towards objectivism, whilst non-formal educational practices in the form of retraining or capacity building activities among out-of-school persons, are more constructivist.

Though COL largely falls within the constructivist domain as stated earlier, it is obvious, looking at practical applications, that some components of objectivist pedagogy such as direct knowledge transfer by way of lesson notes and recommended readings, individual learning, and objective assessments by way of quizzes, are often included. Merrill calls this approach "moderate constructivism" (Merrill, 1991, p. 99). Thus, whilst recommending the adoption of moderate constructivism by organizations, the advice also is that non-formal COL developers, particularly those in developing countries, need to orient learning processes more towards the constructivist end of the continuum. This is because, non-formal education is most often aimed at helping address immediate and long-term societal challenges which can vary in complexity. Non-formal educators should therefore adopt models and strategies that will promote self-directed learning, build on learners' prior knowledge and experiences, allow learners to bring multiple perspectives to bear on issues, and be situated in learners' real-life contexts, whilst ensuring that basic knowledge and skills are directly transferred.

Practical examples of such approaches, which can be facilitated by online technologies, include:

1. **Cognitive Apprenticeships:** enculturating authentic practices into learners through activities akin to craft apprenticeships (Brown, Collins, & Duguid, 1989). Authentic activities that reflect the ways in which knowledge and skills are used in practice, not only help promote deep learning through the development of critical thinking skills, but also help

improve learning retention and performance (Smart & Cappel, 2006). Another rationale for the integration of authentic activities in learning is that people generally have difficulties transfering knowledge and skills learnt in abstraction to real-life contexts, and so when learning processes are carried out within realistic contexts, there will be more positive learning outcomes (Picciano, 2002; Watkins, 2005).

Cognitive apprenticeship learning thus typically starts with selecting real-world situations or tasks that are grounded in learner needs, proceeding with a deliberate objectivist approach to deliver content and fundamental principles, and then using expert practitioners to model and help facilitate learning. This can be a recursive process (if need be), but the experts eventually scale back their "coaching" activities as learners progressively become more proficient.

2. **Anchored Instruction:** creating situations in which learners, through sustained experiences, can grapple with the problems and opportunities that experts encounter (Cognition and Technology Group at Vanderbilt, 1990). The goal of this problem-based approach is to have learners "experience what it is like to grow from novices who have only rudimentary knowledge to relatively sophisticated experts who have explored an environment from multiple points of view" (Cognition and Technology Group at Vanderbilt, 1990, p.9). Videos depicting problem situations serve as the anchors, and all the resources and scaffolding that learners need in order to solve the problem(s) are made available to learners. This makes it easier for learners to manage in the learning environment with limited time or limited resources.

3. **Situated Cognition:** embedding learning within the individual's everyday living/professional activities. This calls for implementing strategies that allow learners to

choose their own learning paths, but still work collaboratively to apply concepts on the job. This approach works well with people in culturally organized settings (Driscoll & Carliner, 2005), and is thus suitable for training employees within specific organizations. Indeed, Dixon (1997) articulates a dimension of this approach by using the metaphor of a hallway i.e. places where collective meaning is constructed through dialogue between organizational members. Dixon outlines seven critical elements of hallway learning as: (1) reliance on discussions, not lectures; (2) egalitarian participation; (3) encouragement of multiple perspectives; (4) nonexpert-based dialogue; (5) use of a participant-generated database; (6) creation of shared experiences; and (7) creation of unpredictable outcomes (p.28).

4. **Cognitive Flexibility:** presenting the same items of knowledge in a variety of ways by using nonlinear (ill-structured) learning processes The major goal of this is to help learners develop the ability to approach issues through multiple perspectives, and therefore better understand various situations (Godshalk, Harvey, & Moller, 2004). This also affords learners the opportunity to acquire complex knowledge structures and develop cognitively flexible processing skills. Hypertext and hypermedia learning components delivered through websites are particularly suitable for fostering cognitive flexibility.

All the above-mentioned approaches place the learner at the center of all activities, and asMcKeachie (2002) observes, persons who are motivated to learn through such learner-centered approaches, "will choose tasks that enhance their learning, will work hard at those tasks, and will persist in the face of difficulty in order to attain their goals" (p. 19). In seeking to implement any of these therefore, the developing world COL developer,, must first make sure that each prospective participant has the capacity to communicate effectively online, both in terms of technology availability and use, and ability to deal with the varying challenges of communicating electronically. Some strategies that can be adopted to aid learners in this direction are enumerated in the latter part of this article.

Pedagogical theories and their implications can serve as guides for implementing flexible non-formal COL programs in ways that can help build competence, hone leadership skills, support creativity, build social capital and widen participation at the community level (Franklin & Hosein, 2009). By acquiring such knowledge, skills and competences, working adults in the developing world can be more effective in contributing to community development both individually and collectively.

Media Effect Theories

The debate as to whether or not media by themselves have any significant impact on learning and training outcomes has been a long-standing one. For one school of thought, media is simply a vehicle of delivering instruction, and hence does not influence learning outcomes. Clark (2001, as cited in Rice, Hiltz, & Spencer, 2005) exemplifies this thinking by metaphorically asserting that "media do not influence learning any more than the truck that delivers groceries influences the nutrition of a community" (p. 215). Thus, to Clark, it does not matter whether instruction is delivered by slide-tape show or by a computer, it is the content and the organizational instructional strategy that is important (Shoffner, Jones, & Harmon, 2000). The counter argument (e.g., Kozma, 2001) is that, certain media may be better suited to support certain specific types of content and/or specific pedagogies, hence media effects under such circumstances cannot be ignored. Indeed, in extending Clark's metaphor, Shoffner, Jones, and Harmon (2000, para 13) remark that "if you are

moving ice cream in Mississippi in August, the difference between a flatbed truck and a refrigerated one is crucial."

In recent times however there appears to be little controversy in this regard as media technologies are advancing, and it is becoming clear that when applied appropriately, certain types of media technologies can indeed influence learning in both the cognitive and affective domains (Christopher, Thomas, & Tallent-Runnels, 2004; Sullivan, 2002). Several media effect theories have therefore been put forward, and some of these can be adapted and applied to help establish frameworks for developing and implementing context-based COL processes.

These media effect theories are; (1) social presence - the degree to which a medium is perceived as conveying the actual physical presence of the communicating participants (Short, Williams, & Christie, 1976, as cited in Rice et al., 2005); and (2) media richness -the extent to which a medium can support language variety, feedback, nonverbal cues and learning (Rice, Hiltz, & Spencer, 2005). Conceptually therefore, face-to-face interaction represents the highest level of social presence and media richness, with the age-old print-based correspondence-style of distance learning representing the lowest level. All other technology-enabled communication and interactions are located anywhere in between these two extremes.

With regard to learning and training, social presence theory argues that different media foster different levels of perceived intimacy and immediacy, with a greater perceived social presence having an intensifying effect on media users, increasing involvement, task performance, persuasion, social interaction etc. (Lombard, Ditton, & Reich, 1997). Surveys and experimental studies have found that greater perceived social presence, as afforded by a particular medium, e.g., television or audio and video conferencing systems, results in greater learner satisfaction with socio-emotional tasks such as persuasion, resolving conflicts, maintaining friendly relations etc. (Hackman & Walker, 1990).

Media richness theory on its part establishes that characteristics of media vary in terms of their ability to support task uncertainty and ambiguity, and so when the information processing capabilities of a medium match information processing demands, task performance will improve (Rice, 1992). In other words, as Rice (1992) explains, "performance is not assured by any particular organizational design, but is contingent on an appropriate match between contextual variables (such as task demands) and organizational arrangements (such as communication structures and media)."

The underlying principle of both social presence and media richness theories is contingency theory (Hiltz et al., 2000). Thus a good match between the characteristics of any medium that will be employed in any particular situation, and the communication activities required, should lead to more positive outcomes. For example, videoconference applications rank very high in social presence and media richness, and will thus be more effective if they are employed in situations that require high communication and collaborative activities. They will probably add little value if used to deliver lengthy speeches. It is thus possible that a particular medium might be "too lean" for some particular tasks, and yet "too rich" for others. In both cases, performance is not expected to be optimal.

With regard to COL, the inclusion of some form of media or the other should therefore vary on a case-by-case basis. Research has reported both successes and failures in cases involving the application of some particular media in different learning contexts. For instance, though media richness and social presence theories predict that having online pictures of other learners available to class members should result in stronger and faster bonding between learners, Walther, Slovacek and Tidwell (2001) found in a study involving several student teams that introducing

pictures after group members had developed a sense of bonding through text only communication tended to dampen affinity. Interestingly however, for new unacquainted teams, pictures promoted swift formation of feelings of affection between group members.

Other studies involving the incorporation of other media such as audio and video in asynchronous communication also yielded mixed results, with participants in one study expressing satisfaction about how making audio recorded presentations represented a positive learning experience (Bargeron et al., 2002), whilst in another study at the New Jersey Institute of Technology in 2001, subjects reportedly found text correspondence to be more convenient than audio (Rice et al., 2005).

All these findings indicate that there is no clearly established cause-effect relationship between the use (or non-use) of any particular medium and success in learning or performance. Specific types of media can however both afford and constrain learning in their own particular ways, and in COL, whatever media is employed should be directly relevant to the instructional and learning processes. As Clark and Craig (2001, as cited in Rice et al., 2005) concludes;

The best implementation strategy is to identify what instructional technologies (methods) are suitable for what goals, and to find the media functionalities (available in a variety of communication media) that best support these methods, in order to lower costs and time whilst increasing access (p. 231).

Media technologies commonly adopted in COL environments include asynchronous text discussion boards, e-mail, synchronous chat, picture galleries, video conferencing, asynchronous audio and video clips, and assessment tools. Computer programs that provide a single platform for the integration of most of these technologies are currently available. Known as Learning Management Systems (LMS), Course Management Systems (CMS) or Virtual Learning Environments (VLE), these web-based applications enable COL developers implement most of the prior-mentioned constructivist learning approaches. They also offer instructors the opportunity to undertake a range of such housekeeping tasks as registering and tracking individual learning participants' online activities, receiving their digital artifacts, and also assessing learning outcomes. LMSs can thus be used as focal points for all technologies that can provide the requisite social presence and media richness needed for specific learning situations - from the lowest to the highest possible levels.

Several LMSs (both proprietary and open source) have thus been widely adopted by most education institutions and other organizations all over the world as the main platform for COL delivery. Notable examples of these are *Blackboard* which is proprietary, and *Moodle* which is open source (Bennett, 2003). For organizations within developing countries wishing to implement constructivist COL practices, the following are recommended:

- Adopt a single LMS, particularly the open source alternatives (e.g., *Moodle* and *Sakai*) as they work effectively in supporting basic online communication such as e-mail and text-based discussions as well as more advanced multimedia technologies, and most importantly, are free.

- Make a moderate investment to have the system reside elsewhere in the world where it can be guaranteed to be up and running all the time. As LMSs have web-based user-interfaces, all that the instructors and learning participants need is internet access, even if intermittent, and effective collaborative learning can take place.

- LMSs also support learning objects (content that can be used and re-used), and so for organizations that offer periodic training using particular content, developers should consider creating learning objects and loading these into the LMS.

Incidentally, within the developing world context of inadequate infrastructure and lack of round-the-clock access to online technologies by most individuals, it is possible that a single LMS platform might not be providing the flexibility and seamlessness that learners require to remain motivated. Developing world organizations therefore need to explore ways of engaging other media technologies in their COL practices. One such recommended technologies is text messaging via cellular phones. Cell phone penetration is currently very rapid in the developing world, and with communities such as mobileactive. org actively trying to increase the effectiveness of Non-Governmental Organizations (NGOs) through mobile technology (Vendel, 2009), non-formal COL developers need to leverage these technologies to effectively support learning and training. Using text messaging to augment the LMS can thus help sustain online learning in the event of other temporary technology setbacks such as power outages etc. (Asunka & Chae, 2009).

Regarding media effects on learning, the overarching principle is that media use vis-à-vis learning processes and outcomes is a case-by-case situation. In addition, the constructivist nature of COL calls for active learner participation and interactivity, flexible learning paths, and in some cases, optional learning outcomes. Thus for learning organizations where the desirable outcomes of their COL practices are high quality learning and increased productivity (and not exam grades or course credits as pertains in formal education), all available technologies need to be deployed effectively to motivate and engage learners. Some other recommendations that can assist COL instructors in this direction thus include:

- Using e-mail extensively - to provide information and for acknowledging enquiries and submissions

- Using blogs and wikis to provide commentaries that will "provoke" learners to respond, and also as platforms for collective creation of content.

- Including downloadable videos and audio, but only if they enhance content or serve as a main anchor for specific activities. If possible, text transcripts of such resources should be provided.
- Encouraging critical thinking by giving challenging tasks that can be accomplished in multiple ways - text, websites, videos etc.
- Making sure that all participants within particular collaborative groups have equitable access to all media technologies, or encouraging groups to use the medium that is common to all members as their main medium of communication.
- Providing printable text in most cases, as this is still the most desirable form of learning even for people engaged in COL.
- Introducing occasional face-to-face meetings if all learning participants are within one geographical location. Participation in these should however be voluntary.
- Using synchronous interaction media such as webinars and electronic whiteboards only if learning takes place within an organization's local area network (LAN) where high bandwidth is assured.

Group Interaction/Social Influence Theories

Several explanations on how participating in group activities helps members to learn have been put forward by researchers and education practitioners. The most common of these are two; the socio-emotional and the cognitive dimensions (Benbunan-Fich et al., 2005). In terms of the socio-emotional aspects, Hiltz points out that:

Group members learn by virtue of mediating socio-emotional variables (such as motivation, reduced anxiety, or satisfaction) that create an emotional or intellectual climate favorable to learning. When working with peers instead of alone (or with the instructor), anxiety and uncertainty are reduced as learners find their ways through complex or new tasks. These effects tend to increase motivation and satisfaction with the learning process in general (Hiltz, 2000, p. 107).

Through group activities therefore, learners build self-esteem, learn to accommodate diverse opinions on issues, enhance their communication and listening skills, exhibit reduced anxiety towards collaborative activities, and generally develop skills needed in workforce and other out-of-school settings (Taylor, 2004).

With regard to the cognitive explanations, cognitive psychologists including Piaget, Vygotsky and Bruner, have all emphasized the social nature of learning, and how group collaborative processes directly influence cognition. Group discussions for instance, have been demonstrated to be capable of providing cognitive scaffolding that is essential for higher order thinking. Other spontaneous group activities such as conversations, conflicts or disagreements (and efforts being made to avoid or resolve them), multiple perspectives, self-explanations (together with explanations to others) and internalization of concepts conveyed from more knowledgeable peers, all contribute towards the group members' cognitive development (Benbunan-Fich et al., 2005; Stacey, 2005).

Webb and Sugrue (1997) also report that, among groups with both above-average and below-average students, the higher level of discussion translated into an advantage in achievement tests for the below-average students when students were tested on a group basis and also individually. Heller, Keith, and Anderson (1992) also demonstrate in one study that students in collaborative groups significantly outperformed a control group where students worked individually.

Not all studies have however concluded that working in small groups is beneficial for learning. Indeed Brookfield and Preskill (1999) point out that collaborative group approaches to learning can sometimes become "emotional battlegrounds" as individuals strive to express their own identity within the group context, and be individually responsible for their own learning (Dirkx & Smith, 2004). Several studies have therefore reported either a lack of enthusiasm on the part of students to work in groups (e.g., Dirkx & Smith, 2004), or very frequently, do not work as well as is expected of them.

This notwithstanding, the cognitive, social and psychological benefits of collaborative group learning have been demonstrated to be quite substantial (Stacey, 2005; Taylor, 2004), and even though these conclusions have been based mostly on research on face-to-face learning groups, there is reason (and evidence) to believe that the online environment can also provide the social setting needed for effective group collaboration.

Group interactions in online courses mostly involve asynchronous written text facilitated and moderated by both instructors and learners. The benefits of this approach have been attributed to the fact that, no single person or group can dominate the conversation, whilst hostile and bullying participants are less likely to be disruptive and intimidating to others as non-verbal cues are absent (Roberts, 2005). Most learners have therefore been reported to perceive online discussions as more equitable and more democratic in comparison with face-to-face discussions.

Also, because of the asynchronous nature, online discussions affords participants the opportunity to reflect on others' contributions before writing, as well as on their own before posting, and this creates a certain level of mindfulness and a culture of metacognition in online courses (Rice, Hiltz, & Spencer, 2005). Asynchronous written dialogue therefore represents one of the core activities of COL.

Based on this understanding therefore, though online group work can often involve the use of sophisticated technologies such as video conferencing, synchronous audio and text discussions etc, within the context of limited technologies, asynchronous text discussion should be enough to facilitate effective group activities. The challenge however is motivating learners to participate in such discussions in meaningful and productive ways, and not just for the purpose of satisfying some external requirements.

Actions that can be taken to ensure prospective learners or trainees develop the requisite online personalities for online dialogue and collaboration, and also participate effectively include:

- Defining norms and clear codes of conduct
- Providing different channels of communication between learners and between individual learners and the instructor(s)
- Keeping groups as heterogeneous as possible i.e., in terms of gender, ability, cultural backgrounds etc.)
- Allowing for a range of member roles within groups
- Allowing for and facilitating subgroups within group collaborative activities
- Allowing participants to resolve their own disputes
- Providing timely feedback and responses to inquiries
- Treating technology availability as the bottom line i.e. ensuring that technology access and availability is not a barrier to communication (Asunka & Chae, 2009)

FUTURE RESEARCH DIRECTIONS

Developmental organizations seeking to implement collaborative online learning and training practices have to contend with a lot of challenges as this mode of learning represents a paradigm shift in educational activities. Identifying and addressing these challenges as they relate to specific contexts should therefore be of prime importance. This is even more imperative in the developing world where the lack of adequate technology infrastructure and other socio-economic issues can further exacerbate the challenges. Conceptual, and more importantly, empirical research work aimed at evolving best practice frameworks will thus go a long way in helping organizations develop and implement effective online learning solutions.

In line with this, one important area that should be considered by COL researchers is the learner perspective. It is known that the total commitment and participation of learners is crucial for successful learning outcomes in COL courses. Indeed, there are reports of failures of some COL courses due to a lack of understanding of the learners' characteristics and perceptions about the helpfulness, accessibility, and usability of the learning resources and technologies. In these studies, the learners reported such unpleasant experiences as communication breakdowns and technical difficulties, ambiguous instructions, unwillingness of other learners to participate in group assignments, and the general feeling of 'disconnect' due to the lack of face-to-face interactions (Jonassen, Howland, Moore, & Marra, 2003; Rice, Hiltz, & Spencer, 2005). Organizations who implement COL should therefore carry out empirical studies in tandem with the learning activities so as to establish learner attitudes, attributes and general perceptions of the learning activities and technological affordances. Findings of such studies will collectively help establish best practice design and implementation frameworks.

A second area of critical importance in non-formal COL that requires further research attention is context. Unlike formal education where most of the learning takes place within the school setting, decontextualized from daily life and work, much of adult learning takes place within the socio-cultural settings in which the learners live and work. Each adult's learning situation thus differs from others, and as COL can potentially involve individuals originating from, or residing in different parts of the world, it is crucial to understand how common environments could be established for effective and productive dialogue between learners. Studies regarding this issue could be accomplished in a number of ways e.g., following a specific group of learners as they engage in different COL programs, or surveying workers who have been involved in several COL activities, and documenting their experiences and perceptions.

Another suggested area of non-formal COL research is the learning process. As an adult's learning is closely tied to his or her life situation, adults likely will not be inclined to learn anything that they perceive as not being meaningful. Working adults within organizations might be motivated to learn new ideas and skills if that will enhance their performance. Knowledge, and the technologies that can be employed in learning processes are however in a state of flux, and this means employees will be demanding new or updated knowledge within shorter periods of time. Additionally, motivation to learn will increase if the learning processes are seamlessly integrated with the emerging technologies that people are increasingly getting attached to. Learning content and processes therefore need to be constantly revised and also integrated with emerging technologies such as social networking and mobile computing technologies as these are becoming more ubiquitous. Organizations hoping to remain viable learning organizations should therefore continuously develop and pilot future-oriented COL solutions so they can arrive at their own best-practice frameworks, rather than waiting to try solutions that have emerged out of other contexts.

CONCLUSION

This article contributes to the discussion on what it takes to provide flexible online multimedia learning environments that are appropriate, workable and acceptable to non-formal learners in the developing world. Specifically, the article aims to serve as a resource support and guide to organizations who, though working within the technological constraints prevalent in many parts of the developing world, still wish to implement online learning to aid in their training and capacity building activities.

Arguing that successful COL processes and outcomes begin with a full understanding of the various underlying theories by all stakeholders, the article elaborates extensively on pedagogical, media/technology effects and group interaction theories, and how these can potentially influence COL practices in non-formal education and training. In so doing, the article also reviews findings on some studies pertaining to the application of these theories and evolves several recommendations and strategies that non-formal educators can adopt to help make their COL initiatives succeed.

On the whole, the emphasis of this article is that implementing non-formal COL within the context of limited access and inadequate supporting technologies can present unique challenges, and should therefore not simply follow the developed world models, but should be based on appropriate and contextual interpretations and applications of the underlying theories, and on findings of sound empirical studies conducted within that context.

REFERENCES

Ally, M. (2008). Foundations of educational theory for online learning. In Anderson, T. (Ed.), *The theory and practice of online learning* (pp. 15–44). Edmonton, UK: AU Press.

Asunka, S. (2008). Online learning in higher education in Sub-Saharan Africa: Ghanaian university students' experiences and perceptions. *International Review of Research in Open and Distance Learning*, *9*(3), 1–23.

Asunka, S., & Chae, H. S. (2009). Strategies for teaching online courses within the Sub-Saharan African context: An instructor's recommendations. *MERLOT Journal of Online Learning and Teaching*, *5*(2), 372–379.

Bargeron, D., Grudin, J., Gupta, A., Sanocki, E., Li, F., & Leetiernan, S. (2002). Asynchronous collaboration around multimedia applied to on-demand education. *Journal of Management Information Systems*, *18*(4), 117–145.

Barkley, E. F., Cross, K. P., & Major, C. H. (2004). *Collaborative learning techniques: A handbook for college faculty*. San Francisco, CA: Jossey-Bass.

Bates, A. W. T. (2005). *Technology, e-learning and distance education* (2nd ed.). New York, NY: Routledge.

Benbunan-Fich, R., Hiltz, S. R., & Harasim, L. (2005). The online interaction learning model: An integrated theoretical framework for learning networks. In Hiltz, S. R., & Goldman, R. (Eds.), *Learning together online: Research on asynchronous learning networks* (pp. 19–37). Mahwah, NJ: Lawrence Erlbaum.

Bennett, S. (2003). Supporting collaborative project teams using computer-based technologies. In Roberts, T. S. (Ed.), *Online collaborative learning: Theory and practice* (pp. 1–27). Hershey, PA: Information Science Reference. doi:10.4018/978-1-59140-174-2.ch001

Bernstein, A. (2008). *Objectivism in one lesson: An introduction to the philosophy of Ayn Rand*. Lanham, MD: Hamilton Books.

Brookfield, S. D., & Preskill, S. (1999). *Discussion as a way of teaching: Tools and techniques for democratic classrooms*. San Francisco, CA: Jossey-Bass.

Brown, J. S., Collins, A., & Duguid, P. (1989). Situated cognition and the culture of learning. *Educational Researcher*, *18*(1), 32–42.

Bruffee, K. A. (1999). *Collaborative learning: Higher education, interdependence and the authority of knowledge* (2nd ed.). Baltimore, MD: Johns Hopkins University Press.

Christopher, M. M., Thomas, J. A., & Tallent-Runnels, M. K. (2004). Raising the bar: Encouraging high level thinking in online discussion forums. *Roeper Review, 26*(3), 166–171. doi:10.1080/02783190409554262

Clark, R. E. (2001). Media are "mere vehicles": The opening argument. In Clark, R. E. (Ed.), *Learning from media: Arguments, analysis, and evidence* (pp. 1–12). Charlotte, NC: Information Age Publishing.

Clark, R. E., & Craig, T. (2001). What about media effects on learning? In Clark, R. E. (Ed.), *Learning from media: Arguments, analysis and evidence* (pp. 89–101). Charlotte, NC: Information Age Publishing.

Cognition and Technology Group at Vanderbilt. (1990). Situated cognition and the culture of learning. *Educational Researcher, 3*(9), 32–42.

Dirkx, J. M., & Smith, R. O. (2004). Thinking out of a bowl of spaghetti: Learning to learn in online collaborative groups. In Roberts, T. S. (Ed.), *Online collaborative learning: Theory and practice* (pp. 132–159). Hershey, PA: Information Science Reference.

Dixon, N. M. (1997). The hallways of learning. *Organizational Dynamics, 25*(4), 23–34. doi:10.1016/S0090-2616(97)90034-6

Driscoll, M., & Carliner, S. (2005). *Advanced web-based training strategies*. San Francisco, CA: Pfeiffer.

Engvig, M. (2006). *Online learning: All you need to know to facilitate and administer online courses*. Cresskill, NJ: Hampton Press.

Fosnot, C. T. (2005). *Constructivism: Theory, perspectives and practice*. New York, NY: Teachers College Press.

Franklin, M., & Hosein, R. (2009). Flexible education and community development. In Marshall, S., Kinuthia, W., & Taylor, W. (Eds.), *Bridging the knowledge divide: Educational technology for development* (pp. 3–21). Charlotte, NC: Information Age Publishing.

Gardner, P. (1996). Demographic and attitudinal trends: The increasing diversity of today's and tomorrow's learner. *Journal of Cooperative Education, 31*(2-3), 58–82.

Godshalk, V. M., Harvey, D. M., & Moller, L. (2004). The role of learning tasks on attitude change using cognitive flexibility hypertext systems. *Journal of the Learning Sciences, 13*(4), 507–526. doi:10.1207/s15327809jls1304_2

Hackman, M., & Walker, K. (1990). Instructional communication in the televised classroom: The effects of system design and teacher immediacy on student learning and satisfaction. *Communication Education, 39*(3), 196–209. doi:10.1080/03634529009378802

Heller, P., Keith, R., & Anderson, S. (1992). Teaching problem solving through cooperative grouping: Group versus individual problem solving. *American Journal of Physics, 60*, 671–683.

Hiltz, S. R. (1994). *The virtual classroom: Learning without limits via computer networks*. Norwood, NJ: Abex.

Hiltz, S. R., Coppola, N., Rotter, N., Turoff, M., & Benbunan-Fich, R. (2000). Measuring the importance of collaborative learning for the effectiveness of ALN: A multi-measure, multi-method approach. *Journal of Asynchronous Learning Networks, 4*(2), 103–125.

Johnson, D. W., & Johnson, R. T. (1975). *Learning together and alone: Cooperation, competition and individualization*. Upper Saddle River, NJ: Prentice-Hall.

Jonassen, D. H., Howland, J. L., Moore, J. L., & Marra, R. M. (2003). *Learning to solve problems with technology: A constructivist perspective* (2nd ed.). Upper Saddle River, NJ: Merrill.

Kozma, R. (2001). Learning with media. In Clark, R. E. (Ed.), *Learning from media: Arguments, analysis, and evidence* (pp. 179–198). Charlotte, NC: Information Age Publishing.

Leidner, D., & Jarvenpaa, S. (1995). The use of information technology to enhance management school education: A theoretical view. *Management Information Systems Quarterly, 19*, 265–291. doi:10.2307/249596

Lombard, M., Ditton, T., & Reich, R. (1997). The role of screen size in viewer responses to television fare. *Communication Reports, 10*(1), 95–106.

McKeachie, W. (2002). *McKeachie's teaching tips: Strategies, research, and theory for college and university teachers* (11th ed.). Boston, MA: Houghton Mifflin.

Merriam, S. B., & Brockett, R. G. (1997). *The profession and practice of adult education: An introduction*. San Francisco, CA: Jossey-Bass.

Merrill, M. D. (1991). Constructivism and instructional design. In Duffy, T. M., & Jonassen, D. H. (Eds.), *Constructivism and the technology of instruction: A conversation* (pp. 99–114). Mahwah, NJ: Lawrence Erlbaum.

Murphy, P., Anzalone, S., Bosch, A., & Moulton, J. (2002). *Enhancing learning opportunities in Africa: Distance education and information and communication technologies for learning*. Retrieved from http://siteresources.worldbank.org/INTAFRREGTOPDISEDU/Resources/enhancing.pdf

Pallof, R., & Pratt, K. (1999). *Building learning communities in cyberspace*. San Francisco, CA: Jossey-Bass.

Picciano, A. G. (2002). Beyond student perceptions: Issues interaction, presence and performance in an online course. *Journal of Asynchronous Learning Networks, 6*, 20–41.

Relan, A., & Gillani, B. B. (1997). Web-based instruction and the traditional classroom: Similarities and differences. In Khan, B. H. (Ed.), *Web-based instruction* (pp. 41–46). Englewood Cliffs, NJ: Educational Technology Publications.

Rice, R. E. (1992). Task analyzability, use of new media, and effectiveness: A multi-site exploration of media richness. *Organization Science, 3*, 475–500. doi:10.1287/orsc.3.4.475

Rice, R. E., Hiltz, S. R., & Spencer, D. H. (2005). Media mixes and learning networks. In Hiltz, S. R., & Goldman, R. (Eds.), *Learning together online: Research on asynchronous learning networks* (pp. 215–237). Mahwah, NJ: Lawrence Erlbaum.

Roberts, T. S. (2005). Computer-supported collaborative learning in higher education: An introduction. In Roberts, T. S. (Ed.), *Computer-supported collaborative learning in higher education* (pp. 1–18). Hershey, PA: IGI Global.

Schrum, L. M., & Levin, B. B. (2009). *Leading 21st-century schools: Harnessing technology for engagement and achievement*. Thousand Oaks, CA: Corwin Press.

Shoffner, M. B., Jones, M., & Harmon, S. W. (2000). Paradigms restrained: Implications of new and emerging technologies for learning and cognition. *Journal of Electronic Publishing, 6*.

Short, J., Williams, E., & Christie, B. (1976). *The social psychology of telecommunications*. London, UK: Wiley.

Simmons, D. E. (2002). The forum report: E-learning adoption rates and barriers. In Rossett, A. (Ed.), *The ASTD E-learning handbook* (pp. 19–23). New York, NY: McGraw-Hill.

Slavin, R. E. (1987). *Cooperative learning: Student teams* (2nd ed.). Washington, DC: National Educational Association.

Smart, K. L., & Cappel, J. J. (2006). Students' perceptions of online learning: A comparative study. *Journal of Information Technology Education, 5*, 201–219.

Stacey, E. (2005). A constructivist framework for online collaborative learning: Adult learning and collaborative learning theory. In Roberts, T. S. (Ed.), *Computer supported collaborative learning in higher education* (pp. 140–161). Hershey, PA: IGI Global.

Sullivan, P. (2002). It's easier to be yourself when you are invisible: Female college students discuss their online classroom experiences. *Innovative Higher Education, 27*, 129–143. doi:10.1023/A:1021109410893

Taylor, V. (2004). Online group projects: Preparing the instructors to prepare the students. In Roberts, T. S. (Ed.), *Computer supported collaborative learning in higher education*. Hershey, PA: IGI Global. doi:10.4018/978-1-59140-408-8.ch002

Unesco Institute for Statistics. (2007). *Regional literacy rates for youths (15-24) and adults (25+)*. Retrieved from http://stats.uis.unesco.org/unesco/TableViewer/ tableView.aspx?ReportId=201

Vendel, M. (2009). *Universal mobile interface: The importance of the mobile phone to developing countries*. Retrieved from http://universalmobileinterface.wordpress.com/ 2009/04/07/ the-importance-of-the-mobile-phone-to-developing-countries/

Vygotsky, L. (1978). *Mind in society*. Boston, MA: Harvard University Press.

Walther, J. B., Slovacek, C. L., & Tidwell, L. C. (2001). Is a picture worth a thousand words? Photographic images in long-term and short-term computer-mediated communication. *Communication Research, 28*(1), 105–134. doi:10.1177/009365001028001004

Watkins, K. E., & Marsick, V. J. (1993). *Sculpting the learning organization: Lessons in the art and science of systemic change*. San Francisco, CA: Jossey-Bass.

Watkins, R. (2005). Developing interactive e-learning activities. *Performance Improvement, 44*, 5–7. doi:10.1002/pfi.4140440504

This work was previously published in the International Journal of Adult Vocational Education and Technology, Volume 2, Issue 4, edited by Victor C.X. Wang, pp. 43-57, copyright 2011 by IGI Publishing (an imprint of IGI Global).

Chapter 16
Information Technology and Fair Use

Lesley Farmer
California State University - Long Beach, USA

ABSTRACT

Intellectual pursuit and the recognition of ideas is a central concept. Copyrights protect the rights of intellectual creators while balancing those rights with the needs for access. As technologies have expanded, and production has become more sophisticated, the legal regulations surrounding their use have become more complex. With the advent of the interactive web 2.0 and increased resource sharing, as well as growth in distance learning opportunities, complying with the legal use of information technology can be daunting. In any case, leaders and other educators should be aware of the more important aspects of technology-related copyright laws and regulations. This article provides an overview of copyright law and fair use for educational research purposes. It explains different options for intellectual production and sharing, and notes administrative actions to support copyright compliance.

INTRODUCTION

In today's digital world, leaders and other educators can manipulate a wide variety of information for authentic projects. In the process, everyone needs to acknowledge the idea creators and their intellectual property.

As technologies have expanded, and their production has become more sophisticated, the legal regulations surrounding their use have become more complex. With the advent of the interactive web 2.0 and increased resource sharing, as well as growth in distance learning opportunities, complying with the legal use of information technology can be daunting. In any case, leaders and other educators should be aware of the more important aspects of technology-related copyright laws and regulations. This paper provides an overview of copyright law and fair use for educational research purposes.

DOI: 10.4018/978-1-4666-2062-9.ch016

LEGAL BACKGROUND

A central aspect of education is intellectual pursuit and the recognition of great minds. Yet teachers bemoan the rise in cheating, which technology facilitates. On their part, students have a more lax attitude about intellectual property. Particularly with Web 2.0, which fosters collaborate knowledge generation, identifying the originator of an idea can be difficult to ascertain.

The publishing world further complicates the intellectual property picture. Reporters are demanding personal credit and remuneration for their contributions. Publishers create copyright agreements to cover authorship rights based on format. Multimedia copyright laws can be very specific: restricting resizing or other image manipulation, stipulating the length of music or video that can be copied legitimately. Fortunately, education falls under the umbrella of Fair Use, so restrictions are loosened up a bit in order to support personal research.

Although intellectual property is sometimes used interchangeably with copyright, the former is a broader concept. Copyright protects creative and original ideas that are recorded in tangible form. Other U. S. intellectual property deals with trademarks, patents, trade secrets, and licenses.

Copyright laws seek solutions to give authors fair compensation for sharing their work. Begun as a way to give scientists and inventors lead time to prevent others from using their work without permission, copyright laws in the United States have become more far-ranging. For example, in-house writers such as newspaper reporters now demand personal credit and remuneration for their contributions. In this digital age, copyright laws have become more complex.

The chief statute driving copyright law is the Copyright Act of 1976, which become effective in 1978. Several factors were included for the first time in this piece of legislation: a codification of fair use, the right for an author to receive copyright for an unpublished work, and the divisibility of authors' rights. The Act includes definitions, delineates what is copyrightable, and describes copyright rights and limitations.

The Digital Millennium Copyright Act (DMCA) was added to the Act in 1998, largely to conform to international treaties (note that no international copyright law exists) that dealt with technological issues, particularly online material. DMCA limits database company liability, and addresses digital preservation.

Educators and leaders also need to know about the 2002 Technology, Education, and Copyright Harmonization (TEACH) Act, which impacts copyright usage in distance education or in cases where digital information is transmitted as a supplement face-to-face instruction. Displays and performances can be disseminated only for the period of the course and only to those students who are enrolled in the course. Likewise, if teachers copy an article for a face-to-face class, then they can link to the same article online, depending on the magazine database license agreement. A better solution is for the teacher to provide the citation, and ask the students to access the article themselves from the library's database collection. However, the teacher should *not* download the whole magazine issue just because it is technically possible; that action probably does not comply with copyright law.

Further complicating matters, different countries have different copyright guidelines, so information accessed from around the world may be subject to conflicting laws; when in doubt, users should be overly conservative.

Particularly with the advent of Web 2.0 in which students can produce and disseminate information publicly, copyright applications are stricter. A few examples of technology-relevant copyright practices follow.

- Images should not be resized, cropped, or changed in context without explicit permission.

- Photos of recognizable people require written permission if they are to be broadcast.
- Scanning or digitizing work is considered reproducing it, and requires prior permission if shared publicly. Other rights may be covered by patent law, such as copying code.
- Music and video downloads can be very problematic. It is wisest to use pre-approved sites such as iTunes.
- Computer program appearance, graphics and sound may be protected from copying, depending on the company's licensing agreements.
- Slander and libel can occur on social networking sites such as MySpace and Facebook; students might not realize that they can be held legally responsible for their comments, and even arrested and prosecuted.
- Information about health and legal issues should include a disclaimer so the author is not held legally responsible in case the reader uses that information and experiences negative results.
- Each database aggregator and disseminator (such as video streaming) has a unique licensing agreement that covers copyright issues. A good rule of thumb is to apply the most conservative guidelines in order to avoid case-by-case decisions.

Just as technology changes, so too does the law relative to copyright. Bills continue to be put forth to amend codes, such as 2009 H.R. 801 Fair Copyright in Research Works Act. Questions continue to arise about the status of orphan works, those copyrighted works whose authors are difficult or impossible to find. Other laws also exist to support copyright law such as anti-piracy, codified as the Family and Entertainment Copyright Act of 2005.

Fair Use

Fortunately, educational institutions enjoy more freedom in the use of copyrighted materials because of the intent of that use: teaching and personal research without market compensation. These fair use exemptions are listed in Section 107 of 17 United States Code 106:

1. The purpose and character of the use, including whether such use is of commercial nature or is for nonprofit educational purposes;
2. The nature of the copyrighted work;
3. Amount and substantiality of the portion used in relation to the copyrighted work as a whole; and
4. The effect of the use upon the potential market for or value of the copyrighted work.

The expansion of digital resource has further complicated copyright laws and Fair Use. The ease and speed of digital duplication can tempt the most honest user. Especially when software "suites" facilitate repurposing of information (such as turning a PowerPoint into an outline word processed document), it can be difficult to explain how to use digital materials within copyright limits. How does format define information? How does multimedia incorporation change the nature and intellectual property of each information element? These issues can lead to valuable learning moments during which students can understand the nuanced nature of digital information. The National Council of Teachers of English has developed a code of best practices in fair use for media literacy education, which can serve as a useful set of guidelines (http://www.ncte.org/positions/statements/fairusemedialiteracy).

Certainly, students and teachers alike need to cite sources accurate to credit the original creators, but it is no substitute for asking permission. Basically, asking permission requires finding the author of the work, identifying the specific information to be used (full citation, including which section of the document), the purpose of the use, and the extent of use (e.g., how, where and frequency). Copyright clearinghouses (e.g., http://www.copyright.com) can also help users obtain permission.

Fortunately, user-friendly guidelines about fair use are available. The American Library Association for Information Technology Policy has developed two online copyright educational tools that focus on fair use (http://www.wo.ala.org/districtdispatch/?p=3207). The Copyright Advisory Office of Columbia University Libraries' Information Services has developed a useful fair use checklist that can help the education community respect intellectual property while researching and generating ideas: http://www.copyright.columbia.edu/fair-use-checklist#.

PROJECT CHECKLIST

As multimedia and digital resources are incorporated into presentations, particularly as these products are broadcast online, the school community needs to follow more stringent copyright guidelines. The Washington State Library (2008) has developed a checklist of factors to consider when thinking about using and publishing information. Their first point is probably the most salient: ownership of physical and digital objects doesn't guarantee use rights.

- Who owns the material? Have you made a good faith effort to find the owner? Who controls access to the physical items? Who will control access to the digital items?
- Are there written agreements as to construction, ownership, and access to the digital collections?
- Determine copyright and permissions status; are the materials owned outright? Can the rights to publish the materials digitally be obtained?
- What percentage of the materials will need research or requests for permissions? What

will be the added cost of devoting staff time to obtaining permissions?
- Is the material in the public domain or covered by copyright that your organization has legally obtained?
- Remember, any original student work cannot be digitized or published without a signed permission form from the student or their guardian if they are a minor.
- Address copyright, permission to copy on your own digital site. Post a statement to guide use of materials on your digital Web site.
- Provide contact information for users of your Web site.

THE CREATIVE COMMONS

A growing interest in the creative "information commons" reflects a philosophy that "information yearns to be free" and that accessible information leads to expanded discourse, knowledge and progress. Public domain documents have exemplified this philosophy for over a century, and government publications carry on this tradition in the spirit of civic engagement.

A welcome alternative is the Creative Commons (http://www.creativecommons.org), which enables people to upload and share data with the understanding that any use requires cited acknowledgment, and any changes to the data also need to be uploaded and cited within the Creative Commons. This proactive strategy recognizes the benefits of collaborative knowledge building. In 2005 the International Federation of Library Associations and Institutions (IFLA) called upon the World Summit on the Information Society Summit to promote a global Information Commons where all people could access and disseminate information without restrictions. Two main approaches to the creative commons have emerged: 1) contributing and modifying original information, and 2) facilitating the *sharing* of information.

The idea of a creative commons can be expanded across systems, disciplines, even national boundaries. Creative Commons provides an extensive directory of federated repositories (http://wiki.creativecommons.org/Content_Directories). One of the advantages of federated collaborations is that each site typically controls copyright and licensing issues. Nevertheless, these consortia initiatives require careful, thorough planning, not only in terms of technical requirements but also in terms of fiscal and governance issues.

A recent development related to the Creative Commons is the Open Textbook Initiative. In an effort to the make textbooks more affordable, the Higher Educational Opportunity Act of 2008 supported the development of open textbooks. Textbook publishers, such as Flat World Knowledge, offer free online access to textbooks under a Creative Commons license, and low-cost fees for printing copies. In addition, these textbooks are often repurposed so that instructors can essentially create customized texts for their courses. While this option certainly attracts students and instructors, some authors are not so keen on this practice because they get little or no fiscal remuneration for the materials they create. Instead, they must be satisfied with possible increase in visibility and reputation, and derive satisfaction from contributing to the field in a timely manner.

Similarly, "open source" is a growing approach to software development, which impacts intellectual property rights, mainly in the areas of patents and licensing. The term emerged with Netscape's code, which was openly released in 2006 for others to use freely. At this point, the largest repository of open source code, Source-Forge, has over a million registered users. Open source code has been the basis for many social networking applications such as wikis and blogs.

TECHNOLOGY-BASED INFORMATION PACKAGES

Individuals and institutions routinely "package" information together as a way to synthesize the best resources for their clientele. For instance, course "readers" have been a mainstay for years. Copyright permission has always been a part of that production process. Several general copyright issues loom when dealing with technology aspects of packaged information.

- **Content:** Does the entity have permission to copy, download, digitize, modify, excerpt, or package information? What limitations exist on such practices: e.g., length of time to keep the copy, number of copies (sometimes within a specified timeframe), extent of copying (such as percentage of the entire worm), access rights, purpose limitations (such as referral vs. personal research vs. resale), format

- **Format:** Packaging information, such as software installation instructions, for internal use, is a much different issue than scanning published cartoons for a public website. Even if the entity gets permission to copy an image, that permission might not extend to resizing or cropping the image. Copyright owners might not permit content to be reformatted or repurposed with reason, since changing context can result in different interpretations of the information. Likewise, pinning up candid student pictures in the faculty mail room requires a different level of permission than broadcasting those same pictures on the Internet, particularly if any under-age students are shown. Indeed, because of stalking and other criminal behaviors, few institutions show captioned pictures of their staff, particularly in online environments.

- **Liability:** Entities need to read licensing agreements carefully to make sure that their packaging efforts comply with the legal language. Users need equitable access, proper authorization, and confidentiality; moreover, no profits can be incurred (Farb & Riggio, 2004). Once entities start to extract and synthesize information, even with permission, they stand to risk being sued. For instance, health information might be followed by some user with unpleasant results. Especially in the areas of law and health, entities need to make sure that they post a disclaimer that they are not legal or health professionals (unless so licensed). Even the software used to package information is likely to entail legal right for its use, particularly if the product is web-based and disseminated externally. The North Carolina State Library Web Portal Collection Development Policy addresses a number of these issues (http://www.ncecho.org/dig/digguidelines.shtml).

In addition, specific types of information packages have unique copyright implications, as detailed here.

Linking Sources

The naïve user would like a single-stop searching tool that would link all relevant material: primary sources, secondary sources, print, web-based, audiovisual. While a one-stop tool is probably not feasible in the near future (despite Google's intention), smaller-scale reference linking has become an attractive way to add value to information, and facilitate information services. There are several ways to link sources:

- Between citations (e.g., databases)
- Within sources (e.g., hyperlinks)
- Between sources and applications (e.g., course management systems)
- Between sources and services (e.g., e-reserves).

Usually, metadata provides the basis for these actions. More recently, Digital Object Identifiers (DOI) provide an international standards-based "system for persistent and actionable identification and interoperable exchange of managed information on digital networks" (http://www.doi.org).

Links may be categorized as either static (created as a permanent link) or dynamic (created in response to user action). Normally, information packagers pursue dynamic solutions where linking can occur without full control of the resources. This approach is attractive in theory, but may threaten vendors who are less comfortable about open access. Furthermore, as entities create documents that include links, be it at the citation or source level, they need to consider how the source information is captured and authenticated, processing between links, and hosting services. All entities and related protocols need to be interoperable as well as legally compliant (Van de Sompel & Hochstenbach, 1999). Certainly, links within the same website are permissible, but sometimes links to a different website may require permission from the owner of that site; the law is not clear about that issue.

Repositories

Increasingly, institutions and organizations are developing digital repositories, either storing data or storing the documents themselves. In both cases, these services manage and disseminate digital resources. The scope of repositories can range from a single program to international consortia. The value of repositories lies in the quality of use of their content, so identifying desired kinds of documents and collecting high-quality materials are key functions. Key technology management issues of a repository follow:

- Maintaining the data without damage or alteration: storage and security requirements
- Providing "physical" access to the data, including extracting of it from the archive:

authentification, verification, identification, metadata harvesting software

- Ensuring that the user can understand and interpret the data: display/rendering software and preservation planning
- Ensuring long-term stability: technology planning and data maintenance (Wheatley, 2004).

In structuring repositories, entities need to consider three layers: storage, database, and application, each of which may have copyright implications. The Academic and Research Libraries of the American Library Association developed an institutional repository SPEC toolkit to help librarians with policies and procedures (http://www.arl.org/sc/models/repositories/index.shtml).

One promising practice in digitizing materials is systemwide technology initiatives, usually in the form of federated repositories of archival materials. DSpace (http://www.DSpace.org) is an Open Archive Initiative that provides guidelines for digitizing, cataloging, storing, and disseminating unique digital sources. This open source solution emphasizes the need for technical expertise and planning. Nevertheless, the *content within* the repository still needs copyright oversight.

Knowledge management (KM) consists of managing the knowledge of an organization, usually collecting, storing, organizing, and disseminating explicit information such as documents with the intent that others will use that information: an internal repository. Particularly in today's society where in-house knowledge may be proprietary and employees may leave after a short time, making tacit knowledge explicit through the use of a knowledge management system offers an effective way to coalesce expertise. Because they are internal, such KM repositories normally do not require copyright permission, although institutions should set up policies and procedures that delineate levels of access and authorization protocols. As some of the documents may be permitted to be

access externally, dealing with copyright permissions from the start is a good practice.

E-Publishing

For decades, in order to inform their constituents, institutions and organizations have created documents for their own members and for the public. These might be as simple as a guide to the library or as sophisticated as a peer-reviewed journal. In the digital world, these entities need to be aware of copyright for e-publishing.

- Stanford University Library's HighWire Press, which publishes almost a thousand e-journals. The press prides itself in its efforts to incorporate multimedia, hyperlinks, interactivity, and powerful search engines. Although they publish some free online articles, the press hosts digital content on behalf of many publishers, each of which has specific terms of use. HighWire's notice states: "Unless explicitly stated otherwise, content on HighWire's publishing platform, including content accessible without charge, cannot be copied, re-purposed, displayed on other websites, reprinted, redistributed, entered into a database, modified, used to create derivative works or otherwise re-used without the specific permission of its publisher" (http://highwire.stanford.edu/about/terms-of-use.dtl).
- Since 2004, the E-Press has operated as a separate department within the Swedish Linköping University Library. It publishes digital conference proceedings, databases, journals, series, theses, and reports. The press states that it will maintain availability of their publications for 25 years, and their authors retain individual copyrights.

In a few cases, one of the impetuses is financial gain, but for the majority of e-publishers the goal is dissemination of information on topics of interest to their clientele. To this end, open access journals have become quite attractive: they are relatively inexpensive to create (except for labor costs of editing and layout) and disseminate, can include digital features not available in print format such as sound, and may be more timely to publish than print versions. The Budapest Open Access Initiative (2002) asserts that

Removing access barriers to this literature will accelerate research, enrich education, share the learning of the rich with the poor and the poor with the rich, make this literature as useful as it can be, and lay the foundation for uniting humanity in a common intellectual conversation and quest for knowledge.

On the other hand, copyright issues connected with maintaining a permanent collection of the e-publications may be overlooked. Furthermore, if indexing services do not receive a copy of the journal, then access to the information will become even more limited. The best guide to scholarly e-publishing is Bailey's *Open access bibliography: Liberating scholarly literature with e-prints and open access journals* (http://www. digital-scholarship.com/oab/oab.htm).

WEB 2.0/SOCIAL NETWORK

Web 2.0 signals a new level of complexity in copyright. Web 2.0 essentially covers social networking: the interactive Internet. It fosters collaborative work, which results in collective intelligence. Determining the author and ways to recompense the use of web 2.0 works presents a real challenge legally. Furthermore, these documents are often dynamic in nature so that the content may change moment to moment. What, indeed, is the basis of copyright? At best, it would need to be based on a time-stamped version that acknowledges both the time of the creation as well as the time that someone accessed it to use it.

Some people assume that all document on the Internet are free, which assumption is clearly wrong, as discussed above. In some cases, the document creators function on a creative commons agreement, or publish a statement of use. Wikipedia is a good example. It has what it calls a "copyleft" agreement, which states: "Wikipedia content can be copied, modified, and redistributed so long as the new version grants the same freedoms to others and acknowledges the authors of the Wikipedia article used" (http://en.wikipedia. org/wiki/Wikipedia:Copyrights). Most of Wikipedia's articles are co-licensed under the Creative Commons Attribution-Sharealike 3.0 Unported License and the GNU Free Documentation License. Wikipedia states that each image notes its legal usage basis.

Blogs are usually the work of a person or group, and are in a recorded form, so they follow normal copyright laws by default. That argument would then also apply to comments that followers make. Of course, the blogger can provide further guidance, be it a statement about being in public domain or a explicit clause that bars anyone from reproducing any of the material in any format.

Podcasts and videocasts consist of compressed audio and video files that are then broadcast by the creator or an aggregator such as iTunes. Again, these are recorded documents so are assumed to fall within copyright laws. 'Casts can be easily downloaded and shared, so it is wise to contact the originator or from a reputable Internet site. Difficulties tend to arise when someone uses copyrighted sources (particularly commercial music and videos) to create a mash-up or other kind of derivative work. It can be as simple as videotaping a toddler dancing to a Bruce Springsteen song, and then uploading it to YouTube. Unless the videotaper got written permission from Sesame Street to use that song, the broadcasting that that video constitutes illegal usage if for no other reason than that the song writer and producer should be paid royalties every time the video with the music is played. If the videotaper wants to avoid legal action, he or she should either get permission or not upload or broadcast the video; instead, that video can be recorded for home use, and friends can come over to see the bouncing baby bopper. The Podcasting legal guide (http://wiki.creativecommons.org/Podcasting_Legal_Guide) by Vogel, Marlick and the Berman Center provides current in-depth information on legal uses of these media.

Social bookmarking sites, such as Delicious and LibraryThing, provide a means to store and describe ("tag") URLs for later retrieval and use. Similar to a bibliography, a list of lists falls under copyright law. Therefore, the creator of each list has the right to determine who can use it and the conditions of its use. To some degree, that can be controlled through the settings that the originator chooses. Usually, each overarching social bookmarking site has a policy about the use of the site as a whole and the use of individual bookmark collections.

RSS means "really simple syndication," and an RSS feed is a means to gather information from other websites to a central location. Every single website that offers an RSS service has its own copyright policy about legal use. Of course, if the originating news is in the public domain and is copied from an open source or creative commons/copyleft site, then that information can be used freely. One can even broadcast that information via his or her own RSS feed; however, it is usually safer to keep one's personal RSS feeder private and avoid copyright problems altogether. In terms of copyright law, "really simple" is not really simple.

File sharing is a central feature of social networking, as evidenced by the high use of Flickr and YouTube in particular. Without explicit permission, only the owner of the files can reproduce with work, create derivative works, distribute copies of the work to the public, display or perform the work publicly (including by digital transmission). Therefore, such files cannot be integrated into a school DVD for sale or placed on an institutional website or played at a public meeting. In short, one should read each file-sharing site's copyright

guidelines before downloading documents (Talab & Butler, 2007).

ADMINISTRATIVE ISSUES

Because everyone has to comply with copyright law, it behooves everyone to be knowledgeable about it, but it can be difficult to keep current. In the final analysis, administrators are responsible for such compliance. Understanding copyright, particularly as it applies to technology, enables administrators to address the risks of technology as they optimize its benefits. Discovery Educator Network Director Hall Davidson (http://www.halldavidson.net/) suggests ways that administrators can avoid copyright problems.

1. Develop, implement and enforce technology policies and procedures that include a code of ethics.
2. Review technology policies and procedures with the entire educational community.
3. Hire a technology manage to maintain records about licenses and registration information for technology.
4. Teach and reinforce legal and ethical technology use.

Training

To help the educational community remain in compliance, librarians sometimes provide training about copyright because of their role as information managers. More information about copyright is located online. Institutions should also maintain a reviewed bibliography of copyright resources that can be consulted easily.

U.S. Copyright Office
http://www.copyright.gov
Provides copyright forms and regulations, and a searchable database of copyright registrations

American Library Association Copyright

http://www.ala.org/ala/issuesadvocacy/copyright/index.cfm

Good information and links about legislation, intellectual property, and international copyright activities

Columbia University Libraries Information Services Copyright Advisory Office

http://copyright.columbia.edu

Well-respected site targeted to librarians and educators

University Of Texas

http://utsystem.edu/ogc/IntellectualProperty/crpindex.htm

Many links on copyright issues; they have a good crash course tutorial at http://www.lib.utsystem.edu/copyright/

Stanford University Libraries Copyright & Fair Use

http://fairuse.stanford.edu

Focuses on fair use, the public domain, and the permissions process

Copyright Website

http://www.benedict.com

Provides general copyright information for education and digital resource creators

Copyright for Educators

http://www.koce.org/classroom/copyright.htm

Public television site designed to help educators learn about fair use

Intellectual Property Legal Center

http://www.cetus.org/fairindex.html

Provides information on several aspects of intellectual property, with a separate section on ebooks

New York State Education Department Office of College and University Evaluation

http://www.highered.nysed.gov/ocue/ded/resources.html

Useful links about distance education: organization support, learning design, learner support, intellectual property, and disabilities

Cybercrime

http://www.cybercrime.gov

Computer crime and intellectual property section of the Criminal Division of the U. S. Department of Justice

Software & Information Industry Association

http://www.siia.net/index.php?option=com_content&view=article&id=77&Itemid=7

Their Anti-Piracy Division campaign tries to balance enforcement with education

Digital Rights Management

As digital resources grow in number and percentage in institutions, the function of digital asset management has grown in complexity. How do institutions keep track of all their electronic resources as well as make sure that they are effectively stored and retrieved? Especially in today's Web 2.0 world, digital asset management has to address interactivity options and social networking features, such as push technology RRS feeds, comment/messaging options, incorporation of faculty repositories, enterprise mash-ups, and user-customizable folksonomy "shells." While some of these features are low-cost plug-ins, their management and incorporation into the library's digital collection system can involve sophisticated technical support, which is usually *not* inexpensive. Furthermore, such customizations need to be well documented and maintained.

Within that scope, the field of digital rights management (DRM) has become increasingly important. Broadly speaking, DRM deals with the exact rights that each digital content has: who holds those rights and under which circumstances, who has authority to access that content and how that can be insured as well as preventing non-authorized people access (Calhoun, 2005). Complying with intellectual property regulations is very difficult; so digital rights management technologies are being employed to control content use. While automated systems conveniently take care of authentification issues and facilitate fair royalties compensation, they can also and may jeopardize privacy rights and leak into discriminatory profiling practices. E-resources sometimes are not device-neutral, so rights are sometimes given for just one operating system, which belies the concept of intellectual property. Installation of DRM-protected content can be burdensome, and may malfunction, preventing authorized access. At the other end of the process, when the access key to DRM-protected content is lost or the device becomes obsolete, the content itself becomes unreadable, even if it has been paid for legally. DRM can also pose problems for users with special needs. Furthermore, these DRM digital tools are not standardized. In short, DRM technology may be unavoidable when purchasing some digital resources, but needs to be carefully used (Houghton-Jan, 2007).

Even without considering DRM technology, digital rights management can be complicated Libraries are usually the body that deals with commercial digital resources, and a few are now dealing with institutional e-documents. Within that scope, subscription databases (including e-book aggregators) constitute the major copyright effort because each vendor has a unique set of license agreements. Farb and Riggio (2004) list basic elements of most contracts: scope, completeness of content, duration, warranties, indemnification, access, confidentiality, sharing, archiving, disability compliance, and usage statistics. Increasingly, libraries are considering "leasing with an option to buy" licenses as a way to insure access through backfile ownership; licensing a database with no copyright to the content beyond the date of the license is no longer attractive.

Libraries and their institutions are embracing the creative commons arena of electronic journals. Particularly as the academic community pursues research venues, providing efficient access to e-journals is a logical function for academic libraries. The Scholarly Publishing and Academic Resources Coalition (SPARC) (http://www.arl.org/sparc), founded in 1998, exemplifies a collab-

orative library approach to disseminating research. Because of such open interchanges, more citations have been included in studies, and scientific advances have been accelerated (Lawrence, 2001).

FUTURE TRENDS

Copyright law tends to react to new technologies and practices, so it is unlikely that it will proactively change. Nevertheless, technology will continue to change and expand, so the law will need to accommodate such changes. In addition, technology has also impacted the interchange of information, from the local to the international level, which will affect copyright law at least indirectly. Both technology as a whole and the phenomenon of resource sharing is already impacting the publishing model, which may have startling implications for copyright. In the face of such change, it seems almost laughable to consider that current copyright law allows for proprietary rights for 70 years after the author's death in some cases. This practice may need to change in light of digital realities.

Interactive technology corners the market in terms of copyright issues. As noted above, determining the recordable version of a document when multiple users can edit it almost simultaneously can be a copyright nightmare. As web 3.0 emphasizes the relations between documents, those relationship themselves might fall under copyright just as bibliographies and links can.

The core concept of a work also needs further scrutiny as works are manifested in so many different formats and appearances. Right now, an e-book might be licensed to be readable on a single device; is that fair if the content itself exists separately from that device? How different does the document have to be in order to be considered a separate work?

International aspects also impact copyright in several ways. At present, no international copyright law exists. How, then, are royalties handled when publishers are international or offer translations of works? It is done by international treaties or agreements, usually on a case-by-case basis. Right now, Disney licenses some merchandise abroad, which products are not allowed in the U.S. because of copyright restrictions; foreign entities can sell them to U.S. buyers, who cannot buy the items stateside. Such inequities need to be addressed.

As mentioned above, documents and repositories are increasingly the products of collective intelligence. As this practice expands in global environments, copyright law may need to become international so that authors can be fairly compensated. Theoretically, virtual worlds are associated with the country in which the software is based, but such boundaries may also come into question as documents are created in those virtual realities by people in other countries. Again, copyright law may need to be handled internationally.

Publishing itself is undergoing internal scrutiny as it develops new models of production and diffusion. Format issues, particularly as one idea is manifested in several ways, make fair remuneration difficult to ascertain. Particularly as product buyers and licensees share these documents, such as libraries and organizations, determining what is a fair royalty can be problematic. Micro-payments for access and downloading or printing are slowly being incorporated, but the models for fair rights still need to be hammered out.

CONCLUSION

Gone are the days of copyright limits of fourteen years, which was calculated on the average age of a generation. Somehow the spirit of the U.S. Constitution "to promote the progress of science and useful arts, by securing for limited times to authors and inventors the exclusive right to their respective writings and discoveries (Article 1, Section 1, Clause 8) seems to have been left behind.

Nevertheless, educators and other researchers have the strength of fair use behind them so they can promote an effective learning environment, be it face-to-face or virtual. In addition, collaborative practices such as the Creative Commons promote intellectual sharing in order to advance their fields.

Technology has significantly expanded the intellectual arena in terms of production and sharing of information. In response, copyright law has tried to codify intellectual property rights to balance the rights of the creator and appropriate access to information. Such laws are often format-specific, reflecting both the nature of the medium as well as the perspectives of their producers. Dissemination models have also changed drastically, so how the information buyer uses that information constitutes another can of copyright worms. Adding the international dimension that technology facilitates, copyright law cannot help but seem instantly out of date.

At the least, leaders and other educators need to keep abreast of copyright issues, and try to comply with them in an ever-changing environment.

REFERENCES

Budapest Open Access Initiative. (2002). *Budapest open access initiative*. Retrieved from http://www.soros.org/openaccess/read.shtml

Calhoun, T. (2005). DRM: The challenge of the decade. *Campus Technology*, 18-20.

Farb, S., & Riggio, A. (2004). Medium or message? A new look at standards, structures, and schemata for managing electronic resources. *Library Hi Tech*, *22*(2), 144–152. doi:10.1108/07378830410524576

Houghton-Jan, S. (2007). Imagine no restrictions. *School Library Journal*, 53–54.

Talab, R., & Butler, R. (2007). Shared electronic spaces in the classroom. *TechTrends*, *51*(1), 12–14. doi:10.1007/s11528-007-0004-1

Van de Sompel, H., & Hochstenbach, P. (1999). Reference linking in a hybrid library environment. *D-Lib Magazine*, *5*(4). doi:10.1045/april99-van_de_sompel-pt1

Wheatley, P. (2004). *Institutional repositories within the context of digital preservation*. York, UK: Digital Preservation Coalition.

This work was previously published in the International Journal of Adult Vocational Education and Technology, Volume 2, Issue 1, edited by Victor C.X. Wang, pp. 1-12, copyright 2011 by IGI Publishing (an imprint of IGI Global).

Chapter 17
Adult Education and Sustainable Learning Outcome of Rural Widows of Central Northern Nigeria

Lantana M. Usman
University of Northern British Columbia, Canada

ABSTRACT

In northern Nigeria, widows' identities and status are defined within the mores, norms, traditional religions, and legal institutions of the cultures of the community. The ethnic cultural laws are oppressive and retrogressive. The nexus of these cultural pressures trigger discriminatory practices that deny school attending widows' access, and completion of primary and secondary levels of education, leaving them literacy bankrupt and unskilled to fend for themselves and their children. These experiences motivated an all women Community Based Organization (CBO) to establish a Widows Training School to educate widows in vocational skills and basic literacy and numeracy. This paper examines research that was conducted with a sample of former graduates and attendees of the Widows Training School (WTS). The study is based on a qualitative educational research orientation, and the case study design. Multi-modal data were derived from Focused Group Interviews (FGIs) and Non Participant Observation (NPO) with a sample population of the widows. Data analysis engaged the qualitative process of transcription, categorization, and generation of codes that were merged into major themes, and presented in the as socio cultural status of the widows in the community; historical foundation, nature and curriculum implementation of the school; and the facets of sustainable learning outcome of the widows.

DOI: 10.4018/978-1-4666-2062-9.ch017

INTRODUCTION

In Nigeria, adult education is a part of the nation's educational policy, and considered pathway to basic literacy, numeracy, and for poverty alleviation (Federal Ministry of Education of Nigeria, 2000; Omolewa, 1981, 1997). Specific to women adult education, vocational training is greatly emphasized, considering women's cultural role as secondary providers of children's physiological needs, and as nurturers of the family (Blueprint of Women's Education in Nigeria, 1986; Omolewa, 1997). To expand and reinforce the goals of adult education on women at the state, federal, and local levels, previous Nigerian First Ladies (NFLs) established active Vocational Training Project Centers (VTPC) that implemented vocational training projects for rural and urban women. One outstanding rural based vocational training project was the 1987 Better Life for Rural Women (BLRW), whose popularity garnered international recognition by UNESCO and UNIFEM (Babangida, 2005). Currently, the federal Ministry of Women Affairs and the Women's Commission facilitate women's vocational adult education through local government departments of women and youth across the nation. Regardless of these initiatives, it is significant to note that rural women's level of participation is still low, thereby marginalizing their access and attainment of basic literacy and vocational skills that will lead them to progressive and sustainable life style that will change their poor social and economic conditions in the community. To change the situation, an all women Community Based Organization (CBO) was established as the first residential Widows Training School in the rural central northern Nigerian state of Kaduna. The primary aim of the school is to provide vocational skills training, basic literacy and numeracy (at the primary school level), and counseling services for the widows. The secondary purpose of the school is to facilitate graduates to become socially and economically empowered, and self-reliant. The school expects the graduates to not only sustain their learning outcome as new

'small scale entrepreneurs', but to use their basic literacy to access information that will assist them utilize state based legal services to fight back the oppression and discrimination emanated to them by the traditional legal system; as well as exercise and enjoy their human rights and privileges to live independent life styles that are free from cultural victimization and oppression. Since the inception of the Widows Training School (WTS) a research study had never been conducted. So far, my research study is the first to undertake an assessment performance of the school's program and its learning outcome on the widows. Hence, the purpose of this article is to provide an evidence based report on not only the performance of the school, but the extent to which the widows' learning outcomes are sustained in their home communities. In doing so, a cursory look at the extent to which the goals and purpose of the school have been achieved are analyzed, with the anticipation that further research on the school and with similar organizations that focus on the development of widows in the rural area of the country, and indeed the Sub-Sahara African region.

The contextualization presents an overview of my research procedures, followed by a synopsis on the socio-cultural status, and the social and economic realities of the widows. The latter elaborates on the learning motivation for vocational skills and literacy acquisition of the widows. A description of the historical foundations of the school, the nature and implementation of the curriculum are discussed in relation to Adult Educational Theories (AET) of Knox' Proficiency Theory (KPT) (Knox, 1977), and Jarvis Learning Process Theory (JLT) (Jarvis, 1995; 1987) on adult learners' self-determination, intentionality, and rationality. The latter are re-situated to the widows' learning motivations, teaching, and learning praxis. In discussing the major findings of the study excerpts of the widows Focus Group Interviews (FGIs) are cited to support their claims and experiences on the facets of sustainable learning outcome and learning motivation. The concluding section provides a summation of the entire discussion, a reflection of the widows learning challenges, and the shortcoming of the school vocational disciplines. It is anticipated that the data "might be helpful for the administrators of the organization in determining expansion plans" (Slavin, 2007, p. 152) as well as allied stake holders such as the state and local governments, international donors and multilateral organizations connected to the development of rural marginalized population as women.

Research Procedures

The study orientation was based on the qualitative educational research, and the case study design. Within the typology of Case Study Designs (CSDs), the Historical Case Study (HCS) design was adopted to analyze the historical foundation, nature and curriculum implementation of the Widows' Training School (WTS). My choice of the research design provides a "better understanding of a particular case, its uniqueness or ordinariness that makes the case interesting" (Stake, 1994; Berg, 2003, p. 256). In addition, the general merits associated with case study on extensive data access, flexibility to data collection procedures, and thorough appraisal of the study (Bodgan & Biklen, 2003; Marshal & Rossman, 1999), and the "illumination of a societal concern under investigation" (Patton, 2002, p. 213), were considered for the choice of the research design. However, the fact that a research study had not been undertaken on the Widows Training School (WTS) became the primary purpose of the study, which was to evaluate "the program or policy for possible recommendation to practitioners for a useful practice to solve the problem [under investigation]" (McEwan & McEwan, 2003, p. 21). In addition, the secondary purpose aims at evaluating the impact, and efficacies of the school's program on the widows as well as the performance of the school management on the growth and lapses of its programs.

As common with qualitative case study designs on study framework, open research questions were postulated as; what are the aims, and purposes of establishing the WTS in the community? What are the widows' motivating factors to the enrolment, participation, and completion of the school programs? To what extent has the school programs provided social and economic empowerment and learning sustenabilities for the widows? How has the learning outcome changed the family and community perception of the widows and their new acquired status as self reliant and emerging entrepreneurs? In what ways do the widows use their acquired basic literacy and numeracy for personal growth? What forms of synergies exist between the Widows' Training School and the local government educational boards? Widows' Training School (WTS) and business outlets of graduates of the school within the sub-urban and rural parts of the community served as research sites. Ethical considerations were undertaken through the acquisition of written and verbal consent of all the participants. To further gain the trust of the widows and teachers of the school, I solicited for further cooperation of the school principal to serve as a gatekeeper, and as a witness during my classroom observations. Confidentiality, none-malfeasance, and fidelity of the participants were addressed with the use of pseudonyms to protect their identities in the course of data analysis, and in reporting the study in this article (Bodgan & Biklen, 2003).

Purposeful qualitative sampling as the "maximal variation sampling of which sample individuals differ in some characteristics or trait as age groups, gender etc" (Creswell, 2005, p. 204) was used to select (25) widow participants within the age range of 18-30 as the population sample. Within the selected sample, six (6) of the school-attending widows are challenged by HIV/AIDs disease. Multi-modal data were derived from of the Focused Group Interviews (FGIs), and the Non-Participant Observation (NPO) techniques. The use of FGIs took cognizance of its compatibility and parity advantage in doing research with women participants as reiterated by Callahan (1983) that "the women's participation and the flow of ideas and information would be enhanced by being able to listen to each other's experience and to interact with each other…A group interview format facilitates women building on each other's ideas and augments the identification of patterns through their shared experience" (p. 38).

Socio-Cultural Status of Widows in the Community

Most ethnic groups of Sub-Sahara Africa describe the social status and identities of widows within a cultural context. Widows' lived experiences are defined by traditional rights, laws, and mores, which serve as framework to socialization in the family and communities (Adukwu-Bogun, 2004; Cattell, 1997; Kore, 2005). Specific to Nigeria's ethnic groups, the embedded traditional social and legal structures from pre-colonial and post-colonial times continue to limit and violate the human rights of widows (Ewelukwa, 2002). These unviable traditional cultural practices reflect the norms of traditional patriarchy, which not only humiliate the widows, but also perpetuate injustices on them and relegating them into lower status in the community (Potash, 1986). The major effects of such systemic practices is the suppression of their voices, which are not only silenced, but unheard, and under-represented at the family, community, national and at the international level in the discourse of gender issues (Assembly of African Union, 2003; Division for the Advancement of Women, 1980; Ezer, 2007; Kirwen, 1979; Okoye, 1995). While some may argue that the adoption of Christianity and Islamic religions have to some extent regulated the injustices emanated on widows by traditional institutions, and that the 'new' religious practices provide support, care, and nurturing for widows by its members. Nonetheless, the extent to such care is not only questionable, but negotiable, depending on the level of commitment of members of these religious communities, and family members of the widows practicing the religious principles and doctrines on the issues of widows (Abu, 1998; Kirwen, 1979). The preceding discussion provides

a brief synopsis of the socio-economic realities of young widow participants of my study.

In central northern Nigeria, widows are subjected to traditional discriminatory practices that range from physical and mental abuses, to banishment from the late husband's extended families (Kore, 2005; Muller, 1986). The cruelest of the traditional practices experienced by most widows of the region, is the process of disinheriting widows and their children from their late husband's assets, thereby relegating them to the pangs of poverty and deprivation. The material deprivation expose the widows to severe mental and emotional health challenges such as periodic hallucinations, which are similar health symptoms experienced by other widows across developed countries (Parks, 1964). These unnecessary cultural demands are further compounded with the pressure of recycling the widows in arranged re-marriages to adult male relative of the late husband. Such socio-cultural arrangements reduce widows to 'commodities' and deprives them from inheriting any assets of their late spouses (Kore, 2005; Okoye, 1995). In another argument, proponents of widow inheritance believe that the traditional marriage inheritance will retain the 'wealth' (material and children, as the latter is considered a primary source of wealth in the region) within the deceased husband's family. In another dimension, considering the rural economies of the region as agrarian, with heavy reliance and dependence on the extended family labor, with women providing cheap and unpaid labor as wives and daughters, subletting widows to leave the extending family units is a loss of primary cheap labor on the family farm, which is guarded against by male heads of households (Abu, 1998; Adukwu-Bogun, 2004; Kore, 2005; Muller, 1986). Hence, women who become widows are desperately re-cycled through re-marriages within the extended family so as to continue the utilization of their unpaid labor on the family farms. With these informal economic variables, the lived experiences of rural widows of the region does not only shape and re-define the status of widows, but display their material poverty and deprivation as most of them live below the poverty line. Because they posses no income generating skills such as literacy and numeracy that will enable them emancipate themselves from such traditional forms of family dependency, they will continue to be servitude to informal economic bondage as farm and allied domestic laborers (Kore, 2006; Okoye, 1995; Potash, 1986).

On the other hand, the 'sense' or "justification" of the traditional practices of widows' arranged re-marriages within the late husband's extended family aim at family continuity through procreation, as the widow is expected and must continue the reproductive 'duties' to protect and increase the deceased husbands lineage by having more children with the 'brother' of her former husband, while the latter is expected to 'protect' the widow from becoming 'promiscuous' (Muller, 1986; Okoye, 1995). Further cultural 'reasoning' to this parochial arrangement is based on the belief that the widows' benefit more, as they are not only provided the company of 'responsible partners 'for social security, but provided unlimited 'material support' by the new spouse (Abu, 1998; Cattel, 1997; Ewelukwa, 2002). The widows' lack of voice or inability to grant their consent to such uncivil marriage arrangements demonstrates not only a violation of their fundamental human rights to private life, but an illustration of their social disempowerment, thereby facilitating their dependency on the extended family unit members. Such myopic new life style renders widows voiceless, and limit their chances of becoming free and independent or self reliant economically and socially. These cultural undertakings are one of the many facets of irregularities of orthodox patriarchal practices of the region, which holds the notion of 'male' gender to be 'responsible' in the 'nurturing' of the feminine gender. This notion may not be a bad role assumption, but the fact that the practice dwells on 'forces' that coerce, or mandate widows to absolute submission and compliance to such orthodox social arrangements without their consent, nor attempting to negotiate boundaries and degree of 'male nurturing' of the widows is what many

African womanists and feminists consider as the violation of the widows human rights (Adukwu-Bogun, 2004; Assembly of African Union, 2003; Division for the Advancement of Women, 1980; Ezer, 2007).

These traditional discriminatory practices violates widows' civil rights and liberty of social engagement stated in the Protocol of the African Charter on Human and Peoples Rights on the Rights of Women and Widows Rights in Article 20 that stated: "States/Parties shall take appropriate legal measures to ensure that widows enjoy all human rights through the implementation of the following provisions: a) that widows are not subjected to inhuman, humiliating or degrading treatment; b) a widow shall automatically become the guardian and custodian of her children, after the death of her husband, unless this is contrary to the interests and the welfare of the children; c) a widow shall have the right to remarry, and in that event, to marry the person of her choice" (Assembly of African Union in Maputo, 2003).

Other social forms of discrimination of widows include ex-communicating and isolating them from the public during the period of mourning, as well as and prohibiting members of the public to buy or sell to the widows (Adukwu-Bogun, 2004). The cumulative impact of these forms of maltreatment is not only an economic strangulation of the widows, but a psychological torture that inflicts and induce health challenges such as mental psychosis, hallucinations, high blood pressure, black outs, and hemorrhage in extreme cases (Parkes, 1964; Rees, 1971). In isolation practices of the widows of the region reinforces the traditional adage of the region that "women should be seen and not heard" in public places (Adukwu-Abogun, 2004, p. 26).

The acceptance of these discriminatory practices by the widows are attributed to their lack of being economically empowered, as well as having low literacy levels so as to prevent access to information and to use legal services (Division for the Advancement of Women, 1980). While there is no single source of international law of non–discrimination, agencies as the International Covenant on Civil and Political Rights, and the International Covenant on Economic, Social and Cultural Rights require countries to guarantee gender equality and prohibit discrimination. The traditional prevalence of widowhood rites and practices, coupled with the fact that women are the victims of these horrendous practices, exemplifies the unequal gendered power relations, especially in the developing countries of Sub-Sahara Africa (Cattel, 1997; Ezer, 2007; Kirwen, 1979).

Even though regional attempts are made to regulate all forms of discriminatory practices against African women through the African Charter on Human and Peoples Rights' Article 18(3) that states: "The state shall ensure the elimination of every discrimination against women, and also ensure the protection of the rights of the women and children as stipulated in the international declaration and conventions". The practical application of the African Union Charter on the welfare of the widows differs from nation to nation, considering the differences in culture and traditions of states. Such implementations create loopholes for the interpretation of customary laws, therefore not solving the discriminatory practices experienced by most widows in Africa, and specifically in rural central part of northern Nigeria. In addition, the lack of adequate systemic legal practices that serve as checks and balances in dealing with issues of discrimination against widows has led to the intervention of women Non Governmental Organizations (NGOs) to provide financial legal fees to support some widows to addresses the injustices in civil courts. However, these gestures are limited, as the NGOs are overwhelmed by the population of widows with many incidences that require redress. Other NGO's have provided widows with survival 'hand outs' such as cash, clothes and food, while some assist widows with micro loans that will help them start small businesses, with the aim of empowering them socially and economically (Esin, 2005). An all women Community Based Organization (CBO) in central northern Nigeria adopted a more rural

focus. They are the group that founded the first rural Widow Training School (WTS) to provide vocational skills training, and basic literacy for rural widows in that region (Gwamruwa, 1980). The preceding discussion provides a synoptic narrative of the historical foundation, nature, characteristics, curriculum implementation process, and learning outcome of the school for the widows.

HISTORICAL FOUNDATION, NATURE, AND CURRICULUM IMPLEMENTATION OF THE SCHOOL

The Widows' Training School (WTS) was founded by the Community Based Organization (CBO) called the Zumuntan Matan ECWA in 1979. The organization was made up of six pioneer rural women from the Evangelical Church of West Africa (ECWA). Subsequently, male executives of the church supported the effort of the association by providing land and substantial funds for the building of the Widow Training School (WTS) in Samaru Kataf. The school is a residential type, with dormitories partitioned into cubicles that accommodate a widow and her two young children that are under the age of ten. The essence of creating a home-friendly environment for the widows was not only necessary, but mandatory as many of them are often rendered semi-homeless by hostile in-laws, while those allowed to keep their 'homes' have decided to temporary leave while attending WTS in order to allow existing in-laws hostilities to subside (FGIs M-A-W #1004). The school compound has two large halls that accommodate equipment and student's participation in vocational subjects' practicum as: sewing, cooking, knitting, audio-visual technology. In addition, the school farm is within the school compound and accommodates agricultural oriented subjects in gardening vegetables, grains, and fruits, piggery, poultry and fishery farms. Situating the farms within proximity of the widows' hostels provides the feeling of 'home-village' environment. At the centre of the school's compound are two buildings that accommodate seven classrooms, and two rooms that serve as the principal's office and teachers' staffroom.

A female principal, who is also a widow, heads the school leadership. The management of the school is supported by a board of ten (10) male and female members, from various professions across the state, in addition to the traditional ruler of the environment. On the other hand, instructional duties and responsibilities are managed by ten (10) faculty members including eight women, six (natives) and two Canadian missionary teachers, and two are male teachers, who also multi-task as handy men. The female teachers serve as role models for the widows. Specific vocational subject teachers in subjects as Health Education and Maternal Childcare are often provided to the school from the state teaching hospital, while Home Economics Department of Kaduna State Development Project. Samaru-Kataf supplies Home Economics and Food and Nutrition teachers (Gwamruwa, 1980). The schools' collaboration with the government agencies is minimal, but effective, as the synergy demonstrate government's support in not only transforming the lives of the widows, but a way of contributing state's resources in alleviating poverty amongst rural women.

Objectives of the School. The school's primary objective is to train and graduate widows in vocational skills and "to help learners gain opportunities to earn basic or traditional income" (Indabawa & Mpofu, 2005, p. 85). These vocational skills are gender specific and include: sewing, baking, knitting, cooking, embroidery, subsistence agriculture, poultry etc (Gwamruwa, 1980). The school management believes that the acquisition of vocational skills will empower widows to become small-scale entrepreneurs for sustainable development of self, and the family (Stromquist, 1988). The preemption of this objective has been tested in other rural women adult education studies by Bhasin (1992). The women's "recognition of their contribution and knowledge, will help self-respect and dignity, enabling them to become more economically in-

dependent and self-reliant, reducing their burden of work, especially at home…." (Bhasin, 1992, p. 20). The secondary objective of the school is to provide the widows with basic literacy education as "the acquisition of the skills of reading, writing and numeration at basic levels, in a particular language, local or foreign" (Indabawa & Mpofu, 2006, p. 85). The level of basic literacy provided to the widows is at the primary school level, which not only provide them basic literacy and numeracy, but motivates them to aspire and pursue secondary school education in the future, especially the younger widows (Gwamruwa, 1980). The schools' goal concerning the widows' literacy attainment is to make them functional literates, and to enable them to assist their primary school children in them in their home work, especially those children residing with the widows in the school dormitories. The school also believes that through basic literacy, the widows can exercise their right to access and use state based information on legal services to solve their social problems that are family oriented.

The schools' curriculum is made of vocational disciplines as, Domestic Science, Home Economics, Agriculture; Tailoring, Bakery, Cookery, Textile processing, Florist Education; Food and Nutrition, Decoration (indoor and outdoor), Restaurant Management, Arts and Craft, and the 4Rs (Reading, Writing, Arithmetic and Religion). The primary school subjects include English language, Health Education (maternal and child care focus), Social Studies and Book Keeping. The medium of instructions in the first year is Hausa language, the lingua franca and mother tongue of the social environment, while the second year teaches both English and Hausa languages concurrently. Learning in the mother tongue is traditional to Africa's informal teaching and learning processes (Fafunwa, 1963), as "a person learns better in the mother tongue because of an undisputable accord between the spirit of language and the mentality of the people who speak it" (Diop, 2000; Fasokun, Katahoire, & Oduaran, 2005, p. 119).

In sum, the planning, foundation, nature and the development of the schools' curriculum policies and processes compliment the UN recommendation that schools must consider among other things, the background, interests, knowledge, attitudes, skills and the conditions of learners' lives, and those of their immediate and extended families (UNESCO, 2001). Establishing a welcoming and friendly school environment along traditional living style of the community is not only creating 'normalcy' for the widows, but provide them with safe social and private spaces that will restore 'peace' in their troubled emotional state and that of their children. Regardless of the input of the CBOs, the facts that state government support is marginal, and disappointing, as their actions are in conflict with the widows' pursuit of education and poverty alleviation in the implementation of UN Millennium Development Goals (MDGs) (Nwosu, 2010). The political negligence of widows' welfare is worrisome, and requires prompt attention by women themselves. This can be achieved through increasing female participation in politics, as their participation will, to some extent, provide rural and urban women a voice in the state. The proceeding discussion relates the major findings of the study on the learning motivation of the widows, effective teaching and learning process of the teachers, and the measurable facets of sustainable learning outcome experienced by the widows. Excerpts of the widow's interview data are cited to substantiate their claim of positive learning experiences.

DISCUSSION OF MAJOR FINDINGS

The qualitative analysis of the data identified major themes that are central to teaching, the learning process and the learning outcomes. This information provides a better understanding of the extent to which the schools' programs, objectives, and goals have been attained. The major themes on the learning motivation of the widows were identified as the effective teaching strategies of the curriculum,

its perception, and accommodation by the widows. The sustainable learning outcomes of the widows are explained by the data analysis. These findings are discussed with excerpts of the widows' comments from the FGIs (Focus Group Interviews). There were three major groups included in the FGIs and they are: Teenage Widows (T-W), Late Adolescent Widows (L-A-W), and Middle Aged Widows (M-A-W).

What are widows' learning motivations? Across Sub-Sahara Africa, formal and informal adult education has purpose, aims and objectives, which can be stated in form of questions as: why and how do adult learners learn? Various reasons arise as to why adult learners want to learn. Knowles (1975) indicates motivation to learn as a response to life events, while Fasokun (1984) (Fasokun, Katahoire, & Oduaran, 2005) explained that "adults in Africa are motivated to learn in order to maintain or establish social relationships, to serve others, to satisfy a personal interest, to advance their careers, to earn money or to meet external expectations" (p. 23). Within the region, informal adult education are vocation based, and associated to indigenous apprenticeship system, whose purpose or motivation is to enable learners to acquire functional and sustainable skills that will support their overall survival to old age (Fafunwa, 1963). These learning motivations are related to socio-economic needs and wants of the learners, with the teaching and learning process allowing the learners to apply the process and outcomes in their daily life, and as a feature of applied learning (Oduaran, 2000, p. 28).

One of the major responses of the widows was that their motivation to learn and master one or two vocational skills that will enable them sustain them economically so they can support themselves and their children. A teenage widow stated,

All of us have no trade, nor education to sustain us and our orphans. Most if not all of us married early according to tradition, and did not complete primary school. We do not know anything more than farming on the family farms, now that our husbands are no more; we are forced to fend for

ourselves. Even those of us who work on the family farms for our in-laws, we are not rewarded with the share of the farm products for consumption or sale. The only solution is to return to school, get some vocational skills that will assist us stand by our selves (FGIs T-W #1001).

There above comment is economic based. In view of their poverty level, the issue of daily survival is their primary preoccupation, which is not only rational reason motivating their learning, but also goal oriented. This facilitates their intrinsic and extrinsic learning motivation in and outside the classrooms. Another motivating learning factor of the widows included the social dynamics of learning. The fact that all of them share similar lived experiences; they draw inspirations from each other by encouraging and supporting each others' learning efforts through interpersonal counseling and communication to boost self esteem, and encourage each other to attain self actualization by completing their studies. A middle-aged widow added:

Even though we leave in our separate rooms in the dormitory, we often come together and pray, and talk personal concerns for a more collective solution. It allows us the opportunity to strengthen each other. In many cases, we use such moments to as each other support on our schoolwork, i.e., Arithmetic, English and Health Education that are challenging. Sometimes one of us may fall sick and unable to do their share of daily routine task on the school farm as the piggery, poultry etc, the remaining ones will multitask to cover the sick students' task of the day. The concerns for each other strengthen our motivation to continue learning and at the same time socialize and communicate as families" (FGIs/ M-A-W #1003).

Apparently, the peer support system of the widows is a primary learning motivation as reiterated above. One additional motivation of the widows learning is the acquisition of counseling (religious and formal) services that will heal their battered emotional psyche that are caused by spousal be-

reavement, maltreatment of in-laws, and worries about their children's survival and sustainability. Nonetheless, the school counseling-pastoral unit, whose members include the school principal, a clergy, a trained female counselor, and a serving member of the school board offer inspirations and counseling services to the widow, This added counseling ensures the women retain their learning focus, aspirations, and goals for learning. The school based counseling services are not only appreciated by the widows, but also more often looked forward to. In one of the comments of the adolescent widows, it was stated that:

More often, we experience some emotional setbacks that disturb our learning engagement. These occur when we either visit our families to see our other children, and find them in uncared and hungry situation; we become very upset and unfocused in our studies. The principal and the counseling group will calm us down and assist us with food and clothing to send it to the children, so we can re-direct our study attention and focus on why we are here (FGIs/L-A-W #1002).

The widows also identified the school environment as a motivating factor to their learning. Most of them find the school environment to be 'friendly' and 'safe'. They not only have personal social spaces, but also they can distant themselves from the social reminders of their loss away from bullying in-laws. Most of them are motivated by their teachers, whom they see as role models and significant others. Their teachers are pillars to lean on, especially when challenged by difficult learning tasks in the curriculum and in aspects of their social life. In sum, the learning motivations of the widows are both intrinsic and extrinsic. These factors are all focused on the learning outcomes, which many believe is the core learning motivation to their steady attendance and participation in all vocational and basic literacy curriculums. Generally, the motivational purpose of widows learning is to enable them solve real life problems. The question then is, to what extent do the curriculum delivery mechanism support their learning motivation? and what are the efficacies of the delivery system on the widows? The answers to these questions are discussed below.

Andragogy and the widows' learning style. The teaching strategy for adult learners is referred as andragogy, "the art and science of helping adults to learn" (Knowles 1980, p. 38). The application of andragogy considers the understanding of adult development of which "their perception of time changes from one of postponed application of knowledge to immediacy of application, and accordingly their orientation towards learning shifts from one of the subject-centeredness to one of problem-centeredness (Knowles, 1980, p. 38). Furthermore, Fasokun, Katahoire, and Oduaran (2005) state that andragogy facilitates self-directed learning, which requires adult learners to be treated with care so as to avoid their withdrawal from the learning programs. In discussing the application of andragogy on the widows' at WTS, this paper will use Knox's Proficiency Theory [KPT] (1980) and Jarvis's Learning Process Theory [JLPT] (1995) of adult learning to explain the learning motivation and style of the widows.

In helping adult widows with andragogy, the findings reflect on the observational data on curriculum implementation by the teachers. In basic literacy subjects such as Writing, WTS teachers use journal writing to encourage the widows to write on their personal experiences, or "what has happened to an individual unexpectedly" (Fasokun, Katahoire, & Oduaran, 2005, p. 60). Jarvis' Learning Process Theory (JLPT) of adult learning states that the beginning of learning for adult learners' starts with their personal experience, and that these experiences are recovered from memory and applied to prevailing challenges allowing people to learn differently because of the discrepancies in their life experiences (Jarvis, 1995). The theory reinforces the social context of learning (Jarvis, 1987) which not only allows students active participation as individualized learners, but encourages learners [as

the widows] to reflect on their written experiences, develop strategies on how to solve experiences they consider as problems, thereby, encouraging them to be active problem solvers. As noted by Fasokun, Katahoire, and Oduaran (2005), the African perspectives of adult learning is that "there is a belief that all experiences educate, whether such experiences are pleasant or unpleasant" (p. 57). The focus is that adult learners accumulate a growing reservoir of experiences that becomes an increasing resource for learning (Knowles, 1980, p. 38). Furthermore, the classroom observational data revealed how WTS teachers facilitate students into applying their previous informal educational experiences into learning vocational subjects such as agricultural education, especially the practical perspectives. Considering the fact that most of the women have been involved with such agricultural activities, they are building on already acquired skill levels. Their previous learning increases the performance of the widows in these subject areas. Reflecting further on the approach Knox's Proficiency Theory [KPT] (Knox, 1980) explains how teacher's focus on the learners' proficiency (learners past and present characteristics, knowledge, skills and traditional values), the aspirations of adult learners, and the role of facilitators are crucial in helping adult learners to learn. In applying this theoretical framework to the widow adult learners, who's 'values' and 'interests' reflect the general environment on agricultural education as gardening, subsistence agriculture, poultry and domestic animal husbandry are reinforced in the teachers' open teaching approach. Their teachers allow the widows to apply their traditional skills side-by-side to the modern methods in the practical aspects of the vocational subjects. Grenier (1998) stated that African adults tend to store indigenous knowledge in their memories and express this knowledge in agricultural practices and animal breeding.

Other facets of andragogy applied by teachers of WTS were connected to Knox's reference to general environment and value teaching approach for adult learners (Knox, 1980). With the case of the widows, the social environment that are connected to cultural values, were put into consideration by teachers as a means of helping them to learn 'taboo' oriented curricula contents in subjects as Healthcare education, reproduction, sex education, maternal-child health care, HIV/AIDs education amongst other issues. How then did the teachers assist the widows to learn these 'taboo' oriented curricula without both sides embarrassed, or attaining maximum active teaching-learning engagement and comprehension? Based on my series of classroom observations, teachers' often teach the content by supporting the message with personal stories, experiences, or visual real life movies to facilitate a better understanding of the content by the widows, and to minimize level of embarrassment; teachers of the same gender presented the material. The teachers' delivery strategy allow the widows to share with the teacher and classmates their personal experiences as well, thereby making the classroom discourse all inclusive, active, and participatory.

In taking cognizance of the learners cultural values of age, grade, socialization, and communication process, WTS female teachers teach curricula content that are cultural sensitive, otherwise considered as "taboo' by using group teaching techniques. The teachers divide the widows according to their age grade range, especially when using visuals as videos, or guest speaker presentations as health workers on curricula content on reproduction, sex education, Sexually Transmitted Diseases (STD), etc. The teachers' approaches are not only feminizing instruction, but the content of study so as to enable the widows to freely connect with the learning content as well as the teachers. The teaching-learning praxis enabled the widows to seek content based clarification without feeling embarrassed, as compared to when the curricula content are taught by male teachers of the WTS or invited community based guess speakers. It is considered a cultural taboo for women and men to engage in open sex oriented discussion whether in

the public places as the classroom or otherwise in the region. Additionally, merit goes to the teachers' cultural sensitivity in their androgogical approach that respects to some extent the gender socialization of the widows' culture.

As part of the delivery mechanism of WTS teachers, the data noted how teachers use more formative assessments that are individual problem based. For example problem solving projects, collaborative group work, observational data, exhibitions, hands on experiments, peer and self-assessments in the vocational subjects, while literacy based subjects involve drama, debate, cultural dances, oral presentations, journaling. This approach relates learners' task performance that coincides or relates to real life settings. The assessment format measures, and identify widow's academic progress, thereby creating more opportunities for them to succeed academically. To further engage widows' general environment as recommended by Knox' theory, WTS teachers' assessment approach use the community members as the target social environment by inviting them into the school compound during teacher-student exhibitions of learning products from vocational subjects as the agricultural products, knitted sweaters, bakery products amongst others. The aim of using exhibition is to showcase the widows learning portfolio for the public to appreciate their learning input, as well as purchase some of the products, which will bring income for the widows, as well as increase the widows learning motivation and self esteem. A middle age widow group member stated:

When we exhibit our learning products from the poultry, fishery, sweaters etc for members of the public, they are always surprised at our hands on learning efforts. Usually, the products are bought at the end of the exhibition, which provide some financial income for us. We get encouraged and work harder to produce good learning products, and always look forward for the next exhibition (FGIs/M-A-W, #1003).

The above excerpt illustrates widows' perception and acceptance of their teachers' use of andragogy to facilitate their learning engagement and success. In sum, the teacher's application of andragogy is consistent with the normative pattern of indigenous African adult education learning of the apprenticeship system, of which the teacher assume the role of a facilitator as well as model the curriculum while the, learners observe, and imitate the teachers through hands-on, in order to attain mastery of the curriculum. In addition, teachers approach of connecting the widows to their previous experience and memories through self written, biographies, stories, oral narratives and practices of indigenous agricultural skills are considered pathways to knowledge construction and retention in the formal and informal setting across Sub-Sahara Africa (Chilisa & Preece, 2005; Indabawa & Mpofu, 2006; Nafukho, Amutabi, & Otunga, 2005).

FACETS OF WIDOWS' SUSTAINABLE LEARNING OUTCOME

So far, my research findings did not only identify the schooling effects on the widows, but identified the extent to which the organizational purpose and objectives of the WTS have been achieved. Indeed, the findings affirmed that both organizational [school] and self-objectives (widows) and purpose of schooling at the WTS have to some extent been achieved. First, the impact of the widows' acquired basic literacy and numeracy was identified on their proficiencies in reading in the local language, and in English scripture based textbooks, and school based textbooks at the end of their second year in the school, and after graduating. Many of the widows are able to write their school journals on their daily life experiences, as well as write letters to relatives. As one middle age woman stated:

Most times when I am emotionally disturbed, I write my children letters of encouragement, I use

to quote scriptures I would want them to read, in doing so, I am not only communicating with my boys, but improving daily my writing skills, which assist me in my school work (FGIs/M-A-W #1003).

In addition, the practice of their acquired literacy effect is evident on the academic support they provide to their children, as many of them assist their lower primary school children with their school homework. The graduates of WTS use their acquired vocational skills to become small-scale entrepreneurs or small business owners such as food vendors, bakers, exotic fruit, vegetable farmers, or poultry, fishery, piggery farmers, etc. In the voice of one of the most successful widows in fishery farming, she stated:

I am more than thankful for graduating from the widows' school. My interest was fish farming, and as a student, I made sure my final practicum project was on that. I noticed my hand is good with that farming. On graduating, I started the project from my rented house backyard, which eventually required more space, as I had more fish production that I ever imagined. I am glad to say that I not only supply the community with fish, but travel to the big cities and supply fish to top class restaurants in hotels like Hilton, Nicon Noga and Ramada. I have 15 women and men working in my big fish farm I developed from a piece of land I bought. I always remember my humble beginning with the school. So from time to time, I send fish to the widows to feed their children, as well as donate cash to the school (FGIs/M-A-W/#1004.

In addition to the above success story, widows like those cited above, use their new status and income to invest in their children's education. They do this by enrolling them in private Christian schools around the community, or pay for private tutors for their children to be coached in subjects like English, Math, and Science. The acts is grounded on the widows' beliefs that through sound education, their children will be offered better job opportunities in the professions, as well as manage their businesses at a more sophisticated level or a modern based approach. They strongly feel that the children's' higher educational dividend will expand and promote the family businesses, as well as prevent the children from depending on the extended family members for support (Kore, 2005). Indeed, even those of them attending WTS often sell products of their vocational subjects (i.e., eggs, fish, chicken, cardigans) to members of the public so as to generate income and support their orphans. These measures are driven by their determination to be self-reliant and economically independent in order to improve the quality of their life and that of their children. The process empowers the widows economically so that they can afford such items as food that, thereby meets their physiological needs.

Furthermore, the study identified the impact of widows learning outcomes on learning continuities of five (5) former graduates of WTS. The widows furthered their education by graduating from Women Teacher's College, a high school that prepares females to teach in the lower elementary schools. These widows are currently serving as native language public primary school teachers within the local government. Their new positions as civil public workers enable them to earn a monthly income that will sustain their daily physiological needs such as food and clothing for themselves and their children. The success of this new group of "widow teachers" serve as motivation to learning focus and carrier aspirations to those widows attending WTS, as most of them expressed the desire to pursue high school education after graduating from Widow's Training School (WTS) programs.

The widows' economic self-reliance is one of the goals of establishing the WTS, which to the satisfaction of this study has been achieved by most of the widows who took part. Indeed, the level of sustainability has motivated the state government to award yearly stipend to the school, and this gesture is in compliance to the state, and indeed Nigeria's, commitment to the Millennium Development Goals on education for the eradication of poverty, targeted for 2015 by UN (UNESCO, 2003).

Additionally, the dividend of the widows' literacy and numeracy attainment was evidenced in their participatory civic engagement as voters at the village and state political activities. During the course of my fieldwork, a graduate of the WTS ran for the position of a local government councilor. The entire WTS teachers and students' population, and other widows within the constituency participated in campaigning and voting for the candidate. This involvement of the school contributed to the election success of the widow candidate. Thus, the school not only played an important role of sensitizing the political support of one of their own, (considering the fact that the candidate has shared lived experience with the other widows), but the widows trusted the candidacy of one of their own to represent their interests. They also trust her to represent their voice in grassroot political forum, especially in annulling traditional discriminatory laws against widows as a political policy and process. The political support provided to the widow political candidate was the first political breakthrough for the widows, according to the school principal. The principal added that, the political behavior of the widows since then has been sustained and promoted at every opportunity. The success to embrace change in political behavior by WTS widows served as the awakening process that is crucial with "oppressed individuals, who come to know that it is through social reconstruction they can participate in construction" (Barakett & Cleghorn, 2008, p. 89). The praxis of such political participation is described as conscientization or critical consciousness by Friere (1970). However, despite the success of the widows' political participation at that time, traditional leaders or local chiefs as custodians of customary laws were less enthused, as some of them believe the widows' political participation is anti-tradition. The local chiefs also view this as weakening the patriarchal structures of male political leadership that was handed by the ancestors. These retrogressive views of the traditional leaders are systemic excuses that are used to further oppress widows not only in Nigeria, but also for the most parts of ethnic Sub-Sahara Africa (Ewelukwa, 2002; Ezer, 2007; Okoye, 1995; Schildkrout, 1986).

Other facets of social empowerment derived by the widows learning outcomes include the ability to build new social relationships and networks amongst themselves and their children that were sustained even after graduating from the school. These relationships have bonded the widows and facilitate their socialization process. These bounds encourage, support and mentor each other on coping strategies of their situations. Such peer support systems have restored widows' self-esteem, provided them self-efficacy to face their changed life situation as single parents. Indeed, graduates of WTS often return to the school to mentor the younger widows, thereby bonding them in and outside the school that in essence results to life friendship and strong interpersonal communications.

In addition to social empowerment of the widows, the study noted their new ability in observing good modern child healthcare, and management of common ailments, general hygiene and sanitation practices. Health literacy subjects of the school curriculum demands that the widows put into practice what they learn. When on the school premises, resident students are required to maintain a high standard of hygiene, and general sanitation. Indeed, the widows' dormitories are kept clean at all times. The school farm products (i.e., fruits and vegetables, eggs etc.) augment the food and nutrition of the widows and their growing children. High nutrition have prevented their children from kwashiorkor disease, as well as prevented the degenerating immunity of the widows suffering from HIV/Aids. Seasonal immunization against children's five killer diseases (i.e., polio, whooping cough, cholera, meningitis, etc.) are administered to the women and their children by the school and local government hospital health workers The school ensures adequate supervision of the women's healthcare practices on hygiene of their bodies, especially the management of reproductive cycles

by providing them with free sanitary materials. Six women who participated in my study with HIV/AIDs are provided special routine checks on their health in the local hospitals and the school infirmary. In addition, the affected widows are provided with sanitary towels and disinfectants to arrest the acute liquid flow associated with the brutal later stage of the disease. These acquired health routines have been sustained by the infected widows, thereby improving their general health quality and that of their children, which in the past they were unable to attain, had they not been enrolled in WTS. In sum, the dividends of the widows learning outcomes have not only improved the quality of lives of the widows and their children, but provide the school management the commitment to sustain those changes experienced by the women.

CONCLUSION

Women's literacy and general education are often social policy phenomenoum that are prone to governmental debates across national and international borders, and continue to gain the attention of global body such as the United Nation (UNESCO, 2003). In developing countries of Sub-Sahara Africa, the focus on marginalized women groups such as the rural widows is not only an urgent need to protect their fundamental human rights to education, but a pathway to ameliorate their suffering from social and economic poverty. It is also to expose their plight on the traditional legal frameworks that deny them freedom to private life and the need for civil legal system that will arrest their plight. Indeed, the discussion articulated the historical foundations, curriculum implementation, and the impact of learning outcome for sustainable development of sample of widowed students who attend and graduated from the Widows Training School. The discussion synthesized the extent to which the school's objectives and the learning motivation of widows' have been achieved and sustained. These narratives ascertained that both have not only been achieved, but exceeded the expectations of the study participants. Nonetheless, the lack of state government's financial support of the WTS, and for the widows, especially in the area of capacity building of the vocational programs that are technology oriented (i.e., typewriting, photography etc.) is a setback to exposing the widows with more opportunities to skills profiting jobs that are currently a the move of the modern times.

As stated by Jean de la Fontein, education is the discovery of man's ignorance, indeed, the attainment of basic literacy of the widows and the involvement of prominent male members of the urban community (i.e., elites and business men serving as board members of WTS) has to some extent change the patriarchal cultural ignorance related to the status, identities, role expectations and functions of widows in the ethnic region. Such cooperation re-situate the psychology of adult learning, which enables adults as members of the community to have input on the nature and outcome of their learning, so as to facilitate self and community development (Fasokun, Katahoire, & Oduaran, 2005). The slogan "educate a girl/woman is to educate a family and a nation" is indeed measurable from excerpts of the study's from the Focus Group Interview (FGIs) of the widows, especially the applied aspects of their sustainable learning outcome in social and economic perspectives. It is the resolve of this discussion that state and federal governments of Nigeria and other nations across Sub-Sahara Africa still practicing traditional cultural norms that are disempowering rural widows. Establishing widow training schools that will provide them with vocational skills for economic self-reliance and empowerment is seen as a way to provide widows and their children with a better life. It is also a way to enable them to access basic functional literacy skills that will expose and enable them to access information on free legal services that will challenge the customary laws that inhibit them from freedom to an independent family life and systemic discrimination practices.

REFERENCES

Abu, T. (1998). *Parent in-law's attitude towards widows and widows' adjustment*. Unpublished Bachelor of Arts thesis, ECWA Theological Seminary, Jos, Africa.

Adukwu-Bogun, N. S. (2004). *The challenges of widowhood*. Suleija, Nigeria: By-Shop Ltd.

Assembly of African Union. (2003). *Protocol to the African charter on human and peoples' rights on the rights of women in Africa*. Retrieved from http://www.achpr.org/english/women/protocol-women.pdf

Babangida, M. (2005). *Celebrating two decades of Nigeria's better life programme: 1985 2005*. Retrieved from http://www.dawodu.com/mba-bangida1.htm

Berg, L. B. (2004). *Qualitative research methods for the social sciences*. Boston, MA: Allyn & Bacon.

Bhasin, K. (1992). Education for women's empowerment: Some reflections. *Adult Education and Development, 39*, 11–24.

Blueprint of Women's Education in Nigeria. (1986). *Proceedings of the national workshop on the production of a Blueprint on women's education in Nigeria*. Lagos, Nigeria: Federal Government Printers.

Bodgan, R. C., & Biklen, S. K. (2003). *Qualitative research for education: An introduction to theories and methods* (4th ed.). Boston, MA: Ally & Bacon.

Cattel, G. M. (1997). African widows, culture and social change: Case studies from Kenya. In Sokolovsky, J. (Ed.), *The cultural context of aging* (pp. 71–98). Westport, CT: Bergin & Garvey.

Chilisa, B., & Preece, J. (2005). *Research methods for adult educators in Africa*. Hamburg, Germany: UNESCO Institute for Education.

Creswell, W. J. (2005). *Educational research, planning, conducting, and evaluating qualitative and quantitative research* (2nd ed.). Upper Saddle River, NJ: Prentice Hall/Pearson.

Division for the Advancement of Women. (1980). *Convention on the elimination of all forms of discrimination against women (CEDAW)*. Retrieved from http://www.un.org/womenwatch/daw/cedaw/

Eisner, I. E. W., & Peshkin, A. (Eds.), *Qualitative inquiry in education* (pp. 121–152). New York, NY: Teachers College Press.

Esin, H. (2005). *Women urged to pick interest in vocational training*. Retrieved from http://allafrica.com/stories/200512140580.html

Ewelukwa, U. U. (2002). Post-colonialism, gender, customary injustice: Widows in African societies. *Human Rights Quarterly, 24*(2), 424–486. doi:10.1353/hrq.2002.0021

Ezer, T. (2007). Swaziland widows fighting for their rights. *HIV/AIDS. Policy Review, 12*(23), 72–73.

Fafunwa, B. (1963). African education and social dynamics. *West African Journal of Education, 7*(2), 66–70.

Fasokun, T., Katahoire, A., & Oduaran, A. (2005). *The psychology of adult learning in Africa*. Hamburg, Germany: UNESCO Institute for Education.

Federal Ministry of Education of Nigeria. (2000). *National policy on education*. Lagos, Nigeria: NERC Press.

Grenier, L. (1998). *Working with indigenous knowledge: A guide for researchers*. Ottawa, ON, Canada: Development Research Center.

Gwamruwa. (1980). *Mujailar makarantar* [History of widows training school]. Kaduna, Nigeria: Bada Group Nigeria.

Hurd, D. M. (1987). *The poverty of widows: Future prospects*. Retrieved from http://www.nber.org/papers/w2326

Indabawa, S., & Mpofu, S. (2006). *The social context of adult learning in Africa*. Hamburg, Germany: UNESCO Institute for Education.

Jarvis, P. (1987). *Adult learning in the social context*. London, UK: Crown Helm.

Jarvis, P. (1995). *Adult and continuing education: Theory and practice*. London, UK: Routledge.

Kirwen, C. M. (1979). *African widows*. New York, NY: Mary Knoll & Orbis Books.

Knowles, M. (1980). *The modern practice of adult education: From pedagogy to andragogy*. Chicago, IL: Chicago Association Press.

Knox, B. A. (1977). *Adult development and learning*. San Francisco, CA: Jossey Bass.

Kore, D. (2005). *Mai kare gwamraye da marayu* [Protector of widows/widowers and orphans]. Jos, Nigeria: The African Christian Textbooks.

Marshall, C., & Rossman, G. B. (1999). *Designing qualitative research* (3rd ed.). Thousand Oaks, CA: Sage.

McEwan, K. E., & McEwan, J. P. (2003). *Making sense of research. What is good, what is not, and how to tell the difference*. Thousand Oaks, CA: Sage.

Muller, J. (1986). Where to live? Widow's choices among the Rukuba. In Potash, B. (Ed.), *Widows in African societies: Choices and constrains* (pp. 175–192). Stanford, CA: Stanford University Press.

Nafukho, F., Amutabi, N. M., & Otunga, R. (2005). *Foundations of adult education in Africa*. Hamburg, Germany: UNESCO Institute for Education.

Nudel, R. A. (1986). *Starting over: Help for young widows and widowers*. New York, NY: Dadd, Mead & Co.

Nwosu, N. (2010). *Millennium development goals (MDGs): Our journey so far*. Retrieved from http://www.nigeriamasterweb.com/paperfrmes.html

Okoye, U. P. (1995). *Widowhood: A natural cultural tragedy*. Enugu, Nigeria: Nucik Publishers.

Omolewa, M. A. (1981). *Adult education practice in Nigeria*. Ibadan, Nigeria: Evans Brothers.

Omolewa, M. A. (1997). Literacy, income generation, and poverty alleviation. *CARESON Journal of Research and Development*, *1*(1), 1–17.

Parkes, M. C. (1964). Effects of bereavement on physical mental health: A study of medical records of widows. *British Medical Journal*, *2*(5404), 274–279. doi:10.1136/bmj.2.5404.274

Patton, M. Q. (2002). *Qualitative research and evaluation methods* (3rd ed.). Thousand Oaks, CA: Sage.

Rees, D. W. (1971). The hallucination of widowhood. *British Medical Journal*, *4*(5778), 37–41. doi:10.1136/bmj.4.5778.37

Robinson, H. J. (1995). Grief response, coping processes, and social support of widows: Research with Roys' Model. *Nursing Science Quarterly*, *8*(4), 158–164. doi:10.1177/089431849500800406

Schildkrout, E. (1986). Widows in Hausa society: Ritual phase or social status. In Potash, B. (Ed.), *Widows in African societies: Choices and constrains* (pp. 131–152). Stanford, CA: Stanford University Press.

Slavin, E. R. (2007). *Educational research: In an age of accountability*. Boston, MA: Pearson.

Street, B. (2007). *Literacy and development: Ethnographic perspectives*. London, UK: Routledge.

Stromquist, P. N. (1988). Women's education in development: From welfare to empowerment. *Convergence*, *21*(4), 5–16.

UNESCO. (2001). *Handbook: Non-formal adult education facilitators*. Bangkok, Thailand: UNESCO Asian-Pacific Programme of Education for All.

UNESCO. (2003). *World education forum: Final report*. Paris, France: UNESCO.

Wolcott, F. H. (1990). On seeking-and-rejecting –validity in qualitative research. In Eisner, E. W., & Peshkin, A. (Eds.), *Qualitative inquiry in education* (pp. 121–152). New York, NY: Teachers College Press.

This work was previously published in the International Journal of Adult Vocational Education and Technology, Volume 2, Issue 2, edited by Victor C.X. Wang, pp. 25-41, copyright 2011 by IGI Publishing (an imprint of IGI Global).

Chapter 18
Transformative Learning

Victor C. X. Wang
Florida Atlantic University, USA

Patricia Cranton
University of New Brunswick, Canada

ABSTRACT

The theory of transformative learning has been explored by different theorists and scholars. However, few scholars have made an attempt to make a comparison between transformative learning and Confucianism or between transformative learning and andragogy. The authors of this article address these comparisons to develop new and different insights to guide Web-based teaching and learning. Indeed, as Web-based teaching and learning has become popular in the 21ˢᵗ century, the theory of transformative learning should help Web-based teaching and learning. The authors of this article demonstrate different ways whereby the theory of transformative learning can be used to stimulate critical self-reflection and potentially transformative learning.

INTRODUCTION

Mention of transformative learning immediately reminds scholars and learners of its chief proponent, Jack Mezirow who is Emeritus Professor of Adult and Continuing Education, Teachers College, Columbia University, Former Chairman, Department of Higher and Adult Education, and Director for Adult Education. It was Mezirow who popularized the theory of transformative learning in the early 1980s. Mezirow's theory is such that individuals' meaning perspectives are transformed through a process of construing and appropriating new or revised interpretations of the meaning of an experience as a guide to awareness, feeling and action (Jarvis, 2002, p. 188). Later, several scholars expanded the theory of transformative learning. Cranton (2006) and King (2005) both focused on understanding how transformative learning can be fostered in practice. Other scholars worked to develop the theory in different directions in response to critiques of Mezirow's earlier work.

DOI: 10.4018/978-1-4666-2062-9.ch018

In this paper, we first provide an overview of Mezirow's theory, followed by a discussion of some of the theoretical perspectives that have arisen since Mezirow (1991) published is foundational text in the area. We then set transformative learning into the context of adult learning in general and, more specifically, demonstrate its relation to andragogy. We explore the connection between transformative learning and Confucianism, and then examine the kinds of reflection that are central in transformative learning theory. Finally, we reflect on implications for transformative learning in web-based teaching and learning.

MEZIROW'S THEORY OF TRANSFORMATIVE LEARNING

Jack Mezirow's (1991, 2000) perspective reflects a rational approach to transformative learning emphasizing a critical and objective analysis of an interpretation of experience. The discussion in this section draws on Cranton and Taylor (in press). Transformative learning is seen as a process whereby previously uncritically assimilated habits of mind are called into question and revised so as to be more open, permeable, and better justified (Mezirow, 2000). Based to some extent on Habermas' communicative theory, the theory assumes that there is need among all humans to understand and make meaning of their experiences. The theory is constructivist in nature, so the assumption is made that there are no fixed truths and change is continuous. People cannot always be confident of what they know or believe, so they look for ways to better understand their world and themselves. As Mezirow (2000) puts it, adults have a need to understand "how to negotiate and act upon our own purposes, values, feelings and meanings rather than those we have uncritically assimilated from others—to gain greater control over all lives as socially responsible clear thinking decision makers" (p. 8). Over time, this leads to better justified beliefs about the self and the world external to the self.

In transformative learning theory, a person's frame of reference includes the assumptions and expectations that underlie his or her thinking, beliefs, and actions. A frame of reference is composed of two dimensions, habits of mind and a point of view. Habits of mind are habitual means of thinking, feeling, and acting influenced by underlying cultural, political, social, educational, and economic assumptions about the world. The habits of mind get expressed in a particular point of view. They often develop uncritically in childhood through socialization and acculturation with family, teachers, and through other significant relationships. Over time, in conjunction with numerous congruent experiences, a frame of reference becomes reified, providing a rationalization for an often irrational world. It offers criteria for evaluating the world adults interact with, based on a set of cultural and psychological assumptions. These assumptions give meaning to experience, but they are subjective, and they can distort thoughts and perceptions, skewing reality.

Frames of reference act as a lens or filter when a person encounters a new experience. That is, if a person has a particular view about the role of women in society or what marriage should mean, then that person will view women or marriage through the lens of his or her beliefs and values. When an individual comes upon a new experience that is discrepant with those beliefs and values, he or she can either disregard the new experience or begin to critically question frame of reference he or she held previously. This process can be gradual and cumulative, or it may be dramatic and epochal. The event that stimulates the critical questioning has been called a "disorienting dilemma" (Mezirow, 1991), though that term is used less often in the current literature.

In his original study of women returning to higher education, Mezirow (1978) identified a series of phases in the process the women went through. These are: a disorienting dilemma (returning to school), a self-examination with feelings of guilt or shame, critical reflections of assumptions, the dialoguing in concert with others, exploration and experimentation with new roles and ideas, developing a course of action, acquiring new skills and knowledge, trying on new roles, developing competence, and overtime developing a more inclusive and critical worldview. These phases have been confirmed in the research, but not all phases have been found in every study, and the order shifts in some circumstances.

Mezirow's theory has been criticized for being too rational, too much focused on the individual, and for neglecting emotional, imagination, and social change. These critiques have led scholars to propose a variety of extensions to the theory and, in some cases, alternative perspectives. These perspectives are summarized in the next section.

THEORETICAL PERSPECTIVES

Since Mezirow's early work, and especially in the last ten years, many other theorists have entered the scene, introducing a variety of alternative interpretations of transformative learning. Transformative learning theory is, as Mezirow (2000) suggests, a "theory in progress." Some theorists, including Mezirow, focus on the individual, and others are interested in the social context of transformative learning, social change as a goal, or the transformation undergone by groups and organizations. Although this appears to be a great divide in theoretical positions, there is no reason that both the individual and the social perspectives cannot peacefully coexist.

Within the focus on individual transformation, there is Mezirow's cognitive and rational approach. In contrast to this is the extrarational approach, or as labeled by others (Taylor, 2005), the depth psychology approach. Extrarational perspectives substitute imagination, intuition, and emotion for critical reflection (Dirkx, 2001). Depth psychology theorists (Boyd & Myers, 1988; Dirkx, 2001) define transformation in relation to the Jungian concept of individuation, in which individuals bring the unconscious to consciousness as they differentiate

Self from Other and simultaneously integrate Self with the collective.

Also within the individual focus is a developmental perspective. As is the case in developmental psychology in general, transformative learning in this framework describes shifts in the way we make meaning—moving from a simplistic reliance on authority through to more complex ways of knowing or higher orders or consciousness (Kegan, 2000). Belenky and Stanton (2000) fall within this perspective in that they report on a similar change in epistemology, but they emphasize connected knowing (through collaboration and acceptance of others' views) rather than autonomous, independent knowing.

According to Wang (2004, 2007), Mezirow's theory of transformative learning has been widely criticized for focusing too narrowly on individual transformation. Social change has long been a goal of adult and higher education. Some transformative learning theorists see ideology critique as central to transformation. Brookfield (2000) goes so far as to say that critical reflection without social action is "self-indulgent" and "makes no real difference to anything" (p. 143). Taylor (2005) and Fisher-Yoshida, Geller, and Schapiro (2009) call this the social-emancipatory approach to transformation and connect it with Freire's (1970) work.

In spite of the critiques of Mezirow's work and the proliferation of alternative perspectives, the theory of transformative learning (Mezirow, 1978, 1990, 1991, 1997, 2000) has been widely applied to various groups of adult learners simply because this theory is capable of explaining how adult learners make sense or meaning of their experiences, hence perspective transformation, which is the heart and soul of this very popular theory in the field. Not only is this transformative learning popular in North America, it is also welcomed in Europe as it has been interpreted as the theory of reflectivity.

Over the years, multiple journal articles, international conferences have examined, critiqued transformative learning in an effort to further apply it in practice. However, little has been written regarding how scholars have turned to theory of transformative learning. Were there similar theories prior to its existence in the field of adult learning?

THE GENERAL CONTEXT OF ADULT LEARNING

Over the decades since Lindeman's (1926) *The Meaning of Adult Education* was published, adult learning theory has evolved into a complex, multifaceted set of theoretical perspectives. Adult learning has been described consistently as a process that is different from children's learning since Malcolm Knowles (1975, 1980) made that distinction. In the 1970s and 1980s, adult learning was described as voluntary (individuals choose to become involved), self-directed, experiential, and collaborative. Adults "going back to school" were thought to be anxious and lacking in self-esteem based on their earlier childhood experiences in education. Brundage and MacKeracher (1980) provide a good example of the early efforts to define principles of adult learning. During that time, adult learning was seen to be a cognitive process that led to the acquisition of skills and knowledge. Early writings on transformative learning reflected this general trend (Mezirow, 1981). Instructional design and program planning models focused on setting objectives, finding appropriate learning strategies, and objective assessment of the learning. Knowles (1980) advocated that the learner be involved in making instructional design decisions, but aside from that, the process did not deviate much from instructional design in any other setting.

Things began to change after the publication of Brookfield's (1986) *Understanding and Facilitating Adult Learning*. He critiqued the automaton approach to meeting learner needs and discussed the political dimensions of self-directed learning (Brookfield, 1993). Attention began to be paid to the social context of adult learning and to learning that goes beyond cognitive processes. As Merriam (2008) points out, adult learning theory began to draw on situated cognition theory, feminist theory, critical social theory, and postmodern theory. Adult learning is now described in relation to embodied learning, the emotions, spirituality, relational learning, arts-based learning, and storytelling. Non-western perspectives, which reject Western dichotomies such as mind-body and emotion-reason, are contributing to an interest in holistic approaches to understanding adult learning (Merriam & Sek Kim, 2008).

The evolution of transformative learning theory has paralleled and been strongly influenced by the development of adult learning theory in general. As Gunnlaugson (2008) suggests, we are now in the "second wave" of theory development in the field of transformative learning; that is, we are moving toward the integration of the various factions of the theory and into a more holistic perspective.

ANDRAGOGY

Prior to the emergence of transformative learning theory, andragogy was the central model that addressed how adults learn and how their instructors can better help them learn. Andragogy was first coined by a German grammar school teacher by the name of Alexander Kapp in 1833 and was later popularized by the father of adult education, Malcolm Knowles (1970, 1973, 1975) in the United States. Although a popular model in the field, it is not without criticisms. One of the criticisms is that it fails to take into consideration social settings that adult learners are engaged in their learning (Wang & Bott, 2003-2004). Because of these criticisms, some scholars have turned to other theories. Mezirow took the initiative and launched the study of transformative learning in the late 1970s. Thereafter, a provocative theory of transformative learning was advanced.

CONFUCIAN HUMANISM

Mezirow based his theory on his interpretation of Habermasian critical theory and Marxist socialism (as cited in Wang, 2004-2005, p. 17). As scholars further probe the theory of transformative learning, it was discovered that transformative learning was contained in Confucian seminal humanism advanced twenty-five centuries ago (Wang & King, 2006, 2007). It was in the *The Great Learning* (Zhu, 1992) that Confucius addressed self-transformation in order for humans to realize not only the moral goodness and the cosmic creativity that embraces the universe in its entirety (Tu, 1979). Although such is the case, Mezirow never mentioned Confucius in his publications. It was Wang and King (2006, 2007) who made a bold comparison between Confucius and Mezirow. Thereafter, a connection between Mezirow's theory of transformative learning and Confucianism was discovered. Both Confucianism and Mezirow's theory of transformative learning strive to help learners achieve growth and development (Merriam, 2004). Growth and development of learners are explained differently by Confucius and Mezirow. To Confucius, this may mean authentic persons or sages and one's sagehood may be realized via self-criticism or the rectification of the mind. To Confucius, learning could not occur without silent reflection (as cited in Wang & King, 2006, 2007). Without making any reference to Confucianism, Mezirow suggested that critical reflection is key in the theory of transformative learning. Mezirow was interested in fundamental change in perspective (or perspective transformation) that transforms the way that an adult understands and interacts with his or her world. Therefore, critical reflection or reflective thinking is the foundational activity that supports and cultivates such "perspective transformations" (as cited in Wang & King, 2006, 2007).

While both Confucius and Mezirow interpreted transformative learning from different angles, the goal is the same, that is, to help learners achieve growth and development in Merriam's terms. As Wang and King (2006, 2007) noted, "although

Confucius was the first educator and/or philosopher to define reflection twenty-five centuries ago, Mezirow should be credited with categorizing three types of reflection and seven levels of reflectivity" (p. 261). Without Mezirow's groundbreaking efforts, both adult educators and learners would find it hard to apply the theory of transformative learning to life. The next section will help readers better understand the theory of transformative learning.

THREE TYPES AND SEVEN LEVELS OF REFLECTION IN TRANSFORMATIVE LEARNING

Through extensive research, Mezirow identified three types of reflection: content reflection (i.e., an examination of the content or description of a problem); process reflection (i.e., checking on the problem-solving strategies); premise reflection (i.e., questioning the problem). In other words, content reflection relates to "what." Process reflection relates to "How." Premise reflection relates to "Why." Indeed, critical reflection cannot occur without learners asking questions using such words as "what," "how," and "why." According to Mezirow, the three types of reflection help learners think reflectively upon their external situations. How about one's inner experience as addressed by Confucius twenty-five centuries ago? Mezirow put forward seven levels of reflectivity that focus and explain learners' inner experience. As noted by Jarvis (1987, p. 91), the seven levels of reflectivity include:

1. **Reflectivity**: an awareness of a specific perception, meaning, behavior, or habit;
2. **Affective reflectivity**: awareness of how the individual feels about what is being perceived, thought, or acted upon;
3. **Discriminant reflectivity**: the assessment of the efficacy of perception, thought, action or habit;

4. **Judgmental reflectivity**: making and becoming aware of value judgments about perception, thought, action or habit;
5. **Conceptual reflectivity**: self-reflection which might lead to questioning of whether good, bad or adequate concepts were employed for understanding or judgment;
6. **Psychic reflectivity**: recognition of the habit of making percipient judgments on the basis of limited information;
7. **Theoretical reflectivity**: awareness that the habit for percipient judgment or for conceptual inadequacy lies in a set of taken-for-granted cultural or psychological assumptions which explain personal experience less satisfactorily than another perspective with more functional criteria for seeing, thinking or acting.

A closer examination of Mezirow's seven levels of reflectivity implies reflection involves only affective and cognitive aspects. On the other hand, Confucius's silent reflection involves the whole person. It seems that Confucius's silent reflection is even closer to the three commonly accepted objectives of learning: learning results in change in cognitive domain, affective domain and psychomotor domain. Yet, Mezirow's perspective transformation is even more important in the field of adult learning simply because perspective transformation may lead to further change in one's cognitive domain, affective domain and psychomotor domain. This is probably why people say, "change your thought and you change your world." It is obvious such a saying is closely related to Mezirow's perspective transformation. Perspective transformation is a prerequisite for change in other domains as a result of learning on the part of the learners.

IMPLICATIONS FOR WEB-BASED TEACHING AND LEARNING

There are no particular teaching methods that guarantee transformative learning in either face-to-face or web-based teaching and learning. A provocative statement, a story told by a fellow student, or an argument made in an article can all stimulate critical self-reflection and potentially transformative learning. Often neither we as teachers nor the transforming student can pinpoint just what it was that initiated or sustained the process.

It is and environment of challenge which underlies fostering transformation, not a specific method. Given that, we can look for ways to create an environment of challenge. Not challenge alone--it must be combined with safety, support, and a sense of learner empowerment.

In order to bring about a catalyst for transformation, we need to expose students to viewpoints that may be discrepant with their own. Films, documentaries, novels, short stories, poems, music, and art often portray unusual perspectives in dramatic and interesting ways. With recent advances in technologies for web-based teaching and learning, it is easy to incorporate such materials into a course.

Whenever possible, we should use readings to present ideas from more than one point of view. We need to encourage students to seek out controversial or unusual ways of understanding a topic. During an online discussion, students can be asked to search for material that presents an opposing point of view and bring that into the discussion.

Critical questioning can be helpful in encouraging learners to articulate their assumptions. The facilitator of an online course needs to be involved and present for this to happen (students seem unlikely to ask critical questions of each other for fear of offending their peers). Questions are crafted so as to encourage people to describe what they believe and how they came to believe it. For example, the educator might ask, "Do you believe intelligence declines with age?" followed by "How would you describe intelligence?" and "Is your view based on your own experience or the experience of someone you know?" or "What have you read or heard that supports that view?"

To encourage critical self-reflection, we need to provide the opportunity for students to question their assumptions--to examine what they think and how they feel, to consider the consequences of holding certain assumptions. In many ways, the web-based environment is ideal for encouraging critical reflection. There is always "time to think" in response to others' comments, and it is easy to look for evidence in support of or in opposition to a particular point of view.

Reflective journals are widely used in adult education and, for some but not all students, are a good vehicle for critical self-reflection. Learners may choose to keep a reflective journal as a course project, where they reflect on the nature and content of the online discussions. Students who are not familiar with keeping journals may need some guidance, such as not only report on what happened, but also include their thoughts, reactions, and feelings and pay special attention to writing about why they think or feel as they do. Dialogue journals where students write to each other or blogs are another way to extend the sharing of perspectives.

Modeling critical self-reflection as the educator may be one of the most important things we can do. We should make a point of openly questioning our own perspectives and support students' efforts to do the same. Although it may seem uncomfortable at first, especially if we are used to being the voice of authority in the classroom, a questioning atmosphere can quickly become quite natural. What we have to try to do in our teaching is to create safe and enjoyable ways for people to try on different points of view--ways of acting out or talking about alternatives. One simple strategy is to ask students to write letters or memos from a different perspective. Managers could write from the perspective of a staff member; nurses from the perspective of a patient, and so on. Learners can share these letters online to create further diversity in the points of view available for discussion.

Teaching for transformation is setting the stage and providing the opportunity. When it comes down to students actually revising their assumptions or larger frames of reference, there is little we can do aside from giving support. The process may be painful for some, and we need to acknowledge this, or it may be joyous for others, and we can celebrate with the student. The important thing here is to be available, to "be there" for the student by e-mail or even telephone. Whenever possible, we should make the time for one-on-one interaction with a student who is changing her beliefs. We can also encourage students to connect with each other through a class listserv or social networking.

CONCLUSION

The theory of transformative learning is such an important development in the field of adult learning. One may ask, "is it better than andragogy?" No single theory is the best theory in the field of adult learning. As one theory fails to guide one's action in the field, an alternative theory should be sought. Upon this basis of thinking, the theory of transformative learning does bring synergy to the field of adult learning.

To better understand andragogy, one has to make the distinction between the education of adults (andragogy) and the education of children. Teachers are charged with the responsibility of teaching students "critical thinking skills." Critical thinking would not be possible without critical reflection. These two are so intertwined that one cannot occur without the other. Therefore, it is safe to claim, "like andragogy, the theory of transformative learning is such a useful and powerful theory that it helps learners achieve growth and development." More importantly, the theory of transformative learning leads to the possibility of creating new knowledge and skills via critical reflection. Therefore, the value of such a theory is self-explanatory.

REFERENCES

Belenky, M., & Stanton, A. (2000). Inequality, development, and connected knowing. In Mezirow, , J. (Eds.) et al., *Learning as transformation: Critical perspectives on a theory in progress* (pp. 71–102). San Francisco, CA: Jossey-Bass.

Boyd, R. D., & Myers, J. B. (1988). Transformative education. *International Journal of Lifelong Education, 7*, 261–284. doi:10.1080/0260137880070403

Brookfield, S. D. (1986). *Understanding and facilitating adult learning*. San Francisco, CA: Jossey-Bass.

Brookfield, S. D. (1993). Self-directed learning, political clarity, and the critical practice of adult education. *Adult Education Quarterly, 43*(4), 227–242. doi:10.1177/0741713693043004002

Brookfield, S. D. (2000). Transformative learning as ideology critique. In Mezirow, J., et al. (Eds.), *Learning as transformation: Critical perspectives on a theory in progress* (pp. 125–148). San Francisco, CA: Jossey-Bass.

Brundage, D., & MacKeracher, D. (1980). Adult learning principles and their application to program planning. Toronto, ON, Canada: Ontario Institute for Studies in Education.

Cranton, P. (2006). *Understanding and promoting transformative learning* (2nd ed.). San Francisco, CA: Jossey-Bass.

Cranton, P., & Taylor, E. W. (in press). Transformative learning. In Jarvis, P. (Ed.), *International encyclopedia of learning*. London, UK: Routledge.

Dirkx, J. (2001). Images, transformative learning and the work of soul. *Adult Learning, 12*(3), 15–16.

Fisher-Yoshida, B., Geller, K. D., & Schapiro, S. A. (2009). *Innovations in transformative learning: Space, culture, and the arts*. New York, NY: Peter Lang.

Freire, P. (1970). *Pedagogy of the oppressed*. New York, NY: Herder and Herder.

Gunnlaugson, O. (2008). Metatheoretical prospects for the field of transformative learning. *Journal of Transformative Education, 6*(2), 124–135. doi:10.1177/1541344608323387

Jarvis, P. (1987). *Adult learning in the social context*. New York, NY: Croom Helm.

Jarvis, P. (2002). *International dictionary of adult and continuing education*. London, UK: Kogan Page.

Kegan, R. (2000). What 'form' transforms? A constructivist-developmental approach to transformative learning. In Mezirow, J., (Eds.) et al., *Learning as transformation: Critical perspectives on a theory in progress* (pp. 35–70). San Francisco, CA: Jossey-Bass.

King, K. P. (2005). *Bringing transformative learning to life*. Malabar, FL: Krieger.

Knowles, M. S. (1970). *The modern practice of adult education: Andragogy versus pedagogy*. New York, NY: Association Press.

Knowles, M. S. (1975). *Self-directed learning: A guide for learners and teachers*. New York, NY: Association Press.

Knowles, M. S. (1980). *The modern practice of adult education: From pedagogy to andragogy*. New York, NY: Cambridge.

Knowles, M. S., & Hulda, F. (1973). *Introduction to group dynamics*. Chicago, IL: Follett.

Lindemann, E. (1926). *The meaning of adult education*. New York, NY: New Republic.

Merriam, S. B. (2004). The role of cognitive development in Mezirow's transformational learning theory. *Adult Education Quarterly, 55*(1), 60–68. doi:10.1177/0741713604268891

Merriam, S. B. (2008). Adult learning theory for the twenty-first century. In Merriam, S. B. (Ed.), *Third update on adult learning theory* (pp. 93–98). San Francisco, CA: Jossey-Bass.

Merriam, S. B., & Sek Kim, Y. (2008). Non-Western perspectives on learning and knowing. In Merriam, S. B. (Ed.), *Third update on adult learning theory* (pp. 71–81). San Francisco, CA: Jossey-Bass.

Mezirow, J. (1978). Education for perspective transformation: Women's re-entry programs in community colleges. New York, NY: Teacher's College, Columbia University.

Mezirow, J. (1981). A critical theory of adult learning and education. Adult Education, 32, 3–24. doi:10.1177/074171368103200101d oi:10.1177/074171368103200101

Mezirow, J. (1990). Fostering critical reflection in adulthood: A guide to transformative and emancipatory learning. San Francisco, CA: Jossey-Bass.

Mezirow, J. (1991). Transformative dimensions of adult learning. San Francisco, CA: Jossey-Bass.

Mezirow, J. (1997). Transformative learning: Theory to practice. In P. Cranton (Ed.), *Transformative learning in action. New Directions in Adult and Continuing Education* (no. 74, pp. 5-12). San Francisco, CA: Jossey-Bass.

Mezirow, J. (Ed.). (2000). Learning as transformation: Critical perspectives on a theory in progress. San Francisco, CA: Jossey-Bass.

Mezirow, J. (2000). Transformative learning. In Mezirow, J., (Eds.) et al., *Learning as transformation* (pp. 1–33). San Francisco, CA: Jossey-Bass.

Tu, W. M. (1979). *Humanity and self-cultivation: essays in Confucian thought*. Berkeley, CA: Asian Humanities Press.

Wang, V. (2004-2005). Adult education reality: three generations, different transformation The impact of social context: three generations of Chinese adult learners. *Perspectives: The New York Journal of Adult Learning, 3*(1), 17–32.

Wang, V., & Bott, P. A. (2003-2004). Modes of teaching of Chinese adult educators. *Perspectives: The New York Journal of Adult Learning, 2*(2), 32–51.

Wang, V., & King, K. P. (2006). Understanding Mezirow's theory of reflectivity from Confucian perspectives: A model and perspective. *Radical Pedagogy, 8*(1), 1–17.

Wang, V. C. X. (2004). Philosophy, role of adult educators, and learning How contextually adapted philosophies and the situational role of adult educators affect learners' transformation and emancipation. *Journal of Transformative Education, 2*(3), 204–214. doi:10.1177/1541344604265105

Wang, V. C. X., & King, K. P. (2007). Confucius and Mezirow—Understanding Mezirow's theory of reflectivity from Confucian perspectives: A model and perspective. In King, K. P., & Wang, V. C. X. (Eds.), *Comparative adult education around the globe* (pp. 253–275). Hangzhou, China: Zhejiang University Press.

Zhu, W. Z. (1992). Confucius and traditional Chinese education: An assessment. In Hayhoe, R. (Ed.), *Education and modernization: The Chinese experience* (pp. 3–22). New York, NY: Pergamon Press.

This work was previously published in the International Journal of Adult Vocational Education and Technology, Volume 2, Issue 4, edited by Victor C.X. Wang, pp. 58-66, copyright 2011 by IGI Publishing (an imprint of IGI Global).

Compilation of References

Mezirow, J. (Ed.). (2000). *Learning as transformation: Critical perspectives on a theory in progress.* San Francisco, CA: Jossey-Bass.

Abu, T. (1998). *Parent in-law's attitude towards widows and widows' adjustment.* Unpublished Bachelor of Arts thesis, ECWA Theological Seminary, Jos, Africa.

Adukwu-Bogun, N. S. (2004). *The challenges of widowhood.* Suleija, Nigeria: By-Shop Ltd.

Alexander, B. (2006). Web 2.0: a new wave of innovation for teaching and learning? *EDUCAUSE Review, 41*(2), 33–44.

Ally, M. (2008). Foundations of educational theory for online learning. In Anderson, T. (Ed.), *The theory and practice of online learning* (pp. 15–44). Edmonton, UK: AU Press.

Altschuld, J. W. (1993). *Delphi technique: Lecture, evaluation methods: Principles of needs assessment II.* Columbus, OH: Ohio State University.

Anderson, T. (2004). Toward a theory of online learning. In T. Anderson & F. Elloumi (Eds.), *Theory and Practice of Online Learning* (pp. 33-60). Athabasca, AB, Canada: Athabasca University. Retrieved from http://cde.athabascau.ca/online_book/index.html

Anderson, T. (2007, June 25-29). Social Learning 2.0. In *Proceedings of ED-MEDIA 2007: World Conference on Educational Multimedia, Hypermedia & Telecommunications,* Vancouver, BC, Canada. Retrieved from http://www.slideshare.net/terrya/educational-social-software-edmedia-2007/

Anderson, K. M., & Avery, M. D. (2008). Faculty teaching time: A comparison of web-based and face-to-face graduate nursing courses. *International Journal of Nursing Education Scholarship, 5*(1), 1–12.

Andersson, L. M., & Pearson, C. M. (1999). Tit for tat? The spiraling effect of incivility in the workplace. *Academy of Management Review, 24,* 452–471. doi:10.2307/259136

Arch, A. (2008). *Web accessibility for older users: A literature review.* Retrieved from http://www.w3.org/TR/wai-age-literature/

Argote, L., & Ingram, P. (2000). Knowledge transfer: A basis for competitive advantage in firms. *Organizational Behavior and Human Decision Processes, 82*(1), 150–169. doi:10.1006/obhd.2000.2893

Aspin, D. N., & Chapman, J. D. (2000). Lifelong learning: Concepts and conceptions. *International Journal of Lifelong Education, 19*(1), 2–19. doi:10.1080/026013700293421

Assembly of African Union. (2003). *Protocol to the African charter on human and peoples' rights on the rights of women in Africa.* Retrieved from http://www.achpr.org/english/women/protocolwomen.pdf

Asunka, S. (2008). Online learning in higher education in Sub-Saharan Africa: Ghanaian university students' experiences and perceptions. *International Review of Research in Open and Distance Learning, 9*(3), 1–23.

Asunka, S., & Chae, H. S. (2009). Strategies for teaching online courses within the Sub-Saharan African context: An instructor's recommendations. *MERLOT Journal of Online Learning and Teaching, 5*(2), 372–379.

Atler, C., & Adkins, C. (2001). Improving the writing skills of social work students. *Journal of Social Work, 37*(3), 493–505.

Aula, A. (2005). User study on older adults' use of the Web and search engines. *Universal Access in the Information Society, 4*(1), 67–81. doi:10.1007/s10209-004-0097-7

Australian National Training Authority. (2000). *Turning on learning communities*. Canberra, Australia: Australian National Training Authority.

Babangida, M. (2005). *Celebrating two decades of Nigeria's better life programme: 1985 2005*. Retrieved from http://www.dawodu.com/mbabangida1.htm

Badaracco, J. L. (1998). The discipline of building character. In *Harvard business review on leadership* (pp. 89–114). Boston: Harvard Business School Publishing.

Bargeron, D., Grudin, J., Gupta, A., Sanocki, E., Li, F., & Leetiernan, S. (2002). Asynchronous collaboration around multimedia applied to on-demand education. *Journal of Management Information Systems, 18*(4), 117–145.

Barkley, E. F., Cross, K. P., & Major, C. H. (2004). *Collaborative learning techniques: A handbook for college faculty*. San Francisco, CA: Jossey-Bass.

Barnes, C., & Tynan, B. (2007). The adventures of Miranda in the brave new world: learning in a Web 2.0 millennium. *ALT-J. Research in Learning Technology, 15*(3), 189–200.

Baron, R. A., & Neuman, J. H. (1996). Workplace violence and workplace aggression: Evidence on their relative frequency and potential clauses. *Aggressive Behavior, 22*, 161–173. doi:10.1002/(SICI)1098-2337(1996)22:3<161::AID-AB1>3.0.CO;2-Q

Bates, A. W. T. (2005). *Technology, e-learning and distance education* (2nd ed.). New York, NY: Routledge.

Bax, M. R. N., & Hassan, M. N. (2003). *Lifelong learning in Malaysia*. Paper presented at the IIEP/UNESCO KRIVET International Policy Seminar, Seoul, Korea.

Bean, J. P., & Metzner, B. S. (1985). A conceptual model of nontraditional undergraduate student attrition. *Review of Educational Research, 55*(4), 485–540.

Beaudoin, M. F. (2003). Distance education leadership for the new century. *Online Journal of Distance Learning Administration, 6*(2).

Becker, R. L. (1981). *Reading-free vocational interest inventory: Manual*. Columbus, OH: Elbern.

Becker, S. A. (2004a). A study of web usability for older adults seeking online health resources. *ACM Transactions on Computer-Human Interaction, 11*(4), 387–406. doi:10.1145/1035575.1035578

Becker, S. A. (2004b). E-Government visual accessibility for older adults users. *Social Science Computer Review, 22*(1), 11–23. doi:10.1177/0894439303259876

Beetham, H., McGill, L., & Littlejohn, A. (2009). *Thriving in the 21st century: Learning literacies for the Digital Age*. Retrieved from http://elearning.jiscinvolve.org/wp/2009/06/11/thriving-in-the-21st-century-learning-literacies-for-the-digital-age/: JISC, UK

Belcher, W. L. (2009). Reflections on ten years of teaching writing for publication to graduate students and junior faculty. *Journal of Scholarly Publication, 40*(2), 184–200. doi:10.3138/jsp.40.2.184

Belenky, M., & Stanton, A. (2000). Inequality, development, and connected knowing. In Mezirow, , J. (Eds.) et al., *Learning as transformation: Critical perspectives on a theory in progress* (pp. 71–102). San Francisco, CA: Jossey-Bass.

Benbunan-Fich, R., Hiltz, S. R., & Harasim, L. (2005). The online interaction learning model: An integrated theoretical framework for learning networks. In Hiltz, S. R., & Goldman, R. (Eds.), *Learning together online: Research on asynchronous learning networks* (pp. 19–37). Mahwah, NJ: Lawrence Erlbaum.

Bennett, S. (2003). Supporting collaborative project teams using computer-based technologies. In Roberts, T. S. (Ed.), *Online collaborative learning: Theory and practice* (pp. 1–27). Hershey, PA: Information Science Reference. doi:10.4018/978-1-59140-174-2.ch001

Bennis, W. (1989). *On becoming a leader*. Wilmington, MA: Addison-Wesley Publishing Company.

Bennis, W., & Nanus, B. (1997). *Leaders' strategies for taking charge* (2nd ed.). New York: Harper Collins Publishers.

Berg, J., Berquam, L., & Christoph, K. (2007). Social networking technologies: a "poke" for campus services. *EDUCAUSE Review*, *42*(2), 32–44.

Berg, L. B. (2004). *Qualitative research methods for the social sciences*. Boston, MA: Allyn & Bacon.

Berkman, N., DeWalt, D., Pignone, M., Sheridan, S., Lohr, K., & Lux, L. (2004). *Literacy and health outcomes (Tech. Rep. No. AHRQ 04-E007-2)*. Rockville, MD: Agency for Healthcare Research and Quality.

Bernstein, A. (2008). *Objectivism in one lesson: An introduction to the philosophy of Ayn Rand*. Lanham, MD: Hamilton Books.

Berry, J. W. (1980). Acculturation as varieties of adaptation. In Padilla, A. (Ed.), *Acculturation: Theory, models and some new findings* (pp. 9–25). Boulder, CO: Westview.

Berry, J. W., & Annis, R. C. (1974). Accultruative stress: The role of ecology, culture and differentiation. *Journal of Cross-Cultural Psychology*, *5*, 382–405. doi:10.1177/002202217400500402

Bhasin, K. (1992). Education for women's empowerment: Some reflections. *Adult Education and Development*, *39*, 11–24.

Bloom, B. S. (Ed.). (1956). *Taxonomy of educational objectives*. London, UK: Longman.

Blueprint of Women's Education in Nigeria. (1986). *Proceedings of the national workshop on the production of a Blueprint on women's education in Nigeria*. Lagos, Nigeria: Federal Government Printers.

Blythe, S. (2001). Designing online courses: User-centered practices. *Computers and Composition*, *18*, 329–346. doi:10.1016/S8755-4615(01)00066-4

Bodgan, R. C., & Biklen, S. K. (2003). *Qualitative research for education: An introduction to theories and methods* (4th ed.). Boston, MA: Ally & Bacon.

Boxler, H. N. (2004). Grounded practice: Exploring criticalities in a job reeducation setting. *Adult Education Quarterly*, *54*(3), 210–223. doi:10.1177/0741713604263052

Boyd, R. D., & Myers, J. B. (1988). Transformative education. *International Journal of Lifelong Education*, *7*, 261–284. doi:10.1080/0260137880070403

Bransford, J., Brown, A., & Cocking, R. (1999). *How people learn: Brain, mind, experience, and school*. Washington, DC: National Academies Press.

Brennan, J., Mills, J., Shah, T., & Woodley, A. (1999). *Part-time students and employment: Report of a survey of students, graduates and diplomats*. London, UK: Centre for Higher Education Research & Information, Open University Quality Support Centre.

Bresó, I., Gracia, F. J., Latorre, F., & Peiró, J. M. (2008). Development and validation of the team learning questionnaire. *Organizational Behavior and Management*, *14*(2), 145–160.

Brockett, R. B., & Hiemstra, R. (1991). *Self-direction in adult learning: Perspectives on theory, research, and practice*. London, UK: Routledge.

Brookfield, S. (2006). *The skillful teacher*. New York, NY: John Wiley & Sons.

Brookfield, S. D. (1986). *Understanding and facilitating adult learning*. San Francisco, CA: Jossey-Bass.

Brookfield, S. D. (1991). On ideology, pillage, language and risk: Critical thinking and tensions of critical practice. *Studies in Continuing Education*, *13*(1), 1–14. doi:10.1080/0158037910130101

Brookfield, S. D. (1993). Self-directed learning, political clarity, and the critical practice of adult education. *Adult Education Quarterly*, *43*(4), 227–242. doi:10.1177/0741713693043004002

Brookfield, S. D. (1995). *Becoming a critically reflective teacher*. San Francisco, CA: Jossey-Bass.

Brookfield, S. D. (2000). Transformative learning as ideology critique. In Mezirow, J., et al. (Eds.), *Learning as transformation: Critical perspectives on a theory in progress* (pp. 125–148). San Francisco, CA: Jossey-Bass.

Brookfield, S. D., & Preskill, S. (1999). *Discussion as a way of teaching: Tools and techniques for democratic classrooms*. San Francisco, CA: Jossey-Bass.

Brown, J. S., Collins, A., & Duguid, P. (1989). Situated cognition and the culture of learning. *Educational Researcher*, *18*(1), 32–42.

Bruffee, K. A. (1999). *Collaborative learning: Higher education, interdependence and the authority of knowledge* (2nd ed.). Baltimore, MD: Johns Hopkins University Press.

Brundage, D., & MacKeracher, D. (1980). Adult learning principles and their application to program planning. Toronto, ON, Canada: Ontario Institute for Studies in Education.

Bryant, T. (2006). Social software in academia. *EDUCAUSE Quarterly, 29*(2), 61–64.

Budapest Open Access Initiative. (2002). *Budapest open access initiative.* Retrieved from http://www.soros.org/openaccess/read.shtml

Bui, K. V. T. (2002). First-generation college students at a four-year university: Background characteristics, reasons for pursuing higher education, and first-year experiences. *College Student Journal, 36*(1), 3–11.

Burnham, M. A., Hough, R. L., Karno, M., Escobar, J. I., & Telles, C. A. (1987). Acculturation and lifetime prevalence of psychiatric disorders among Mexican Americans in Los Angeles. *Journal of Health and Social Behavior, 28*, 59–102.

Burton-Jones, A. (2009). Minimizing method bias through programmatic research. *Management Information Systems Quarterly, 33*, 445–471.

Butin, D. W. (2010). *The education dissertation.* Thousand Oaks, CA: Corwin.

Cagle, H. H., Fisher, D. G., Senter, T. P., Thurmond, R. D., & Kastar, A. J. (2002). *Classifying skin lesions of injection drug users: A method for corroborating disease risk.* Rockville, MD: Center for Substance Abuse Treatment, Substance Abuse and Mental Health Services Administration.

Caldwell, B., Cooper, M., Guraino Reid, L., & Vanderheiden, G. (Eds.). (2004). *Web content accessibility guidelines 2.0 (WCAG).* Retrieved from http://www.w3.org/WAI/GL/WCAG20/

Calhoun, T. (2005). DRM: The challenge of the decade. *Campus Technology*, 18-20.

Candy, P. C. (1991). *Self-direction for lifelong learning.* San Francisco, CA: Jossey-Bass.

Cantwell, R., Archer, J., & Bourke, S. (2001). A comparison of the academic experiences and achievement of university students entering by traditional and nontraditional means. *Assessment & Evaluation in Higher Education, 26*(3), 221–234. doi:10.1080/02602930120052387

Carney-Crompton, S., & Tan, J. (2002). Support systems, psychological functioning, and academic performance of nontraditional female students. *Adult Education Quarterly, 52*(2), 140–154. doi:10.1177/0741713602052002005

Carrillo, F. J. (2003). *A note on knowledge-based development* (Tech. Rep. No. CSC2003-07). Monterrey, Mexico: The World Capital Institute.

Carrillo, F. J. (2002). Capital systems: Implications for global knowledge agenda. *Journal of Knowledge Management, 6*(4), 379–399. doi:10.1108/13673270210440884

Carrillo, F. J. (2004). Capital cities: A taxonomy of capital accounts for knowledge cities. *Journal of Knowledge Management, 8*(5), 28–46. doi:10.1108/1367327041058738

Carrillo, F. J. (Ed.). (2006). *Knowledge cities: Approaches, experiences and perspectives.* Oxford, UK: Butterworth-Heinemann/Elsevier.

Casey, C. (2006). A knowledge economy and a learning society: A comparative analysis of New Zealand and Australian experiences. *British Journal of Comparative Education, 36*(3), 343–357.

Cattel, G. M. (1997). African widows, culture and social change: Case studies from Kenya. In Sokolovsky, J. (Ed.), *The cultural context of aging* (pp. 71–98). Westport, CT: Bergin & Garvey.

Chafkin, M. (2010). *Telecommuting by the numbers.* Retrieved from http://www.inc.com/magazine/20100401/telecommuting-by-the-numbers.html

Chance, N. A. (1965). Acculturation, self-identification and personality adjustment. *American Anthropologist, 67*, 372–393. doi:10.1525/aa.1965.67.2.02a00050

Chatzkel, J. (2006). Greater phoenix as a knowledge capital. In Carrillo, F. J. (Ed.), *Knowledge cities: Approaches, experiences and perspectives* (pp. 135–144). Oxford, UK: Butterworth-Heinemann/Elsevier.

Chen, C. C., & Eastman, W. (1997). Toward a civic culture for multicultural organizations. *The Journal of Applied Behavioral Science, 33*, 454–470. doi:10.1177/0021886397334003

Chen, X., & Carroll, C. D. (2007). *Part-time undergraduates in postsecondary education: 2003-04*. Washington, DC: National Center for Education Statistics.

Chilisa, B., & Preece, J. (2005). *Research methods for adult educators in Africa*. Hamburg, Germany: UNESCO Institute for Education.

Chinese Government. (1996, August 29). *Decree for protecting the right of senior citizens*. Retrieved from http://www.gov.cn/banshi/2005-08/04/content_20203.htm

Choi, S. D. (2003). *Changing skills formation and lifelong learning in South Korea*. Unpublished doctoral dissertation, University of London, London, UK.

Choy, S. (2002). *Nontraditional undergraduates: Findings from the condition of education, 2002*. Washington, DC: U.S. Department of Education, National Center for Education Statistics.

Christopher, M. M., Thomas, J. A., & Tallent-Runnels, M. K. (2004). Raising the bar: Encouraging high level thinking in online discussion forums. *Roeper Review, 26*(3), 166–171. doi:10.1080/02783190409554262

Cisco. (2010). *The learning society*. Retrieved from http://tools.cisco.com/search/JSP/search-results.get?strQueryText= the+learning+society+& Search+All+cisco.com= cisco.com&language= en&country= US&thissection= f&accessLevel= Guest

Clark, R. E. (2001). Media are "mere vehicles": The opening argument. In Clark, R. E. (Ed.), *Learning from media: Arguments, analysis, and evidence* (pp. 1–12). Charlotte, NC: Information Age Publishing.

Clark, R. E., & Craig, T. (2001). What about media effects on learning? In Clark, R. E. (Ed.), *Learning from media: Arguments, analysis and evidence* (pp. 89–101). Charlotte, NC: Information Age Publishing.

Clayton, M. (1997). Delphi: A technique to harness expert opinion for critical decision-making tasks in education. *Educational Psychology, 17*(4), 373. doi:10.1080/0144341970170401

Cochran, J. (2007). Reactions to Western educational practice: Adult education in Egypt. In King, K. P., & Wang, V. C. X. (Eds.), *Comparative adult education around the globe* (pp. 85–111). Hangzhou, China: Zhejiang University Press.

Cognition and Technology Group at Vanderbilt. (1990). Situated cognition and the culture of learning. *Educational Researcher, 3*(9), 32–42.

Cohen, J. (1988). *Statistical power for the behavioral sciences* (2nd ed.). Hillsdale, NJ: Erlbaum.

Community College Survey of Student Engagement (CCSSE). (2008). *High expectations and high support*. Austin, TX: The University of Texas at Austin.

Conceição, S. C. O., & Baldor, M. J. (2009, October). *Faculty workload for online instruction: Individual barriers and institutional challenges*. Paper presented at the Midwest Research-to-Practice Conference in Adult, Continuing, and Community Education, Chicago.

Conderman, G., Morin, J., & Stephens, T. (2005). Special education student teaching practices. *Preventing School Failure, 49*(3), 5–10. doi:10.3200/PSFL.49.3.5-10

Conole, G. (2008). listening to the learner voice: The ever changing landscape of technology use for language students. *ReCALL, 20*, 124–140. doi:10.1017/S0958344008000220

Cortina, L. M., Magley, V. J., Williams, J. H., & Langhout, R. D. (2001). Incivility in the workplace: Incidence and impact. *Journal of Occupational Health Psychology, 6*, 64–80. doi:10.1037/1076-8998.6.1.64

Cotugna, N., Vickery, C. E., & Carpenter-Haefele, K. M. (2005). Evaluation of literacy level of patient education pages in health-related journals. *Journal of Community Health, 30*(3), 213–219. doi:10.1007/s10900-004-1959-x

Council of Graduate Schools. (2010). *Ph.D. completion and attrition: Policies and procedures to promote student success*. Washington, DC: Council of Graduate Schools.

Courtney, S. (2001). Technology and culture of teaching and learning. In Lieberman, D., & Wehlberg, C. (Eds.), *To Improve the Academy* (Vol. 19, pp. 232–249). Bolton, MA: Anker Publishing.

Cramer, K. D., & Wasiak, H. (2006). *Change the way you see everything: Through asset-based thinking*. Philadelphia: Running Press.

Cranton, P. (1992). *Working with adult learners*. Middletown, OH: Wall & Emerson.

Cranton, P. (2006). *Understanding and promoting transformative learning* (2nd ed.). San Francisco, CA: Jossey-Bass.

Cranton, P. (2010). Working toward self-evaluation. In Wang, V. C. X. (Ed.), *Assessing and evaluating adult learning in career and technical education* (pp. 1–11). Hershey, PA: IGI Global. doi:10.4018/978-1-61520-745-9.ch001

Cranton, P., & Taylor, E. W. (in press). Transformative learning. In Jarvis, P. (Ed.), *International encyclopedia of learning*. London, UK: Routledge.

Creighton, C., Parks, D., & Creighton, L. (2008). *Mentoring doctoral students: The need for pedagogy*. Retrieved from http://cnx.org/content/m14516/1.3/

Creswell, J. W. (2003). *Research design: Qualitative, quantitative, and mixed methods approaches* (2nd ed.). Thousand Oaks, CA: Sage.

Creswell, W. J. (2005). *Educational research, planning, conducting, and evaluating qualitative and quantitative research* (2nd ed.). Upper Saddle River, NJ: Prentice Hall/Pearson.

Crews, T., & Bodenhamer, J. (2009). Preparing student teaching interns: Advice from current business educators. *Delta Pi Epsilon Journal*, *51*(1), 43–55.

Cyphert, F. R., & Gant, W. L. (1971). The delphi technique: A case study. *Phi Delta Kappan*, *52*, 272–273.

D'Andrade, R. (2001). A cognitivist's view of the units debate in cultural anthropology. *Cross-Cultural Research*, *35*, 242–257. doi:10.1177/106939710103500208

Dalkey, N. C., Rourke, D. L., Lewis, R., & Snyder, D. (1972). *Studies in the quality of life*. Lexington, MA: Lexington Books.

Darkenwald, G., & Merriam, S. (1982). *Adult education: Foundations of practice*. New York, NY: Harper Collins.

Darling-Hammond, L., Hammerness, K., Grossman, P., Rust, F., & Shulman, L. (2005). The design of teacher education programs. In Darling-Hammond, L., & Bransford, J. (Eds.), *Preparing teachers for a changing world: What teachers should learn and be able to do* (pp. 390–441). San Francisco, CA: Jossey-Bass.

De Valero, Y. R. (2001). Departmental factors affecting time-to-degree and completion rates at one land grant institution. *The Journal of Higher Education*, *72*(3), 341–367. doi:10.2307/2649335

Delbecq, A. L., Van de Ven, A. H., & Gustafson, D. H. (1975). *Group techniques for program planning*. Glenview, IL: Scott Foresman.

Delors, J. (1998). *Learning the treasure within*. Paris, France: UNESCO.

Deming, W. E. (2000). *The new economics: For industry, government, education*. Cambridge, MA: MIT Press.

Dennen, V. P., Darabi, A. A., & Smith, L. J. (2007). Instructor-learner interaction in online courses: The relative perceived importance of particular instructor actions on performance and satisfaction. *Distance Education*, *28*(1), 65–79. doi:10.1080/01587910701305319

Department for Education. (2003). *The skills for life survey: A national needs and impact survey of literacy, numeracy and ICT skills*. Retrieved from http://www.dcsf.gov.uk/research/data/uploadfiles/RB490.pdf

Department of Polytechnic and Community College Education. (2009). *Quick facts*. Retrieved from http://www.portal.mohe.gov.my/portal/page/portal/ExtPortal/IPT/POLITEKNIK/files/QuickfactApril09.pdf

Derry, S., & Lesgold, A. (1996). Toward a situated social practice model for instructional design. In Berliner, D. C., & Calfee, R. C. (Eds.), *Handbook of Educational Psychology* (pp. 787–806). New York: Simon & Schuster Macmillan.

Desjardins, R., Rubenson, K., & Milana, M. (2006). *Unequal chances to participate in adult learning: International perspectives*. Paris, France: UNESCO Institute for Educational Planning.

Dever, M., Hager, K., & Klein, K. (2003). Building the university/public school partnership: A workshop for mentor teachers. *Teacher Educator*, *38*(4), 245–255. doi:10.1080/08878730309555321

Dewey, J. (1961). *Democracy and education*. New York, NY: Macmillan.

Diaz, D. P. (2002). *Online drop rates revisited*. Retrieved from http://technologysource.org/article/online_drop_rates_revisited/

DiBiase, D., & Rademacher, H. (2005). Scaling up: Faculty workload, class size, and student satisfaction in a distance learning course on Geographic Information Sciences. *Journal of Geography in Higher Education*, *29*(1), 139–158. doi:10.1080/03098260500030520

Dickinson, A., Smith, M. J., Arnott, J. L., Newell, A. F., & Hill, R. L. (2007). Approaches to web search and navigation for older computer novices. In *Proceedings of the SIGCHI Conference on Human Factors in Computing Systems*, San Jose, CA (pp. 281-290).

Dickinson, A., Eisma, R., Gregor, P., Syme, A., & Milne, S. (2005). Strategies for teaching older people to use the World Wide Web. *Universal Access in the Information Society*, *4*(1), 3–15. doi:10.1007/s10209-003-0082-6

Dickinson, A., & Gregor, P. (2006). Computer use has no demonstrated impact on the well-being of older adults. *International Journal of Human-Computer Studies*, *64*(8), 744–753. doi:10.1016/j.ijhcs.2006.03.001

Dickinson, K., & Maynard, E. S. (1981). *The impact of supported work on ex-addicts* (*Vol. 4*). New York, NY: Manpower Demonstration Research Corporation.

Dillman, D. A. (2000). *Mail and internet surveys: The tailored design method* (2nd ed.). New York: Wiley.

Dirkx, J. (2001). Images, transformative learning and the work of soul. *Adult Learning*, *12*(3), 15–16.

Dirkx, J. M., & Smith, R. O. (2004). Thinking out of a bowl of spaghetti: Learning to learn in online collaborative groups. In Roberts, T. S. (Ed.), *Online collaborative learning: Theory and practice* (pp. 132–159). Hershey, PA: Information Science Reference.

Division for the Advancement of Women. (1980). *Convention on the elimination of all forms of discrimination against women (CEDAW)*. Retrieved from http://www.un.org/womenwatch/daw/cedaw/

Dixon, N. M. (1997). The hallways of learning. *Organizational Dynamics*, *25*(4), 23–34. doi:10.1016/S0090-2616(97)90034-6

Donaldson, J. E., & Graham, S. (1999). A model of college outcomes for adults. *Adult Education Quarterly*, *50*(1), 24–40.

Dori, Y. J., Belcher, J., Bessette, M., Danziger, M., McKinney, A., & Hult, E. (2003). Technology for active learning. *Materials Today*, *6*(12), 44–49. doi:10.1016/S1369-7021(03)01225-2

Dowling-Guyer, S., Johnson, M. E., Fisher, D. G., Needle, R., Watters, J., & Anderson, M. (1994). Reliability of drug users' self-reported HIV risk behaviors and validity of self-reported recent drug use. *Assessment*, *1*, 383–392.

Dreher, G. F., & Ryan, K. C. (2000). Prior work experience and academic achievement among first-year MBA students. *Research in Higher Education*, *41*(4), 505–525. doi:10.1023/A:1007036626439

Drewett, R., Knight, R., & Schubert, U. (1992). *The future of European cities: The role of science and technology*. Brussels, Belgium: European Commission.

Driscoll, M., & Carliner, S. (2005). *Advanced web-based training strategies*. San Francisco, CA: Pfeiffer.

Duffy, T. M., & Cunningham, D. J. (2001). Constructivism: Implications for the design and delivery of instruction. In Jonassen, D. H. (Ed.), *Handbook of research for educational communications and technology* (pp. 170–198). Mahwah, NJ: Erlbaum.

Dulayakasem, U. (2005). *Past/future of non-formal education management*. Bangkok, Thailand: Monitoring and Evaluation Group, The Office of Non-formal Education Administration.

Dyer, W. G., & Dyer, J. H. (1987). *Team building*. Reading, MA: Addison-Wesley.

Edmondson, A. C., Dillon, J. R., & Roloff, K. S. (2007). Three perspectives on team learning: Outcome improvement, task mastery, and group process. *Academy of Management Annals, 1,* 269–314. doi:10.1080/078559811

Edmondson, A. C., & Nembhard, I. M. (2009). Product development and learning in project teams: The challenges are the benefits. *Journal of Product Innovation Management, 26*(2), 123–138. doi:10.1111/j.1540-5885.2009.00341.x

Edson, J. (2007). Curriculum 2.0: user-driven education. *The Huffington Post.* Retrieved from http://www.huffingtonpost.com/jonathan-edson/curriculum-20-userdri_b_53690.html

Education Resources Institute & Institute for Higher Education Policy. (1997). *Missed opportunities: A new look at disadvantaged college aspirants.* Washington, DC: Education Resources Institute & Institute for Higher Education Policy.

Eisner, I. E. W., & Peshkin, A. (Eds.), *Qualitative inquiry in education* (pp. 121–152). New York, NY: Teachers College Press.

Elias, J. L., & Merriam, S. B. (2005). *Philosophical foundations of adult education* (3rd ed.). Malabar, FL: Krieger Publishing.

Emery, V. K., Edwards, P. J., Jacko, J. A., Moloney, K. P., Barnard, L., Kongnakorn, T., et al. (2003). Toward achieving universal usability for older adults through multimodal feedback. In *Proceedings of the Conference on Universal Usability,* Vancouver, BC, Canada (pp. 46-53).

English, L. M. (2009). *International encyclopedia of adult education.* Adelaide, Australia: National Centre for Vocational Education Research (NCVER).

Engvig, M. (2006). *Online learning: All you need to know to facilitate and administer online courses.* Cresskill, NJ: Hampton Press.

Ergazakis, K., Karnezis, K., Metaxiotis, K., & Psarras, J. (2004). Towards knowledge cities conceptual analysis and success stories. *Journal of Knowledge Management, 8*(5), 5–15. doi:10.1108/13673270410558747

Ergazakis, K., Metaxiotis, K., Psarras, J., & Askounis, D. (2006). An emerging pattern of successful knowledge cities' main features. In Carrillo, F. J. (Ed.), *Knowledge cities: Approaches, experiences and perspectives* (pp. 3–16). Oxford, UK: Butterworth- Heinemann/Elsevier.

Esin, H. (2005). *Women urged to pick interest in vocational training.* Retrieved from http://allafrica.com/stories/200512140580.html

European Foundation for the Improvement of Living and Working Conditions. (2010). *Physical and psychological violence at the workplace.* Dublin, Ireland: Author.

Ewelukwa, U. U. (2002). Post-colonialism, gender, customary injustice: Widows in African societies. *Human Rights Quarterly, 24*(2), 424–486. doi:10.1353/hrq.2002.0021

Ezer, T. (2007). Swaziland widows fighting for their rights. *HIV/AIDS. Policy Review, 12*(23), 72–73.

Fafunwa, B. (1963). African education and social dynamics. *West African Journal of Education, 7*(2), 66–70.

Faillos, C. A. (2006). Adult education and the empowerment of the individual in a global society. In Merriam, S. B., Courtney, B. C., & Cervero, R. M. (Eds.), *Global issues and adult education: Perspectives from Latin America, Southern Africa, and the United States* (pp. 15–29). San Francisco, CA: Jossey-Bass.

Fairchild, E. E. (2003). Multiple roles of adult learners. *New Directions for Student Services, 102,* 11–16. doi:10.1002/ss.84

Farb, S., & Riggio, A. (2004). Medium or message? A new look at standards, structures, and schemata for managing electronic resources. *Library Hi Tech, 22*(2), 144–152. doi:10.1108/07378830410524576

Faris, R. (1998). *Learning communities: Cities, towns and villages preparing for a 21st century knowledge-based economy.* Retrieved from http://members.shaw.ca/rfaris/LC.htm

Faris, R. (2006). *Learning cities: Lessons learned.* Retrieved from http://members.shaw.ca/rfaris/docs/VLC%20Lessons%20Learned.pdf

Faris, J., & Peterson, W. (2000). *Learning-based community development: Lessons learned for British Columbia*. Victoria, BC, Canada: Ministry of Community Development, Cooperatives and Volunteers.

Farkas, C. M., & Wetlaufer, S. (1998). The ways executive officers lead. In *Harvard business review on leadership* (pp. 115–146). Boston: Harvard Business School Publishing.

Farmer, L. (2011). Career and technical education technology: Three decades in review and technological trends in the future. In Wang, V. C. X. (Ed.), *Definitive readings in the history, philosophy, practice and theories of career and technical education* (pp. 216–231). Hershey, PA; Hangzhou, China: Information Science Reference and Zhejiang University Press.

Fasokun, T., Katahoire, A., & Oduaran, A. (2005). *The psychology of adult learning in Africa*. Hamburg, Germany: UNESCO Institute for Education.

Federal Ministry of Education of Nigeria. (2000). *National policy on education*. Lagos, Nigeria: NERC Press.

Fenske, R. H., Porter, J. D., & Dubrock, C. P. (2000). Tracking financial aid and persistence of women, minority, and needy students in science, engineering, and mathematics. *Research in Higher Education, 41*(1), 67–94. doi:10.1023/A:1007042413040

Fenwick, T. (2008). Understanding relations of individual--collective learning in work: A review of research. *Management Learning, 39*(3), 227. doi:10.1177/1350507608090875

Fischer, G. (2001). Lifelong learning and its support with new media. In Smelser, N. J., & Baltes, P. B. (Eds.), *International encyclopedia of social and behavioral sciences, discipline cognitive psychology and cognitive science* (pp. 8836–8840). Oxford, UK: Pergamon.

Fisher, D. G., Kuhrt-Hunstiger, T. I., Orr, S., & Davis, D. C. (1999). Hepatitis B validity of drug users' self-report. *Psychology of Addictive Behaviors, 13*(1), 33–38. doi:10.1037/0893-164X.13.1.33

Fisher-Yoshida, B., Geller, K. D., & Schapiro, S. A. (2009). *Innovations in transformative learning: Space, culture, and the arts*. New York, NY: Peter Lang.

Fives, H., Hamman, D., & Olivarez, A. (2007). Does burnout begin with student teaching? Analyzing efficacy, burnout, and support during the student-teaching semester. *Teaching and Teacher Education, 23*, 916–934. doi:10.1016/j.tate.2006.03.013

Fletcher, E., Mountjoy, K., & Bailey, G. (in press). Exploring concerns of business student teachers. *Delta Pi Epsilon Journal*.

Flores, P. (2006). Implementation of the capital system for a knowledge city. In Carrillo, F. J. (Ed.), *Knowledge cities: Approaches, experiences and perspectives* (pp. 75–84). Oxford, UK: Butterworth- Heinemann/Elsevier.

Fosnot, C. T. (2005). *Constructivism: Theory, perspectives and practice*. New York, NY: Teachers College Press.

Fox, S., & Stallworth, L. E. (2010). The battered apple: An application of stress-emotion-control/support theory to teachers' experience of violence and bullying. *Human Relations, 63*, 927–954. doi:10.1177/0018726709349518

Franklin, M., & Hosein, R. (2009). Flexible education and community development. In Marshall, S., Kinuthia, W., & Taylor, W. (Eds.), *Bridging the knowledge divide: Educational technology for development* (pp. 3–21). Charlotte, NC: Information Age Publishing.

Freimuth, V. S. (1979). Assessing the readability of health education messages. *Public Health Reports, 94*(6), 568–570.

Freire, P. (2003). *Pedagogy of the oppressed*. New York, NY: Continuum International Publishing.

French, M. T., Dennis, M. T., McDougal, G. L., Karuntzos, G. T., & Hubbard, R. L. (1992). Training and employment programs in methadone treatment: Client needs and desires. *Journal of Substance Abuse Treatment, 9*, 293–303. doi:10.1016/0740-5472(92)90022-G

Friedman, L. N. (1978). *The Wildcat experiment: An early test of supported work in drug abuse rehabilitation*. Washington, DC: U. S. Government Printing Office.

Fritz, C., & Miller, G. (2003). Concerns expressed by student teachers in agriculture. *Journal of Agricultural Education, 44*(3), 47–53. doi:10.5032/jae.2003.03047

Fryer, R. H. (1997). *Learning for the twenty first century (the Fryer report)*. London, UK: DFEE.

Fuller, F., Parsons, J., & Watkins, J. (1974, April). *Concerns of teachers: Research and reconceptualization.* Paper presented at the Annual Meeting of the American Educational Research Association, Chicago, IL.

Fuqua, D. R., & Newman, J. L. (1989). An examination of the relation between career subscales. *Journal of Counseling Psychology, 36,* 487–491. doi:10.1037/0022-0167.36.4.487

Gagne, R. M., Wager, W. W., Golas, K. C., & Keller, J. M. (2005). *Principles of instructional design* (5th ed.). Stamford, CT: Thomson Learning.

Gal, N. (2006). The role of practicum supervisors in behavior management education. *Teaching and Teacher Education, 22,* 377–393. doi:10.1016/j.tate.2005.11.007

Gardner, H. (1984). The development of competence in culturally defined domains: A preliminary framework. In Shweder, R. A., & LeVine, R. A. (Eds.), *Culture theory: Essay on mind, self, and emotion* (pp. 257–275). New York: Cambridge University Press.

Gardner, P. (1996). Demographic and attitudinal trends: The increasing diversity of today's and tomorrow's learner. *Journal of Cooperative Education, 31*(2-3), 58–82.

Gaytan, J. (2009). Analyzing online education through the lens of institutional theory and practice: the need for research-based and –validated frameworks for planning, designing, delivering, and assessing online instruction. *Delta Pi Epsilon Journal, 51*(2), 62–75.

Gerontological Society of Shanghai (GSS). (2006). *Guideline for design senior accessible website (for trial).* Retrieved from http://www.shanghaigss.org.cn/news_view.asp?newsid=2400

Gibson, C. C. (1998). The distance learner's academic self-concept. In Gibson, C. (Ed.), *Distance learners in higher education: Institutional responses for quality outcomes* (pp. 65–76). Madison, WI: Atwood.

Giddens, A. (1984). *The constitution of society.* Oxford, UK: Polity Press.

Gliner, J. A., & Morgan, G. A. (2000). *Research methods in applied settings: An integrated approach to design and analysis.* Mahwah, NJ: Lawrence Erlbaum.

Godshalk, V. M., Harvey, D. M., & Moller, L. (2004). The role of learning tasks on attitude change using cognitive flexibility hypertext systems. *Journal of the Learning Sciences, 13*(4), 507–526. doi:10.1207/s15327809jls1304_2

Golde, C. M. (2000). Should I stay or should I go? Student descriptions of the doctoral attrition process. *Review of Higher Education, 23*(2), 199–227.

Goodman, E., & Moed, A. (2006, November 4-8). Community in mashups: the case of personal geodata. In *Proceedings of the 20th ACM Conference on Computer Supported Cooperative Work*, Banff, AB, Canada. Retrieved from http://mashworks.net/images/5/59/Goodman_Moed_2006.pdf

Goodnough, K., Osmond, P., Dibbon, D., Glassman, M., & Stevens, K. (2009). Exploring a triad model of student teaching: Pre-service teacher and cooperating teacher perceptions. *Teaching and Teacher Education, 25*(2), 285–296. doi:10.1016/j.tate.2008.10.003

Graham, S. W., Donaldson, J. F., Kasworm, C., & Dirkx, J. (2000). *The experiences of adult undergraduate students—what shapes their learning?* Retrieved from http://www.eric.ed.gov/ ERICWebPortal/ search/ detailmini.jsp?_nfpb=true&_&ERICExtSearch_SearchValue_0=ED440275&ERICExtSearch_ SearchType_0= no&accno= ED440275

Greenberg, E., Dunleavy, E., & Kutner, M. (2008). Literacy behind bars: Results from the 2003 national assessment of adult literacy prison survey, executive summary. *Journal for Vocational Special Needs Education, 30*(2), 16–19.

Greene, M. (2001). *Variations on a blue guitar.* New York, NY: Teachers College Press.

Grenier, L. (1998). *Working with indigenous knowledge: A guide for researchers.* Ottawa, ON, Canada: Development Research Center.

Grimes, S. K. (1995). Targeting academic program to student diversity utilizing learning styles and learning-study strategies. *Journal of College Student Development, 36,* 422–430.

Grossman, P., Schoenfeld, A., & Lee, C. (2005). Teaching subject matter. In Darling-Hammond, L., & Bransford, J. (Eds.), *Preparing teachers for a changing world: What teachers should learn and be able to do* (pp. 201–231). San Francisco, CA: Jossey-Bass.

Grow, G. O. (1991). Teaching learners to be self-directed. *Adult Education Quarterly, 41*(3), 125–149. doi:10.1177/0001848191041003001

Gunnlaugson, O. (2008). Metatheoretical prospects for the field of transformative learning. *Journal of Transformative Education, 6*(2), 124–135. doi:10.1177/1541344608323387

Guthrie, J. W., & Marsh, D. D. (2009). Introduction to the special issue on the education doctorate. *Peabody Journal of Education, 84*, 1–2. doi:10.1080/01619560802679518

Guzman, B. (2001). *The Hispanic population.* Washington, DC: U.S. Department of Commerce.

Gwamruwa. (1980). *Mujailar makarantar* [History of widows training school]. Kaduna, Nigeria: Bada Group Nigeria.

Hackman, M., & Walker, K. (1990). Instructional communication in the televised classroom: The effects of system design and teacher immediacy on student learning and satisfaction. *Communication Education, 39*(3), 196–209. doi:10.1080/03634529009378802

Hake, B. (1999). *Learning to survive in late modernity: From emancipation to employability in the learning society.* International Jahrbuch der Erwachsenenbildung.

Hamman, D., Olivarez, A., Lesley, M., Button, K., Chan, Y., Griffith, R., & Elliot, S. (2006). Pedagogical influence of interaction with cooperating teachers on the efficacy beliefs of student teachers. *Teacher Educator, 42*(1), 15–29. doi:10.1080/08878730609555391

Hammonds, K., Jackson, S., DeGeorge, G., & Morris, K. (1997). *The new university: A tough market is reshaping colleges.* Retrieved from http://www.businessweek.com/1997/51/b3558139.htm

Hase, S., & Kenyon, C. (2000). *From andragogy to heutagogy.* Retrieved from http://ultibase.rmit.edu.au

Hasson, F., Keeney, S., & McKenna, H. (2000). Research guidelines for the Delphi survey technique. *Journal of Advanced Nursing, 32*(4), 1008–1015.

Heifetz, R. A., & Laurie, D. L. (1998). The work of leadership. In *Harvard Business Review on Leadership* (pp. 171–198). Boston, MA: Harvard Business School Publishing.

Heller, P., Keith, R., & Anderson, S. (1992). Teaching problem solving through cooperative grouping: Group versus individual problem solving. *American Journal of Physics, 60*, 671–683.

Hendrix, C. (2000). Computer use among elderly people. *Computers in Nursing, 18*(2), 62–71.

Hermalin, J. A., Steer, R. A., Platt, J. J., & Metzger, D. S. (1990). Risk characteristics associated with chronic unemployment in methadone clients. *Drug and Alcohol Dependence, 26*, 117–125. doi:10.1016/0376-8716(90)90118-X

Hersey, P., & Blanchard, K. (1969). *Management of organizational behavior: Utilizing human resources.* Englewood Cliffs, NJ: Prentice-Hall.

Hilton, J. (2006). The future for higher education: sunrise or perfect storm. *EDUCAUSE Review, 41*(2), 58–71.

Hiltz, S. R. (1994). *The virtual classroom: Learning without limits via computer networks.* Norwood, NJ: Abex.

Hiltz, S. R., Coppola, N., Rotter, N., Turoff, M., & Benbunan-Fich, R. (2000). Measuring the importance of collaborative learning for the effectiveness of ALN: A multi-measure, multi-method approach. *Journal of Asynchronous Learning Networks, 4*(2), 103–125.

Hogh, A., Henriksson, M. E., & Burr, H. (2005). A 5-year follow-up study of aggression at work and psychological health. *International Journal of Behavioral Medicine, 12*, 256–265. doi:10.1207/s15327558ijbm1204_6

Hohn, M. D. (1998). Why is change so hard? Theories and thoughts about the organizational change process. *Focus on Basics, 2*, 1–8.

Holden, M., & Connelly, S. (2004). The learning city: Urban sustainability education and building toward WUF legacy. In Oberlander, H. P. (Ed.), *The Vancouver working group discussion papers for the world urban forum on sustainability* (pp. 1–54). Ottawa, ON, Canada: The Canadian Institute of Planners, Government of Canada.

Holland, J. L. (1996). *Self-directed search: Job finder*. Odessa, FL: Psychological Assessment Resources.

Holland, J. L., Daiger, D. C., & Power, P. G. (1980). *My vocational situation: Description of an experimental diagnostic form for the selection of vocational assistance*. Palo Alto, CA: Consulting Psychologist Press.

Holland, J. L., Fritzsche, B. A., & Powell, A. B. (1994). *Self-directed search, technical manual*. Odessa, FL: Psychological Assessment Resources.

Holland, J. L., Gottfredson, D. C., & Power, P. G. (1980). Some diagnostic scales for research in decision making and personality: Identity, information, and barriers. *Journal of Personality and Social Psychology, 39*, 1191–1200. doi:10.1037/h0077731

Home, A. M. (1998). Predicting role conflict, overload and contagion in adult women university students with families and jobs. *Adult Education Quarterly, 48*(2), 85–97. doi:10.1177/074171369804800204

Horn, L. J., & Carroll, C. D. (1996). *Nontraditional undergraduates: Trends in enrollment from 1986 to 1992 and persistence and attainment among 1989-90 beginning postsecondary students. Postsecondary Education Descriptive Analysis Reports: Statistical Analysis Report*. Washington, DC: U.S. Government Printing Office.

Hoskins, S. L., & Newstead, S. E. (1997). Degree performance as a function of age, gender, prior qualifications and discipline studied. *Assessment & Evaluation in Higher Education, 22*(3), 317. doi:10.1080/0260293970220305

Houghton-Jan, S. (2007). Imagine no restrictions. *School Library Journal, 53*–54.

Howell, S. L., Williams, P. B., & Lindsay, N. K. (2003). Thirty-two trends affecting distance education: An informed foundation for strategic planning. *Online Journal of Distance Learning Administration, 6*(3).

Hsiao, K. P. (1992). *First-generation college students*. Los Angeles, CA: ERIC Clearinghouse for Junior Colleges.

Hsieh, C., & Knight, L. (2008). Problem-based learning for engineering students: An evidence-based comparative study. *Journal of Academic Librarianship, 34*(1), 25–30. doi:10.1016/j.acalib.2007.11.007

Hsu, M. H., Chen, I. Y. L., Chiu, C. M., & Ju, T. L. (2007). Exploring the antecedents of team performance in collaborative learning of computer software. *Computers & Education, 48*(4), 700–718. doi:10.1016/j.compedu.2005.04.018

Huerta-Macias, A. G. (2003). Meeting the challenge of adult education: A bilingual approach to literacy and career development. *Journal of Adolescent & Adult Literacy, 47*(3), 218–226.

Hughes, M. (1993). *Career-oriented program activities and learning experiences that promote achievement of middle-grade education goals*. Unpublished doctoral dissertation, Ohio State University, Columbus, OH.

Hunter, M. (2010, May 7). Anatomical ridicule raises body-scanning concerns. *CNN Travel*, p. A2.

Hurd, D. M. (1987). *The poverty of widows: Future prospects*. Retrieved from http://www.nber.org/papers/w2326

Hutton, S., & Gates, D. (2008). Workplace incivility and productivity losses among direct care staff. *AAOHN Journal, 56*, 168–175. doi:10.3928/08910162-20080401-01

Illeris, K. (2004). *The three dimensions of learning*. Malabar, FL: Krieger Publishing.

Imel, S. (1999). *Work force education: Beyond technical skills (Trends and issues alert no. 1)*. Columbus, OH: ERIC Clearinghouse on Adult, Career, and Vocational Education.

Indabawa, S., & Mpofu, S. (2006). *The social context of adult learning in Africa*. Hamburg, Germany: UNESCO Institute for Education.

Inman, W. E., & Mayes, L. D. (1999). The importance of being first: Unique characteristics of first-generation community college students. *Community College Review, 26*(4), 3–22. doi:10.1177/009155219902600402

International Association of Education Cities. (2009). *Members cities of the IAEC*. Retrieved from http://www.bcn.es/edcities/aice/estatiques/angels/sec_iaec.html

Isaacs, W. (1997). *Dialogue and the art of thinking together: A pioneering approach to communicating in business and in life*. New York, NY: Doubleday.

Ishitani, T. T. (2006). Studying attrition and degree completion behavior among first-generation college students in the United States. *The Journal of Higher Education*, *77*(5), 861–885. doi:10.1353/jhe.2006.0042

Jarvis, P. (1987). *Adult learning in the social context*. New York, NY: Croom Helm.

Jarvis, P. (1995). *Adult and continuing education: Theory and practice*. London, UK: Routledge.

Jarvis, P. (2002). *International dictionary of adult and continuing education*. London, UK: Kogan Page.

Jarvis, P. (2002). Teaching styles and teaching methods. In *The theory & practice of teaching* (pp. 22–30). London: Kogan Page.

Jarvis, P. (2002). *The theory & practice of teaching*. London, UK: Kogan Page.

Jarvis, P. (2004). *Adult education and lifelong learning: Theory and practice* (3rd ed.). London, UK: Routledge.

Jenkins, H. (2007). *Confronting the challenges of participatory culture: media education for the 21st Century*. Chicago: MacArthur Foundation. Retrieved from http://www.digitallearning.macfound.org/atf/cf/%7B7E45C7E0-A3E0-4B89-AC9C-E807E1B0AE4E%7D/JENKINS_WHITE_PAPER.PDF

Johnson, D. W., & Johnson, R. T. (1975). *Learning together and alone: Cooperation, competition and individualization*. Upper Saddle River, NJ: Prentice-Hall.

Johnson, L. G., Schwartz, R. A., & Bower, B. L. (2000). Managing stress among adult women students in community colleges. *Community College Journal of Research and Practice*, *24*, 289–300. doi:10.1080/106689200264079

Johnson, M. E., Fisher, D. G., Davis, D. C., & Cagle, H. H. (1995). Reading abilities of drug users in Anchorage, Alaska. *Journal of Drug Education*, *25*(1), 73–80. doi:10.2190/0314-YCWJ-LX7T-HWL3

Johnson, M. E., Fisher, D. G., Davis, D. C., Cagle, H. H., Rhodes, F., & Booth, R. (1996). Assessing reading level of drug users for HIV and AIDS prevention purposes. *AIDS Education and Prevention*, *8*, 323–334.

Johnson, M. E., Fisher, D. G., & Reynolds, G. L. (1999). Reliability of drug users' self-report of economic variables. *Addiction Research*, *7*, 227–238. doi:10.3109/16066359909004385

Johnson, M. E., Mailloux, S. L., & Fisher, D. G. (1997). The readability of HIV/AIDS educational materials targeted to drug users. *American Journal of Public Health*, *87*(1), 112–113. doi:10.2105/AJPH.87.1.112

Johnson, M. E., Reynolds, G. L., & Fisher, D. G. (2001). Employment status and psychological symptomatology among drug users not currently in treatment. *Evaluation and Program Planning*, *24*, 215–220. doi:10.1016/S0149-7189(01)00011-8

Jonassen, D. H., Howland, J. L., Moore, J. L., & Marra, R. M. (2003). *Learning to solve problems with technology: A constructivist perspective* (2nd ed.). Upper Saddle River, NJ: Merrill.

Kamler, B., & Thomson, P. (2008). The failure of dissertation advice books: Toward alternative pedagogies for doctoral writing. *Educational Researcher*, *37*(8), 507-514.

Kania-Gosche, B. (2010, September). Using the principles of adult learning to facilitate self-directed dissertation writing. In *Proceedings of the 29th Annual Mid West Research to Practice Conference on Adult, Continuing, Community, and Extension Education*, East Lansing, MI.

Kasl, E., Marsick, V. J., & Dechant, K. (1997). Teams as learners: A research-based model of team learning. *The Journal of Applied Behavioral Science*, *33*(2), 227. doi:10.1177/0021886397332010

Kasworm, C. (1990). Adult undergraduates in higher education: A review of past research perspectives. *Review of Educational Research*, *60*(3), 345–375.

Kasworm, C., Polson, C., & Fishback, S. (2002). *Responding to adult learners in higher education*. Malabar, FL: Krieger.

Katz, I. R., & Macklin, A. S. (2007). Information and communication technology (ICT) literacy: integration and assessment in higher education. *Systemics. Cybernetics and Informatics*, *5*(4), 50–55.

Keating, D. P., & Hertzman, C. (1999). *Developmental health and the wealth of nations: Social, biological and educational dynamics*. New York, NY: Guildford Press.

Kegan, R. (2000). What 'form' transforms? A constructivist-developmental approach to transformative learning. In Mezirow, J., (Eds.) et al., *Learning as transformation: Critical perspectives on a theory in progress* (pp. 35–70). San Francisco, CA: Jossey-Bass.

Kember, D. (1999). Integrating part-time study with family, work and social obligations. *Studies in Higher Education*, *24*, 109–124. doi:10.1080/03075079912331380178

Kennedy, G., Dalgarno, B., Bennett, S., Judd, T., Gray, K., et al. (2008). *Immigrants and Natives: Investigating differences between staff and students' use of technology*. Paper presented at Hello! Where are you in the landscape of educational technology? 25th Annual Conference of the Australasian Society for Computers in Learning in Tertiary Education (ASCILITE), Melbourne, Australia.

Kent, S. (2001). Supervision of student teachers: Practices of cooperating teachers prepared in a clinical supervision course. *Journal of Curriculum and Supervision*, *16*(3), 228–244.

Killian, J., & Wilkins, E. (2009). Characteristics of highly effective cooperating teachers: A study of their backgrounds and preparation. *Action in Teacher Education*, *30*(4), 67–83.

Kim, K. A. (2002). Exploring the meaning of "nontraditional" at the community college. *Community College Review*, *30*(1), 74–89. doi:10.1177/009155210203000104

Kim, K. A., Hagedorn, M., & Williamson, J. (2004). *Participation in adult education and lifelong learning 2000-01 (Tech. Rep. No. NCES 2004-50)*. Washington, DC: U.S. Government Printing Office.

King, K. P. (2000). Educational technology that transforms: Educators' transformational learning experiences in professional development. In *Proceedings of the 42nd Annual Adult Education Research Conference*, Vancouver, BC, Canada.

King, J. E. (2003). Nontraditional attendance and persistence: The cost of students' choices. *New Directions for Higher Education*, (121): 69–84. doi:10.1002/he.102

King, K. P. (2005). *Bringing transformative learning to life*. Malabar, FL: Krieger.

Kirshner, D., & Whitson, J. A. (1997). *Situated cognition: Social, semiotic, and psychological Perspectives*. Mahwah, NJ: Erlbaum.

Kirwen, C. M. (1979). *African widows*. New York, NY: Mary Knoll & Orbis Books.

Kitayama, S. (2002). Culture and basic psychological processes—toward a system view of culture: Comment on Oyserman et al. *Psychological Bulletin*, *128*(1), 89–96. doi:10.1037/0033-2909.128.1.89

Kluever, R. C. (1997). Students' attitudes toward the responsibilities and barriers of doctoral study. *New Directions for Higher Education*, *99*, 47–56. doi:10.1002/he.9904

Knight, D., Durham, C. C., & Locke, E. A. (2001). The relationship of team goals, incentives, and efficacy to strategic risk, tactical implementation, and performance. *Academy of Management Journal*, *44*(2), 326–338. doi:10.2307/3069459

Knight, R. V. (1989). City development and urbanization: Building the knowledge-based city. *Urban Affairs Annual Reviews*, *35*, 223–242.

Knight, R. V. (1992). *The future of European cities: The role of science and technology, part IV: Cities as Loci of knowledge-based development (Tech. Rep. No. FOP 379)*. Brussels, Belgium: European Commission.

Knight, R. V. (1995). Knowledge-based development: Policy and planning implications for cities. *Urban Studies (Edinburgh, Scotland)*, *32*(2), 225–260. doi:10.1080/00420989550013068

Knowles, M. S. (1975). *Self-directed learning: A guide for learners and teachers*. New York, NY: Association Press.

Knowles, M. S. (1980). *The modern practice of adult education: From pedagogy to andragogy* (2nd ed.). New York, NY: Cambridge Books.

Knowles, M. S. (1984). *Andragogy in action*. San Francisco, CA: Jossey-Bass.

Knowles, M. S. (1986). *Using learning contracts*. San Francisco, CA: Jossey-Bass.

Knowles, M. S. (1989). *The making of an adult educator*. San Francisco, CA: Jossey-Bass.

Knowles, M. S., Holton, E., & Swanson, A. (2005). *The adult learner* (6th ed.). Oxford, UK: Butterworth-Heinemann/Elsevier.

Knowles, M. S., & Hulda, F. (1973). *Introduction to group dynamics*. Chicago, IL: Follett.

Knox, B. A. (1977). *Adult development and learning*. San Francisco, CA: Jossey Bass.

Kore, D. (2005). *Mai kare gwamraye da marayu* [Protector of widows/widowers and orphans]. Jos, Nigeria: The African Christian Textbooks.

Ko, S., & Rossen, S. (2001). *Teaching online: A practical guide*. Boston: Houghton Mifflin.

Koszalka, T. A., & Ganesan, R. (2004). Designing online courses: A taxonomy to guide strategic use of features available in course management systems (CMS) in distance education. *Distance Education, 25*(2), 243–256. doi:10.1080/0158791042000262111

Kotter, J. P. (1998). What leaders really do. In *Harvard Business Review on Leadership* (pp. 37–60). Boston: Harvard Business School Publishing.

Kozlowski, S., & Ilgen, D. (2007). The science of team success. *Scientific American Mind, 18*(3), 54–61. doi:10.1038/scientificamericanmind0607-54

Kozma, R. (2001). Learning with media. In Clark, R. E. (Ed.), *Learning from media: Arguments, analysis, and evidence* (pp. 179–198). Charlotte, NC: Information Age Publishing.

Kraska, M., & Harris, S. (2007). Cognitive and teaching style preferences of officers attending the Air Force Reserve Office Training Instructor Course. *Journal of Industrial Teacher Education, 44*(5), 5–24.

Kuh, G. D. (2008). *High-impact educational practices: What they are, who has access to them, and why they matter*. Washington, DC: Association of American Colleges and Universities.

Kurniawan, S., & Zaphiris, P. (2005). Research-derived Web design guidelines for older people. In *Proceedings of the 7th International ACM SIGACCESS Conference on Computers and Accessibility*, Baltimore, MD (pp. 129-135).

Kurniawan, S., King, A., Evans, D., & Blenkhorn, P. (2006). Personalising web page presentation for older people. *Interacting with Computers, 18*(3), 457–477. doi:10.1016/j.intcom.2005.11.006

Kutner, M., Greenberg, E., & Baer, J. (2005). *National assessment of adult literacy (NAAL): A first look at the literacy of America's adults in the 21st century (Tech. Rep. No. NCES 2006-470)*. Washington, DC: U.S. Department of Education.

Kutner, M., Greenberg, E., Jin, Y., Boyle, B., Hsu, Y., & Dunleavy, E. (2007). *Literacy in everyday life: Results from the 2003 national assessment of adult literacy*. Washington, DC: U.S. Department of Education.

Kwon, I. T., & Schied, F. M. (2009). *Building communities into lifelong learning cities: The case of the Republic of Korea*. Retrieved from http://www.adulterc.org/Proceedings/2009/proceedings/kwon_schied.pdf

Lantz, A., & Brage, C. (2006). *A learning society/ learning organization*. Paris, France: UNESCO.

Laschinger, H. K., Leiter, M., Day, A., & Gilin, D. (2009). Workplace empowerment, incivility, and burnout: Impact on staff nurse recruitment and retention outcomes. *Journal of Nursing Management, 17*, 309–311.

Laszlo, K. C., & Laszlo, A. (2007). Fostering a sustainable learning society through knowledge-based development. In *Proceedings of the 50th Annual Meeting of the ISSS*.

Latchem, C., & Hanna, D. E. (2001). Leadership in open and flexible learning. In Lathem, C., & Hanna, D. E. (Eds.), *Leadership for 21st Century Learning: Global Perspectives from Educational Innovators* (pp. 53–62). London: Kogan Page Limited.

Lee, K. (2011). Philosopher or philistine? In Wang, V. C. X. (Ed.), *Assessing and evaluating adult learning in career and technical education* (pp. 23–43). Hershey, PA: IGI Global.

Lee, M. J. W., & McLoughlin, C. (Eds.). (2010). *Web 2.0-based e-learning: Applying social informatics for tertiary teaching.* Hershey, PA: Information Science Reference.

Lee, M. J. W., McLoughlin, C., & Chan, A. (2008). Talk the talk: learner-generated podcasts as catalysts for knowledge creation. *British Journal of Educational Technology, 39*(3), 501–521. doi:10.1111/j.1467-8535.2007.00746.x

Lehmann, K., & Chamberlin, L. (2009). *Making the move to elearning: Putting your course online.* Lanham, MD: Rowman & Littlefield.

Leidner, D., & Jarvenpaa, S. (1995). The use of information technology to enhance management school education: A theoretical view. *Management Information Systems Quarterly, 19*, 265–291. doi:10.2307/249596

Leporini, B., & Paternò, F. (2008). Applying Web usability criteria for vision-impaired users: Does it really improve task performance? *International Journal of Human-Computer Interaction, 24*(1), 17–47.

LeVine, R. A. (1984). Properties of culture: Ethnographic view. In Shweder, R. A., & LeVine, R. A. (Eds.), *Culture theory: Essay on mind, self, and emotion* (pp. 67–87). New York: Cambridge University Press.

Levy, S. (2003). Six factors to consider when planning online distance learning programs in higher education. *Online Journal of Distance Learning Administration, 6*(1).

Lewis, T. (1997). America's choice: Literacy or productivity? *Curriculum Inquiry, 27*(4), 391–421. doi:10.1111/0362-6784.00062

Liming, D., & Wolf, M. (2008). *Job outlook by education, 2006-16.* Retrieved from http://www.bls.gov/opub/ooq/2008/fall/art01.pdf

Lim, S., Cortina, L. M., & Magley, V. J. (2008). Personal and workgroup incivility: Impact on work and health outcomes. *The Journal of Applied Psychology, 93*, 95–107. doi:10.1037/0021-9010.93.1.95

Lim, V. K., & Teo, T. S. H. (2009). Mind your e-manners: Impact of cyber incivility on employees' work attitude and behavior. *Information & Management, 46*, 419–425. doi:10.1016/j.im.2009.06.006

Lindemann, E. (1926). *The meaning of adult education.* New York, NY: New Republic.

Lippit, R., & White, R. K. (1958). An experimental study of leadership and group life. In Maccoby, E. E., (Eds.), *Readings in Social Psychology* (3rd ed.). New York: Holt.

Lister, K. (2010). *Telework research network.* Retrieved from http://undress4success.com/research/people-telecommute/

Little, B. L., & Madigan, R. M. (1997). The relationship between collective efficacy and performance in manufacturing work teams. *Small Group Research, 28*(4), 517. doi:10.1177/1046496497284003

Loeb, P., LeVois, M., & Cooper, J. (1981). Increasing employment in ex-heroin addicts II: Methadone maintenance sample. *Behavior Therapy, 12*, 453–460. doi:10.1016/S0005-7894(81)80083-4

Lombard, M., Ditton, T., & Reich, R. (1997). The role of screen size in viewer responses to television fare. *Communication Reports, 10*(1), 95–106.

London, M., & Sessa, V. I. (2007). How groups learn, continuously. *Human Resource Management, 46*(4), 651–670. doi:10.1002/hrm.20186

Longworth, N. (2006). *Learning cities, learning regions, learning communities: Lifelong learning and government.* London, UK: Routledge.

Longworth, N., & Osborne, M. (2010). *Perspectives on learning cities and regions.* Leicester, UK: NIACE.

Lovitts, B. E. (2007). *Making the implicit explicit: Creating performance expectations for the dissertation.* Sterling, VA: Stylus.

Lucas, E. B., Gysbers, N. C., Buescher, K. L., & Heppner, P. P. (1988). My vocational situation: Normative, psychometric, and comparative data. *Measurement & Evaluation in Counseling & Development, 20*, 162–170.

Ludwig, B. (1994). *Internationalizing extension: An exploration of the characteristics evident in a state university extension system that achieves internationalization.* Unpublished doctoral dissertation, Ohio State University, Columbus, OH.

Lynn, G. S., Skov, R. B., & Abel, K. D. (1999). Practices that support team learning and their impact on speed to market and new product success. *Journal of Product Innovation Management, 16*(5), 439–454. doi:10.1016/S0737-6782(98)00071-X

MacArthur, C. A., Konold, T. R., Glutting, J. J., & Alamprese, J. A. (2010). Reading component skills of learners in adult basic education. *Journal of Learning Disabilities, 43*(2), 108–121. doi:10.1177/0022219409359342

Mailloux, S. L., Johnson, M. E., Fisher, D. G., & Pettibone, T. J. (1995). How reliable is computerized assessment of readability. *Computers in Nursing, 13*(5), 221–225.

Malone, T. F., & Yohe, G. W. (2002). Knowledge partnership for sustainable, equitable, and stable society. *Journal of Knowledge Management, 6*(4), 368–378. doi:10.1108/13673270210440875

Marshall, C., & Rossman, G. B. (1999). *Designing qualitative research* (3rd ed.). Thousand Oaks, CA: Sage.

Martinez, A. (2006). A comparative framework for knowledge cities. In Carrillo, F. J. (Ed.), *Knowledge cities: Approaches, experiences and perspectives* (pp. 17–30). Oxford, UK: Butterworth-Heinemann/Elsevier.

Matuga, J. M. (2001). Electronic pedagogical practice: The art and science of teaching and learning on-line. *Journal of Educational Technology & Society, 4*(3), 77–84.

Matuga, J. M. (2005). The role of assessment and evaluation in context: Pedagogical alignment in online courses. In Williams, D. D., Howell, S. L., & Hricko, M. (Eds.), *Online Assessment, Measurement and Evaluation* (pp. 316–330). Hershey, PA: Information Science Reference.

Matuga, J. M. (2007). Self-regulation and online learning: Theoretical issues and practical challenges to support lifelong learning. In Inoue, Y. (Ed.), *Online Education for Lifelong Learning* (pp. 146–168). London: Information Science Publishing.

McAvoy, J., & Butler, T. (2007). The impact of the Abilene Paradox on double-loop learning in an agile team. *Information and Software Technology, 49*(6), 552–563. doi:10.1016/j.infsof.2007.02.012

McCarthy, A., & Garavan, T. N. (2008). Team learning and metacognition: A neglected area of HRD research and practice. *Advances in Developing Human Resources, 10*(4), 509–524. doi:10.1177/1523422308320496

McCaslin, M., & Hickey, D. T. (2001). Self-regulated learning and academic achievement: A Vygotskian view. In Zimmerman, B. J., & Schunk, D. H. (Eds.), *Self-regulated learning and academic achievement: Theoretical perspectives* (pp. 227–252). Mahwah, NJ: Erlbaum.

McCullough, M., Carolane, R., & Hetherington, B. (2003). The experience so far. In *Proceedings of the 43rd Annual National Conference Adult Learning Australia*, Canberra, Australia (pp. 297-311).

McEwan, K. E., & McEwan, J. P. (2003). *Making sense of research. What is good, what is not, and how to tell the difference.* Thousand Oaks, CA: Sage.

McGivney, V. (2004). Understanding persistence in adult learning. *Journal of Open and Distance Learning, 19*(1), 33–46. doi:10.1080/0268051042000177836

McInerney, M. J., & Fink, L. D. (2009). Team-based learning enhances long-term retention and critical thinking in an undergraduate microbial physiology course. *Journal of Microbiology & Biology Education, 4*(1).

McKeachie, W. (2002). *McKeachie's teaching tips: Strategies, research, and theory for college and university teachers* (11th ed.). Boston, MA: Houghton Mifflin.

McLoughlin, C., & Lee, M. J. W. (2008). Future learning landscapes: transforming pedagogy through social software. *Innovate: Journal of Online Education, 4*(5). Retrieved from http://innovateonline.info/index.php?view=article&id=539

Mehlinger, H. D., & Powers, S. M. (2002). *Technology and teacher education: A guide for educators and policymakers.* Boston: Houghton Mifflin Company.

Merriam, S. B. (2001). Andragogy and self-directed learning: Pillars of adult learning theory. *New Directions for Adult and Continuing Education, 89*, 3–13. doi:10.1002/ace.3

Merriam, S. B. (2004). The role of cognitive development in Mezirow's transformational learning theory. *Adult Education Quarterly, 55*(1), 60–68. doi:10.1177/0741713604268891

Merriam, S. B. (2005). How adult life transitions foster learning and development. *New Directions for Adult and Continuing Education, 108*, 3–13. doi:10.1002/ace.193

Merriam, S. B. (2008). Adult learning theory for the twenty-first century. In Merriam, S. B. (Ed.), *Third update on adult learning theory* (pp. 93–98). San Francisco, CA: Jossey-Bass.

Merriam, S. B., & Brockett, R. G. (1997). *The profession and practice of adult education: An introduction.* San Francisco, CA: Jossey-Bass.

Merriam, S. B., & Caffarella, R. S. (1999). *Learning in adulthood.* San Francisco, CA: Jossey-Bass.

Merriam, S. B., & Sek Kim, Y. (2008). Non-Western perspectives on learning and knowing. In Merriam, S. B. (Ed.), *Third update on adult learning theory* (pp. 71–81). San Francisco, CA: Jossey-Bass.

Merrill, M. D. (1991). Constructivism and instructional design. In Duffy, T. M., & Jonassen, D. H. (Eds.), *Constructivism and the technology of instruction: A conversation* (pp. 99–114). Mahwah, NJ: Lawrence Erlbaum.

Mezirow, J. (1978). Education for perspective transformation: Women's re-entry programs in community colleges. New York, NY: Teacher's College, Columbia University.

Mezirow, J. (1981). A critical theory of adult learning and education. Adult Education, 32, 3–24. doi:10.1177/074171368103200101doi:10.1177/074171368103200101

Mezirow, J. (1990). Fostering critical reflection in adulthood: A guide to transformative and emancipatory learning. San Francisco, CA: Jossey-Bass.

Mezirow, J. (1985). A critical theory of self-directed learning. In Brookfield, S. (Ed.), *Self-directed learning: From theory to practice: New directions for continuing education, No. 25.* San Francisco, CA: Jossey-Bass.

Mezirow, J. (1990). *Fostering critical reflection in adulthood: A guide to transformative and emancipatory learning.* San Francisco, CA: Jossey-Bass.

Mezirow, J. (1991). *Transformative dimensions of adult learning.* San Francisco, CA: Jossey-Bass.

Mezirow, J. (2000). Transformative learning. In Mezirow, J., (Eds.) et al., *Learning as transformation* (pp. 1–33). San Francisco, CA: Jossey-Bass.

Mezirow, J. (Ed.). (2000). *Learning as transformation: Critical perspectives on a theory in progress.* San Francisco, CA: Jossey-Bass.

Milby, J. B., Schumacher, J. E., Wallace, D., Vuchinich, R., Mennemeyer, S. T., & Kertesz, S. G. (2010). Effects of sustained abstinence among treated substance-abusing homeless persons on housing and employment. *American Journal of Public Health, 100*, 913–918. doi:10.2105/AJPH.2008.152975

Miller, B., McCardle, P., & Hernandez, R. (2010). Advances and remaining challenges in adult literacy research. *Journal of Learning Disabilities, 43*(2), 101–107. doi:10.1177/0022219409359341

Mintzberg, H. (1998). The manager's job: Folklore and fact. In *Harvard Business Review on Leadership* (pp. 1–36). Boston: Harvard Business School Publishing.

Moreno, S. (1993). *Spanish reading comprehension test.* San Diego, CA: Moreno Educational Co.

Morrell, R. W. (2005). The process of construction and revision in the development of a model site for use by older adults. *Universal Access in the Information Society, 4*(1), 24–38. doi:10.1007/s10209-003-0085-3

Morris, L., & Cranford, S. (2007). Toward a knowledge society in the context of a knowledge economy: Where will we go and how we get there? A global perspective. In *Proceedings of the Commission on International Adult Education and the American Association for Adult and Continuing Education Conference*, Norfolk, VA (pp. 137-149).

Morstain, B., & Smart, J. (1977). A motivational typology of adult learners. *The Journal of Higher Education, 48*(6), 665–679. doi:10.2307/1979011

Mowday, R. T., Steers, R. M., & Porter, L. W. (1979). The measurement of organizational commitment. *Journal of Vocational Behavior, 14*, 224–247. doi:10.1016/0001-8791(79)90072-1

Mullen, C. (2006). *Best writing practices for graduate students: Reducing the discomfort of the blank screen.* Retrieved from http://cnx.org/content/m14054/1.2/

Muller, J. (1986). Where to live? Widow's choices among the Rukuba. In Potash, B. (Ed.), *Widows in African societies: Choices and constrains* (pp. 175–192). Stanford, CA: Stanford University Press.

Murphy, P., Anzalone, S., Bosch, A., & Moulton, J. (2002). *Enhancing learning opportunities in Africa: Distance education and information and communication technologies for learning.* Retrieved from http://siteresources.worldbank.org/INTAFRREGTOPDISEDU/Resources/enhancing.pdf

Murphy, D. A., Roberts, K. J., Hoffman, D., Molina, A., & Lu, M. C. (2003). Barriers and successful strategies to antiretroviral adherence among HIV-infected monolingual Spanish-speaking patients. *AIDS Care, 15*(2), 217–230. doi:10.1080/0954012031000068362

Nafukho, F., Amutabi, N. M., & Otunga, R. (2005). *Foundations of adult education in Africa.* Hamburg, Germany: UNESCO Institute for Education.

Nagel, D. (2009). 10.5 Million preK-12 students will attend classes online by 2014. *The Journal: Transforming Education through Technology.* Retrieved from http://thejournal.com/articles/2009/10/28/10.5-million-prek-12-students-will-attend-classes-online-by-2014.aspx

Nahm, E., Resnick, B., & Covington, B. (2006). Development of theory-based, online health learning modules for older adults: Lessons learned. *CIN: Computers, Informatics. Nursing, 24*(5), 261–268.

National Assessment of Adult Literacy (NAAL). (2003). *The 2003 national assessment of adult literacy.* Retrieved from http://nces.ed.gov/naal/

National Center for Education Statistics. (2003). *National assessment of adult literacy.* Washington, DC: U.S. Department of Education.

National Center for Education Statistics. (2009). *Fast facts.* Retrieved from http://nces.ed.gov/fastfacts/display.asp?id+98

National Center for Education Statistics. (2010). *The condition of education 2010.* Washington, DC: U.S. Department of Education.

National Center for Educational Statistics. (1998). *First-generation students: Undergraduates whose parents never enrolled in postsecondary education.* Washington, DC: U.S. Department of Education.

National Center for Victims of Crime. (2010). *Workplace violence.* Retrieved October 16, 2010, from http://www.ncvc.org/ncvc/Print.aspx

National Economic and Social Development Board, Office of the Prime Minister. (2007). *The tenth national economic and social development plan 2007-2011* (pp. 1–18). Bangkok, Thailand: National Economic and Social Development Board.

National Higher Education Research Institute (NHERI). (2007). *The effectiveness of academic programmes at higher educational institutions (HEIs) towards lifelong learning.* Retrieved from http://www.usm.my/ipptn/fileup/ Lifelong%20Learning.pdf

National Institute on Aging (NIA) & National Library of Medicine. (NLM). (2002). *Making your Web site senior-friendly: A checklist.* Retrieved from http://www.nlm.nih.gov/pubs/checklist.pdf

National Institute on Drug Abuse. (1991). *Risk behavior assessment.* Rockville, MD: National Institute on Drug Abuse (Community Research Branch).

National Institute on Drug Abuse. (1993). *Risk behavior assessment questionnaire.* Rockville, MD: National Institute on Drug Abuse.

Nerad, M., & Miller, D. S. (1997). The institution cares: Berkley's efforts to support dissertation writing in the humanities and social sciences. *New Directions for Higher Education, 99,* 75-90.

Nettles, M. T., & Millett, C. M. (2006). *Three magic letters: Getting to Ph.D.* Baltimore, MD: Johns Hopkins University Press.

Neuman, J. H., & Baron, R. A. (1998). Workplace violence and aggression: Evidence concerning specific forms, potential causes, and preferred targets. *Journal of Management, 24,* 391–419. doi:10.1016/S0149-2063(99)80066-X

New Media Consortium. (2007). *A global imperative: the report of the 21st Century literacy summit.* Retrieved from http://www.nmc.org/pdf/Global_Imperative.pdf

Nielsen, J. (2000). *Why you only need to test with 5 users.* Retrieved from http://www.useit.com/alertbox/20000319.html

Nielsen, J. (2005). *Lower-literacy users.* Retrieved from http://www.useit.com/alertbox/20050314.html

Nilsson, P., & van Driel, J. (2010). Teaching together and learning together–Primary science student teachers' and their mentor' joint teaching and learning in the primary classroom. *Teaching and Teacher Education, 26*(6), 1309–1318. doi:10.1016/j.tate.2010.03.009

Nohria, N., & Berkley, J. D. (1998). Whatever happened to the take-charge manager? In *Harvard Business Review on Leadership* (pp. 199–222). Boston: Harvard Business School Publishing.

Northouse, P. G. (2007). *Leadership theory and practice* (4th ed.). Thousand Oaks, CA: Sage.

Nudel, R. A. (1986). *Starting over: Help for young widows and widowers.* New York, NY: Dadd, Mead & Co.

Nwosu, N. (2010). *Millennium development goals (MDGs): Our journey so far.* Retrieved from http://www.nigeriamasterweb.com/paperfrmes.html

O'Reilly, T. (2005). *What is Web 2.0: design patterns and business models for the next generation of software.* Retrieved from http://www.oreillynet.com/pub/a/oreilly/tim/news/2005/09/30/what-is-web-20.html

Oblinger, D. G., & Oblinger, J. L. (Eds.). (2005). *Educating the net generation.* Washington, DC: EDUCAUSE.

OECD. (1998). *High level seminar on competitive strength and social cohesion through learning cities and regions: Concepts, developments, evaluation.* Paris, France: Center for Research and Innovation.

OECD. (2003). *ICT and Economic Growth: Evidence from OECD countries, industries and firms.* Paris: Author.

Office of the Education Council. (2004). *Learning city.* Bangkok, Thailand: Educational Standards and Learning Development Bureau.

Office of the Education Council. (2008). *Research study on evaluation process of education for learning society promotion.* Bangkok, Thailand: Ministry of Education.

Okoye, U. P. (1995). *Widowhood: A natural cultural tragedy.* Enugu, Nigeria: Nucik Publishers.

Olgren, C. H. (1998). Improving learning outcomes: The effects of learning strategies and motivation. In Gibson, C. C. (Ed.), *Distance learners in higher education: Institutional responses for quality outcomes* (pp. 77–95). Madison, WI: Atwood Publishing.

Omolewa, M. A. (1981). *Adult education practice in Nigeria.* Ibadan, Nigeria: Evans Brothers.

Omolewa, M. A. (1997). Literacy, income generation, and poverty alleviation. *CARESON Journal of Research and Development, 1*(1), 1–17.

Organista, P. B., Organista, K. C., & Kurasaki, K. (2002). The relationship betwen acculturation and ethnic minority mental health. In Chun, K. M., Organista, P. B., & Marín, G. (Eds.), *Acculturation: Advances in theory, measurement, and applied research* (pp. 139–161). Washington, DC: American Psychological Association.

Osika, E. (2006). The concentric support model: A model for planning and evaluation of distance learning programs. *Online Journal of Distance Learning Administration, 9*(3). Retrieved from http://www.westga.edu/~distance/ojdla/fall93/osika93.htm.

Padula, M. A. (1994). Reentry women: A literature review with recommendations for counseling and research. *Journal of Counseling and Development, 73,* 10–16.

Pallof, R., & Pratt, K. (1999). *Building learning communities in cyberspace.* San Francisco, CA: Jossey-Bass.

Parker, J. (2009). Adult learning and CTE: A shared history influenced by technology. In Wang, V. C. X. (Ed.), *Definitive readings in the history, philosophy, practice and theories of career and technical education* (pp. 215–234). Hershey, PA: IGI Global.

Parker, J. (2010). Technology as integral to a new paradigm of adult education. *International Journal of Adult Vocational Education and Technology, 1*(2), 10–18. doi:10.4018/javet.2010040102

Parker-Katz, M., & Bay, M. (2008). Conceptualizing mentor knowledge: Learning from the insiders. *Teaching and Teacher Education, 24*(5), 1259–1269. doi:10.1016/j.tate.2007.05.006

Parkes, M. C. (1964). Effects of bereavement on physical mental health: A study of medical records of widows. *British Medical Journal, 2*(5404), 274–279. doi:10.1136/bmj.2.5404.274

Pascarella, E., & Terenzini, P. (1991). *How college affects students*. San Francisco, CA: Jossey-Bass.

Patton, M. Q. (2002). *Qualitative research and evaluation methods* (3rd ed.). Thousand Oaks, CA: Sage.

Pawlowsky, P. (2001). The treatment of organizational learning in management science. *Handbook of Organizational Learning and Knowledge*, 61-88.

Pearson, C. M., Andersson, L. M., & Porath, C. L. (2000). Assessing and attacking workplace incivility. *Organizational Dynamics, 29*, 123–137. doi:10.1016/S0090-2616(00)00019-X

Pena, C., & Almaguer, I. (2007). Asking the right questions: Online mentoring of student teachers. *International Journal of Instructional Media, 34*(1), 105–113.

Pennington, F., & Green, J. (1976). A comparative analysis of program development processes in six professions. *Adult Education, 27*(1), 13–23. doi:10.1177/074171367602700102

Petty, G. C., & Brewer, E. W. (2005). Perspectives of a healthy work ethic in a 21st-century international community. *International Journal of Vocational Education and Training, 13*(1), 93–104.

Piaget, J. (1967). The mental development of the child. In Elkind, D. (Ed.), *Six psychological studies by Piaget*. New York, NY: Random House.

Picciano, A. G. (2002). Beyond student perceptions: Issues interaction, presence and performance in an online course. *Journal of Asynchronous Learning Networks, 6*, 20–41.

Piskurich, G. (2006). *Rapid instructional design*. New York, NY: John Wiley & Sons.

Platt, J. J. (1995). Vocational rehabilitation of drug abusers. *Psychological Bulletin, 117*, 416–433. doi:10.1037/0033-2909.117.3.416

Platt, J. J., Husband, S. D., Hermalin, J., Cater, J., & Metzger, D. (1993). A cognitive problem-solving employment readiness intervention for methadone clients. *Journal of Cognitive Psychotherapy, 7*, 21–33.

Platt, J. J., Widman, M., Lidz, V., Rubenstein, D., & Thompson, R. (1998). The case for support services in substance abuse treatment. *The American Behavioral Scientist, 41*, 1050–1062. doi:10.1177/0002764298041008003

Poell, R. F., Yorks, L., & Marsick, V. J. (2009). Organizing project-based learning in work contexts: A cross-cultural cross analysis of data from two projects. *Adult Education Quarterly, 60*(1), 77. doi:10.1177/0741713609334138

Pongpaiboon, P. (2007). *Learning society*. Retrieved from http://learners.in.th/blog/yardnapa2/15632

Pope, J. (2006). *Number of students taking online courses rises*. Retrieved from http://www.usatoday.com/tech/news/2006-11-09-online-learning_x.htm

Porath, C. L., & Pearson, C. M. (2010). The cost of bad behavior. *Organizational Dynamics, 39*, 64–71. doi:10.1016/j.orgdyn.2009.10.006

Portes, A., & Rumbaut, R. G. (2001). *Legacies: The story of the immigrant second generation*. Berkeley, CA: Unversity of California Press.

Pratt, D. D. (1988). Andragogy as a relational construct. *Adult Education Quarterly, 38*, 160–181. doi:10.1177/0001848188038003004

Pratt, D. D. (1993). Andragogy after twenty-five years. *New Directions for Adult and Continuing Education*, 57.

Price, D. M. (1999). Philosophy and the adult learner. *Adult Learning, 11*(2), 3–5.

Prichard, J. S., & Ashleigh, M. J. (2007). The effects of team-skills training on transactive memory and performance. *Small Group Research, 38*(6), 696. doi:10.1177/1046496407304923

Puzziferro, M., & Shelton, K. (2009). Supporting online faculty – Revisiting the seven principles (A few years later). *Online Journal of Distance Learning Adminsration, 12*(3). Retrieved from http://www.westga.edu/~distance/ojdla/fall123/puzziferro123.html

Raelin, J. A. (2008). *Work-based learning: Bridging knowledge and action in the workplace*. San Francisco, CA: Jossey-Bass.

Ramirez, R. R., & Cruz, P. D. 1. (2003). *The Hispanic population in the United States: March 2002*. Washington, DC: U.S. Department of Commerce.

Ravert, R. D. (2007). College student preferences for absolute knowledge and perspective in instruction: Implications for traditional and online learning environments. *Quarterly Review of Distance Education, 8*(4), 321–328.

Reay, D. (1998). 'Always knowing' or 'never being sure': Institutional and familial habituses and higher education choice. *Journal of Education Policy, 13*, 519–529. doi:10.1080/0268093980130405

Reay, D. (2002). Class, authenticity and the transition to higher education for mature students. *The Sociological Review, 50*(3), 398–418. doi:10.1111/1467-954X.00389

Rees, D. W. (1971). The hallucination of widowhood. *British Medical Journal, 4*(5778), 37–41. doi:10.1136/bmj.4.5778.37

Reio, T. G. Jr, & Ghosh, R. (2009). Antecedents and outcomes of workplace incivility: Implications for human resource development and practice. *Human Resource Development Quarterly, 20*, 237–264. doi:10.1002/hrdq.20020

Relan, A., & Gillani, B. B. (1997). Web-based instruction and the traditional classroom: Similarities and differences. In Khan, B. H. (Ed.), *Web-based instruction* (pp. 41–46). Englewood Cliffs, NJ: Educational Technology Publications.

Report, H. (2010). *2010 horizon report*. Retrieved from http://wp.nmc.org/horizon2010/

Reynolds, G. L., Theno, S. A., Fisher, D. G., Fenaughty, A. M., Johnson, M. E., & Schlicting, E. G. (1999, November). *Depression and unemployment among Alaskan drug users*. Paper presented at the 127th Annual Meeting of the American Public Health Association, Chicago, IL.

Rhode, J. F. (2009). Interaction equivalency in self-paced online learning environments: An exploration of learner preferences. *International Review of Research in Open and Distance Learning, 10*(1), 1–23.

Rice, R. E. (1992). Task analyzability, use of new media, and effectiveness: A multi-site exploration of media richness. *Organization Science, 3*, 475–500. doi:10.1287/orsc.3.4.475

Rice, R. E., Hiltz, S. R., & Spencer, D. H. (2005). Media mixes and learning networks. In Hiltz, S. R., & Goldman, R. (Eds.), *Learning together online: Research on asynchronous learning networks* (pp. 215–237). Mahwah, NJ: Lawrence Erlbaum.

Richardson, J. T. E. (1994). Mature students in higher education: I. A literature survey on approaches to studying. *Studies in Higher Education, 19*(3), 309–323. doi:10.1080/03075079412331381900

Richardson, J. T. E. (1995). Mature students in higher education: II. An investigation of approaches to studying and academic performance. *Studies in Higher Education, 20*(1), 5–17. doi:10.1080/03075079512331381760

Richardson, J. T. E., & King, E. (1998). Adult students in higher education: Burden or boon? *The Journal of Higher Education, 69*(1), 65–89. doi:10.2307/2649182

Ritt, E. (2008). *Redefining tradition: Adult learners and higher education*. Retrieved from http://eric.ed.gov/ERICWebPortal/ recordDetail?accno=EJ860772

Rivera-Batiz, F. L. (1995). *The impact of vocational education on racial and ethnic minorities*. New York, NY: ERIC Clearinghouse on Urban Education.

Robertson, D. L. (1991). Gender differences in the academic progress of adult undergraduates: Patterns and policy implications. *Journal of College Student Development, 32*, 490–496.

Roberts, T. S. (2005). Computer-supported collaborative learning in higher education: An introduction. In Roberts, T. S. (Ed.), *Computer-supported collaborative learning in higher education* (pp. 1–18). Hershey, PA: IGI Global.

Robinson, H. J. (1995). Grief response, coping processes, and social support of widows: Research with Roys' Model. *Nursing Science Quarterly, 8*(4), 158–164. doi:10.1177/089431849500800406

Rogers, A. (2002). *Teaching adults*. Berkshire, UK: Open University Press.

Rogers, C. R. (1951). *Client-centered therapy*. Boston: Houghton-Mifflin.

Rogers, C. R. (1961). *On become a person*. Boston: Houghton-Mifflin.

Rogers, C. R. (1969). *Freedom to learn*. Columbus, OH: Merrill.

Rogers, C. R. (1980). *A way of being*. Boston: Houghton Mifflin.

Rogler, L. H., Cortés, D., & Malgady, R. G. (1991). Acculturation and mental health status among Hispanics: Convergence and new directions for research. *The American Psychologist*, *46*, 585–597. doi:10.1037/0003-066X.46.6.585

Rogoff, B. (1990). *Apprenticeship in thinking: Cognitive development in social context*. New York: Oxford University Press.

Rosaldo, M. Z. (1984). Toward an anthropology on self and feeling. In Shweder, R. A., & LeVine, R. A. (Eds.), *Culture theory: Essay on mind, self, and emotion* (pp. 137–157). New York: Cambridge University Press.

Rosalso, R. I. Jr. (1999). A note on Geertz as a cultural essayist. In Ortner, S. B. (Ed.), *The fate of "culture": Geertz and beyond* (pp. 30–34). Los Angeles: University of California Press.

Rose, M., & McClafferty, K. A. (2001). A call for the teaching of writing in graduate education. *Educational Researcher*, *30*(2), 27–33. doi:10.3102/0013189X030002027

Ross, H. (1992). Foreign languages education as a barometer of modernization. In Hayhoe, R. (Ed.), *Education and modernization: The Chinese experience* (pp. 239–254). New York, NY: Pergamon Press.

Sadler, T. (2006). "I won't last three weeks": Preservice science teachers reflect on their student-teaching experiences. *Journal of Science Teacher Education*, *17*, 217–241. doi:10.1007/s10972-005-9004-1

Sangsri, S. (2005). *The development of learning communities/ cities for Thai society. Bangkok: Learning policy development group in local wisdom and traveling*. Bangkok, Thailand: Standards and Learning Bureau.

Savelsbergh, C., van der Heijden, B., & Poell, R. F. (2009). The development and empirical validation of a multidimensional measurement instrument for team learning behaviors. *Small Group Research*, *40*(5), 578. doi:10.1177/1046496409340055

Sayago, S., & Blat, J. (2009). About the relevance of accessibility barriers in the everyday interactions of older people with the web. In *Proceedings of the International Cross-Disciplinary Conference on Web Accessibility*, Madrid, Spain (pp. 104-113).

Schein, E. (2010). *Organizational culture and leadership* (4th ed.). San Francisco, CA: Jossey-Bass.

Schifter, C. (2004). Faculty participation in distance education programs: Practices and plans. In Monolescu, D., Schifter, C. C., & Greenwood, L. (Eds.), *The distance education evolution: Issues and case studies* (pp. 22–39). Hershey, PA: Information Science Publishing.

Schildkrout, E. (1986). Widows in Hausa society: Ritual phase or social status. In Potash, B. (Ed.), *Widows in African societies: Choices and constrains* (pp. 131–152). Stanford, CA: Stanford University Press.

Schlicting, E. G., Johnson, M. E., Brems, C., Wells, R., Fisher, D. G., & Reynolds, G. L. (2003). Validity of injecting drug users' self report of Hepatitis A, B, and C. *Clinical Laboratory Science*, *16*(2), 99–106.

Scholtes, P. R., Joiner, B. L., & Streibel, B. J. (2003). *The team handbook* (3rd ed.). Madison, WI: Oriel Incorporated.

Schonfeld, E. (2009). *Techcrunch*. Retrieved from http:// techcrunch.com/ 2009/01/23/ comscore- internet- population- passes- one- billion- top- 15- countries/

Schottenfeld, R. S., Pantalon, M. V., Chawarski, M. C., & Pakes, J. (2000). Community reinforcement approach for combined opioid and cocaine dependence: Patterns of engagement in alternative activities. *Journal of Substance Abuse Treatment*, *18*, 255–261. doi:10.1016/S0740-5472(99)00062-8

Schrum, L. M., & Levin, B. B. (2009). *Leading 21st-century schools: Harnessing technology for engagement and achievement*. Thousand Oaks, CA: Corwin Press.

Schrum, L., & Levin, B. (2009). *Leading 21st Century schools: Harnessing technology for engagement and achievement*. Thousand Oak, CA: Corwin.

Senesh, L. (1991). *Building a learning society.* Retrieved from http://www.ERIC.org

Senge, P. M. (1990). *The fifth discipline: The art and practice of the learning organization.* New York, NY: Doubleday.

Servellen, G. V., Brown, J. S., Lombardi, E., & Herrera, G. (2003). Health literacy in low-income Latin men and women receiving antiretroviral therapy in community-based treatment centers. *AIDS Patient Care and STDs, 17*(6), 283–298. doi:10.1089/108729103322108166

Servellen, G. V., Carpio, F., Lopez, M., Garcia-Teague, L., Herrera, G., & Monterrosa, F. (2003). Program to enhance health literacy and treatment adherence in low-income HIV infected Latino men and women. *AIDS Patient Care and STDs, 17*(11), 581–594. doi:10.1089/108729103322555971

Shanghai Civil Affair Bureau (SCAB). Shanghai Bureau for Senior Citizens' Work (SBSC), & Shanghai Statistic Bureau (SSB). (2009). *2009 annual report of the development of senior citizens' work in Shanghai.* Retrieved from http://www.shanghai60.org.cn/newsinfo.aspx?id=363

Shanghai Civil Affairs Bureau (SCAB). (2009). *2008 aging population and affairs. Monitoring Statistics.* Retrieved from http://www.shmzj.gov.cn/gb/shmzj/node6/node592/node596/userobject1ai22218.html

Shanghai Municipal Committee (SMC). (2006). *Guidelines on promoting the building of a learning society issued by CPC Shanghai Municipal Committee.* Retrieved from http://www.shanghai.gov.cn

Sharit, J., Hernández, M. A., Czaja, S. J., & Pirolli, P. (2008). Investigating the roles of knowledge and cognitive abilities in older adult information seeking on the Web. *ACM Transactions on Computer-Human Interaction, 15*(1), 1–25. doi:10.1145/1352782.1352785

Sharpe, R., Benfield, G., Roberts, G., & Francis, R. (2006). *The undergraduate experience of blended e-learning: a review of UK literature and practice.* York, UK: The Higher Education Academy.

Shepard, D. S., & Reif, S. (2004). The value of vocational rehabilitation in substance user treatment: A cost-effectiveness framework. *Substance Use & Misuse, 39*, 2581–2609. doi:10.1081/JA-200034732

Shirky, C. (2003). *Social software and the politics of groups.* Retrieved November 2, 2010, from http://www.shirky.com/writings/group_politics.html

Shoffner, M. B., Jones, M., & Harmon, S. W. (2000). Paradigms restrained: Implications of new and emerging technologies for learning and cognition. *Journal of Electronic Publishing, 6.*

Short, J., Williams, E., & Christie, B. (1976). *The social psychology of telecommunications.* London, UK: Wiley.

Sibmuenpiam, N. (2003). *The development of learning city model: Local administrative organization, Chonburi Province.* Bangkok, Thailand: Chulalongkorn University.

Silver-Pacuilla, H. (2006). Access and benefits: Assistive technology in adult literacy. *Journal of Adolescent & Adult Literacy, 50*(2), 114–125. doi:10.1598/JAAL.50.2.4

Simmons, D. E. (2002). The forum report: E-learning adoption rates and barriers. In Rossett, A. (Ed.), *The ASTD E-learning handbook* (pp. 19–23). New York, NY: McGraw-Hill.

Sims, R., & Jones, D. (2002, December). *Continuous improvement through shared understanding: Reconceptualizing instructional design for online learning.* Paper presented at ASCILITE 2002, Auckland, New Zealand.

Singh, J., Verbeke, W., & Rhoads, G. K. (1996). Do organizational practices matter in role stress processes? A study of direct and moderating effects for marketing oriented boundary spanners. *Journal of Marketing, 60*, 69–86. doi:10.2307/1251842

Slattery, P. (1995). *Curriculum development in the postmodern era.* New York, NY: Garland Reference Library of Social Science.

Slavin, E. R. (2007). *Educational research: In an age of accountability.* Boston, MA: Pearson.

Slavin, R. E. (1987). *Cooperative learning: Student teams* (2nd ed.). Washington, DC: National Educational Association.

Smart, K. L., & Cappel, J. J. (2006). Students' perceptions of online learning: A comparative study. *Journal of Information Technology Education, 5*, 201–219.

Sork, T. J. (2000). Planning educational programs. In Wilson, A. L., & Hayes, E. R. (Eds.), *Handbook of adult and continuing education* (pp. 171–190). San Francisco, CA: Jossey-Bass.

Spillett, M. A., & Moisiewicz, K. A. (2004). Cheerleader, coach, counselor, critic: Support and challenge roles of the dissertation adviser. *College Student Journal, 38*(2), 246-256.

Spitzer, T. M. (2000). Predictors of college success: A comparison of traditional and nontraditional age students. *NASPA Journal, 38*(1), 82–98.

Stacey, E. (2005). A constructivist framework for online collaborative learning: Adult learning and collaborative learning theory. In Roberts, T. S. (Ed.), *Computer supported collaborative learning in higher education* (pp. 140–161). Hershey, PA: IGI Global.

Steffgen, G., & Ewen, N. (2007). Teachers as victims of school violence-The influence of strain and school culture. *International Journal of Violence and Schools, 3*, 81–93.

Stitt-Gohdes, W. L., & Crews, T. B. (2004). The Delphi technique: A research strategy for career and technical education. *Journal of Career and Technical Education, 20*(2), 1–11.

Street, B. (2007). *Literacy and development: Ethnographic perspectives*. London, UK: Routledge.

Streiff, L. D. (1986). Can clients understand our instructions? *Journal of Nursing Scholarship, 18*(2), 48–52. doi:10.1111/j.1547-5069.1986.tb00542.x

Stromquist, P. N. (1988). Women's education in development: From welfare to empowerment. *Convergence, 21*(4), 5–16.

Su, Y. H. (2007). *The learning society as itself: Lifelong learning, individualization of learning, and beyond education*. Retrieved from http://www.ERIC.org

Sullivan, P. (2002). It's easier to be yourself when you are invisible: Female college students discuss their online classroom experiences. *Innovative Higher Education, 27*, 129–143. doi:10.1023/A:1021109410893

Sutphin, H. (1981). *Positions held by teachers, teacher educators, and state supervisors about selected national issues in agricultural education*. Unpublished doctoral dissertation, Ohio State University, Columbus, OH.

Szirony, G. M. (1997). *MMPI-2 work interference difference among incarcerated substance abusers*. Unpublished doctoral dissertation, Kent State University, Kent, OH.

Tabachnick, B. G., & Fidell, L. S. (2007). *Using multivariate statistics* (5th ed.). Boston, MA: Allyn & Bacon.

Talab, R., & Butler, R. (2007). Shared electronic spaces in the classroom. *TechTrends, 51*(1), 12–14. doi:10.1007/s11528-007-0004-1

Tallent-Runnels, M. K., Thomas, J. A., Lan, W. Y., Cooper, S., Ahern, T. C., & Shaw, S. M. (2006). Teaching courses online: A review of the research. *Review of Educational Research, 76*(1), 93–135. doi:10.3102/00346543076001093

Taniguchi, H., & Kaufman, G. (2005). Degree completion among nontraditional college students. *Social Science Quarterly, 86*(4), 912–927. doi:10.1111/j.0038-4941.2005.00363.x

Taylor, V. (2004). Online group projects: Preparing the instructors to prepare the students. In Roberts, T. S. (Ed.), *Computer supported collaborative learning in higher education*. Hershey, PA: IGI Global. doi:10.4018/978-1-59140-408-8.ch002

Teal, T. (1998). The human side of management. In *Harvard Business Review on Leadership* (pp. 147–170). Boston: Harvard Business School Publishing.

Terenzini, P. T., Springer, L., Yaeger, P. M., Pascarella, E. T., & Nora, P. M. (1996). First-generation college students: Characteristics, experiences, and cognitive development. *Research in Higher Education, 37*(1), 1–22. doi:10.1007/BF01680039

The United Way of Greater Los Angeles. (2004). *Literacy at work: The L.A workforce literacy project*. Los Angeles, CA: Literacy Network of Greater Los Angeles.

Tjosvold, D., Yu, Z., & Hui, C. (2004). Team learning from mistakes: The contribution of cooperative goals and problem-solving. *Journal of Management Studies, 41*(7), 1223–1245. doi:10.1111/j.1467-6486.2004.00473.x

Toffler, A. (1971). *Future shock*. New York: Bantam Books.

Toffler, A. (1980). *The third wave*. New York: Morrow.

Toffler, A. (1990). *Powershift: Knowledge, wealth, and violence at the edge of the 21ˢᵗ century*. New York: Bantam Books.

Tough, A. (1967). Learning without a teacher. *Educational Research Series, 3*.

Tough, A. (1971). *The adult's learning project*. Toronto, ON, Canada: Ontario Institute for Studies in Education.

Trimble, J. (2002). Introduction: Social change and acculturation. In Chun, K. M., Organista, P. B., & Marín, G. (Eds.), *Acculturation: Advances in theory, measurement, and applied research* (pp. 3–13). Washington, DC: American Psychological Association.

Truemen, M., & Hartley, J. (1996). A comparison between the time-management skills and academic performance of mature and traditional-entry university students. *Higher Education, 32*(2), 199–215. doi:10.1007/BF00138396

Tuckman, B. W. (1965). Developmental sequences in small groups. *Psychological Bulletin, 63*, 348–399. doi:10.1037/h0022100

Tuttle, T. (2005). *Part-time students: Enrollment and persistence in state of Indiana*. Bloomington, IN: Indiana Project on Academic Success (IPAS).

Tu, W. M. (1979). *Humanity and self-cultivation: essays in Confucian thought*. Berkeley, CA: Asian Humanities Press.

Twigg, C. (1994). The need for a national learning infrastructure. *Educause, 29*(4-6).

Tyler, R. W. (1949). *Basic principles of curriculum and instruction*. Chicago, IL: University of Chicago Press.

U.S. Census Bureau. (1996). *Population projections of the United States by age, sex, race, and Hispanic origin: 1995 to 2050*. Washington, DC: U.S. Department of Commerce.

U.S. Census Bureau. (2001). *The Hispanic population 2000* (Tech. Rep. No. C2KBR/01-3). Washington, DC: U.S. Department of Commerce.

U.S. Census Bureau. (2010). *Hispanic heritage month 2010: Sept. 15 - Oct. 15*. Retrieved from http://www.census.gov/newsroom/releases/pdf/cb10ff-17_hispanic.pdf

U.S. Department of Health and Human Services. (2004). *Adult and family literacy: Current and future research directions—a workshop summary*. Washington, DC: U.S. Department of Health and Human Services.

Ubell, R. (2010). *Virtual teamwork: Mastering the art and practice of online learning and corporate collaboration*. Hoboken, NJ: John Wiley & Sons. doi:10.1002/9780470615782

Ulschak, F. L. (1983). *Human resource development: The theory and practice of need assessment* (pp. 111–131). Reston, VA: Reston Publishing.

UNESCO Institute for Lifelong Learning (UIL). (2009). *Global report on adult learning and education*. Hamburg, Germany: UNESCO Institute for Lifelong Learning.

Unesco Institute for Statistics. (2007). *Regional literacy rates for youths (15-24) and adults (25+)*. Retrieved from http://stats.uis.unesco.org/unesco/ TableViewer/tableView.aspx?ReportId=201

UNESCO. (1997). *The Hamburg declaration on adult learning*. Paper presented at the Fifth International Conference on Adult Education.

UNESCO. (2001). *Handbook: Non-formal adult education facilitators*. Bangkok, Thailand: UNESCO Asian-Pacific Programme of Education for All.

UNESCO. (2003). *Nurturing the treasure - vision and strategy of the UNESCO institute for education 2002-2007*. Retrieved from http://www.unesco.org/education/uie/pdf/MTS.pdf

UNESCO. (2003). *World education forum: Final report*. Paris, France: UNESCO.

UNESCO. (2005). *Towards knowledge societies*. Retrieved from http://www.unesco.org/en/worldreport

UNESCO. (2009). *Trends in Global Higher Education: Tracking an academic revolution*. Paris: Author.

United Nations. (1981). *Popular participation as a strategy for planning community level action and national development*. New York, NY: United Nations.

Van de Sompel, H., & Hochstenbach, P. (1999). Reference linking in a hybrid library environment. *D-Lib Magazine*, *5*(4). doi:10.1045/april99-van_de_sompel-pt1

Van den Bossche, P., Gijselaers, W. H., Segers, M., & Kirschner, P. A. (2006). Social and cognitive factors driving teamwork in collaborative learning environments: Team learning beliefs and behaviors. *Small Group Research*, *37*(5), 490. doi:10.1177/1046496406292938

Vartia, M. A. (2001). Consequences of workplace bullying with respect to the well-being of its targets and the observers of bullying. *Scandinavian Journal of Work, Environment & Health*, *27*, 63–69.

Vendel, M. (2009). *Universal mobile interface: The importance of the mobile phone to developing countries.* Retrieved from http://universalmobileinterface.wordpress.com/ 2009/04/07/ the-importance-of-the-mobile-phone-to-developing-countries/

Vines, J. A., & Mandell, C. J. (1999). Characteristics of female alcohol and drug substance users engaged in treatment programs. *Journal of Applied Rehabilitation Counseling*, *30*, 35–43.

Von Krogh, G., Nonaka, I., & Ichijo, K. (2000). *Enabling knowledge creation: New tools for unlocking the mysteries of tacit understanding.* New York, NY: Oxford University Press.

Vygotsky, L. (1978). *Mind in society.* Boston, MA: Harvard University Press.

Waggoner, C. (2003). Teachers behaving badly. *The American School Board Journal*, *90*(8), 29–31.

Wagner, D. A., & Venezky, R. L. (1999). Adult literacy: The next generation. *Educational Researcher*, *28*(1), 21–29.

Walters, S. (2005). Learning region. In English, L. M. (Ed.), *International encyclopedia of adult education* (pp. 360–362). Hampshire, UK: Palgrave Macmillan.

Walther, J. B., Slovacek, C. L., & Tidwell, L. C. (2001). Is a picture worth a thousand words? Photographic images in long-term and short-term computer-mediated communication. *Communication Research*, *28*(1), 105–134. doi:10.1177/009365001028001004

Wang, V. (2003). *Principles of adult education.* Boston, MA: Pearson.

Wang, V. (2005). Adult education reality: Three generations, different transformation the impact of social context: Three generations of Chinese adult learners. *New York Journal of Adult Learning*, *3*(1), 17–32.

Wang, V. C. (2010). Critical components of curriculum development for career and technical education instructors in the United States. *International Journal of Adult Education and Technology*, *1*(1), 72–89. doi:10.4018/javet.2010100905

Wang, V. C. X. (2005). Perceptions of the teaching preferences of online instructors. *Journal on Excellence in College Teaching*, *16*(3), 33–53.

Wang, V. C. X. (2006). *Essential elements for andragogical styles and methods: How to create andragogical modes in adult education.* Boston: Pearson Education.

Wang, V. C. X. (2007). Chinese knowledge transmitters or western learning facilitators adult teaching methods compared. In King, K. P., & Wang, V. C. X. (Eds.), *Comparative adult education around the globe* (pp. 113–1370). Hangzhou, China: Zhejiang University Press.

Wang, V. C. X. (2008). *Facilitating adult learning: A comprehensive guide for successful instruction.* Boston, MA: Pearson Education.

Wang, V. C. X., & Farmer, L. (2008). Adult teaching methods in China and Bloom's taxonomy. *International Journal for the Scholarship of Teaching and Learning*, *2*(2), 1–15.

Wang, V. C. X., & King, K. (2009). *Building workforce competencies in career and technical education.* Charlotte, NC: Information Age Publishing.

Wang, V. C. X., & King, K. (Eds.). (2008). *Innovations in career and technical education: Strategic approaches towards workforce competencies around the globe.* Charlotte, NC: Information Age Publishing.

Wang, V., & Bott, P. A. (2004). Modes of teaching of Chinese adult educators. *New York Journal of Adult Learning*, *2*(2), 32–51.

Wang, V., & King, K. P. (2006). Understanding Mezirow's theory of reflectivity from Confucian perspectives: A model and perspective. *Radical Pedagogy*, *8*(1), 1–17.

Wang, V., & Sarbo, L. (2004). Philosophy, role of adult educators, and learning how contextually adapted philosophies and the situational role of adult educators affect learners' transformation and emancipation. *Journal of Transformative Education, 2*(3), 204–214. doi:10.1177/1541344604265105

Watkins, K. E., & Marsick, V. J. (1993). *Sculpting the learning organization: Lessons in the art and science of systemic change*. San Francisco, CA: Jossey-Bass.

Watkins, K., & Marsick, V. (1990). *Informal and incidental learning in the workplace*. London, UK: Routledge.

Watkins, R. (2005). Developing interactive e-learning activities. *Performance Improvement, 44*, 5–7. doi:10.1002/pfi.4140440504

Weaver, D., & Stanulis, R. (1996). Negotiating preparation and practice: Student teaching in the middle. *Journal of Teacher Education, 47*(1), 27–36. doi:10.1177/0022487196047001006

Web Accessibility Initiative (WAI). (1999). *Accessibility guidelines*. Retrieved from http://www.w3.org/wai

Wendler, C., Bridgeman, B., Cline, F., Millett, C., Rock, J., Bell, N., & McAllister, P. (2010). *The path forward: The future of graduate education in the United States*. Princeton, NJ: Educational Testing Service.

Wenger, D. M. (1987). Transactive memory: A contemporary analysis of the group mind. *Theories of Group Behavior*, 185-208.

Wertsch, J. V. (1985). *Vygotsky and the social formation of mind*. Cambridge, MA: Harvard University Press.

Westby, C. (1997). There's more to passing than knowing the answers. *Language, Speech, and Hearing Services in Schools, 28*(3), 274–286.

West, S. (2008). The utilization of vocational rehabilitation services in substance abuse treatment facilities in the U.S. *Journal of Vocational Rehabilitation, 29*, 71–75.

Wheatley, M. (1999). *Leadership and the new science: Discovering order in a chaotic World* (2nd ed.). San Francisco, CA: Berrett-Koehler Publishers.

Wheatley, P. (2004). *Institutional repositories within the context of digital preservation*. York, UK: Digital Preservation Coalition.

Wheeler, S., Yeomans, P., & Wheeler, S. (2008). The good, the bad and the wiki: Evaluating student-generated content for collaborative learning. *British Journal of Educational Technology, 39*(6), 987–995. doi:10.1111/j.1467-8535.2007.00799.x

White, R. (n.d.). *Four myths about online learning*. Retrieved from http://www.learnnc.org/lp/pages/2720

White, L. A. (1975). *The concept of cultural systems: A key to understanding tribes and nations*. New York: Columbia University Press.

Wick, D. A. (2004). Older adults and their information seeking. *Behavioral & Social Sciences Librarian, 22*(2), 1–26. doi:10.1300/J103v22n02_01

Windham, C. (2005). The student's perspective. In Oblinger, D. G., & Oblinger, J. L. (Eds.), *Educating the Net Generation* (pp. 5.1–5.16). Washington, DC: EDUCAUSE.

Wirz, D. (2004). Students' learning styles vs. professors' teaching styles. *Inquiry, 9*(1).

Wiseman, L., & McKeown, G. (2010). *Multipliers: How the best leaders make everyone smarter*. New York, NY: HarperCollins.

Witkin, B. R. (1984). *Assessing needs in educational and social programs*. San Francisco, CA: Jossey-Bass.

Wolcott, F. H. (1990). On seeking-and-rejecting – validity in qualitative research. In Eisner, E. W., & Peshkin, A. (Eds.), *Qualitative inquiry in education* (pp. 121–152). New York, NY: Teachers College Press.

World Bank. (1998). *Knowledge for development*. Retrieved from http://www.worldbank.org/wdr/wdr98

World Education Services. (2006). *WES grade conversion guide*. Toronto, ON, Canada: World Education Services.

Wu, W. L., Hsu, B. F., & Yeh, R. S. (2007). Fostering the determinants of knowledge transfer: A team-level analysis. *Journal of Information Science, 33*(3), 326–339. doi:10.1177/0165551506070733

Yarnit, M. (1998). *Learning towns and cities-survey.* Hershey, PA: IGI Global.

Yeatman, A. (1995). Making supervision relationships accountable: Graduate student logs. *Australian Universities'. RE:view*, *2*, 9–11.

Zaleznik, A. (1998). Managers and leaders: Are they different? In *Harvard Business Review onLeadership* (pp. 61–88). Boston: Harvard Business School Publishing.

Zhu, W. Z. (1992). Confucius and traditional Chinese education: An assessment. In Hayhoe, R. (Ed.), *Education and modernization: The Chinese experience* (pp. 3–22). New York, NY: Pergamon Press.

Zimmerman, B. J. (1986). Becoming a self-regulated learner: Which are the key subprocesses? *Contemporary Educational Psychology*, *11*, 307–313. doi:10.1016/0361-476X(86)90027-5

Zimmerman, B. J. (1994). Dimensions of academic self-regulation: A conceptual framework for education. In Schunk, D. H., & Zimmerman, B. J. (Eds.), *Self-regulation of learning and performance: Issues and educational implications* (pp. 3–20). Hillsdale, NJ: LEA.

Zimmerman, B. J. (2001). Theories of self-regulated learning and academic achievement: An overview and analysis. In Zimmerman, B. J., & Schunk, D. H. (Eds.), *Self-regulated learning and academic achievement: Theoretical perspectives* (pp. 1–38). Mahwah, NJ: Erlbaum.

Zimmerman, B. J., & Paulsen, A. S. (1995). Self-monitoring during collegiate studying: An Invaluable tool for academic self-regulation. In Pintrich, P. R. (Ed.), *Understanding self-regulated learning* (pp. 13–27). San Francisco: Jossey-Bass.

About the Contributors

Victor C. X. Wang, Ed.D., is an Associate Professor of Educational Leadership and Research Methodology at Florida Atlantic University, USA. Wang's research and writing activities have focused on workforce education, the foundations of adult education, adult teaching and learning, training, transformative learning, cultural issues in vocational and adult education, distance education, human performance technology, instructional/administrative leadership, and curriculum development. He has published over 130 journal articles, book chapters, and books during the past nine years and has been a reviewer for five national and international journals. Currently he serves as the editor in chief of the International Journal of Adult Vocational Education and Technology. He has won many academic achievement awards from universities in China and in the United States, including the Distinguished Faculty Scholarly & Creative Achievement Award in 2009. Wang taught extensively as a Professor in Chinese universities prior to coming to study and work in the United States in 1997. He has taught adult learners English as a second language, Chinese, computer technology, vocational (career and technical education) and adult education courses, research methods, administrative leadership, human resource management and curriculum development for the past 21 years in university settings. He has had extensive experience chairing and mentoring Doctoral dissertations. Three of the books he has written and edited have been adopted as required textbooks by major universities in the United States and in China. In addition, numerous universities worldwide, including some Ivy League universities, have cataloged his books and journal articles.

* * *

Stephen Asunka holds MA and Ed.D degrees in Instructional Technology and Media from Teachers College, Columbia University, New York, and is currently the Director of Instructional Technology at Regent University College of Science & Technology in Ghana. Stephen is passionate about online (distance) learning, particularly as it pertains to higher education in developing countries that are grappling with inadequate technology infrastructure and resources. His research therefore focuses on evolving best practice online pedagogical strategies and instructor/learner activities and attitudes that will not only make higher education more accessible, but also result in more positive learning outcomes under developing world conditions.

Glenn Bailey is an Associate Professor in the Department of Marketing at Illinois State University. His research interest includes investigating the preparation of business education teachers.

Suwithida Charungkaittikul, Ph.D student and Faculty member in Non-Formal Education, Department of Educational Policy, Management, and Leadership, Faculty of Education, Chulalongkorn University, Bangkok, Thailand, has been awarded two research grants from Graduate School, Chulalongkorn University: (1) The 11th Annual Scholarship for Chulalongkorn University 90th Anniversary (Academic Year 1/2010) Ratchada Pisek Sompoch Fund (The 90th Year Chulalongkorn University Scholarship); and, (2) The 1st Ph.D. Scholarship in Support of Dissertation-Research Scholarship Aboard (D-RSAB) for her research dissertation to study *"The Scenario of a Learning Society Model toward promoting a Positive Paradigm Shift for Communities."* She has spent a year working and studying with Dr. John A. Henschke, Chair of Doctoral Program in Andragogy Emphasis Specialty, Instructional Leadership, School of Education, Lindenwood University, St. Charles, Missouri, USA. Her advisor is Associate Professor Archanya Ratana-Ubol, Ph.D., and co-advisors are Associate Professor John A. Henschke, Ed.D., and Pan Kimpee, Ph.D.

Lesley Farmer, Professor at California State University Long Beach, coordinates the Librarianship program. She earned her M.S. in Library Science at the University of North Carolina Chapel Hill, and received her doctorate in Adult Education from Temple University. Dr. Farmer has worked as a librarian in K-12 school settings as well as in public, special and academic libraries. She chaired the Education Section of the Special Libraries Association, and is the International Association of School Librarianship Vice-President of Association Relations. Dr. Farmer is a Fulbright Scholar, and has received a university Distinguished Scholarly Activity Award, several professional association awards, and national/international grants. Dr. Farmer's research interests include information literacy, assessment, collaboration, and educational technology. A frequent presenter and writer for the profession, Dr. Farmer has published two dozen professional books, and over a hundred professional book chapters and articles. Her most recent books are Your School Library: Check It Out!, published by Libraries Unlimited in 2009; and NealSchuman Technology Management Handbook for School Library Media Centers, co-authored with Marc McPhee in 2010.

Dennis G. Fisher holds a Ph.D. from the University of Illinois, Urbana, and completed post-doctoral work at the University of California, Los Angeles. Dr. Fisher is currently Professor of Psychology and Director of the Center for Behavioral Research and Services at California State University, Long Beach. Since 1990, he has authored or coauthored approximately 200 publications and presentations, primarily in the areas of drug abuse and HIV prevention.

Edward C. Fletcher Jr. is an Assistant Professor in the Department of Adult, Career and Higher Education at the University of South Florida. His research interests are three-fold: (a) longitudinally studying the effects of high school curriculum tracking with regard to postsecondary and labor market outcomes in adulthood; (b) examining the preparedness of business education teachers and teacher candidates; and (c) exploring the status, curricula, and issues of current U.S. graduate programs (Master's and Doctoral) in Career and Technical Education and Workforce Education.

Steven A. Freeman, PhD, is a professor in the Agricultural and Biosystems Engineering Department and associate director of the Center for Excellence in Learning and Teaching at Iowa State University. He coordinates the occupational safety option of the industrial technology degree program for the department. His research interests are in agricultural and workplace safety and the scholarship of teaching and learning.

Xiaoqing Gu is associate professor of learning technology in East China Normal University, Shanghai, China. Her research interests cover learning system design, evaluation and application.

Yesenia Guzman, M. A. is a graduate of the California State University, Long Beach Master of Arts in Research (M.A.R.) degree from the Department of Psychology. She is currently employed as a bilingual interviewer and HIV pre- and post-test counselor.

Colin R. Harbke earned his doctorate in experimental psychology at Washington State University and his bachelor's degree from the University of Alaska Anchorage. He is currently an assistant professor of psychology at Western Illinois University. He teaches in the areas of statistics and research methodology. His primary research interests pertain to students' growth in self-efficacy for math, science, and statistics.

Lila Holt is currently conducting research on incorporating computational thinking to promote self-directed learning. As a PhD candidate at the University of Tennessee her area of interest is instructional technology with a concentration in adult learning.

Norhayati Ibrahim is a doctoral student in the Agricultural and Biosystems Engineering Department's industrial and agricultural technology degree program at Iowa State University. She is on leave from the Department of Polytechnics and Community Colleges Education, Malaysia, where she serves as assistant director. Her research interests are in adult technical education and higher education initiatives to help non-traditional university students succeed in their studies.

Mark E. Johnson received his Ph.D. in Counseling Psychology from the University of California, Santa Barbara. He is a Professor of Psychology and Director of the Center for Behavioral Health Research and Services at the University of Alaska, Anchorage. Dr. Johnson's current research interests include research ethics, substance abuse prevention, and rural healthcare disparities.

Beth Kania-Gosche, PhD, is currently teaching in the Educational Leadership department at Lindenwood University in St. Charles, MO. She teaches educational research courses and coordinates the last six hours of dissertation writing for doctoral students. She serves on many doctoral committees and runs workshops to help students with the writing aspect of the dissertation. She was previously a high school English teacher and Gateway Writing Project summer fellow. In May of 2009, she graduated with her Ph.D. in Educational Studies from Saint Louis University, where she was previously an instructor.

Julia M. Matuga received a Bachelor and Master of Science degree in Curriculum Studies from Indiana University, Bloomington and worked as a K-12 art teacher for five years before returning to graduate school. Julia earned her doctorate in Educational Psychology with an emphasis in Learning, Cognition, and Instruction from Indiana University (IU), Bloomington. While a graduate student at IU, Julia taught her first online course and became interested in how students learn online. Julia is currently the Associate Dean of Graduate Studies and External Programs and Associate Professor of Educational

Psychology at Bowling Green State University (BGSU). She oversees the development of online courses and programs within the College of Education and Human Development at BGSU. She has published book chapters and research articles on self-regulation and assessment within online learning environments.

Catherine McLoughlin joined ACU in 2002 and is currently Coordinator of SIMERR ACT, the Research Centre for Science, Information Technology and Mathematics Education for Rural and regional Australia (SiMERR) at the School of Education, Canberra. Dr McLoughlin teaches at undergraduate and postgraduate levels in the areas of educational psychology, teaching methodologies and research methods. Catherine is the author and co-author of over 200 refereed publications, including journal articles, book chapters and conference papers on a wide range of topics related to e-learning, design of culturally relevant learning environments, the evaluation of learning technologies, cognitive psychology and learner engagement. Dr. McLoughlin is editor of the *Australian Journal of Educational Technology* and she is on the editorial boards of a number of leading international journals in the field of educational technology.

Kathy Mountjoy is an Assistant Professor in the Department of Marketing at Illinois State University. Her research interest includes investigating the preparation of business education teachers.

Judith Parker, Ed.D., is an adjunct Assistant Professor in Organization and Leadership at Teachers College/Columbia University in New York teaching graduate courses that are totally on-line, totally classroom and blended delivery formats. She has earned a doctorate, Ed.D.degree, and an M.S. degree in Adult and Continuing Education from Teachers College/Columbia University, an M.S. degree in physics from Purdue University in Indiana, and a B.S. degree in physics and mathematics from Notre Dame College in Ohio. She has presented numerous papers at conferences globally including the Academy of Management, American Association of Physics Teachers, American Society of Training and Development, College Industry Education Conference, Quality and Productivity Management Association, Business and Multimedia Conference in Ireland, Lisbon 2000 European Conference on ODL Networking for Quality Learning, and World Open Learning for Business Conferences in the UK. Judith has been published in the "Compendium on Uses of Distance Learning Technologies in Engineering Education" the "Journal of the International Association for Continuing Engineering Education" and the "International Journal of Adult Vocational Education and Technology". She has authored chapters in Workplace Training and Learning: A Cross-Cultural Perspective; Definitive Readings in the History, Philosophy, Practice and Theories of Career and Technical Education; Integrating Adult Learning and Technology for Effective Education: Strategic Approaches; Handbook of Research on E-Learning Applications for Career and Technical Education: Technologies for Vocational Training and the Encyclopedia of Information Communication Technologies and Adult Education Integration. Judith has over 20 years' experience in leadership positions within global business organizations. She has worked extensively with technical managers and technical employees in Asia and Europe in leadership education and training and technical employee skill development by using an action-learning model and integrating distance learning technologies with classroom sessions. She has been elected a Fellow of the American Association for the Advancement of Science, and has received the American Association of Physics Teachers Innovative Teaching Award and the Park College Educational Partnership Award.

William C. Pedersen, Ph.D. is an Associate Professor in the Department of Psychology at California State University, Long Beach. He teaches in the areas of statistics and social psychology. Dr. Pedersen's research is primary focused on factors that impact aggressive behavior and violence with additional lines of research in the areas of both intergroup relations and evolutionary psychology (specifically gender differences in mating strategies).

Sandra Poirier has a broad background in education with more than 15 years experience in public sectors located in culturally diverse international environments. She has worked as a secondary teacher, cooperative extension agent, and a university teacher educator in the United States, Canada, Caribbean, and the Middle East. Her strengths include creating innovative educational programs within a cultural context and identifying appropriate outreach efforts to solve problems with positive results. She has been recognized for her ability to work effectively building community partnerships towards a common goal, creating hybrid and online courses to meet the changing needs of students, and creatively evaluating the learning outcomes of the students. She has been employed at Middle Tennessee State University as an associate professor in the Department of Human Sciences since 2005. In 2008 she was awarded the MTSU Distinguished Distance Learning Educator and in 2009 the Outstanding Career and Technical Post-Secondary Instructor Award in Tennessee.

Stephanie M. Reio is a senior justice administration major at the University of Louisville. Her interests include interpersonal and workplace violence, prisoner rehabilitation, and resiliency. She is currently interning at the Probation and Parole Office in District 16, Louisville, KY.

Thomas G. Reio, Jr. is Associate Professor of Adult Education and Human Resource Development in the Department of Leadership and Professional Studies at Florida International University in Miami, Florida. Tom earned his PhD in Adult and Continuing Education from Virginia Polytechnic Institute and State University. He was first runner-up for the Malcolm S. Knowles Dissertation-of-the-Year with his dissertation that investigated the connections among adult curiosity, workplace learning, and job performance. He is presently editor of *Human Resource Development Review* and co-editor of *New Horizons in Adult Education and Human Resource Development*. He is the immediate past Quantitative Methods Editor for *Human Resource Development Quarterly*. He has been involved for a number of years in conducting research on educational and psychological principles such as motivation and emotions, and how they impact learning and performance in formal and informal contexts. His research concerns curiosity and risk-taking motivation, workplace incivility and violence, workplace socialization processes, workplace incivility, entrepreneurship, and workplace learning. He is currently actively engaged in research investigating curiosity and risk taking throughout the lifespan. He has been involved extensively in evaluation projects concerning children and adults in both the public and private sector. His work has been published in leading journals in education, business, and psychology. These journals include *Journal of School Psychology, Personality and Individual Differences, The Journal of Genetic Psychology, Educational and Psychological Measurement, Journal of Business and Psychology, Journal of Interpersonal Violence, Human Resource Development Quarterly, Journal of Management Development, International Journal of Self-Directed Learning*, and *Teaching and Teacher Education*. He has authored chapters in the *Handbook of Educational Psychology, Emerging Directions in Self-Directed Learning, Teaching and Learning: International Best Practice, and Research on Sociocultural Influ-*

ences on Motivation and Learning. He has over 16 years of experience as a training and development director, organizational consultant, and operations manager.

Grace Reynolds, D.P.A., is Assistant Professor of Health Care Administration and Associate Director of the Center for Behavioral Research and Services at the California State University, Long Beach (CSULB). Dr. Reynolds has published on HIV and sexually transmitted disease testing with health disparities populations and teaches graduate courses in research and quantitative methods.

Mack C. Shelley, II, PhD, is a professor in the Statistics Department and the Political Science Department at Iowa State University, where he serves as director of the public policy and administration program. His research interests include education research and evaluation, social statistics, applied multivariate statistics, public policy, times series, and forecasting.

Lantana Usman is currently a tenured Associate Professor at the University of Northern British Columbia, Prince George, Canada. She obtained her PhD in Educational Administration, Leadership and Policy Studies from the University of Alberta, Canada, and taught as a sessional professor. Her area of research and teaching interest include Educational Policies and Administration, Comparative International Education, Socio-cultural Context of Schooling, Social Studies Education, Economics of Education, Developmental Education (South), Gender and Education, Immigrant and Refugee Education, Multicultural Education, Rural Education (South), and Qualitative Educational Research. She has published in several peer review international journals, with the most recent ones as the International Journal of Educational Management; International Journal of Lifelong Learning; International Journal of Social Economics and International Studies in Educational Administration/Journal of the Commonwealth Council for Educational Administration & Management; book chapters; and international conference publications. She served as a guest associate editor for the International Journal of Diversity in Organizations, Communities and Nations, as well as engaged in active review of manuscripts for the journal, and the International Journal of Educational Management; International Journal of Educational Development; International Journal Of Psychology and Counseling; and International Journal of Political Science and International Relations amongst others. She is a fellow and grant recipient of American Association of University Women International, Delta Kappa Gamma International World Distinguished Women Educators, and Ambassador and Scholar, Rotary International University Teachers amongst others.

Michele M. Wood, PhD, is an Assistant Professor in the Health Science Department at the California State University, Fullerton. Dr. Wood teaches courses in statistics, drug use, and program design and evaluation. She has 20 years experience designing, implementing, and evaluating interventions for substance users.

Deborah G. Wooldridge is a Professor and the Director of the School of Family and Consumer Sciences and the Associate Dean for Research and Field Experiences in the College of Education and Human Development at Bowling Green State University. Dr. Wooldridge served as the Dean of the College of Family Sciences at Zayed University in the United Arab Emirates, as Associate Dean of Education and the Coordinator of External Funding at Southeast Missouri State University. She was a middle school and high school teacher in Oklahoma. Deborah was a Fulbright Senior Scholar at the

University of Bahrain in the Kingdom of Bahrain and has done consulting with Ministries of Education and Ministries of Labor and Social Affairs in Oman, Kuwait, Bahrain and the United Arab Emirates, as well as acting as a liaison for UNICEF officials in Saudi Arabia for the Dubai and Abu Dhabi areas. She has a Ph.D. in resource management and consumer sciences from Texas Woman's University and a B.S. and M.S. in Education from the University of Oklahoma. During her career in higher education she has published, secured international, federal and state funding for research and community partnership projects. Her research interests are cultural and social issues of the family, learning outcomes assessment and curriculum redesign and assessment.

Mary Ziegler is an Associate Professor in Adult Learning and has been at the University of Tennessee for more than eighteen years. She is widely published in the area of adult literacy and has recently conducted studies on making meaning in virtual environments.

Index

R

radical philosophy 15
Ralph Tyler model 84-85
Reading-Free Vocational Interest Inventory (R-FVII) 143, 146
reflection and action 101
Risk Behavior Assessment (RBA) 75, 145
rituals of participation 32

S

Self-Directed Search (SDS) 143, 146
senior friendly 44, 51
social influence theories 195
Spanish reading comprehension test 74
students
    dependent variable 111
    independent variables 111
student teaching 172-173
substance abuse treatment 144
sustainable learning 216, 226

T

teacher candidates 172-173
teacher education 180

team-based work 94-95
team cohesion 102
team efficacy 102
team learning 95
team politics 101
Technology, Education, and Copyright Harmonization (TEACH) Act 203
text-based technology 100
traditional instructional leadership 83-84
transactive memory system 96
transformative learning 232, 235
transliteracies 5

V

Virtual Learning Environments (VLE) 2
vocational assessment 145
vocational skills 216
Vocational Training Project Centers (VTPC) 216

W

Web 2.0 209
Widows Training School (WTS) 215-217
workplace incivility 58
Workplace Incivility Scale (WIS) 62